Workshop on Cognitive Modeling and Computational Linguistics (CMCL 2019)

Minneapolis, Minnesota, USA
7 June 2019

ISBN: 978-1-5108-8783-1

NAACL HLT 2019

**Cognitive Modeling
and Computational Linguistics**

Proceedings of the Workshop

June 7, 2019
Minneapolis, USA

Workshop sponsored by:
University of Pisa - CoLing Lab

Laboratoire Parole et Langage - Aix-en-Provence

Institute of Language, Communication and Brain, Marseille

Order copies of this and other ACL proceedings from:

Association for Computational Linguistics (ACL)
209 N. Eighth Street
Stroudsburg, PA 18360
USA
Tel: +1-570-476-8006
Fax: +1-570-476-0860
acl@aclweb.org

ISBN 978-1-948087-96-4

Introduction

Since its inaugural meeting in 2010, the Cognitive Modeling and Computational Linguistics workshop has served as a unique venue for research at the intersection of cognitive science and natural language processing. Previous CMCLs have highlighted work on developing parsers based on different grammar formalisms; computational accounts of human language acquisition, comprehension, or production; and modeling the representation of concepts in a cognitively relevant way. This year, we have received 31 paper submissions, 18 of which were accepted as regular workshop papers (58%). Two cross-submissions have been accepted for a poster presentation.

The 2019 meeting of the Cognitive Modeling and Computational Linguistics (CMCL) workshop follows in the tradition of many CMCLs past. We are proud to have selected a broad spectrum of talks and topics this year, ranging from parsing models, to models of sentence comprehension, to speech production, to distributional semantics methods. We are also proud to host a poster session that is larger than in previous years, increasing the reach of our workshop and allowing us to support more junior researchers and more works in progress.

Our invited speakers come from both industry and academic research backgrounds. Attendees are participating from across the globe.

Support for CMCL comes from a wide range of academic sponsors, without whom we would not have been able to sponsor four travel awards, a best paper award, and partially offset the costs of participation of our invited speakers. As such we gratefully acknowledge support from the Institute of Language, Communication and Brain (ILCB), Marseille; Laboratoire Parole et Langage (LPL), Aix-en-Provence; and Computational Linguistics Laboratory (Coling Lab), Pisa.

Organizers:

Emmanuele Chersoni, The Hong Kong Polytechnic University
Cassandra Jacobs, University of Toronto
Alessandro Lenci, University of Pisa
Tal Linzen, Johns Hopkins University
Laurent Prévot, Aix-Marseille Université
Enrico Santus, MIT

Invited Speakers:

Dr. Klinton Bicknell, Research Scientist, Duolingo
Dr. Leila Wehbe, Assistant Professor, Carnegie Mellon University

Program Commitee Members:

Raquel Garrido Alhama,Max Planck Institute for Psycholinguistics
Philippe Blache, Aix-Marseille Université
Marc Brysbaert, Ghent University
Francesca Carota, Max Planck Institute for Psycholinguistics
Christos Christodoulopoulos, Amazon
Eunjin Chun, The Hong Kong Polytechnic University
Robert Daland, Apple
Barry Devereux, Queen's University Belfast
Brian Dillon, University of Massachusetts
Micha Elsner, Ohio State University
Thomas Francois, Université Catholique de Louvain
Robert Frank, Yale University
Stella Frank, University of Edinburgh
Thomas Graf, Stony Brook University
John Hale, University of Georgia
Jeffrey Heinz, Stony Brook University
Joshua Herring, Periodic Inc.
Yu-Yin Hsu, The Hong Kong Polytechnic University
Tim Hunter, UCLA
Samar Husain, Indian Institute of Technology Delhi
Gaja Jarosz, University of Massachusetts Amherst
Shalom Lappin, King's College London
Gianluca Lebani, University of Utrecht
Pavel Logacev, Bogazici University
Alessandro Lopopolo, Radboud University of Nijmegen
Karl David Neergaard, Aix-Marseille Université
Sebastian Padó, University of Stuttgart
Vito Pirrelli, ILC-CNR Pisa
Stephen Politzer-Ahles, The Hong Kong Polytechnic University
Jean-Philippe Prost, Université Montpellier 2
Zhen Qin, The Hong Kong Polytechnic University
Giulia Rambelli, University of Pisa

Carlos Ramisch, Aix-Marseille Université
Roi Reichart, Technion University
Asad Sayeed, University of Gothenburg
William Schuler, Ohio State University
Olga Seminck, Université Paris-Sorbonne – Paris IV
Marco Silvio Giuseppe Senaldi, Scuola Normale Superiore di Pisa
Cory Shain, Ohio State University
Shravan Vasishth, University of Potsdam
Aline Villavicencio, University of Essex
Titus Von Der Malsburg, University of Potsdam
Victoria Yaneva, University of Wolverhampton
Frances Yung, Saarland University
Alessandra Zarcone, Frauenhofer IIS Erlangen

Table of Contents

The Active-Filler Strategy in a Move-Eager Left-Corner Minimalist Grammar Parser
Tim Hunter, Miloš Stanojević and Edward Stabler 1

Priming vs. Inhibition of Optional Infinitival "to"
Robin Melnick and Thomas Wasow 11

Simulating Spanish-English Code-Switching: El Modelo Está Generating Code-Switches
Chara Tsoukala, Stefan L. Frank, Antal van den Bosch, Jorge Valdes Kroff and Mirjam Broersma
20

Surprisal and Interference Effects of Case Markers in Hindi Word Order
Sidharth Ranjan, Sumeet Agarwal and Rajakrishnan Rajkumar 30

Modeling Hierarchical Syntactic Structures in Morphological Processing
Yohei Oseki, Charles Yang and Alec Marantz 43

A Modeling Study of the Effects of Surprisal and Entropy in Perceptual Decision Making of an Adaptive Agent
Pyeong Whan Cho and Richard Lewis 53

Modeling Long-Distance Cue Integration in Spoken Word Recognition
Wednesday Bushong and T. Florian Jaeger 62

Toward a Computational Multidimensional Lexical Similarity Measure for Modeling Word Association Tasks in Psycholinguistics
Bruno Gaume, Lydia Mai Ho-Dac, Ludovic Tanguy, Cécile Fabre, Bénédicte Pierrejean, Nabil Hathout, Jérôme Farinas, Julien Pinquier, Lola Danet, Patrice Péran, Xavier De Boissezon and Mélanie Jucla 71

Dependency Parsing with your Eyes: Dependency Structure Predicts Eye Regressions During Reading
Alessandro Lopopolo, Stefan L. Frank, Antal van den Bosch and Roel Willems 77

A Framework for Decoding Event-Related Potentials from Text
Shaorong Yan and Aaron Steven White 86

Testing a Minimalist Grammar Parser on Italian Relative Clause Asymmetries
Aniello De Santo 93

Quantifiers in a Multimodal World: Hallucinating Vision with Language and Sound
Alberto Testoni, Sandro Pezzelle and Raffaella Bernardi 105

Frequency vs. Association for Constraint Selection in Usage-Based Construction Grammar
Jonathan Dunn 117

The Development of Abstract Concepts in Children's Early Lexical Networks
Abdellah Fourtassi, Isaac Scheinfeld and Michael Frank 129

Verb-Second Effect on Quantifier Scope Interpretation
Asad Sayeed, Matthias Lindemann and Vera Demberg 134

Neural Models of the Psychosemantics of 'Most'
Lewis O'Sullivan and Shane Steinert-Threlkeld 140

The Role of Utterance Boundaries and Word Frequencies for Part-of-speech Learning in Brazilian Portuguese Through Distributional Analysis
Pablo Picasso Feliciano de Faria 152

Using Grounded Word Representations to Study Theories of Lexical Concepts
Dylan Ebert and Ellie Pavlick 160

Conference Program

Friday, June 7, 2019

9:00–9:15   *Welcome to the Workshop*

9:15–10:15   *Session 1: Invited Talk: Klinton Bicknell*

10:15–10:45   *Session 2: Talks: Session 1*

10:15–10:45   *The Active-Filler Strategy in a Move-Eager Left-Corner Minimalist Grammar Parser*
Tim Hunter, Miloš Stanojević and Edward Stabler

10:45–11:00   *Coffee Break*

11:00–12:00   *Session 3: Talks: Session 2*

11:00–11:30   *Priming vs. Inhibition of Optional Infinitival "to"*
Robin Melnick and Thomas Wasow

11:30–12:00   *Simulating Spanish-English Code-Switching: El Modelo Está Generating Code-Switches*
Chara Tsoukala, Stefan L. Frank, Antal van den Bosch, Jorge Valdes Kroff and Mirjam Broersma

12:00–13:00   *Lunch Break*

13:00–14:30   *Session 4: Talks: Session 3*

13:00–13:30   *Surprisal and Interference Effects of Case Markers in Hindi Word Order*
Sidharth Ranjan, Sumeet Agarwal and Rajakrishnan Rajkumar

13:30–14:00   *Modeling Hierarchical Syntactic Structures in Morphological Processing*
Yohei Oseki, Charles Yang and Alec Marantz

14:00–14:30 *A Modeling Study of the Effects of Surprisal and Entropy in Perceptual Decision Making of an Adaptive Agent*
Pyeong Whan Cho and Richard Lewis

14:30–15:30 ***Session 5: Poster Session***

Modeling Long-Distance Cue Integration in Spoken Word Recognition
Wednesday Bushong and T. Florian Jaeger

Toward a Computational Multidimensional Lexical Similarity Measure for Modeling Word Association Tasks in Psycholinguistics
Bruno Gaume, Lydia Mai Ho-Dac, Ludovic Tanguy, Cécile Fabre, Bénédicte Pierrejean, Nabil Hathout, Jérôme Farinas, Julien Pinquier, Lola Danet, Patrice Péran, Xavier De Boissezon and Mélanie Jucla

Dependency Parsing with your Eyes: Dependency Structure Predicts Eye Regressions During Reading
Alessandro Lopopolo, Stefan L. Frank, Antal van den Bosch and Roel Willems

A Framework for Decoding Event-Related Potentials from Text
Shaorong Yan and Aaron Steven White

Testing a Minimalist Grammar Parser on Italian Relative Clause Asymmetries
Aniello De Santo

Quantifiers in a Multimodal World: Hallucinating Vision with Language and Sound
Alberto Testoni, Sandro Pezzelle and Raffaella Bernardi

Frequency vs. Association for Constraint Selection in Usage-Based Construction Grammar
Jonathan Dunn

The Development of Abstract Concepts in Children's Early Lexical Networks
Abdellah Fourtassi, Isaac Scheinfeld and Michael Frank

Verb-Second Effect on Quantifier Scope Interpretation
Asad Sayeed, Matthias Lindemann and Vera Demberg

Neural Models of the Psychosemantics of 'Most'
Lewis O'Sullivan and Shane Steinert-Threlkeld

Friday, June 7, 2019 (continued)

15:30–15:45   *Coffee Break*

15:45–16:45   *Session 6: Talks: Session 4*

15:45–16:15   *The Role of Utterance Boundaries and Word Frequencies for Part-of-speech Learning in Brazilian Portuguese Through Distributional Analysis*
Pablo Picasso Feliciano de Faria

16:15–16:45   *Using Grounded Word Representations to Study Theories of Lexical Concepts*
Dylan Ebert and Ellie Pavlick

16:45–17:45   *Session 7: Invited Talk: Leila Wehbe*

The Active-Filler Strategy in a Move-Eager Left-Corner Minimalist Grammar Parser

Tim Hunter
Department of Linguistics
UCLA
timhunter@ucla.edu

Miloš Stanojević
School of Informatics
University of Edinburgh
m.stanojevic@ed.ac.uk

Edward P. Stabler
Samsung Research America
California, USA
stabler@ucla.edu

Abstract

Recent psycholinguistic evidence suggests that human parsing of moved elements is 'active', and perhaps even 'hyper-active': it seems that a leftward-moved object is related to a verbal position rapidly, perhaps even before the transitivity information associated with the verb is available to the listener. This paper presents a formal, sound and complete parser for Minimalist Grammars whose search space contains branching points that we can identify as the locus of the decision to perform this kind of active gap-finding. This brings formal models of parsing into closer contact with recent psycholinguistic theorizing than was previously possible.

1 Introduction

Minimalist Grammars (MGs) (Stabler, 1997, 2011) provide an explicit formulation of the central ideas of contemporary transformational grammar, deriving from Chomsky (1995). They have allowed formal insights into syntactic theory itself (Kobele, 2010; Kobele and Michaelis, 2011; Hunter, 2011; Graf, 2013), and there has been some work using MGs as the basis for psycholinguistic modeling. But this psycholinguistic work has focused primarily on sentence-processing at a relatively high level of abstraction, considering various measures of the workload imposed by different kinds of sentences — either information-theoretic metrics (Hale, 2003, 2006; Yun et al., 2015), or metrics based on memory load (Kobele et al., 2012; Graf and Marcinek, 2014; Brennan et al., 2016) — rather than the algorithmic-level questions of how derivations are pieced together incrementally.

A significant amount of experimental sentence-processing work aims to investigate exactly these kinds of algorithmic-level questions as they apply to long-distance syntactic dependencies, for example filler-gap dependencies between a moved wh-phrase and its base position. This is the kind of syntactic construction that MGs are particularly well-placed to describe (in contrast to simpler formalisms such as context-free grammars where parsing is well-studied), but it has been difficult to connect the experimental psycholinguistic work with any incremental, algorithmic-level MG parsing algorithms. Most parsing strategies proposed by psycholinguists have not been easy to relate to formal models of parsing.

2 Motivation and Background

A significant problem that confronts the human sentence-processor is the treatment of *filler-gap* dependencies. These are dependencies between a pronounced element, the *filler*, and a position in the sentence that is not indicated in any direct way by the pronunciation, the *gap*. A canonical example is the kind of dependency created by wh-movement, for example the one shown in (1).

(1) What did John buy ___ yesterday?

The interesting puzzle posed by such dependencies is that a parser, of course, does not get to "see" the gap: it must somehow determine that there is a gap in the position indicated in (1) on the basis of the properties of the surrounding words, for example the fact that 'what' must be associated with a corresponding gap, the fact that 'buy' takes a direct object, etc.

Experimental psycholinguistic work has uncovered a number of robust generalizations about how the human parsing system decides where to posit gap sites in amongst the pronounced elements as it works through a sentence incrementally. One conceivable strategy would be to posit gaps "only as a last resort, when all other structural hypotheses about that part of the sentence have been tried and

Proceedings of the Workshop on Cognitive Modeling and Computational Linguistics, pages 1–10
Minneapolis, USA, June 7, 2019. ©2019 Association for Computational Linguistics

have failed" (Fodor, 1978, p.433). But the strategy that comprehenders actually employ is essentially to treat gaps as a "first resort", or what has become known as the "active filler" or "active gap-finding" strategy: hypothesize that there is a gap in any position where there might be one, and retract this hypothesis if subsequent input provides bottom-up evidence disconfirming it (Fodor, 1978; Stowe, 1986; Frazier and Clifton, 1989). Specifically, there is reason to believe that the dependency in (1) is constructed before the parser encounters 'yesterday'. A primary piece of evidence for this is the so-called "filled-gap effect": in a sentence like (2), we observe a reading slowdown at 'books' (Stowe, 1986).

(2)   What did John buy books about ___ yesterday?

This slowdown is what one might expect if a dependency between 'what' and the object-position of 'buy' is constructed — actively, as a first resort — before the comprehender reads past 'buy', and then has to be retracted when 'books' is read. (What was hypothesized to be a gap position is in fact filled, hence "filled-gap effect".)

This basic generalization prompts a number of questions about the details of when and how this sort of hypothesizing of a gap takes place: in particular, one can ask what counts as a position where there "might be" a gap, and how this strategy interacts with the intricate grammatical constraints upon the relevant long-distance dependencies. See for example Traxler and Pickering (1996), Phillips (2006), Staub (2007), Wagers and Phillips (2009), and Omaki et al. (2015), among many others, for investigations of these issues.

At present it is difficult for the generalizations emerging from this experimental work to be framed in terms of the workings of a parser for contemporary transformational grammars. Consider for comparison the earlier empirical work on attachment preferences and garden path theory (e.g. Frazier and Clifton, 1996): since the focus was on grammatical relationships that were local in phrase-structural terms, the strategies being discovered could be understood as strategies for searching through the hypothesis space induced by the operations of a context-free parser. For example, the garden-path effect in (3) can be interpreted as evidence that given the locally ambiguous prefix 'When Fido scratched the vet', readers pursue the analysis in (4a) rather than the one in (4b).

This is an instance of the Late Closure preference.

(3)   When Fido scratched the vet (and his new assistant) removed the muzzle.

(4)   a. When [$_s$ Fido scratched the vet] [$_s$ ...]
       b. When [$_s$ Fido scratched] [$_s$ the vet ...]

Another way to put this is to say that after the word 'scratched', a bottom-up parser has the choice between performing a reduce step (to analyze this verb as a complete, intransitive VP) or performing a shift step (supposing that other remaining input will also be part of the VP), and it prefers the latter. See Figure 1, where the initial empty sequence of stack elements is indicated by ϵ. If we suppose that the parser first explores the branch of the search space shown on the left in Figure 1, corresponding to the structure in (4a), then the disruption observed at the word 'removed' in (3) can be linked to the idea that this word triggers backtracking to the branching point shown in the diagram, so that the alternative intransitive-verb analysis in (4b) can be constructed by following the other branch.

In principle, it should be possible to give an analogous description of the active filler strategy for positing gaps: we can imagine a description of the parser's search space that allows us to state preferences for one kind of transition (the kind that interrupts "local processing" and posits a gap associated with an earlier filler) over another (the kind that continues working with local material). This is difficult at present, however, because there are relatively few formal models of parsing that treat both long-distance dependencies and local dependencies in a cohesive, integrated manner. Aside from this technical hurdle, however, the active filler strategy can be regarded as having the same form as the Late Closure preference: just as humans' first guess given the prefix 'When Fido scratched the vet' is (4a) rather than (4b), their first guess given the prefix 'What did John buy' is (5a) rather than (5b).

(5)   a. What did John buy ___ ...
       b. What did John buy ...

3   Minimalist Grammars

A Minimalist Grammar (Stabler, 1997, 2011) is defined with a tuple $G = \langle \Sigma, B, Lex, C, \{\text{MERGE}, \text{MOVE}\} \rangle$, where Σ is the **vocabulary**, B is a set of **basic features**, Lex

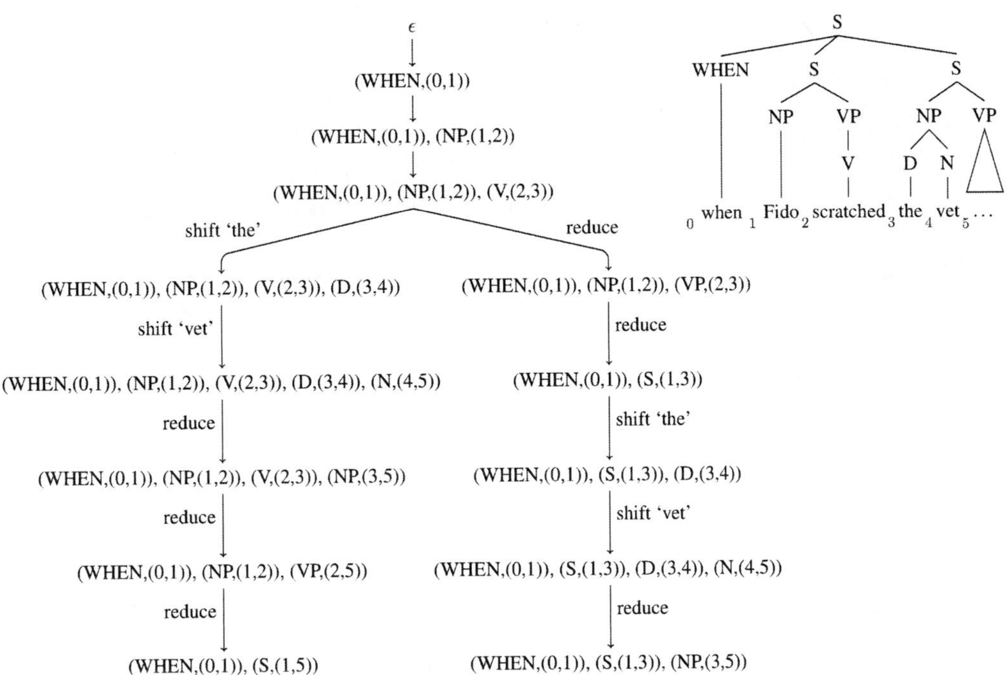

Figure 1: Part of the search space for the locally-ambiguous prefix '$_0$ When $_1$ Fido $_2$ scratched $_3$ the $_4$ vet $_5$' in a bottom-up shift-reduce parser. The left branch is the route favoured by Late Closure (Frazier and Clifton, 1996). The garden-path effect in (3) can be seen as a consequence of the reanalysis required when a parser searches this left branch first.

is a finite **lexicon** (as defined just below), $C \in B$ is the **start category**, and MERGE and MOVE are the generating functions. The basic features of the set B are concatenated with prefix operators to specify their roles, as follows:

categories, selectees $= B$
selectors $= \{=f \mid f \in B\}$
licensees $= \{-f \mid f \in B\}$
licensors $= \{+f \mid f \in B\}$

Let F be the set of role-marked **features**, that is, the union of the categories, selectors, licensors and licensees. Let $T = \{::, :\}$ be two **types**, indicating "lexical" and "derived" structures, respectively. Let $\mathbb{C} = \Sigma^* \times T \times F^*$ be the set of **chains**. Let $E = \mathbb{C}^+$ be the set of **expressions**; intuitively, an expression is a chain together with its "moving" sub-chains, if any. Finally, the **lexicon** $Lex \subset \Sigma^* \times \{::\} \times F^*$ is a finite set. The functions MERGE and MOVE are defined in Table 1. Note that each MERGE rule deletes a selection feature $=f$ and a corresponding category feature f, so the result on the left side of each rule has two features less than the total number of features on the right. Similarly, each

MOVE rule deletes a licensor feature $+f$ and a licensee feature $-f$. The rules (understood as functions from right-to-left, or "bottom-up") have pairwise disjoint domains; that is, an instance of a right side of a rule is not an instance of the right side of any other rule. The set of all **structures** that can be derived from the lexicon is $S(G) = \mathrm{closure}(Lex, \{\mathrm{MERGE}, \mathrm{MOVE}\})$. The set of **sentences** $L(G) = \{s \mid s \cdot C \in S(G)$ for some type $\cdot \in \{:, ::\}\}$, where C is the "start" category.

Two simple derivations are shown in Figures 2 and 3. These trees have elements of the grammar's lexicon (not shown separately) at their leaves. At each binary-branching node we write the structure that results from applying MERGE to the structures at the daughter nodes; and at each unary-branching node we write the structure that results from applying MOVE to the structure at the daughter node.

The lowest MERGE step shown in Figure 2, for example, combines (via MERGE3, specifically) the lexical items for 'buy' and 'what'; the d category feature on 'what' can satisfy the first of the =d se-

merge is the union of the following 3 rules, each with 2 elements on the right, for strings $s, t \in \Sigma^*$, for types $\cdot \in \{:, ::\}$ (lexical and derived, respectively), for feature sequences $\gamma \in F^*$, $\delta \in F^+$, and for chains $\alpha_1, \ldots, \alpha_k, \iota_1, \ldots, \iota_l$ $(0 \leq k, l)$ (MERGE1) lexical item s selects non-mover t to produce the merged st $$st : \gamma, \alpha_1, \ldots, \alpha_k \quad \rightarrow \quad s ::= f\gamma \quad t \cdot f, \alpha_1, \ldots, \alpha_k$$ (MERGE2) derived item s selects a non-mover t to produce the merged ts $$ts : \gamma, \alpha_1, \ldots, \alpha_k, \iota_1, \ldots, \iota_l \quad \rightarrow \quad s :=f\gamma, \alpha_1, \ldots, \alpha_k \quad t \cdot f, \iota_1, \ldots, \iota_l$$ (MERGE3) any item s selects a mover t to produce the merged s with chain t $$s : \gamma, \alpha_1, \ldots, \alpha_k, t : \delta, \iota_1, \ldots, \iota_l \quad \rightarrow \quad s \cdot =f\gamma, \alpha_1, \ldots, \alpha_k \quad t \cdot f\delta, \iota_1, \ldots, \iota_l$$ **move** is the union of the following 2 rules, each with 1 element on the right, for $\delta \in F^+$, such that none of the chains $\alpha_1, \ldots, \alpha_{i-1}, \alpha_{i+1}, \ldots, \alpha_k$ has $-f$ as its first feature: (MOVE1) final move of t, so its $-f$ chain is eliminated on the left $$ts : \gamma, \alpha_1, \ldots, \alpha_{i-1}, \alpha_{i+1}, \ldots, \alpha_k \quad \rightarrow \quad s : +f\gamma, \alpha_1, \ldots, \alpha_{i-1}, t : -f, \alpha_{i+1}, \ldots, \alpha_k$$ (MOVE2) nonfinal move of t, so its chain continues with features δ $$s : \gamma, \alpha_1, \ldots, \alpha_{i-1}, t : \delta, \alpha_{i+1}, \ldots, \alpha_k \quad \rightarrow \quad s : +f\gamma, \alpha_1, \ldots, \alpha_{i-1}, t : -f\delta, \alpha_{i+1}, \ldots, \alpha_k$$

Table 1: **Rules for minimalist grammars** from Stabler 2011, §A.1.

lectors on 'buy', and these two features are deleted in the resulting structure. This resulting structure, like the two above it, consists of two chains: as well as the chain[1] that participates "as usual" in the structure-building steps of combining with the subject and silent complementizer, there is the chain 'what : $-$wh' representing the wh-element that is "in transit" throughout these steps of the derivation. Given this separation of a structure into its component chains, movement amounts to bringing together two chains. The (formally redundant) dashed line in the figure links the MOVE step at the root of the derivation to the structure that gave rise to the 'what' chain that this MOVE step acts on. The last two steps of the derivation effectively *wrap* (Bach, 1979) the components 'John buys' and 'what' around the (as it happens, silent) complementizer.

4 Previous MG Parsers

Stabler (2013) presented the first systematic generalization of incremental/transition-based CFG parsing methods to MGs, specifically a top-down MG parser. This requires a complete root-to-leaf path to a lexical item before it can be scanned, and therefore only allows a filler (e.g. a wh-phrase) to be consumed once we commit to a particular position for the corresponding gap (e.g. matrix sub-

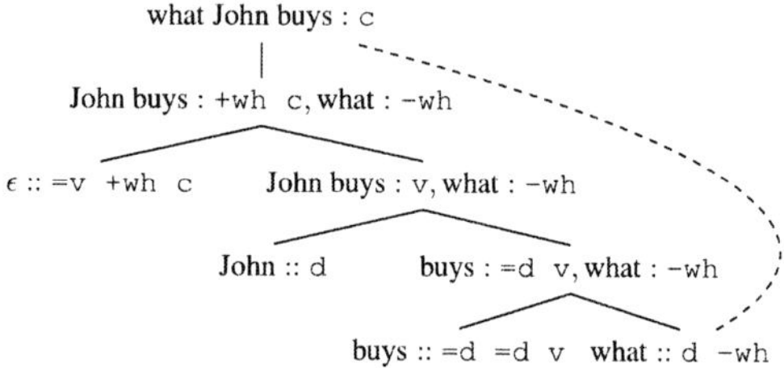

Figure 2: Example derivation for: what John buys

ject position, matrix object position, embedded subject position, etc.). In terms of the tree diagrams like Figures 2 and 3, both the solid-line connection from the root down to a wh-phrase and the dashed-line connection are established before the wh-phrase can be consumed. The ambiguity-resolution question raised by filler-gap dependencies therefore amounts to a choice between competing analyses that diverged before the filler was consumed, rather than a choice of how to extend a particular analysis like in Figure 1. See Hunter (in press) for more detailed discussion.

Stanojević and Stabler (2018) adapt the idea of left-corner parsing from CFGs to MGs. This parser can consume a wh-filler without committing to a particular gap site for it, and therefore — unlike the Stabler (2013) parser — there is a single sequence of steps that it can take to parse a prefix such as 'What does John think' which can be extended with either a subject-gap or object-

---

[1] In traditional terminology, this first chain happens to be a trivial or one-membered chain, i.e. one that does not undergo any movement.

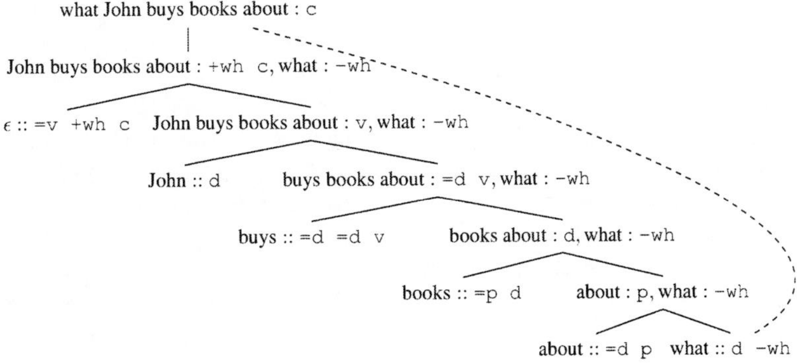

Figure 3: Example derivation for: what John buys books about

gap structure.[2] But it does this without identifying a "filler site" for the wh-phrase either: the wh-phrase, in effect, remains entirely disconnected from the rest of the structure until its gap site is encountered, then the rest of the clause(s) out of which the wh-phrase moves is assembled, and only then is the wh-phrase slotted into its surface position as part of the linking of this clause into its surroundings. In terms of the tree diagrams: while this parser does allow the solid-line connection from the root down to a wh-phrase to be unknown when the wh-phrase is scanned, it constructs the dashed-line connection only after this solid-line connection is eventually established.

The goal here is to adjust the parsing mechanisms of Stanojević and Stabler (2018) so that they produce a search space where the choice points are more in line with the psycholinguistic literature's framing of the choices that confront the human sentence-processing mechanism regarding filler-gap dependencies. With respect to the tree diagrams, we would like a parser that can establish the dashed-line connection down to a wh-phrase at the point where the wh-phrase is consumed, and delay the solid-line connection until later.

5   Move-Eager Left-Corner MG Parsing

We maintain an input buffer and a store. Each item in the store is either an element of the form ((start index, end index) · category), or an implication (written with $\Rightarrow$) from one such element to another. There is a distinguished "top" item in the store; additional items are unordered. We begin with an implication $((0, n) \cdot c) \Rightarrow ((0, n) \text{ ROOT})$ in the store, where c is the starting category of the grammar and 'ROOT' is a distinguished grammar-external symbol.

A SHIFT transition consumes a word from the buffer and puts a corresponding element $((i, i + 1) :: X)$ into the top position in the store, or $((i, i) :: X)$ in the case of shifting an empty string.

We define the other parsing transitions in terms of the five MG grammatical rules in Table 1.

If R is a binary grammatical rule $A \rightarrow B\ C$ and we have B at the top of our store, then the transition relation LC(R) allows us to replace this B with the implication $C \Rightarrow A$; or, if we have C at the top of our store, then LC(R) allows us to replace C with the implication $B \Rightarrow A$. The idea in the latter case is that, since we have already found a C, finding a B in the future is now all that we need to do to establish an A. This is familiar from left-corner CFG parsing, and forms the core of how MERGE steps are parsed (since the MERGE rules are the binary rules). For example, if we have found a preposition spanning from position i to position j, i.e. $((i, j) :: \text{=d p})$, then LC(MERGE1) allows us to replace this with an implication $((j, k) \cdot \text{d}) \Rightarrow ((i, k) : \text{p})$. The right side of this implication has type ':', since it is necessarily non-lexical; the type of the left side is unspecified ($\cdot \in \{:, ::\}$).

Given an implication $X \Rightarrow Y$ somewhere in our store, a central idea from (arc-eager) left-corner parsing is that parsing steps that produce an X can be *connected*, or chained together, with this stored implication to instead produce a Y (and in this case we remove the implication from the store). We can think of $X \Rightarrow Y$ as a fragment of tree

---

[2]Leaving aside questions of how movement dependencies are treated, left-corner parsing is also generally regarded as more psychologically plausible for reasons relating to the memory demands imposed by different kinds of embedding configurations in basic, movement-free structures (Resnik, 1992).

structure that has Y at the root and has an "unfilled" X somewhere along its frontier (or a *context*, a Y tree with an X hole); if there is a step we can take that can produce an X, that X can be plugged in to the tree fragment.

For any parsing transition T, there are four variants $\text{C0}(T)$, $\text{C1}(T)$, $\text{C2}(T)$ and $\text{C3}(T)$ that connect, in slightly varying configurations, the items produced by T itself with implications already in the store.

(6)   a.   If T produces B and we already have $B \Rightarrow A$, then $\text{C0}(T)$ produces A.

    b.   If T produces $B \Rightarrow A$ and we already have $C \Rightarrow B$, then $\text{C1}(T)$ produces $C \Rightarrow A$.

    c.   If T produces $C \Rightarrow B$ and we already have $B \Rightarrow A$, then $\text{C2}(T)$ produces $C \Rightarrow A$.

    d.   If T produces $C \Rightarrow B$ and we already have $B \Rightarrow A$ and $D \Rightarrow C$, then $\text{C3}(T)$ produces $D \Rightarrow A$.

In all cases the relevant pre-existing implications are removed from the store. C0 connects a shifted lexical item with the antecedent of an implication, i.e. the "unfilled" slot at the bottom of some tree fragment. Rules $\text{C1}(T)$ and $\text{C2}(T)$ are similar to function composition, or the **B** combinatory rule of CCG (Steedman, 2000).[3] $\text{C1}(T)$ and $\text{C2}(T)$ differ from each other in whether it is the top or bottom of the fragment newly created by T that connects with a pre-existing fragment; $\text{C3}(T)$ is for the more complicated cases where connections are made at *both* ends of the fragment created by T. See Figure 4.

The place where the parser presented here differs from that of Stanojević and Stabler (2018) is in the treatment of MOVE rules. These are treated as ways to "extend" the other parsing transitions. Given a grammar rule $\text{MOVE}n$ of the form $A \rightarrow B$, if a parsing transition T produces an implication $C \Rightarrow B$, then $\text{MV}n(T)$ produces $C \Rightarrow A$.[4] (The parser of Stanojević and Stabler (2018), in contrast, would wait until C is completed and we simply have B, at which point a standalone MOVE-transition would replace this with A.)

With these rules, we obtain a search space that better allows us to precisely express the active/greedy gap-finding strategies that the psycholinguistic evidence supports. This is illustrated by the traces shown in Figures 5-6.[5]

The first interesting step in Figure 5 is Step 2, which builds the MERGE3 step (i.e. the bottom application of MERGE in Figure 2 discussed earlier) on top of 'what' to produce an implication. Given the actual surroundings of 'what' in Figure 2, (the feature parts of) this implication would be =d =d v $\Rightarrow$ =d v,-wh.[6] But it could also be =dγ $\Rightarrow$ γ,-wh for any other feature-sequence γ (cf. Table 1), so the parser creates an implication where these additional features are left as variables to be resolved by unification later. This is the new store item shown in Step 2, where the start and end positions of the selector of 'what' are likewise unknown and left as variables n_0 and n_1, α_3 is the first feature of γ (which we actually know cannot be a licensor) and α_4 is the rest of γ.[7]

The next step shifts the empty complementizer into the store. The resulting item has no variables, and spans from position 1 to position 1.

Step 4 is perhaps the most complex and interesting step. At its core is the fact that LC(MERGE1) constructs, from the silent complementizer whose features are =v +wh c, an implication from the its complement (features v, plus possible movers) to its parent (features +wh c, plus possible movers). But the right-hand side of this implication is something that MOVE1 can apply to; specifically, MOVE1 applied to +wh c, -wh produces c. So putting these together, MV1(LC(MERGE1)) produces an implication from v,-wh to c. And C2 can chain this together with the initial implication from c to ROOT, to produce an implication from v,-wh to ROOT as the end result. This new store

---

[3]Resnik (1992, p.197) emphasizes this relationship between arc-eager parsing's connect rules and function composition, and the analogy to CCG's function composition operation specifically.

[4]Note that whereas $\Rightarrow$ "points upwards" in the tree, $\rightarrow$ points downwards (cf. Table 1).

[5]An implementation using depth-first backtracking search is available at https://github.com/stanojevic/Move-Eager-Left-Corner-MG-Parser

[6]In these sequences of feature-sequences, spaces bind more tightly than commas.

[7]Leaving the other features of the wh-phrase's selector as variables allows us to remain completely agnostic about the base position of the wh-phrase. But a version of this parser that did not do this would still avoid the problem for the top-down MG parser discussed in Section 4: it would commit to the *immediate* surroundings of the wh-phrase's base position (for which there are only finitely many options) before moving on from consuming the filler, but it would remain agnostic about how far this surrounding material is from the root of the tree. Committing to the immediate surroundings of the wh-phrase would not be unnatural in languages with rich case-marking.

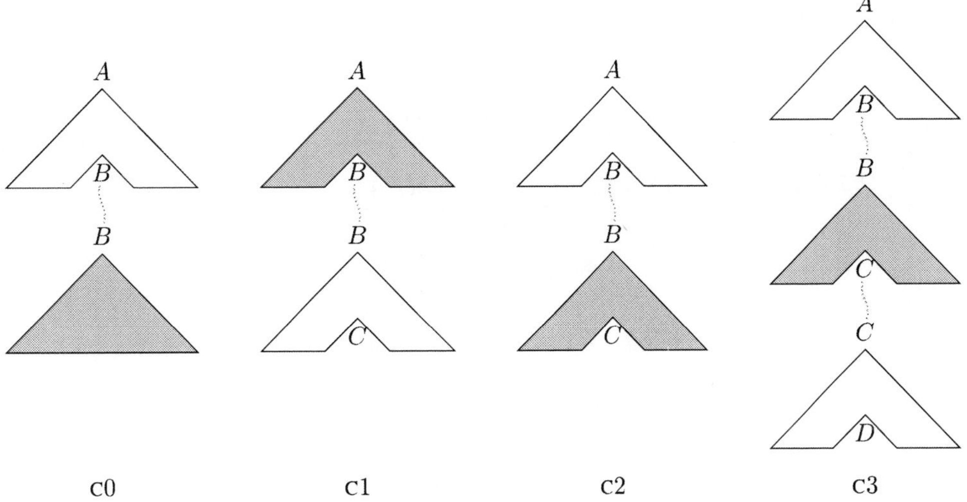

Figure 4: Illustration of connecting operations C0, C1, C2 and C3. The newly created item is shaded in each case.

item in Step 4 says, in effect, that finding a v spanning positions 1 to n_0, out of which has moved the −wh element already found spanning positions 0 to 1, will allow us to conclude that the root of a complete tree spans positions 0 to n_0. The implication established at Step 2 remains in place, unaffected by this step.

Step 6 places 'John' in the subject position: LC(MERGE2) creates an implication from some selector with features =dγ (plus movers, if any) to the parent node with features γ (plus the same movers, if any). By taking γ to be v and taking the relevant movers to be −wh, the right-hand side of this new implication can be unified with the left-hand side of the one established at Step 4; and furthermore, the left-hand side of the new implication can be unified with the right-hand side of the one established at Step 2 (i.e. the parent of the wh-phrase). The new implication is therefore chained together with two existing ones, by C3, to produce an implication simply from =d =d v to ROOT. The left-hand side of this implication is plugged in when we shift the next word, 'buys'.

Particularly important for the goals outlined above is that instead of the C3(LC(MERGE2)) transition in Step 6, the parser also has the option of taking the C2(LC(MERGE2)) transition shown in Step 6' in Figure 6. This transition involves the same MERGE step putting 'John' in the subject position, and connects the resulting structure "upwards" to the sought-after v, −wh in the same way, but *does not* connect the bottom of the resulting

structure to the surroundings of the wh-phrase that were constructed at Step 2. Instead, the sister node of the subject (features =d v, −wh) is left open as the left-hand side of the implication to ROOT, and the implication constructed at Step 2 remains. This is exactly what is required in the sentence being parsed in Figure 6, where the gap is further embedded inside the direct object. But the first five steps are the same in both cases.[8]

The choice between whether to take Step 6 or 6' therefore reflects exactly the choice between whether to follow the active filler strategy or not, just as the the choice between a shift step and a reduce step in Figure 1 reflects the choice between whether to follow the Late Closure strategy or not; recall the discussion of (4) and (5) above. The observed human preference for active gap-finding might therefore be formulated as a preference for C3 transitions over C2 transitions, just as Late Closure effects can be formulated as the result of a preference for shift transitions over reduce transitions. On this view, the filled-gap effect in (2) (i.e. the disruption at 'books') is the result of backtracking out of an area of the search space that a C3 transition led into, corresponding to the analysis in (5a), back to a branching point from which

---

Step	Derivation
0 init	$((0, n_0) \cdot_1 \text{c}) \Rightarrow ((0, n_0)\ \textbf{ROOT})$
1 SHIFT 'what'	$((0, 1) :: \text{d}\ \text{-wh})$ $((0, n_0) \cdot_1 \text{c}) \Rightarrow ((0, n_0)\ \textbf{ROOT})$
2 LC(MERGE3)	$((n_0, n_1) \cdot_2 {=}\text{d}\alpha_3\alpha_4) \Rightarrow ((n_0, n_1) : \alpha_3\alpha_4), ((0, 1) : -\text{wh})\quad \alpha_3 \neq +f_9$ $((0, n_7) \cdot_8 \text{c}) \Rightarrow ((0, n_7)\ \textbf{ROOT})$
3 SHIFT ϵ	$((1, 1) :: {=}\text{v}\ {+}\text{wh}\ \text{c})$ $((n_4, n_5) \cdot_6 {=}\text{d}\alpha_7\alpha_8) \Rightarrow ((n_4, n_5) : \alpha_7\alpha_8), ((0, 1) : -\text{wh})\quad \alpha_7 \neq +f_{13}$ $((0, n_{11}) \cdot_{12} \text{c}) \Rightarrow ((0, n_{11})\ \textbf{ROOT})$
4 C2(MV1(LC(MERGE1)))	$((1, n_0) \cdot_1 \text{v}), ((0, 1), -\text{wh}) \Rightarrow ((0, n_0)\ \textbf{ROOT})$ $((n_3, n_4) \cdot_5 {=}\text{d}\alpha_6\alpha_7) \Rightarrow ((n_3, n_4) : \alpha_6\alpha_7), ((0, 1) : -\text{wh})\quad \alpha_6 \neq +f_8$
5 SHIFT 'John'	$((1, 2) :: \text{d})$ $((1, n_0) \cdot_1 \text{v}), ((0, 1), -\text{wh}) \Rightarrow ((0, n_0)\ \textbf{ROOT})$ $((n_3, n_4) \cdot_5 {=}\text{d}\alpha_6\alpha_7) \Rightarrow ((n_3, n_4) : \alpha_6\alpha_7), ((0, 1) : -\text{wh})\quad \alpha_6 \neq +f_8$
6 C3(LC(MERGE2))	$((2, n_0) \cdot_1 {=}\text{d}\ {=}\text{d}\ \text{v}) \Rightarrow ((0, n_0)\ \textbf{ROOT})$
7 C0(SHIFT) 'buys'	$((0, 3)\ \textbf{ROOT})$

Figure 5: Trace of the parser's progress on 'What John buys', with a gap in object position. Variables are subscripted, and unification of variables when the rules apply is restricted by the indicated inequalities. Note that the (derived, lexical) type indicators are variables when they are introduced before the type is specified.

Step	Derivation
6' C2(LC(MERGE2))	$((2, n_0) : {=}\text{d}\ \text{v}, ((0, 1), -\text{wh}) \Rightarrow ((0, n_0)\ \textbf{ROOT})$ $((n_2, n_3) \cdot_4 {=}\text{d}\alpha_5\alpha_6) \Rightarrow ((n_2, n_3) : \alpha_5\alpha_6), ((0, 1) : -\text{wh})\quad \alpha_6 \neq +f_8$
7' SHIFT 'buys'	$((2, 3) :: {=}\text{d}\ {=}\text{d}\ \text{v})$ $((2, n_4) : {=}\text{d}\ \text{v}, ((0, 1), -\text{wh}) \Rightarrow ((0, n_4)\ \textbf{ROOT})$ $((n_6, n_7) \cdot_8 {=}\text{d}\alpha_9\alpha_{10}) \Rightarrow ((n_6, n_7) : \alpha_9\alpha_{10}), ((0, 1) : -\text{wh})\quad \alpha_{10} \neq +f_{11}$
8' C2(LC(MERGE1))	$((3, n_0) \cdot_1 \text{d}, ((0, 1), -\text{wh}) \Rightarrow ((0, n_0)\ \textbf{ROOT})$ $((n_3, n_4) \cdot_5 {=}\text{d}\alpha_6\alpha_7) \Rightarrow ((n_3, n_4) : \alpha_6\alpha_7), ((0, 1) : -\text{wh})\quad \alpha_7 \neq +f_8$
9' SHIFT 'books'	$((3, 4) :: {=}\text{p}\ \text{d}$ $((3, n_2) \cdot_3 \text{d}, ((0, 1), -\text{wh}) \Rightarrow ((0, n_2)\ \textbf{ROOT})$ $((n_5, n_6) \cdot_7 {=}\text{d}\alpha_8\alpha_9) \Rightarrow ((n_3, n_4) : \alpha_6\alpha_7), ((0, 1) : -\text{wh})\quad \alpha_9 \neq +f_9$
10' C3(LC(MERGE1))	$((4, n_0) \cdot_1 {=}\text{d}\ \text{p}\alpha_8\alpha_9) \Rightarrow ((0, n_0)\ \textbf{ROOT})$
11' C0(SHIFT) 'about'	$((0, 5)\ \textbf{ROOT})$

Figure 6: Trace of the parser's progress on 'What John buys books about', with gap inside a PP inside an object. As anticipated in the discussion of example (5) above, the first five steps, up to and including the shift step that consumes the subject 'John', are the same as in Figure 5, and so we do not repeat them again, showing only how the remaining steps differ.

we can take a C2 transition instead to construct the analysis in (5b).

This general, formal hypothesis of a preference for C3 transitions over C2 transitions has the potential to make predictions about human parsing preferences in domains beyond those that directly prompted the active gap-finding generalization.

6 Conclusion

The main contribution we would like to highlight is that this parser's search space, for sentences containing a filler-gap dependency, is shaped in such a way that it contains branching points corresponding to the choice of whether to (a) posit a gap actively as a first-resort when the opportunity arises, or (b) explore other analyses of the local material first before resorting to positing a gap. This makes it possible to at least *state*, in a precise and general way, the widely-accepted generalization that the human parsing mechanism takes the former option (i.e. adopts the active-filler strategy), and formulate a theory that includes a stipulation to this effect. But if the facts had turned out differently it would have been just as easy to stipulate that the other option is taken instead, and so in this respect we make no claim here to having progressed towards an *explanation* of the observed active-filler generalization. Rather we hope to have pinpointed more precisely what there is to be explained.

This kind of formal instantiation of the active filler idea may also provide a way for variations on the broadly-accepted core idea to be formulated in ways that make precise, distinguishable predictions. For example, looking more closely at Figures 5 and 6, we see that the parser actually posits the gap site before consuming the word that precedes the gap: this happens in Step 6 before shifting 'buys' in Figure 5, and in Step 10' before shifting 'about' in Figure 6. This emerges as a consequence of the fact that, given a binary-branching tree node, a left-corner parser uses one daughter to predict the other (its sister) rather than constructing both independently (as a bottom-up parser would). Since the parser already "knows about" the gap, the way it goes about establishing a structure where the gap and a verb are sisters (if this is what it chooses to do) is by using the gap to predict the verb in its sister position — even though the verb might be usually thought of as appearing to the left of the gap. Although

this perhaps diverges from the most natural understanding of the strategies discussed in the psycholinguistics literature, it appears to be similar to the "hyper-active" gap-finding strategy that Omaki et al. (2015) report some evidence for.

A second way in which the details of Figures 5 and 6 may differ from the usual conception of the active filler strategy is that the filler wh-phrase is integrated into its surface position *after* the complementizer is shifted in Step 3. In a sense it is the +wh feature on the complementizer that really triggers the construction of the MOVE step of the derivation, rather than the filler, and the filler is identified as the moved -wh element only indirectly by virtue of the fact that it covers the required span, from position 0 to position 1. In these sentences with a null complementizer this difference is not really meaningful, but it may be in languages that allow an overt complementizer to co-occur with a fronted wh-phrase.

Finally, one of the most well-known properties of active gap-finding is that it is island-sensitive: humans do not posit gaps in positions which are separated from the filler position by an island boundary (e.g. Traxler and Pickering, 1996; Wagers and Phillips, 2009). In future work we intend to investigate whether this effect might fall out as a natural consequence of certain grammatical encodings of the relevant island constraints.

Acknowledgments

The second author was supported by ERC H2020 Advanced Fellowship GA 742137 SEMANTAX grant. The second and third authors devised and implemented the parser described here; the first author contributed the psycholinguistic motivations and interpretations.

References

Emmon Bach. 1979. Control in Montague Grammar. *Linguistic Inquiry*, 10(4):515–531.

J.R. Brennan, E.P. Stabler, S.E. VanWagenen, W.-M. Luh, and J.T. Hale. 2016. Abstract linguistic structure correlates with temporal activity during naturalistic comprehension. *Brain and Language*, 157-158:81–94.

Noam Chomsky. 1995. *The Minimalist Program*. MIT Press, Cambridge, Massachusetts.

Janet Dean Fodor. 1978. Parsing strategies and constraints on transformations. *Linguistic Inquiry*, 9(3):427–473.

Lyn Frazier and Charles Clifton. 1989. Successive cyclicity in the grammar and the parser. *Languages and Cognitive Processes*, 2(4):93–126.

Lyn Frazier and Charles Clifton. 1996. *Construal*. MIT Press, Cambridge, MA.

Thomas Graf. 2013. *Local and transderivational constraints in syntax and semantics*. Ph.D. thesis, UCLA.

Thomas Graf and Bradley Marcinek. 2014. Evaluating evaluation metrics for minimalist parsing. In *Procs. 2014 ACL Workshop on Cognitive Modeling and Computational Linguistics (CMCL)*, page 2836.

John T. Hale. 2003. *Grammar, uncertainty and sentence processing*. Ph.D. thesis, Johns Hopkins University.

John T. Hale. 2006. Uncertainty about the rest of the sentence. *Cognitive Science*, 30:643–672.

Tim Hunter. 2011. *Syntactic Effects of Conjunctivist Semantics: Unifying Movement and Adjunction*. John Benjamins, Philadelphia.

Tim Hunter. in press. Left-corner parsing of minimalist grammars. In R.C. Berwick and E.P. Stabler, editors, *Minimalist Parsing*. Oxford University Press.

Gregory M. Kobele. 2010. Without remnant movement, MGs are context-free. In *Mathematics of Language 10/11*, LNCS 6149, pages 160–173, NY. Springer.

Gregory M. Kobele, Sabrina Gerth, and John T. Hale. 2012. Memory resource allocation in top-down minimalist parsing. In *Procs. Formal Grammar 2012*, Opole, Poland.

Gregory M. Kobele and Jens Michaelis. 2011. Disentangling notions of specifier impenetrability. In M. Kanazawa, A. Kornai, M. Kracht, and H. Seki, editors, *The Mathematics of Language*, pages 126–142. Springer, Berlin.

Akira Omaki, Ellen F. Lau, Imogen Davidson White, Myles L. Dakan, Aaron Apple, and Colin Phillips. 2015. Hyper-active gap filling. *Frontiers in Psychology*, 6(384).

Colin Phillips. 2006. The real-time status of island phenomena. *Language*, 82:795–823.

Philip Resnik. 1992. Left-corner parsing and psychological plausibility. In *Proceedings of the Fourteenth International Conference on Computational Linguistics (COLING '92)*, pages 191–197.

Edward P. Stabler. 1997. Derivational minimalism. In C. Retoré, editor, *Logical Aspects of Computational Linguistics*, LNCS 1328, pages 68–95. Springer-Verlag, NY.

Edward P. Stabler. 2011. Computational perspectives on minimalism. In Cedric Boeckx, editor, *Oxford Handbook of Linguistic Minimalism*, pages 617–641. Oxford University Press, Oxford.

Edward P. Stabler. 2013. Two models of minimalist, incremental syntactic analysis. *Topics in Cognitive Science*, 5(3):611–633.

Miloš Stanojević and Edward Stabler. 2018. A sound and complete left-corner parser for Minimalist Grammars. In *Procs. Eighth Workshop on Cognitive Aspects of Computational Language Learning and Processing*, pages 65–74.

Adrian Staub. 2007. The parser doesn't ignore transitivity, after all. *Journal of Experimental Psychology: Learning, Memory and Cognition*, 33(3):550–569.

Mark Steedman. 2000. *The Syntactic Process*. MIT Press, Cambridge, MA.

Laurie A. Stowe. 1986. Parsing wh-constructions: Evidence for on-line gap location. *Language and Cognitive Processes*, 1(3):227–245.

Matthew J. Traxler and Martin J. Pickering. 1996. Plausibility and the processing of unbounded dependencies: An eye-tracking study. *Journal of Memory and Language*, 35:454–475.

Matthew W. Wagers and Colin Phillips. 2009. Multiple dependencies and the role of grammar in real-time comprehension. *Journal of Linguistics*, 45:395–433.

Jiwon Yun, Zhong Chen, Tim Hunter, John Whitman, and John Hale. 2015. Uncertainty in the processing of relative clauses in East Asian languages. *Journal of East Asian Linguistics*, 24(2).

Priming vs. Inhibition of Optional Infinitival *to*

Robin Melnick
Pomona College
robin.melnick@pomona.edu

Thomas Wasow
Stanford University
wasow@stanford.edu

Abstract

The word *to* that precedes verbs in English infinitives is optional in at least two environments: in what Wasow et al. (2015) have called the "do-be construction", and in the complement of *help*, explored in the present work. Wasow et al. found that a preceding infinitival *to* increases the use of optional following *to* in the environment they examined, but the use of *to* in the complement of *help* is reduced following *to help*. We examine two hypotheses regarding why the same function word is primed by prior use in one construction and inhibited in another. We then test predictions made by the two hypotheses, finding support for one of them.

1 Introduction

Wasow et al. (2015) investigated factors that influence the optional use of *to* in examples like (1),[1] which Flickinger and Wasow (2013) had dubbed the "do-be construction".

All they do is (to) report gloomy things.[2] (1)

The subject of this construction always contains a relative clause containing a form of the verb *do*; its main verb is a copula; and the copula is followed by a verb phrase, whose inflection must take one of three forms: the one matching the form of *do* (as in 2), the full infinitive form (that is, with *to*, as in 3), or a bare infinitive (without *to*, as in 4).

What we're *doing is going* down the same path. (2)
One thing he *did was to listen*. (3)
The best that can be *done is discuss* this issue. (4)

Wasow et al. found that a variety of factors influence the choice between the last two of these. In particular, the rate of *to* in the post-copula VP is significantly higher than would be expected (given the other factors) when the occurrence of *do* in the subject is infinitival, as in (4)—that is, *to do*. This was attributed to the well-known phenomenon of priming (cf. Branigan and Pickering, 2017 and references cited there).

Another environment in which the infinitival *to* is optional is in VP complements of the verb *help*, with or without noun phrase (NP) object, as in (5).

We helped (them) (to) clear the table. (5)

Descriptive grammars of English (e.g., Peters, 2004:247) often note this peculiarity of *help*, sometimes anecdotally suggesting factors that might influence the use of *to*. Among these is the form of *help*. More specifically, in the words of Lohmann's (2011) quantitative corpus study of this phenomenon, "The bare infinitive is preferred after cases of *to help*." This is just the opposite of priming: A preceding *to* reduces, rather than increases, the use of *to* in this construction. Such anti-priming has been given a number of names in the linguistics literature, including *haplology, the Obligatory Contour Principle* (OCP)*, and horror aequi*. See Walter (2007) for a detailed discussion and many examples of the application of these terms. We will use the term *interference*.

Our question is why a preceding occurrence of infinitival *to* increases the use of *to* in one environment where it is optional, but has the opposite effect in another. What is it about these two constructions that leads to this difference in the use of *to*?

---

[1] All examples in this paper are drawn from the Corpus of Contemporary American English (COCA; Davies, 2008-).

[2] The original token included optional *to* in the source corpus.

Proceedings of the Workshop on Cognitive Modeling and Computational Linguistics, pages 11–19
Minneapolis, USA, June 7, 2019. ©2019 Association for Computational Linguistics

We begin by presenting a multivariate corpus study of *help (to)*, investigating factors that simultaneously influence the use of *to*, interference being just one among several. Section 2 summarizes the compilation and annotation of our sample then presents our statistical model of these data. Section 3 discusses two possible explanations for the opposite influence of a preceding infinitival *to* on the use of a following optional *to* in the two constructions, then further explores a prediction that follows from one of the two hypotheses presented, providing data confirming that prediction.

2   Corpus Study of *help (to)*

Lohmann's earlier study of *help (to)*, as we have termed the construction, was based on a smaller sample (N=1,718) and explored fewer factors of influence than Wasow et al.'s study of *do-be (to)*. The *do-be (to)* work also drew from the Corpus of Contemporary American English (COCA), vs. Lohmann's use of data from the British National Corpus. For better comparison then with the prior results for *do-be (to)*, we have followed Wasow et al. in investigating a similar range of factors, with data drawn from COCA, in the present study using a downloaded version pre-tagged for part of speech, with a total of 520M words divided among five genres: academic, fiction, magazines, newspapers, and spoken.

2.1   Extracting Tokens

We began by programmatically identifying 135K sentences that included a verb-tagged form of *help*. We then passed these sentences through the CoreNLP PCFG constituency parser (version 2.0.2; Klein and Manning, 2003; Manning et al., 2014) to annotate grammatical structure.

Our initial look through several dozen examples found that *help (to)* constructions were represented by a surprising variety of structures in parser output, including a number that we considered to be incorrect. This guided us in crafting a syntactic tree search query (TGrep2; Rohde, 2005) aimed at balancing precision and recall,[3] while still allowing maximal flexibility in terms of any intervening

material: between infinitival *to* and *help* (i.e., "split infinitives"); between *help* (or a direct-object NP) and *to* (if present) preceding the complement verb; or between *to* and the complement verb. We identified 78,283 tokens for further analysis. Checking a random sample (N=100) found precision of 98.3%, recall of 76.3%, yielding F_1 measure 85.9.[4]

2.2   Factors in our Analysis

To model variation in our dependent measure, the presence or absence of *to* before a VP complement of *help*, we began by considering elements analogous to those previously shown to be significantly predictive of optional *to* in the *do-be* construction, including phonological, syntactic, cognitive, and information-theoretic measures. Specifically, we programmatically annotated each token for:

- The primary independent variable (predictor) of interest, whether *help* is preceded by infinitival *to* (again, allowing intervening material). Per Lohmann (2011), infinitival *to* is expected to disfavor optional *to* before complement verb (i.e., interference).

- Accessibility of the complement verb lemma, as reflected by relative frequency within the COCA corpus. This was log-adjusted to account for the Zipfian distribution of verb frequencies, as illustrated in Figure 1.

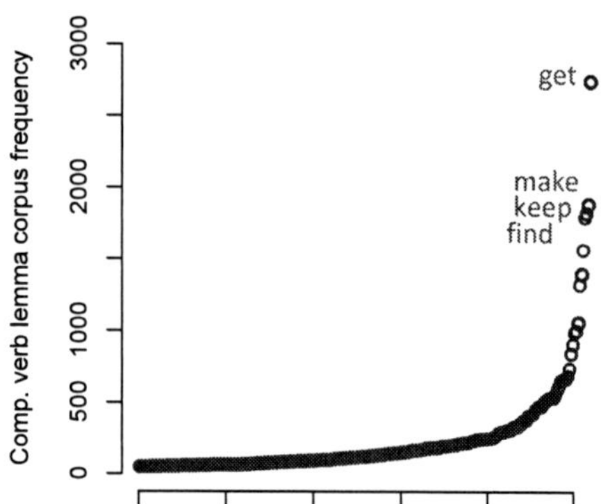

Figure 1: Corpus frequency of *help*-complement verb lemmas. For regression modeling, frequencies are log-adjusted to produce a nearer to linear fit.

---

[3] Of all tokens returned, *precision* is defined as the fraction that were intended targets. Of all intended targets, *recall* is the portion returned by the search.

[4] We randomly selected 100 tokens from our original sample of all COCA sentences that had included a form of *help* and judged that 76 of these represented *help (to)* constructions. Our subsequent tree search query selected 58 of these valid tokens and one non-*help (to)* token, yielding *precision* = 58/59 (0.983), recall = 58/76 (0.763). F_1 is the harmonic mean of *precision* and *recall*, $2pr/(p+r) = 0.859$.

- Predictability of complement verb lemma in context—context here being its likelihood of following *help (to)*—reflected by its relative frequency within the COCA *help (to)* data, once again log-adjusted.

- Intra-token distances, as derived from the constituency parse, including from head noun of subject NP to complement verb, and from head noun of object NP (if present) to complement verb. Head nouns within NP syntactic constituents were identified via the CoreNLP dependency parser (Chen and Manning, 2014).

- Phonological environment of (optional) *to* site. Where complement verb is preceded by optional *to*, we classified the initial segment of whatever word follows *to* (which may be negation, an intervening adverb, or the complement verb itself) into one of four categories: vowels, sibilants, sonorants, or other.[5] We similarly classify the final segment of whatever word precedes *to*. For tokens omitting optional *to*, we classified the initial segment of the complement verb and the final segment of whatever word precedes it. We then annotated each example for whether the given environment was expected, a priori, to favor or disfavor optional *to*. Since *to* is stop-initial, its insertion was expected to be promoted by OCP when preceded and followed by a pair of vowels, sibilants, or sonorants, but disfavored between pairs of "other" segments (i.e., stops, affricates).

- Stress pattern (i.e., prosody), encoded as *clash*, *lapse*, or *other*. As with phonological environment above, we considered the words following and preceding optional *to* if present, or the complement verb and word preceding it where *to* is omitted. *Clash* was coded if the preceding word has final stress and the following word has initial stress. *Lapse* was coded if these are both unstressed.[6]

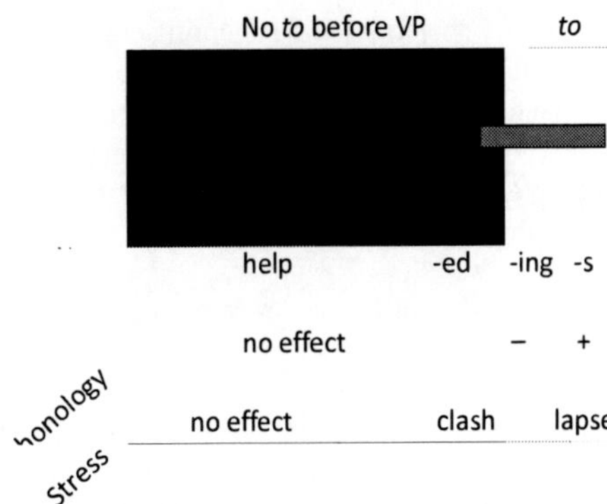

Figure 2: Distribution of categorical variables: (i) presence of infinitival *to* before VP complement; (ii) presence of infinitival *to* before *help*; (iii) presence of direct object NP following *help*; (iv) form of verb *help*; (v) *to*-favoring or disfavoring phonological environment surrounding *to*-site; and (vi) lexical stress environment surrounding *to*-site. X-axis represents number of tokens.

- Surface form of *help* (*help*, *helps*, *helped*, or *helping*).

- Spoken vs. written portion of the corpus.

To these we added measures not modeled in the prior work on the *do-be (to)* construction:

- Animacy of subject.[7]

- Whether or not *help* is negated.

- Whether or not *help* is preceded by a modal auxiliary.

Finally, we encoded an element representing a key difference between *help (to)* and *do-be (to)*:

- Presence of a direct object following *help*.

While the *do-be (to)* construction does not present this option, an object NP following *help* changes the construction's syntactic interpretation. In *help (to)* constructions, *help* is a "control verb", so-called because when followed by a complement verb, *help* functions to control what is understood

---

[5] Assuming phonetic transcriptions extracted from the Carnegie Mellon Pronouncing Dictionary (CMUdict), version 0.7b (2014), for each word.

[6] Drawing once again on information from CMUdict, in this case syllabic stress for each word.

[7] We follow the programmatic animacy-annotation scheme of Melnick 2017, expanding on a technique from Theijssen 2012. As previously noted, a dependency parse identifies the head noun within each subject NP. This is then lemmatized

(via NLTK; Bird et al., 2009) and compared to a static list of animates built from WordNet (Princeton University, 2010) *person* and *animal* terms, a Wikipedia list of notable U.S. companies, and an additional whitelist to capture reflexive pronouns, personal pronouns other than *it* and *them*, and certain impersonal pronouns (*someone*, *everybody*, and so on). Subject head nouns of length greater than two letters in all caps are also marked ANIMATE.

to be the subject of the subordinate VP, but just what that subject is understood to be in any given token depends on whether or not *help* has an object NP. Without an object NP, the subject of the complement verb is understood to be the same as the subject of *help*. For example:

Sunshine helps (to) grow flowers. (6)

In (6), "sunshine" is understood to be the subject of both main verb *help* and complement verb *grow*. In (7), on the other hand, while "sunshine" is again the subject of *help*, object NP "gardeners" is now understood to be the subject of *grow*:

Sunshine helps gardeners (to) grow flowers. (7)

Following annotation, we peformed additional clean-up of the data to improve accuracy. These steps included:

- For the spoken (i.e., transcribed) portion of the corpus only, we excluded tokens where *help* is preceded by *want to, have to,* or *going to,* as we suspect that these transcriptions could represent tokens actually spoken closer

to a one-word [wɑnə] ("wanna"), [hæftə] ("hafta"), or [ɡənə] ("gonna"), that is, without a distinct *to* ([tu]), the potential contributor to an interference effect.

- Limiting analysis to tokens with complement verb lemmas appearing 50 or more times within our sample, in order to improve reliability of relative frequency estimates.

After all adjustments, the final data set for analysis totals 63,593 tokens. Figure 2 shows univariate distributions for several factors laid out above.

2.3 Modeling Variation

To assess the effect of infinitival *to* before *help* (i.e., on the inclusion of infinitival *to* before a following complement verb) while simultaneously controlling for other expected influences, we fit our data with a mixed-effects binary logistic regression model (Pinheiro and Bates, 2000; Bresnan et al., 2007; Baayen et al., 2008), predicting infinitival complement VP from fixed effects for the several factors described above, with a random effect for complement verb lemma.

	Est. β	Std Err	z value	Pr(>|z|)	
Fixed effects					
Form of *help*:					
help	-0.608	0.071	-8.614	< 0.0001	***
helped	-0.722	0.082	-8.787	< 0.0001	***
helping	0.418	0.081	5.179	< 0.0001	***
helps	-0.048	0.083	-0.584	0.5590	
Infinitive *help*	**-2.072**	**0.062**	**-33.436**	**< 0.0001**	***
Object NP present ("object control")	-1.691	0.042	-40.741	< 0.0001	***
Written corpus	-0.212	0.034	-6.256	< 0.0001	***
Modal before *help*	0.265	0.044	5.962	< 0.0001	***
Negated *help*	0.413	0.108	3.825	0.0001	***
Subject animacy	-0.300	0.032	-9.417	< 0.0001	***
Phon.: (−) condition	-0.465	0.045	-10.298	< 0.0001	***
Phon.: (+) condition	0.149	0.052	2.881	0.0040	**
Stress: clash	-0.213	0.039	-5.482	< 0.0001	***
Stress: lapse	0.402	0.052	7.707	< 0.0001	***
Distance, controller↔*to*	0.089	0.016	5.488	< 0.0001	***
Verb availaility	0.255	0.044	5.851	< 0.0001	***
Verb predictability	-0.265	0.036	-7.434	< 0.0001	***
Interactions					
Object NP × Sbj animacy	0.218	0.052	4.181	< 0.0001	***
Object NP × Controller distance	0.085	0.022	3.943	0.0001	***
Object NP × Verb preditability	0.250	0.041	6.081	< 0.0001	***

Table 1: Logistic regression model of *help (to)* construction, fixed effects and interactions, predicting optional *to* before complement verb. Positive beta coefficients promote optional *to*. The outlined row highlights the effect of *to* before *help*, with negative coefficient suggesting inhibition (i.e., interference).

Since the presence or absence of an NP direct object following the main verb *help* affects both a given token's projected syntactic structure and its inter-constituent dependencies (e.g., whether the subject of the complement verb is controlled by the subject or object of *help*), we explored interactions of object NP presence with a handful of other predictors, including subject animacy, distance to complement verb from controller (subject or object of *help*), and both availability and predictability of the complement verb. Stepwise reduction based on significant contribution to model fit retained all main effects and eliminated only the interaction of object presence with complement verb availability. Table 1 presents the resulting model, with pseudo-$R^2 = 0.382$.

The primary observation is that the interference effect of infinitival *help*—i.e., disfavoring optional *to* before a following complement verb—is confirmed here under multivariate control ($\beta = -2.072$, $z = -33.4$, $p < 0.0001$).

While other factors were included chiefly to maximize accuracy of our interference effect estimate, we briefly review their results. Most of the several factors with analogs in Wasow et al.'s model of the *do-be* construction appear to have similar effects here. Written language produces less optional *to* than spoken, presumed to reflect less pressure from online processing demands. Increased distance—in this case, to the complement verb from the subject of *help* or from its direct object, if present—promotes optional *to*, as increased dependency length generates additional processing load (Hawkins, 2004). Increased predictability of a particular complement verb in context (i.e., prior probability of encountering it following *help*) disfavors optional *to*, which we take as an example of the principle of Uniform Information Density (UID; Levy and Jaeger, 2007; Jaeger; 2010). Here, UID would predict that *to* would be more likely to be included where it would serve to spread out the arrival of new information, or *surprisal*, in those cases where the complement verb is *less* predictable in context (i.e., the inverse of predictability). Surprisingly, increased overall corpus frequency of the complement verb—as opposed to its frequency just in the context of the *help (to)* construction— appears to promote optional *to*, counter to its effect in Wasow et al.'s *do-be* results, though exploring this further falls beyond our present scope.

We also find a few significant interactions. The main effect of an animate *help* subject—and thus an animate subject for the complement verb, as well, when *help* has no direct object—appears to disfavor optional *to*, but this effect was largely neutralized in the presence of a direct object. This follows from noting that in such cases, it is the *help* direct object that is interpreted as the subject of the complement verb. The significant distance effect, conversely, was only further enhanced in such "object control" cases. In the context of the shorter dependency length between direct object and following complement verb in these examples, small increases in length had a larger effect. Finally, like the subject animacy effect, the UID effect (predictability of complement verb in context) appears to be largely neutralized in the presence of a direct object.

Figure 3(a) illustrates the relative contribution to model fit for each fixed effect. The presence of an NP object following *help*—with its critical syntactic role, when present, in determining the subject of the complement verb—makes the single largest contribution to model fit, followed by our primary object of study, the interference effect (i.e.,

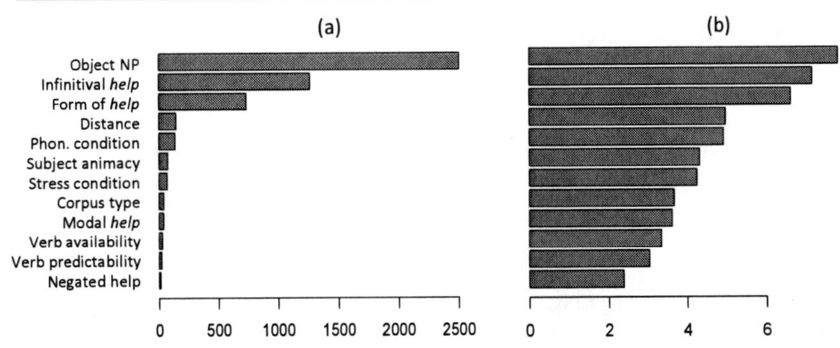

Figure 3: Fixed-effect contributions to fit, as measured by Akaike Information Criterion, log-adjusted in 3(b).

infinitive *to* before *help*). Figure 3(b) presents the same data on a logarithmic scale to better visualize the relative sizes of the smaller contributors.

3 Two Hypotheses

Our model thus confirms under multivariate control the observation that preceding infinitival *to* disfavors optional *to* before a following complement verb, in contrast with the *do-be (to)* construction, where Wasow et al. (2015) had found preceding infinitival *to* favoring optional following *to*—that is, interference in *help (to)* vs. priming in *do-be (to)*. Why do the constructions behave so differently in this respect?

3.1 The Locality Hypothesis

A first hypothesis is that the preceding *to* in the *help* construction tends to be closer to the site of optional *to* than in the *do-be* construction. When no object NP intervenes between infinitival *help* and a VP complement, the site of optional *to* is most often separated from the preceding *to* by just one monosyllabic word. In the *do-be* construction, by contrast, there must be a minimum of two words (*do* and some form of *be*) between infinitival *do* and the site of optional *to*.

Most examples in the linguistics literature of what Walter (2007) calls "repetition avoidance" are very local: avoidance of identical or similar segments, tones, inflections, or words that are adjacent. Hence, it is perhaps natural to conjecture that interference is necessarily a very short-lived effect, and to look for a solution to our puzzle in terms of locality. But the psycholinguistics literature also contains examples of less local interference effects, for example, Ferreira and Firato (2002).

Both our corpus study and that of Wasow et al. found significant effects of the distance to the optional *to* site from an obligatory preceding verb (*do* or *help*). But locality cannot be the full explanation of the difference in the behavior of optional *to* in the two constructions. The interference effect of *to* immediately preceding *help* persists even when an object NP intervenes between *help* and its VP complement. This is confirmed by separately refitting our model to just those tokens with an object NP. The negative influence of preceding *to* on following *to* remains highly significant ($\beta = -1.41$, $z = -17.6$, $p < 0.0001$). In this environment, the optional *to* site following

help is as far from a preceding *to* as in the *do-be* construction, a minimum of two words in each construction and often more, as in (8). Hence, something else must be involved.

Professionals learn how [*to help*] families of young children with visual impairments [*promote*] emergent literacy skills   (8)

3.2 The Function Hypothesis

The second hypothesis was first suggested to us by Emily Bender (p.c.). She noted that the verb *do* that is an obligatory part of the *do-be* construction functions essentially as an elliptical replacement for the post-copula VP. For example, in (1) part of what is predicated of the referent of *they* is that they report gloomy things, and *do* stands in for the VP *report gloomy things*.

Elliptical constructions generally exhibit some structural parallelism between the ellipsis site and the antecedent. The exact nature of the parallelism constraints in such constructions has been the subject of a great deal of linguistic literature over the past half century; see, for example, Hankamer and Sag (1976) and van Craenenbroeck and Merchant (2013). These parallelism constraints presumably assist the listener (or reader) in identifying the antecedent and thus determining the intended interpretation of elliptical expressions. The priming of *to* in the *do-be* construction, then, can be viewed as one component of the expected parallelism in ellipsis.

In contrast, there is no elliptical relationship between the verb *help* and its complement VP. However, when both *help* and its complement are full infinitives (with *to*), it is an instance of self-embedding (also known as recursion)—that is, a construction (in this case, an infinitival VP) directly embedded within another construction of the same type.

It has been known for over half a century (see Miller and Chomsky, 1963:286) that center self-embedding creates severe processing difficulty. Although less attention has been paid to the effect of self-embedding on the edge of a constituent, there is some literature (e.g., Christiansen and MacDonald, 2009) showing that right-branching recursive structures also cause processing difficulty, albeit less than center self-embedding. Without the second occurrence of *to*, *to help* VP is not an instance of self-embedding. Hence, it should not be surprising that we observe interference when *to help* takes a full infinitival complement.

3.3 A Prediction

If the interference effect that we observe in the *help* (*to*) construction is due to avoidance of self-embedding, then it should show up with other verbs that take infinitival complements. Even though *help* is exceptional in allowing the word *to* to be omitted, most other verbs that can take infinitival complements can also occur in other environments. For example, *expect, need, try,* and *want* all can take simple NP objects; *appear, ask,* and *try* can all take a prepositional complement; and *seem* can take an adjectival complement. If speakers avoid embedding infinitival VPs directly under another infinitival VP, the effect should be observable with these other verbs as well. With the other verbs avoiding self-embedding it is not so simple as merely replacing the full infinitival VP with a VP lacking *to*. But other paraphrases that avoid recursion are always possible. Hence, we predict that the rate of occurrence of infinitival VP complements in these other verbs should be lower when the verbs themselves are infinitival (i.e. immediately preceded by *to*) than in other environments.

3.4 Testing the Prediction

To test this prediction, we turn once again to COCA, identifying all verb lemmas ever observed to take an infinitval complement. This yields 10,931 types in the corpus. Further restricting analysis to those verb lemmas appearing more than 1,000 times overall and at least 10 times with an infinitival complement yields 1,019 types. We examined all 70.1M occurances of these verbs, classifying each token into one of four categories: (a) non-infinitival verb, V_1; (b) verb with infinitval complement, V_1 *to* V_2; (c) infinitival verb, *to* V_1; or (d) infinitival verb with infinitval complement, *to* V_1 *to* V_2.[8]

Our prediction can be restated as in (9), the expectation that the conditional probability of the appearance of a complement verb given infinitival main verb should be much less than the conditional probability of complement verb given non-infinitival main verb.

$$p(V_2 \mid to\ V_1) \ll p(V_2 \mid V_1) \qquad (9)$$

This is formulated in (10) in terms of our four-way classification above.

$$\frac{(d)}{(c)} \ll \frac{(b)}{(a)} \qquad (10)$$

In a single metric, we expect the ratio in (11) to be much less than 1.

$$\frac{(d)/(c)}{(b)/(a)} \ll 1 \qquad (11)$$

We found this measure to be less than 1 for 837 of our 1,019 verbs (82.1%), representing 53.4M of 70.1M tokens (76.2%). Across the entire set of verbs, we calculate an aggregate ratio of 0.292. Table 2 presents individual results for ten common verbs that take an infinitival complement, including *help*, in ascending order by ratio value.

Verb	(d/c) / (b/a)
help	0.083
hope	0.104
like	0.131
expect	0.133
appear	0.134
seem	0.154
demand	0.232
need	0.386
ask	0.417
try	0.817

Table 2: Values << 1 suggest an infinitival main verb disfavors appearance with an infinitival complement.

To consider the statistical significance of these findings, we employ McNemar's Chi-Squared test, which corrects for lack of independence of observations, required here as each verb provides tokens in multiple conditions (i.e., in each of our four token classification categories). Of the 837 verbs noted above as disfavoring infinitival recursion (ratio < 1), 824 (98.4%) show a significant result under McNemar's $\chi2$ ($p < 0.05$). Finally, an aggregate test of the full data set finds $\chi2 = 110.04$, df = 1, p < 0.0001.

Infinitival verb self-embedding indeed appears to be strongly disfavored in this large corpus of modern American English, in turn supporting the function hypothesis for the apparent interference effect on optional *to* before a complement verb following infinitival *help*.

---

[8] Without resorting to parsing the entire 520M-word corpus, we limited extractions here, unlike our full *help* study, to tokens without intervening material.

4   Conclusions

Our corpus investigations of optional *to* have shown that both priming and interference occur in the use of the same optional function word. Which one occurs in a given environment is not arbitrary. Rather, it depends on more general properties of those environments: we find priming where repetition can facilitate processing, as it does in elliptical constructions; and we find interference where repetition creates processing difficulty, as it does in self-embedding.

Acknowledgments

We thank Evan Chuu for assistance in data preparation and are grateful for comments from three anonymous reviewers. This work has also benefited from discussions with Emily Bender, Florian Jaeger, and Maryellen MacDonald. Any errors remain our own. Statistical calculations and graphics were developed with R version 3.5.1 (R Core Team, 2018).

References

R. Harald Baayen, Douglas J. Davidson, and Douglas M. Bates. 2008. Mixed-effects modeling with crossed random effects for subjects and items. *Journal of memory and language* 59.4: 390-412.

Steven Bird, Ewan Klein, and Edwin Loper. 2009. *Natural language processing with Python.* Sebastopol, CA: O'Reilly Media.

Holly P. Branigan and Martin J. Pickering. 2017. Structural priming and the representation of language. *Behavioral and Brain Sciences* 40.

Joan Bresnan, Anna Cueni, Tatiana Nikitina, and R. Harald Baayen. 2007. Predicting the dative alternation. In *Cognitive foundations of interpretation*, pp. 69-94. KNAW.

Carnegie Mellon University. 2014. *The Carnegie Mellon Pronouncing Dictionary (CMUdict), version 0.7b.* http://www.speech.cs.cmu.edu/cgi-bin/cmudict

Danqi Chen and Christopher Manning. 2014. A fast and accurate dependency parser using neural networks. In *Proceedings of EMNLP 2014.*

Morten H. Christiansen and Maryellen C. MacDonald. 2009. A usage-based approach to recursion in sentence processing. *Language Learning* 59(1): 126-161.

Jeroen van Craenenbroeck and Jason Merchant. 2013. Ellipsis phenomena. In Marcel den Dikken (ed.), *The Cambridge Handbook of Generative Syntax,* 701-745. Cambridge University Press: Cambridge.

Mark Davies. 2008-. *The Corpus of Contemporary American English (COCA): 560 million words, 1990-present.* https://corpus.byu.edu/coca/

Victor S. Ferreira and Carla E. Firato. 2002. Proactive interference effects on sentence production *Psychonomic Bulletin & Review,* 9(4):795-800.

Daniel Flickinger and Thomas Wasow. 2013. A corpus-driven analysis of the do-be construction. In Philip Hofmeister & Elisabeth Norcliffe (eds) *The Core and the Periphery: Data-Driven Perspectives on Syntax Inspired by Ivan A. Sag,* pp. 35-63. CSLI Publications.

Jorge Hankamer and Ivan A. Sag. 1976. Deep and surface anaphora. *Linguistic Inquiry* 7(3):391-426.

John A. Hawkins. 2004. *Efficiency and complexity in grammars.* Oxford University Press on Demand.

Florian Jaeger. 2010. Redundancy and reduction: Speakers manage information density. *Cognitive Psychology* 61(1):23-62.

Dan Klein and Christopher D. Manning. 2003. Accurate unlexicalized parsing. *Proceedings of the 41st Meeting of the Association for Computational Linguistics,* pp. 423-430.

Roger P. Levy and T. Florian. Jaeger. 2007. Speakers optimize information density through syntactic reduction. In *Advances in neural information processing systems,* pp. 849- 856.

Arne Lohmann. 2011. *Help* vs *help to*: A multifactorial, mixed-effects account of infinitive marker omission. *English Language & Linguistics* 15, no. 3: 499-521.

Christopher D. Manning, Mihai Surdeanu, John Bauer, Jenny Finkel, Steven J. Bethard, and David McClosky. 2014. The Stanford CoreNLP Natural Language Processing Toolkit. In *Proceedings of the 52nd Annual Meeting of the Association for Computational Linguistics: System Demonstrations,* pp. 55-60.

Robin Melnick. 2017. *Consistency in variation: On the provenance of end-weight.* Unpublished Stanford University dissertation.

George Miller and Noam Chomsky.1963. Finitary models of language users. In R. Luce, R. Bush and E. Galanter (eds.) *Handbook of Mathematical Psychology, Vol 2,* 419-93. New York: Wiley.

Pam Peters. 2004. *The Cambridge Guide to English Usage*. Cambridge University Press, Cambridge, England.

José C. Pinheiro and Douglas M. Bates. 2000. *Statistics and computing. Mixed-effects models in S and S-PLUS*. Springer.

Princeton University. 2010. *About WordNet*. http://wordnet.princeton.edu

R Core Team. 2018. *R: A language and environment for statistical computing*. R Foundation for Statistical Computing, Vienna, Austria. URL https://www.R-project.org/.

Douglas L. Rohde. 2005. *Tgrep2 user manual*. http://tedlab.mit.edu/~dr/Tgrep2/tgrep2.pdf

Daphne L. Theijssen. (2012. *Making choices: Modelling the English dative alternation*. Unpublished dissertation, Radboud University Nijmegen.

Mary Ann Walter. 2007. *Repetition avoidance in human language*. Unpublished MIT dissertation.

Thomas Wasow, Roger Levy, Robin Melnick, Hanzhi Zhu, and Tom Juzek. 2015. Processing, prosody, and optional *to*. In Lyn Frazier and Edward Gibson (eds) *Explicit and Implicit Prosody in Sentence Processing*, pp. 133-158. Springer.

Simulating Spanish-English Code-Switching: *El Modelo Está Generating Code-Switches*

Chara Tsoukala
Centre for Language Studies,
Radboud University
c.tsoukala@let.ru.nl

Stefan L. Frank
Centre for Language Studies,
Radboud University
s.frank@let.ru.nl

Antal van den Bosch
KNAW Meertens Institute;
Centre for Language Studies,
Radboud University
a.vandenbosch@let.ru.nl

Jorge Valdés Kroff
Department of Spanish and Portuguese Studies,
University of Florida
jvaldeskroff@ufl.edu

Mirjam Broersma
Centre for Language Studies,
Radboud University
m.broersma@let.ru.nl

Abstract

Multilingual speakers are able to switch from one language to the other ("code-switch") between or within sentences. Because the underlying cognitive mechanisms are not well understood, in this study we use computational cognitive modeling to shed light on the process of code-switching. We employed the Bilingual Dual-path model, a Recurrent Neural Network of bilingual sentence production (Tsoukala et al., 2017) and simulated sentence production in simultaneous Spanish-English bilinguals. Our first goal was to investigate whether the model would code-switch without being exposed to code-switched training input. The model indeed produced code-switches even without any exposure to such input and the patterns of code-switches are in line with earlier linguistic work (Poplack, 1980). The second goal of this study was to investigate an auxiliary phrase asymmetry that exists in Spanish-English code-switched production. Using this cognitive model, we examined a possible cause for this asymmetry. To our knowledge, this is the first computational cognitive model that aims to simulate code-switched sentence production.

1 Introduction

People who speak several languages are able to switch from one language to the other, between or within sentences, a process called code-switching. Code-switching has been studied for decades by theoretical linguists and sociolinguists (e.g., Poplack 1980; Muysken 2000) and more recently by psycholinguists (e.g., Bullock and Toribio 2009). In the past few years it has started being studied with a computational methodology, and it has garnered attention among the natural language processing (NLP) research community. Several NLP applications have emerged, e.g., to detect code-switches (Solorio and Liu, 2008; Guzmán et al., 2017), or to automatically recognize code-switched speech (Yılmaz et al., 2016; Gonen and Goldberg, 2018). Moreover, there are a small number of cognitive computational models relevant to code-switching: Filippi et al. (2014) developed a model of code-switched word production and Janciauskas and Chang (2018), while simulating age of acquisition effects on native Korean speakers of English, reported that the models that had been exposed to English later produced code-switches, i.e., occasionally used Korean words in their predominantly English production.

The underlying mechanisms of code-switching, however, are still not well understood. Therefore, we suggest using computational cognitive modeling to simulate code-switching behavior in multilinguals with the goal of gaining more insight into the process of code-switching. In this work, we have employed a model of bilingual sentence production (Tsoukala et al., 2017) and tested whether it can produce spontaneous code-switches without being trained on code-switched sentences (Experiment 1, Section 3). We wanted to test whether code-switching can be (partially) attributed to internal factors and explained by the distributions of the two languages involved, or whether it is strictly a community-based practice that can only be explained by exposure to code-switches. To test the former, we hypothesized that a model that receives training input in two languages but no code-switched sentences, will nevertheless be able to produce code-switched sentences by combining patterns from the two languages it has been

Proceedings of the Workshop on Cognitive Modeling and Computational Linguistics, pages 20–29
Minneapolis, USA, June 7, 2019. ©2019 Association for Computational Linguistics

trained on. We then employed this model to investigate a specific production phenomenon that occurs in Spanish-English code-switching (Experiment 2). As explained in Section 4, we wanted to test whether the phenomenon of interest is caused by the distributional properties of the two languages. This is something that can be explicitly tested with this model because it is not trained on code-switched input.

To our knowledge, this is the first computational cognitive model that aims to simulate code-switched sentence production.

2 Model

To simulate code-switched sentence production, we first needed to simulate bilingual production. For that purpose, we employed the Bilingual Dual-path model (Tsoukala et al., 2017) and trained it to simulate simultaneous Spanish-English bilinguals, i.e., speakers who acquired both Spanish and English from infancy.

The Bilingual Dual-path model is a modified version of Dual-path (Chang, 2002). We chose to work with, and extend, the Dual-path model because it is one of the most successful and empirically validated cognitive models of sentence production. It has been used to explain a wide range of phenomena in various languages; for an overview see Frank et al. (in press).

2.1 Bilingual Dual-path Model

The Bilingual Dual-path model (Figure 1) is a Recurrent Neural Network (RNN) based on the Simple Recurrent Network (SRN; Elman 1990) architecture. It learns to convert a message into a sentence by predicting the sentence word by word. Dual-path got its name because of its two pathways that influence the production of each word: i) the meaning, or semantic, system that learns to map words onto concepts (and their realization, see below and Section 2.2.1), thematic roles, event semantics and the intended language ("target language"), and ii) the sequencing, or syntactic, system that is an SRN that learns to abstract syntactic patterns. Both paths influence the next word prediction (the "output" layer).

To express a new message (see Section 2.2.4 for examples of messages), the following items are fixed and influence the production of the first word: the to-be-expressed semantic roles have fixed connections with their concepts and realiza-tions, and the relevant "event semantics" and "target language" units are activated. Additionally, the hidden layer's context units are reset to a default value (0.5 in our simulations).

The output word is determined as the word with the highest activation in the output layer. Once an output word has been produced, it is fed back as input (to the "input" layer). During the training phase, the target word is given as input instead of the (potentially different) output word.

The sequencing system is a regular SRN that has one recurrent hidden layer (of 110 units in our simulations) and two 70-unit "compress" layers that are placed between the input word and the hidden layer, and between the hidden layer and the output word.

The meaning system learns to map the input word onto a concept and, whenever relevant, the realization of that concept (PRON for pronoun, INDEF for an indefinite article and DEF for definite articles; see Section 2.2.1 ("Message") for concrete examples).

A difference between this architecture and other RNNs is that whenever a new message needs to be expressed, the network receives fixed connections between concepts and roles; this allows their separation (instead of having a single unit for, e.g., 'AGENT-WOMAN') and, in turn, enables the model to generalize and to produce words in novel roles. For instance, if the concept 'WOMAN' has only been seen as an AGENT in the training set, it can still be correctly expressed in novel roles (PATIENT, RECIPIENT) during the test phase (Chang, 2002).

All layers use the *tanh* activation function, except the output and predicted role layers that use *softmax*. The model is built in Python and can be found at https://github.com/xtsoukala/CMCL19.

2.2 Input Languages

In order to simulate Spanish-English bilingual sentence production, we generated input with relevant properties of the two languages. The sentences (and their messages, see Section 2.2.1) are generated before the training starts, and they are based on the allowed structures (Section 2.2.2). For each part of speech (POS) a randomly selected lexical item (from that POS and target language) is sampled from the lexicon (Section 2.2.3). The advantage of using artificial (miniature) languages is

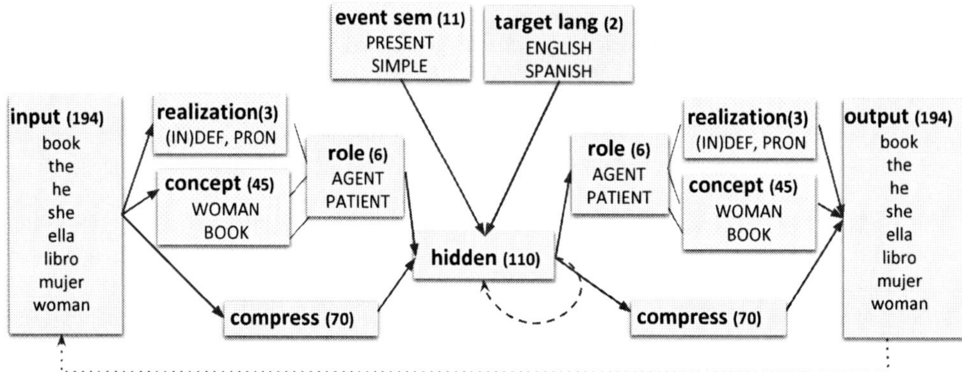

Figure 1: Bilingual Dual-path, the model used in these simulations, is a next-word prediction model that converts messages into sentences. It is based on an SRN (the lower path, via the 'compress' layers) that is augmented with a semantic stream (upper path) that contains information about concepts, thematic roles, event semantics, and the target language.

that we can manipulate the frequency and grammar of the input and isolate (and thereby study) the phenomenon of interest.

2.2.1 Message

The model is trained using generated sentences (as described above) paired with their message that consists of semantics and their realization, event-semantics, and target language, which will be explained in turn below.

In these simulations, the semantics contains information regarding 45 unique concepts and 6 thematic roles: AGENT, AGENT-MODIFIER, PATIENT, ACTION-LINKING, RECIPIENT, and ATTRIBUTE.

ACTION-LINKING is a combined thematic role that can be used for all verb types: action (e.g., 'throws'), linking ('is') and possession ('has'). ATTRIBUTE is an attribute expressed with a linking verb concept ('BE'). AGENT and RECIPIENT can be expressed only with animate nouns.

A concept (e.g., WOMAN for the English word 'woman' or Spanish word 'mujer') is assigned to each thematic role (during the sentence generation process) along with a realization attribute (PRON for pronoun, DEF for definite article, and INDEF for indefinite article) according to the meaning that needs to be expressed. For instance, in the sentence "the woman runs" the message would include "AGENT=WOMAN, DEF", whereas "a woman" would be encoded as "AGENT=WOMAN, INDEF", and "she" as "AGENT=WOMAN, PRON".

Furthermore, the message contains event semantic information (denoted as EVENT-SEM), which gives information regarding the tense (PRESENT, PAST) and aspect (SIMPLE, PERFECT or PROGRESSIVE). The EVENT-SEM layer also contains information regarding the roles needed for that particular message; the model needs to keep track of the roles expressed and make sure that if, e.g., the role of RECIPIENT is activated then the recipient has also been expressed.

Additionally, the message contains information about the target language so that the model knows whether it is learning to produce an English or Spanish sentence.

2.2.2 Structures

The allowed structures for both languages are the following in our simulations:

- SV: Subject - Verb, e.g., "a happy dog runs"; "un perro feliz corre"

- SVO: Subject - Verb - Object, e.g., "the boy is carrying a book"; "el niño está llevando un libro"

- SVDOPP: Subject - Verb - Direct Object - Prepositional Phrase, e.g., "she shows a book to the girl"; "ella muestra un libro a la niña"

- SVIODO: Subject - Verb - Indirect Object - Direct Object: e.g., "she shows the girl a book" (Structure occurs only in English)

- SVPPDO: Subject - Verb - Prepositional Phrase - Direct Object: e.g., "ella muestra a la niña un libro" ("she shows to a girl a book"). Structure only used in Spanish.

The roles can be expressed using either a Noun Phrase (NP) with definite (DEF) or indefinite (IN-DEF) article (e.g., 'the woman', 'a woman'). Additionally, AGENT can be expressed with a pronoun (PRON, e.g. 'she'). NPs optionally contain a modifier (an adjective, e.g., 'a tall woman').

The verbs are either intransitive (e.g., 'sleep'), transitive ('carry'), double transitive ('show'), linking ('is') or possession verb ('has'). The tense is present or past and the aspect is simple, progressive, or perfect. Only the simple past was used whereas the present tense is used with all three aspects:

- simple present: "the man cooks"; "el hombre cocina"

- present progressive: "the man is cooking"; "el hombre está cocinando"

- present perfect: "the man has cooked"; "el hombre ha cocinado"

2.2.3 Bilingual Lexicon

The lexicon consists of 194 words (Table 1): 88 English words, 105 Spanish words, and the shared period ('.') that marks the end of the sentence. The Spanish lexicon is bigger because this language is gendered: for instance, 'tired' is either 'cansado', if it modifies a masculine noun, or 'cansada' for a feminine noun. Syntactic category information (such as 'adjective', 'participle') is not given explicitly; the model learns it through the syntactic path during training.

2.2.4 Input Examples

To illustrate the input, here is an example of the message (excluding the target language):

AGENT=WOMAN, INDEF

AGENT-MOD=TALL

ACTION-LINKING=GIVE

PATIENT=BOOK, DEF

RECIPIENT=GIRL, DEF

EVENT-SEM=SIMPLE,PRESENT,AGENT, AGENT-MOD, PATIENT, RECIPIENT

POS	n	Examples
Verbs	64	
auxiliary	4	is, has, *está, ha*
intransitive	32	walked, swims, *nada*
transitive	12	carries, push, *lleva*
double transitive	12	gives, throws, *da*
possession	4	has, had, *tiene, tenía*
linking [1]	4	is, was, *está, estaba*
Participles [2]	57	eating, eaten, *comido*
Nouns	46	
animate	10	uncle, aunt, *tío, tía*
inanimate	36	pen, book, *libro*
Adjectives	22	busy, *ocupado*
Determiners	6	a, the, *un, una, el, la*
Prepositions	2	to, *a*
Pronouns	4	he, she, *él, ella*

[1] Three of these overlap with the auxiliary verbs.
[2] Nine of these have the same form as a verb; e.g., 'walked' is either a perfect participle or a verb.

Table 1: POS in bilingual lexicon (Spanish in italics)

This message would be expressed linguistically in the following manner in English and Spanish:

- a tall woman gives the girl a book .

- una mujer alta da a la niña un libro . (word-by-word translation: "a woman tall gives to the girl a book")

If the aspect was PROGRESSIVE instead of SIMPLE, on the other hand, the corresponding sentences would be "a tall woman is giving the girl a book"; "una mujer alta está dando a la niña un libro".

The linking verb messages were encoded in the following manner:

AGENT=WOMAN, DEF

ACTION-LINKING=BE

ATTRIBUTE=TIRED

EVENT-SEM=SIMPLE,PRESENT, AGENT, ATTRIBUTE

and expressed as "the woman is tired"; "la mujer está cansada".

2.3 Training

The model was trained on a total of 3040 randomly generated sentence-message pairs in English and

Spanish (training set; 50% [1520 pairs] per language). Recall that no code-switched sentences were given as input.

We ran 60 simulations using different input and different random initial weights per simulation, as the input and the weights are the only non-deterministic parts of the model. The models were trained for 30 epochs, where 1 epoch corresponds to a full iteration of the training set (3040 sentences). At the beginning of each epoch, the training set was shuffled.

The "realization–role" and "role–realization" connection weights were set to 10, and the "concept–role" and "role–concept" to 30. The initial learning rate was 0.10 and linearly decreased over 10 epochs until it reached 0.02; the momentum was set to 0.9. None of the hyper-parameters was optimized for the task, and they do not play a crucial role in the results. We selected the values from Tsoukala et al. (2017) and increased the "concept–role" connections because this resulted in slightly better performance (the current experiments use more concepts).

2.4 Evaluation and Performance Threshold

The correctness of a sentence is determined by whether the correct (and complete) semantic meaning has been expressed in a grammatical sentence but not necessarily in the target syntactic structure. For instance, if the target sentence is "a sad grandfather is showing the book to a girl" and the produced sentence is "a sad grandfather is showing the *pen* to a girl" it is counted as incorrect, whereas if the produced sentence is "a sad grandfather is showing *the girl the book*" it is counted as correct even though it was expressed with a different syntactic structure than the target one. If it is expressed with a different aspect (e.g., perfect instead of progressive) or realization (e.g., pronoun instead of an NP with an indefinite article) it is also marked as incorrect. If the sentence contains code-switches it is marked as correct as long as it expresses the correct meaning, is expressed in one of the allowed structures (Section 2.2.2) and the POS sequence of each phrase (NP, Verb Phase [VP], Prepositional Phrase [PP]) is valid in either language.

For all the experiments, we excluded from the analysis simulations that did not learn to produce at least 75% of the messages correctly according to the criteria above.

3 Experiment 1: Code-Switching

In this study, we investigate whether the Bilingual Dual-path would produce code-switched sentences if trained on Spanish and English (but not code-switched) sentences. We investigate the occurrence of different patterns of code-switching that have been observed in the language use of human bilingual speakers.

3.1 Background

Muysken (2000) proposed the following typology of code-switching:

1. Insertional switching
   Insertions of single words/fixed expressions:

   - lexical (e.g., noun): "I read a *libro*" (I read a book)
   - fixed expressions/ interjections/ idiomatic expressions: "*Oh my god, estamos sin palabras*" (we are speechless)

2. Alternational switching
   Alternation between the two languages, involving multi-word sequences, either between or within sentences:

   - Inter-sentential switching: "I heard you had an accident. *¿Qué pasó?*" (What happened?)
   - Intra-sentential switching: "I had a hard time finding *tu casa esta mañana.*" (your house this morning)

3. Congruent lexicalization
   In cases where the languages share syntactic structures and are highly cognate, it is possible to use the shared syntax and insert lexical items from either language, thus seemingly switching back and forth: e.g., "*Bueno*, in other words, *el* flight *que sale de* Chicago around three o'clock" ('Fine, ... the flight which leaves from ...') (Pfaff, 1979)

3.1.1 Code-Switching by Syntactic Category

In a seminal study, Poplack (1980) observed the Puerto-Rican community in the US. She found that balanced bilinguals produced mostly complex code-switches, such as intra-sentential ones, and few insertions. Switches at the NP were more frequent than switches at the VP and PP, and noun insertions were the most frequent lexical insertion whereas determiner insertions occurred rarely.

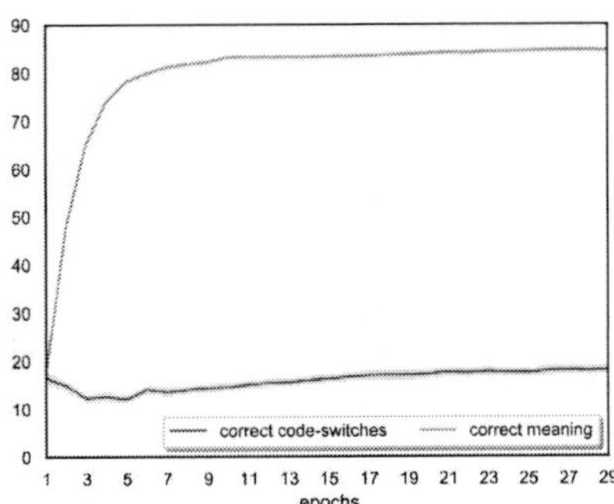

Figure 2: Percentage of correctly produced sentences and of code-switches among those sentences. The shaded area shows the Standard Error of the Mean (SEM) computed over 56 simulations

3.2 Method

To simulate code-switching, we trained the model as described in Section 2.3 and tested it on 760 unseen sentences (test set) that were randomly generated in the same manner as the training set.

During the test ("production") phase we manipulated the model's language control by activating a target language only at the beginning, before the production of the first word, so as to indicate the conversational setting (intended language). After the first word had been produced, we activated both target language nodes, thus allowing the model to produce the sentence in either language or to code-switch.

We excluded from the analysis four models that did not pass the 75% performance threshold (as explained in Section 2.4). The reported results are from the remaining 56 simulations.

3.3 Results

As hypothesized, the model produced code-switches even though it had not been exposed to code-switched input. The model code-switched in 18.09% of the correctly produced sentences (at the last epoch, see Figure 2).

3.3.1 Typology of Code-Switching in the Model's Output

Figure 3 shows the insertions per POS and the alternational code-switched types (per POS at which the first language switch occurred) that were produced by the model at the end of the training (30th epoch). The model produced alternational

switches more frequently than insertional switches (13.57% vs 4.52%).

3.3.2 Examples of Code-Switched Sentences

Insertional code-switches of different syntactic categories are illustrated below:

- Noun insertion:
  Target: un anfitrión feliz ha pateado un bolígrafo . (English: a happy host has kicked a pen)
  Output: un anfitrión feliz ha pateado un *pen* .

- Verb insertion:
  Target: un camarero llevó la llave . (English: a waiter carried the key)
  Output: un camarero *carried* la llave .

- Determiner insertion:
  Target: he is showing the book to the father .
  Output: he is showing *el* book to the father .

- Adjective insertion:
  Target: a man is sad . Output: a man is *triste* .

Examples of alternational switches are provided below:

- Alternation at the determiner (Noun Phrase):
  Target: the uncle has shown a father the toy .
  Output: the uncle has shown *un padre* the toy .

- Alternation at the noun:
  Target: the short boy shows a brother a book .
  Output: the short boy shows a *libro a un hermano* .

- Alternation at the preposition (Prepositional Phrase):
  Target: the tall waiter has given a brother a book .
  Output: the tall waiter has given *a un hermano un libro* .

- Alternation at the auxiliary verb (Auxiliary Phrase):
  Target: the short waiter is showing a dog a toy .
  Output: the short waiter *está mostrando a un perro un juguete* .

Note that in the third example (Prepositional Phrase) the model inserted a preposition when switching, thus adhering to Spanish grammar: The

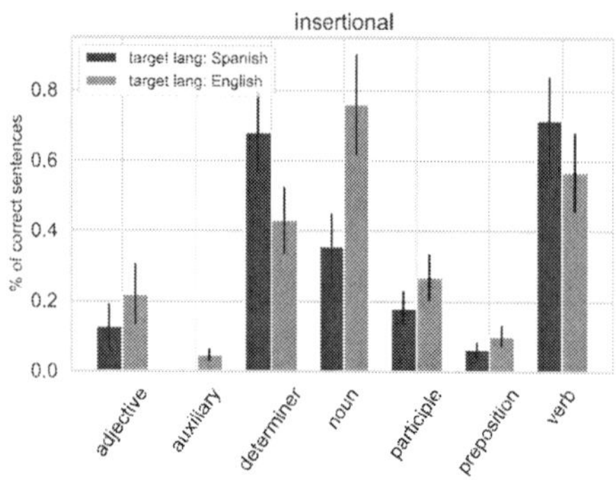 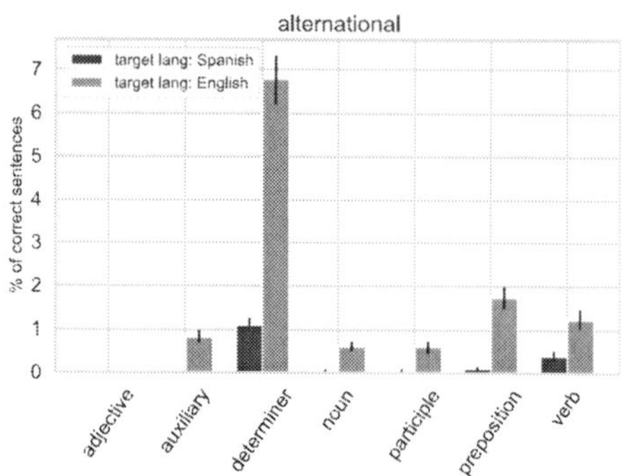

Figure 3: Types of insertional switching (left) and alternational switching (right). For alternational switches, the POS indicates the first point of switch. All values designate the percentage of correctly produced sentences. The error bars show the SEM computed over 56 simulations.

double dative does not exist with the double noun phrase form in Spanish. This cross-linguistic difference is even more relevant in the fourth example (Auxiliary Phrase switch) because the verb is in Spanish and the sentence would have been entirely ungrammatical if the model had not inserted a preposition ("**a** un perro").

3.4 Discussion

The model produced spontaneous code-switches through the manipulation of the target language, without being exposed to code-switched input. This supports the hypothesis that code-switches can occur due to internal and distributional factors, and not only because of exposure to code-switching.

Simulating a balanced bilingual speaker, the model produced mostly alternational switches as opposed to insertional ones. This is in line with Poplack's (1980) observation. Furthermore, alternations at the NP (alternational switch at the determiner) were more likely than alternations at the VP (alternational switch at the verb) or PP (alternational switch at the preposition), which is also in line with the patterns observed by Poplack. However, the model also produced code-switching patterns that are not attested in humans. For instance, the model inserted determiners (1.11% of the correctly produced sentences), especially English determiners in an otherwise Spanish sentence (0.68% of correctly produced sentences). We hypothesize that the model has this preference because determiners in English are not gendered. This means both that the model does not need to select a gendered article and that it prefers to use

the English determiner which has twice the frequency of the Spanish ones (as, e.g., 'the' is the translation of both 'el' and 'la' that are the Spanish definite determiners for masculine and feminine nouns respectively).

In bilingual environments where both languages are used, bilingual speakers start with an intended language that is defined by the conversational environment, but they are capable of communicating using either of their languages, or by code-switching (Grosjean, 2001). The top-down language control manipulation in the model (i.e., activating both target languages) is analogous to manipulating the conversational setting in which a speaker is interacting. Spontaneous code-switches occur when there is no target language preference. We only activate a target language right before the production of the first word so as to set the conversational environment.

4 Experiment 2: Auxiliary Phrase Asymmetry

Our second experiment applies the model to a specific code-switching phenomenon: a production asymmetry that has been observed among Spanish-English communities in the US.

4.1 Background

Spanish-English bilinguals are moderately likely to code-switch in the progressive structure between the Spanish auxiliary "estar" ("to be") and the participle. For instance:

1. *Las personas están* protesting (The people are protesting)

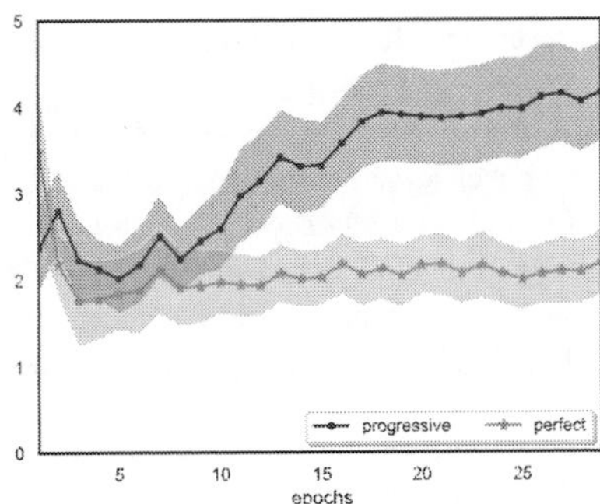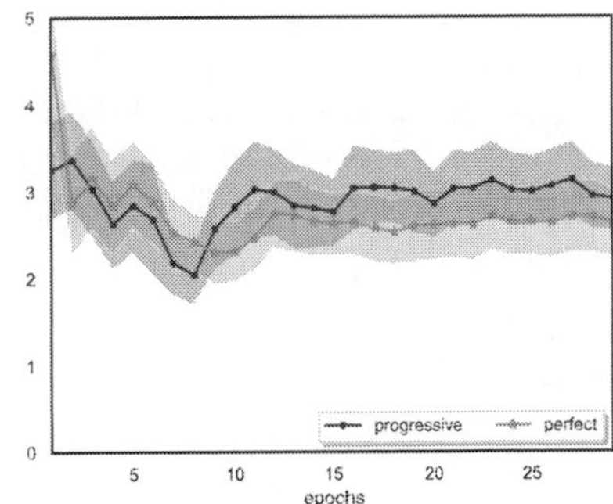

Figure 4: Percentage of Spanish-to-English participle switches for the correctly produced sentences per aspect in the "haber-model" (left) and the "tener-model" (right). Shaded areas show the SEM computed over 47 simulations.

is valid, whereas a switch at the perfect structure is rarely produced between the Spanish auxiliary "haber" ("to have") and the participle:

2. * *Las personas han* protested (The people have protested)

Furthermore, a switch at the auxiliary is likely for both structures: "*Las personas* are protesting", "*Las personas* have protested".

This phenomenon is known as the "auxiliary phrase asymmetry" (Guzzardo Tamargo et al., 2016; Poplack, 1980; Pfaff, 1979), and it has been confirmed both in production through corpus analysis and in comprehension through an eye-tracking-while-reading study (Guzzardo Tamargo et al.).

According to the "grammaticalization account", the source of this asymmetry is that "estar" has more semantic weight and is syntactically more independent as it also functions as a linking verb (e.g., "el enfermero está cansado"; "the nurse is tired"), whereas "haber" is highly grammaticalized as it is almost exclusively used as an auxiliary. The verb of possession in Spanish is "tener" ("el enfermero tiene un libro"; "the nurse has a book"), and "haber" is only used as an auxiliary verb or in archaic formulations (Guzzardo Tamargo et al., 2016). An alternative hypothesis suggested, but not attested, by Guzzardo Tamargo et al. is that the asymmetry emerges from community-supported practice ("exposure-based account"), i.e., speakers must be exposed to the production asymmetry.

4.2 Method

To investigate if the model provides support for the grammaticalization account, we first tested whether the asymmetry would emerge in the model described in Section 2.3; this would imply that the asymmetry can emerge even only from the distributional patterns of the two languages and that the exposure-based account is not necessary to explain the phenomenon, as the asymmetry is not present in the input. Second, we took advantage of the fact that the model input is generated and can therefore be manipulated, and we tested explicitly the grammaticalization hypothesis by replacing all instances of "haber" with "tener", the Spanish main verb "to have", thereby adding semantic weight to the Spanish auxiliary verb.

Specifically, for the first research question we employed again the model described in Section 2.3 ("haber-model"), and we tested it on 1000 novel messages: 500 progressive sentences (e.g., "the boy is kicking a ball") and 500 that were the perfect-tense equivalent of those sentences ("the boy has kicked a ball"). As in the previous experiment (Section 3), we activated both languages after the first word of each sentence had been produced.

For the second model ("tener-model"), we replaced all the instances of "haber" with "tener" in the training set (e.g., "el niño ha comido"; "the boy has eaten" became "el niño tiene comido"). We kept everything else the same (1000 test messages, initialized weights, lexicon size even though "haber" was no longer used, and all the layer sizes), and we ran 60 simulations using the modified input. Because "tener" is also used as an independent main verb with semantic content, we hypothesized that this model will not show the asymmetry.

In order to have a fair comparison between the two models, we only analyzed the simulations that had successfully learned to produce at least 75% of the sentences for both models.[1] Five simulations failed in the "haber-model" model and eight in the "tener-model", thus leading to a total of 47 simulations to be analyzed.

4.3 Results

Even without any manipulations, the "haber-model" showed a strong preference for progressive participle switches: 4.16% vs 2.18% for the perfect participle switches. Figure 4 (left) shows the average percentage of Spanish-to-English participle switches over 47 simulations per aspect (progressive and perfect).

Figure 5 shows the percentage of code-switches at the auxiliary verb and participle for the progressive and perfect structure, after 30 training epochs. In the progressive aspect, the simulations did not show a preference for a switch at the auxiliary; it is equally likely compared to a switch at the participle, thus reflecting prior experimental and corpus-based results (Guzzardo Tamargo et al., 2016). In the perfect structures, on the other hand, a switch at the participle is much less likely than a switch at the auxiliary position.

When tested on the same 1000 messages, the "tener-model" (that substituted the original Spanish auxiliary verb from the "haber-model" for one with more semantic weight) did not show a preference for progressive participle switches (2.91% vs 2.63%; Figure 4, right).

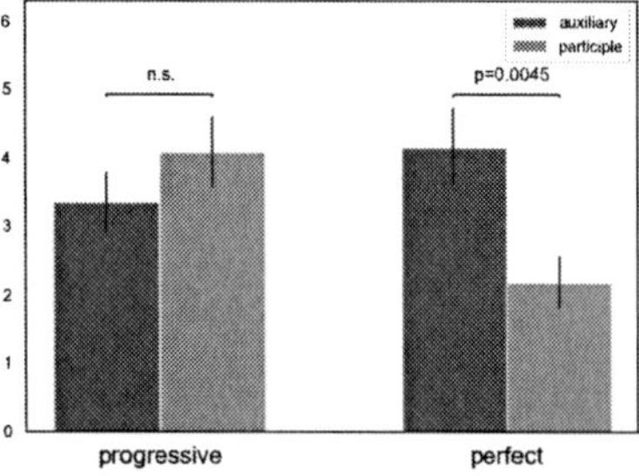

Figure 5: Percentages of code-switches at the auxiliary and participle for the progressive and perfect aspect, after 30 epochs. Error bars show the SEM computed over 47 simulations.

---

[1]The "sameness" of the simulations is judged by the simulation number which indicates the seed for the initialized weights and the generated input.

4.4 Discussion

We tested whether the auxiliary phrase asymmetry in Spanish-English code-switching could be derived from the properties of the two languages. The "haber-model" simulated the attested asymmetry and the "tener-model" tested whether the cause could be attributed to the Spanish auxiliary "haber" that only has a limited, dependent syntactic function (i.e., is more grammaticalized) and is not used as frequently as the English equivalent ("have"). The two simulations confirm that the grammaticalization account could be responsible for the asymmetry.

5 Conclusion

We have presented a novel method to test hypotheses in code-switched sentence production. This computational cognitive model can easily be modified to simulate code-switched production of a different language pair. Additionally, the generated input allows for manipulations that help test other hypotheses about code-switching, for instance the idea that cognates can trigger code-switched speech (Clyne, 1980).

Acknowledgments

The work presented here was funded by the Netherlands Organisation for Scientific Research (NWO) Gravitation Grant 024.001.006 to the Language in Interaction Consortium.

References

Barbara E. Bullock and Almeida Jacqueline Toribio. 2009. Trying to hit a moving target: On the sociophonetics of code-switching. *Multidisciplinary Approaches to Code Switching*, 41:189–206.

Franklin Chang. 2002. Symbolically speaking: A connectionist model of sentence production. *Cognitive Science*, 26:609–651.

Michael G. Clyne. 1980. Triggering and language processing. *Canadian Journal of Psychology/Revue canadienne de psychologie*, 34(4):400.

Jeffrey L. Elman. 1990. Finding structure in time. *Cognitive Science*, 14(2):179–211.

Roberto Filippi, Themis Karaminis, and Michael S.C. Thomas. 2014. Language switching in bilingual production: Empirical data and computational modelling. *Bilingualism: Language and Cognition*, 17(2):294–315.

Stefan L Frank, Padraic Monaghan, and Chara Tsoukala. in press. Neural network models of language acquisition and processing. In Peter Hagoort, editor, *Human Language: from Genes and Brains to Behavior*. The MIT Press.

Hila Gonen and Yoav Goldberg. 2018. Language modeling for code-switching: Evaluation, integration of monolingual data, and discriminative training. *arXiv preprint arXiv:1810.11895*.

François Grosjean. 2001. The bilingual's language modes. In Janet L. Nicol, editor, *One mind, two languages: Bilingual language processing*, pages 1–22. Oxford: Blackwell.

Gualberto A Guzmán, Joseph Ricard, Jacqueline Serigos, Barbara E Bullock, and Almeida Jacqueline Toribio. 2017. Metrics for modeling code-switching across corpora. In *INTERSPEECH*, pages 67–71.

Rosa E. Guzzardo Tamargo, Jorge R. Valdés Kroff, and Paola E. Dussias. 2016. Examining the relationship between comprehension and production processes in code-switched language. *Journal of Memory and Language*, 89:138–161.

Marius Janciauskas and Franklin Chang. 2018. Input and age-dependent variation in second language learning: A connectionist account. *Cognitive Science*, 42:519–554.

Pieter Muysken. 2000. *Bilingual Speech: A Typology of Code-Mixing*. Cambridge University Press.

Carol W. Pfaff. 1979. Constraints on language mixing: intrasentential code-switching and borrowing in Spanish/English. *Language*, pages 291–318.

Shana Poplack. 1980. Sometimes I'll start a sentence in Spanish y termino en Español: toward a typology of code-switching. *Linguistics*, 18(7-8):581–618.

Thamar Solorio and Yang Liu. 2008. Learning to predict code-switching points. In *Proceedings of the Conference on Empirical Methods in Natural Language Processing*, pages 973–981. Association for Computational Linguistics.

Chara Tsoukala, Stefan L. Frank, and Mirjam Broersma. 2017. "He's pregnant": simulating the confusing case of gender pronoun errors in L2. *Proceedings of the 39th Annual Conference of the Cognitive Science Society*, pages 3392–3397.

Emre Yılmaz, Henk van den Heuvel, and David van Leeuwen. 2016. Investigating bilingual deep neural networks for automatic recognition of code-switching Frisian speech. *Procedia Computer Science*, 81:159–166.

Surprisal and Interference Effects of Case Markers in Hindi Word Order

Sidharth Ranjan
IIT Delhi
sidharth.ranjan@cse.iitd.ac.in

Rajakrishnan Rajkumar
IISER Bhopal
rajak@iiserb.ac.in

Sumeet Agarwal
IIT Delhi
sumeet@iitd.ac.in

Abstract

Based on the Production-Distribution-Comprehension (PDC) account of language processing, we formulate two distinct hypotheses about case marking, word order choices and processing in Hindi. Our first hypothesis is that Hindi tends to optimize for processing efficiency at both lexical and syntactic levels. We quantify the role of case markers in this process. For the task of predicting the reference sentence occurring in a corpus (amidst meaning-equivalent grammatical variants) using a machine learning model, surprisal estimates from an artificial version of the language (*i.e.*, Hindi without any case markers) result in lower prediction accuracy compared to natural Hindi. Our second hypothesis is that Hindi tends to minimize interference due to case markers while ordering preverbal constituents. We show that Hindi tends to avoid placing next to each other constituents whose heads are marked by identical case inflections. Our findings adhere to PDC assumptions and we discuss their implications for language production, learning and universals.

1 Introduction

Language universals encode distributional regularities across languages of the world. This study is motivated by the well known correlation between case marking and increased word order flexibility (Sapir, 1921; Blake, 2001), often expressed as an *implicationql universal*[1]. The origin of such universals has been the topic of a long-standing debate in linguistics and cognitive science (Fedzechkina et al., 2012). As the cited work expounds, one view is that language universals emerged due to constraints specific to the

system of language and not related to the other cognitive faculties (Chomsky, 1965; Fodor, 2001). Another view is that languages evolved over time as a consequence of cognitive mechanisms and pressures linked with language use. Thus, cognitive biases related to processing (Hawkins, 2004), learnability (Christiansen and Chater, 2008) and communicative efficiency (Jaeger and Tily, 2011) have been proposed as underlying the systematic similarities and divergences between natural languages.

The Production-Distribution-Comprehension (PDC) account of language processing proposed by MacDonald (2013) is an integrated theory of language production and comprehension that seeks to connect language production with typology and comprehension. It is broadly in the spirit of the second view regarding linguistic universals described above and posits production difficulty as the *sole* factor influencing linguistic form. Hence it is an unconventional approach, contrasting radically with alternative accounts of language use in which language forms are shaped by constraints on language acquisition processes or considerations of facilitating language comprehension for the listeners. Based on PDC assumptions, we formulated two hypotheses linking processing efficiency, case marking, and word order choices at the level of individual speakers (as opposed to the population level) in Hindi, a language having predominantly SOV word order. Hindi has a rich system of case markers along with a relatively flexible word order (Agnihotri, 2007; Kachru, 2006) and thus adheres to the implicational universal stated at the outset.

The PDC principle *Easy First* stipulates that more accessible words are ordered before less accessible words. Accessibility of a word is influenced by its ease of retrievability from memory.

---

[1] "Given X in a particular language, we always find Y" where X and Y are characteristics of the language (Greenberg, 1963).

30

Proceedings of the Workshop on Cognitive Modeling and Computational Linguistics, pages 30–42
Minneapolis, USA, June 7, 2019. ©2019 Association for Computational Linguistics

Inspired by the stated PDC principle, our first hypothesis is that Hindi tends to optimize for processing efficiency at both lexical and syntactic levels. We investigate the role of case markers in this process by comparing the processing efficiency of natural Hindi and an artificial version of Hindi without case markers. Based on the PDC principle of *Reduce Interference*, our second hypothesis is that Hindi orders constituents such that phonological interference caused by case marker repetition is minimized. Interference is the idea that entities with similar properties (like form, meaning, animacy, concreteness and so forth) cause processing difficulties when they occur in proximity. A long line of research attests the role of interference in both production (Bock, 1987; Jaeger et al., 2012) and comprehension (Van Dyke and McElree, 2006; Van Dyke, 2007).

In order to test the stated hypotheses, we deploy a machine learning model to predict the reference sentence occurring in the Hindi-Urdu TreeBank (HUTB) corpus (Bhatt et al., 2009) of written text[2] (Example 1a below), amidst a set of artificially created grammatical variants expressing the same proposition (Examples 1b-1c). Case markers are shown in bold for illustration purposes.

(1) a.   isse pehle jila   upabhokta adalat **ne**
             this before district consumer court ERG
             28 April 1998 **ko** apne faisle   mẽ
             28 April 1998 ON own decision LOC
             company **ko**   nirdesh diyaa thaa ki...
             company DAT direction gave   COMPL
             Earlier, the District Consumer Court had directed the company in its decision on April 28, 1998 that ...

     b.   isse pehle jila upabhokta adalat **ne** apne faisle mẽ 28 April 1998 **ko** company **ko** nirdesh diyaa thaa ki...

     c.   jila upabhokta adalat **ne** isse pehle apne faisle mẽ 28 April 1998 **ko** company **ko** nirdesh diyaa thaa ki...

The variants above have two adjacent *ko*-marked constituents, potentially causing interference during production. So the PDC account would not prefer these sentences on account of production difficulty and instead prefer the reference sentence above. The possibility that speakers chose the reference sentence above so that it would facilitate comprehension for listeners (compared to variant sentences which might be harder to interpret) is not considered by the PDC account.

---

[2]We concede that the use of written data (due to the lack of a publicly available Hindi speech corpus) is a major limitation of our study.

We quantified processing efficiency using surprisal, originally proposed as a measure of language comprehension difficulty by Surprisal Theory (Hale, 2001; Levy, 2008). Consequently, we introduced surprisal estimated from n-gram and dependency parsing models into a logistic regression model for the task of predicting the reference sentence. Our choice of surprisal is inspired by Levy and Gibson (2013), who point out that the desiderata for PDC to become a theory of powerful empirical import is that it should make *quantitative* and *localized* predictions about incremental processing difficulty at each word. They highlight the fact that such a theory already exists, *viz.* the Surprisal Theory of language comprehension mentioned above. A perusal of the literature on information density in language production suggests that surprisal is a reasonable choice to model production difficulty as well.

Information density and surprisal are mathematically equivalent and both quantify the contextual predictability of a linguistic unit. But surprisal is based on different theoretical assumptions about resource allocation in comprehension. Recent research has demonstrated that reduction phenomena at both lexical (Frank and Jaeger, 2008, verb contraction) and syntactic (Jaeger, 2010, *that*-complementizer choice) levels exhibit the drive to minimize variation in information density across the linguistic signal. Moreover, instances of the same word which have greater predictability tend to be spoken faster and with less emphasis on acoustic details (Bell et al., 2009; Pluymaekers et al., 2005). The work cited above uses lexical frequencies or n-gram models over words to estimate contextual predictability. More recently, Demberg et al. (2012) showed that syntactic surprisal estimated from a top-down incremental parser is positively correlated with the duration of words in spontaneous speech, even in the presence of controls including word frequencies and trigram lexical surprisal estimates. Crucial to our study, words which are predictable in context have been interpreted to be more accessible in recent research (Arnold, 2011).

The results of our experiments show that reference sentences tend to minimize both trigram and dependency parser surprisal in comparison to their variants. Further, we show that the prediction accuracies of surprisal estimates derived from an artificially created version of Hindi without any case markers are significantly worse than the corresponding surprisal estimates based on natural Hindi. This experiment demonstrates the crucial contribution of case markers towards the predictive ability of surprisal and confirms our first hypothesis. Subsequently, we demonstrate that Hindi tends to avoid placing together constituents whose heads are marked by the same case marker. Moreover, incorporating predictors based on adjacent case marker sequences in a statistical model significantly improves model prediction accuracy over an extremely competitive baseline provided by n-gram and dependency parser surprisal. Phonological interference is a plausible explanation for this phenomenon and lends credence to our second hypothesis. The Hindi sentence comprehension literature provides only limited support for interference involving case marker sequences (Vasishth, 2003). Hence, it is plausible that this effect is a factor confined to the production system and not related to considerations of language comprehension. Further research using spoken corpora and spontaneous production experiments need to be performed in order to validate the psychological reality of our findings. Given that symbols used in the Hindi orthography have a direct correspondence with the sounds of the language (Vaid and Gupta, 2002), we expect speech to behave similarly.

Our main contribution is that we broaden the typological base of the PDC account of language processing, leveraging its connection with the well established surprisal theory of language comprehension. Levy and Gibson (2013) state that surprisal would enable PDC to be implemented computationally, thus facilitating hypothesis testing on a wide range of linguistic phenomena cross-linguistically. To this end, we set up a computational framework consisting of standard tools and techniques from the field of Natural Language Generation (NLG). Methodologically, the task of referent sentence prediction is a relatively novel way of studying word order and is inspired from the surface realization component of NLG. Recently, using a similar setup, Rajkumar et al. (2016) showed the impact of dependency length on English word order choices.

In this paper, Section 2 provides necessary background and Section 3 provides details of our data sets and models. Section 4 presents our experiments and their results. Finally, Section 5 summa-

Marker	Case (Gloss)	Grammatical Function
ϕ	nominative (NOM)	subject/object
ne	ergative (ERG)	subject
ko	accusative (ACC)	object
	dative (DAT)	subject/indirect object
se	instrumental (INS)	subject/oblique/adjunct
$ka/ki/ke$	genitive (GEN)	subject (infinitives) specifier
$m\tilde{e}/par/tak$	locative (LOC)	oblique/adjunct

Table 1: Hindi case markers (Butt and King, 1996).

rizes the conclusions of our study and discusses the implications of our results for language production and learning.

2 Background

This section offers a brief background on Hindi word order and case marking, surprisal and core assumptions of the PDC account.

2.1 Hindi Word Order and Case Marking

A long line of work (Butt and King, 1996; Kidwai, 2000) has shown that scrambling in Hindi is influenced by factors like discourse considerations (topic, focus, background, and completive information), semantics (definiteness and animacy), and prosody (Patil et al., 2008). Hindi follows the head-marking strategy where case markers are postpositions which attach to noun phrases and encode a range of grammatical functions like subject and object (see Table 1 and case markers in bold in Examples 1a and 2a).

2.2 Surprisal Theory

The Surprisal Theory of language comprehension posits that fine-grained probabilistic knowledge (attained from prior linguistic experience) helps comprehenders form expectations about interpretations of the previously encountered structure as well as upcoming material (Hale, 2001; Levy, 2008). The theory defines surprisal as a measure of comprehension difficulty. In this work, we used the following definitions of surprisal:

1. **n-gram surprisal**: Mathematically, n-gram surprisal of the $(i+1)^{th}$ word, w_{i+1}, based on a traditional n-gram model is given by $S_{i+1} = -\log P(w_{i+1}|w_{i-n+2}, ..., w_{i-1}, w_i)$, as defined by Hale (2001). We estimated n-gram surprisal via trigram models (n=3) over words trained on 1 million sentences from the EMILLE corpus (Baker et al., 2002) using the SRILM toolkit (Stolcke, 2002) with Good-Turing discounting.

2. **Dependency parser surprisal** was computed using the probabilistic incremental dependency parser developed by Agrawal et al. (2017), based on the parallel-

processing variant of the *arc-eager* parsing strategy (Nivre, 2008) proposed by Boston et al. (2011). This parser maintains a set of the k most probable parses at each word as it proceeds through the sentence. The probability of a parser state is taken to be the product of the probabilities of all transitions made to reach that state. This parser can thus be used to define a measure of *dependency parser surprisal*: for the ith word in a sentence, we first define the *prefix probability* α_i as the sum of probabilities of the k maintained parser states at word i:

$$\alpha_i = \sum_{\text{top } k \text{ derivations } d \text{ leading to word } i} Prob(d) \quad (1)$$

The dependency parser surprisal at word i+1 is then computed as:

$$S_{i+1}^{syn} = -\log(\alpha_{i+1}/\alpha_i) \quad (2)$$

The dependency parser surprisal of the $(i+1)^{th}$ word is computed as the negative log-ratio of the sum of probabilities of maintained parser states at word $i+1$ to the same sum at word i. We estimated it using a corpus of 12,000 HUTB projective trees.

2.3 Production-Distribution-Comprehension (PDC) Account

The **Production** component of the PDC account posits three factors of production ease. 1. *Easy First*: Relatively more accessible (ease of memory retrieval and conceptual salience) or available elements are produced earlier in the structure. 2. *Plan Reuse*: Speakers tend to repeat previously used or mentioned structures due to syntactic priming. 3. *Reduce Interference*: Speakers tend to choose words which do not interfere with other words in the utterance plan. These factors compete with each other during the production process to mould language forms.

The **Distribution** component states that the distribution of structures in natural languages reflects a bias towards having a greater number of structures which are easier to produce. Thus PDC attributes the greater frequency of subject relative clauses compared to object relatives across languages to production ease. Finally, the **Comprehension** part of the PDC approach proposes that language comprehension reflects the statistics of the input (*i.e.*, production patterns) perceived by language users. Thus, according to PDC, the greater difficulty involved in comprehending object relative clauses compared to subject relatives (Gibson, 2000) is because of the lower exposure to object relatives by virtue of their lower frequency in the linguistic input to comprehenders. Levy and Gibson (2013) puts forth the idea that surprisal (estimated from corpora) is naturally very compatible with the PDC assumption described above. Maryellen MacDonald and colleagues validate PDC predictions using a series of experiments related to relative clause production and comprehension in many languages (Gennari and MacDonald, 2008, 2009; Gennari et al., 2012).

3 Data and Models

Our data set consists of 8736 reference sentences corresponding to labeled, projective dependency trees in the Hindi-Urdu TreeBank (HUTB) corpus of written Hindi (Bhatt et al., 2009). We generated variants for each reference sentence by randomly permuting the preverbal constituents of the root node of its dependency tree. We selected trees whose roots were verbs. For example, in the tree depicted in Figure 1 (corresponding to Example 1a), we reordered the preverbal constituents immediately dominated by the verb *diyaa* and obtained the variants shown in Examples 1b and 1c. In order to eliminate ungrammatical variants, we excluded variants containing dependency relation sequences of the root word not present in the corpus of HUTB gold standard trees. Dependency relation sequences like *k7t-k1*, *k1-k7t*, *k7t-k7* and *k7-k4* in Figure 1 simulate grammar rules used in grammar-based surface realization systems. We obtained 175801 variants after filtering.

In order to mitigate the imbalance between the number of reference and variant sentences, we transformed the data set using a technique described in Joachims (2002). As per this technique, a binary classification problem can be converted into a pairwise ranking problem by training a classifier on the difference between the feature vectors of a reference sentence and its syntactic choice variants:

$$\mathbf{w} \cdot \phi(Reference) > \mathbf{w} \cdot \phi(Variant) \quad (3)$$

$$\mathbf{w} \cdot (\phi(Reference) - \phi(Variant)) > 0 \quad (4)$$

In Equation 3 above, the $Reference$ data point is predicted to outrank the $Variant$ data point when the dot product of the feature vector of the reference with $\mathbf{w}$ (learned feature weights) is greater than the corresponding product of the variant. The same can be written (Equation 4) as the dot product of $\mathbf{w}$ with the feature vector difference being positive. We created ordered pairs

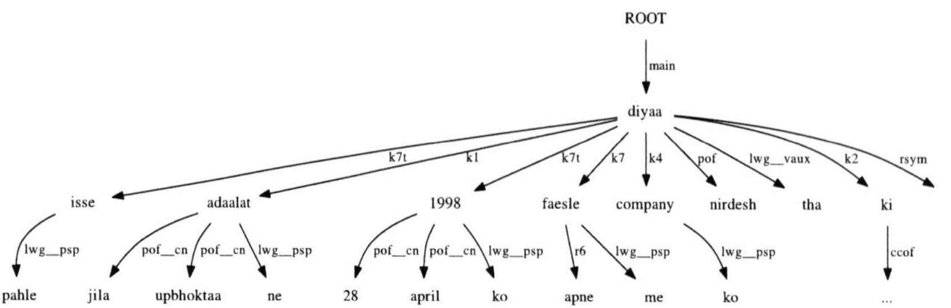

Figure 1: Example HUTB dependency tree (Table 8 in the Appendix provides a glossary of dependency relations)

consisting of the feature vectors of reference and variant sentences. Every reference sentence in the data set was paired with each of its variants (Examples 1a-1b and Examples 1c-1a constitute two such pairs). Then the feature values of the first member of the pair were subtracted from the corresponding values of the second member. Pairs alternate between *reference-variant* (coded as "1") and *variant-reference* (coded as "0"), resulting in a data set consisting of an equal number of classification labels of each kind (see Appendix for a detailed illustration).

4 Experiments

In this section, we describe three experiments to test our hypotheses on the transformed version of our data set consisting of 175801 data points using a logistic regression model. The goal is to predict "1" and "0" labels (as described in the previous section) using a set of cognitively motivated features. We calculated lexical and dependency parser surprisal feature values over entire sentences by summing the log probabilities of the surprisal values of individual words. We carried out 27-fold cross-validation; for each run, a model trained on 26 folds (consisting of 1 fold for hyperparameter tuning) was used to generate predictions about the remaining fold (100 training iterations using lbfgs solver in python *scikit-learn* toolkit-v0.16.1).

4.1 Processing Efficiency Experiments

Here, we test the hypothesis that word order choices in language are optimized for processing efficiency by incorporating trigram and dependency parser surprisal as predictors in a logistic re-

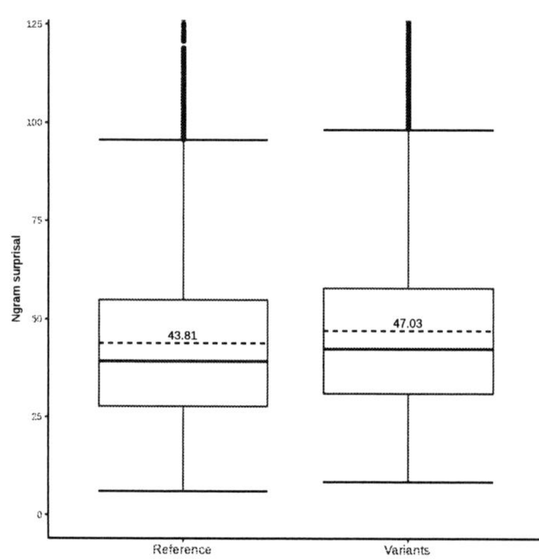

Figure 2: Mean trigram surprisal per sentence of reference and variant sentences (95% confidence intervals indicated)

gression model. A negative regression coefficient for these predictors would imply that corpus sentences have lower surprisal than variants. For the entire corpus, Figure 2 indicates this trend, where the mean trigram surprisal per sentence of the corpus of reference sentences is lower than the corresponding value of all their variants (Figure 4 in the Appendix depicts the same trend for syntactic surprisal). For the task of predicting HUTB reference sentences, both our surprisal measures have a negative regression coefficient, individually as well as in combination (first three rows of Table 2). This confirms our hypothesis that word order choices optimize for processing efficiency. Given our interpretation of low surprisal as denoting ease of accessibility, our first experiment shows that Hindi

Predictor(s)	Accuracy %	Weight(s)
Hindi		
Parser surprisal	62.10	-0.43
Trigram surprisal	89.96	-0.81
Trigram + parser surprisal	90.14	-0.98, -0.43
Caseless Hindi		
Caseless parser surprisal	55.03	-0.29
Caseless trigram surprisal	87.73	-0.83
Caseless trigram + parser surprisal	87.81	-0.93, -0.27

Table 2: Classification accuracies of surprisal for natural and caseless Hindi (175801 data points)

speakers tend to produce sentences by ordering preverbal constituents such that more accessible elements are realized first compared to other competing grammatical variants. This is in line with the PDC *Easy First* principle. Further, the classification accuracies indicate that trigram surprisal estimated from the EMILLE corpus is very effective in modelling syntactic choice (89.96% accuracy). For the same task, Ranjan (2015) reported that trigram surprisal estimated from the HUTB itself (smaller quantity of in-domain data) resulted in a lower accuracy of around 85%. In this context, our results show that a bigger n-gram training set can overcome the limitation of being from a different domain. A qualitative exploration revealed that n-gram model surprisal was particularly effective in reference-variant pairs as shown below (case markers shown in bold):

(2) a. Paakistan **ne** brihaspativaar **ko**
Pakistan ERG Thursday at
kathit taur **par** apne yahaan nirmit paramanu
allegedly indigenous nuclear
hathiyaar dhone **me** saksam krooj
weapons capable LOC carrying cruise
missile **ka** pareekshan kiyaa hai.
missile GEN tested

Pakistan has allegedly tested an indigenous cruise missile capable of carrying nuclear weapons on Thursday.

b. brihaspativaar **ko** Pakistan **ne** kathit taur **par** apne ...

The reference sentence (Example 2a with trigram surprisal of 45.60 hartleys) has the ergative-accusative (*ne-ko*) ordering of case-marked nouns compared to the variant (Example 2b with higher trigram surprisal 47.12) having the opposite ordering of nouns. Overall, 6% of a total of 175 HUTB sentences having ergative and accusative case markers exhibit a non-canonical accusative-ergative order (Agrawal et al., 2017). In both sentences above, the case markers in questions are separated by a single word and hence form part of a single trigram. Thus trigram surprisal is able to model the dominant order successfully

while dispreferring the opposite order seen in Example 2b. Moreover, dependency parser surprisal has much lower classification accuracy compared to trigram surprisal and has a very negligible impact on performance on top of trigram surprisal. Thus, surprisal estimates from an incremental dependency parser are not effective in modelling constituent order choices. This is slightly unexpected as Agrawal et al. (2017) showed that surprisal estimates derived via the dependency parser deployed in our work accounts for per-word reading times for the Potsdam-Allahabad corpus over and above bigram frequencies. Using a similar setup, Rajkumar et al. (2016) showed that for the task of predicting English syntactic choice alternations, PCFG surprisal performed significantly better than n-gram model surprisal and the impact of dependency length is over and above both the aforementioned surprisal predictors. We are in the process of creating a constituency structure treebank for Hindi and plan to experiment with surprisal derived from a constituent-structure parser very soon. In recently completed work, Ranjan et al. (In Preparation) show that for Hindi, dependency length exhibits a weak effect over and above surprisal for predicting corpus sentences amidst artificial variants. Finally, we examined 1022 reference-variant pairs in our dataset where none of our features was able to predict the reference sentence correctly. We isolated cases involving other factors like given-new orders (30% cases), focus or topic considerations (marked by *hi* or *to* markers constituting 10% of cases) and null subjects (7.5%). Such discourse considerations are not encoded in our surprisal estimates (confined to single sentences) and further research can incorporate information about sentences from the preceding context into surprisal estimates.

Note that when considering the relationship between communicative efficiency and word order choices, there is a potential 'levels' problem (Levy, 2018). At the level of evolutionary timescales and entire populations, one might expect the grammar or distributional properties of the language to be adapted for efficiency. But at the level of an individual speaker's production choices, certain measures of efficiency will in turn depend on the extant distribution of linguistic forms. So there is a potential circularity in trying to assess the validity of such measures. Here we seek to model only the lower of these levels, *i.e.,* individual choices over a human lifetime. Hence, all the non-corpus variants we consider are *grammatical*. We assume that the grammar of the language is held fixed, and within the set of possible word order variants of a sentence licensed by that extant grammar, seek to model why speakers may have a greater propensity to produce some variants over others.

4.2 Case Markers and Processing Efficiency

In order to quantify the exact contribution of Hindi case markers towards the predictive accuracy of syntactic and trigram surprisal, we performed similar experiments using an artificial version of the language (*i.e.*, Hindi without case markers). The sentence comprehension literature demonstrates the vital role of case markers in predicting the final verb in verb-final constructions of languages like German (Levy and Keller, 2013) and Japanese (Grissom II et al., 2016). Moreover, in recent years, deploying artificial languages to test hypotheses about language processing and learning has been in vogue in both connectionist modelling (Lupyan and Christiansen, 2002; Everbroeck, 2003) as well as behavioural experiments (Kurumada and Jaeger, 2015; Fedzechkina et al., 2017). Inspired by the cited works, we created a caseless version of Hindi by removing case markers (those listed in Table 1) from both reference and variant sentences. The caseless equivalents of Examples 2a and 2b discussed in the previous section are given below:

(3) a.   Pakistan brihaspativaar kathit taur apne yahaan nirmit paramanu hathiyaar dhone mein saksam krooj missile pareekshan kiyaa hai.

      b.   brihaspativaar Pakistan kathit taur apne ...

Then we estimated surprisal by stripping off case markers from the EMILLE corpus (trigram surprisal) as well as HUTB trees (dependency parser surprisal) so that our surprisal estimates mirrored the patterns in the caseless version of the language faithfully. Both surprisal measures derived from the caseless version of Hindi perform significantly worse than natural Hindi (last three rows of Table 2). Caseless trigram surprisal does 2% worse, while there is a 7% dip in the performance of caseless dependency parser surprisal (McNemar's two-tailed significance $p < 0.001$ for both measures). Thus the caseless language model is not able to predict the reference sentence shown in Example 3a as it awards higher trigram surprisal (45.21),

in comparison to the variant sentence in Example 3b, which has a lower surprisal value (43.74). Figure 3 in the Appendix depicts the lexical surprisal profiles for the examples discussed above (both regular Hindi and caseless equivalents). Dependency parser surprisal also exhibited the same predictions.

Removing any kinds of words (especially function words) will result in a decrease in prediction accuracy. So we compared the prediction accuracy of caseless surprisal with another baseline obtained by removing case markers and all other postpositions (e.g. *ke liye*, *ke dwara*) from both training and test data. Surprisal estimates derived from the case marker and postposition stripped version of Hindi resulted in an extra dip of 0.3% in the accuracy of trigram surprisal and 2.5% for dependency parser surprisal compared to surprisal obtained by stripping just the case markers. Thus even within the set of postpositions, case markers play a significant role in lexical and syntactic predictability and hence processing efficiency. Lack of case markers reduces the overall information content of a sentence for both speaker and hearer. Spontaneous production experiments showed that Japanese speakers tend to omit the optional marker *-o* when the meaning of the sentence is probable in a given context (Kurumada and Jaeger, 2015). However, in cases where the meaning is not plausible, speakers tend to mention the case marker, in spite of entailing greater production effort.

The work of Lupyan and Christiansen (2002) showed that for artificial SOV languages with no case marking, a sequential learning device (Simple Recurrent Network) failed to achieve high accuracy for the task of mapping words to grammatical roles. Their simulations suggest that verb-final languages need a case system for optimal learning as word order is not a reliable cue for grammatical function assignment. Using the miniature artificial language learning paradigm, Fedzechkina et al. (2017) conducted a study where two groups of adult learners were exposed to artificial languages with optional case marking (one fixed order and one flexible order). Learners of the flexible constituent order language produced more case markers than learners of the fixed order language, mirroring typological patterns.

4.2.1 Interference Experiments

In the light of the PDC principle of *Minimize Interference*, we investigate whether interference

Predictor name	Sequence	Distance
ϕ-ne	1	3
ne-ko	1	3
ko-mẽ	1	2
mẽ-ko	1	1
same-seq	0	-
diff-seq	4	-

Table 3: Values of case features extracted from tree in Figure 1.

Case marker sequence	Weight
ϕ-ϕ	**-0.002**
ke-ke	**-0.025**
ko-ko	**-0.291**
mẽ-mẽ	**-0.061**
tak-tak	0.008
par-par	0.231
se-se	0.055
same-seq	-0.009
diff-seq	0.009

Table 4: Learned weights of some case-sequence predictors.

Predictor(s)	Classification accuracy%	Ranking accuracy%
Case distance features	70.79	-
Case sequence features	74.94	-
Random Classifier	-	21.25
Baseline (trigram+parser surprisal)	90.16	55.04
Baseline+Case distance features	90.85***	55.68***
Baseline+Case sequence features	91.13***	56.03***
Baseline+Case distance + sequence features	**91.60*****	**56.16*****

Table 5: Pairwise classification and ranking accuracy (*** denotes McNemar's two-tailed significance $p < 0.001$ over the baseline model).

between NPs whose heads are marked by the same case marker influence preverbal constituent ordering choices in Hindi. Since PDC seeks to link production and comprehension, our experiments are also motivated by prior work on case marker interference in sentence comprehension in SOV languages like Japanese (Lewis and Nakayama, 2001), Korean (Lee et al., 2005) and Hindi (Vasishth, 2003). Our work is directly related to the experiments on identical case marking described in Chapter 3 of Vasishth (2003). In the case of Hindi center-embeddings, this work examined whether NPs having nominal heads marked by identical case markers induce similarity-based interference effects at the subsequent verb as predicted by the Retrieval Interference Theory (Lewis, 1998; Lewis and Nakayama, 2001). The study shows limited support for interference emanating from phonologically similar case markers.

In order to investigate interference caused by case markers in syntactic choice, we designed features based on case markers and incorporated them into our logistic regression model. For each dependency tree, we introduced two types of features associated with preverbal constituents of the root verb. 1. *Case-sequence features*: Counts of case marker sequences associated with the heads of a pair of adjacent constituents. We also introduced generic case-sequence features *same-seq* and *diff-seq* to model the overall trend. For each tree, these features denote the total number of identical and different case markers sequences associated with pairs of adjacent constituents. 2. *Case-distance features*: Number of intervening words between heads of the constituents of root verbs. Here, the feature name is obtained by combining the case markers associated with the constituent heads in question. Constituents which do not have case marked heads are marked as ϕ in order to model

the fact that languages often use adverbial elements or other non-case marked arguments to separate case marked constituents. Table 3 illustrates our case features based on the dependency tree in Figure 1 corresponding to Example 1a.

In isolation, the case-sequence and case-distance features exhibit accuracies around 70% (second column of Table 5). The case sequence and distance features together induce a significant accuracy increase of 1.5% (McNemar's two-tailed significance $p < 0.001$) over a baseline model consisting of lexical and dependency parser surprisal as features. Though this might be a small increase when considered in isolation, we would like to note that our baseline model is extremely competitive (90.16% accuracy). Even dependency parser surprisal did not confer considerable performance gains over and above trigram surprisal as discussed earlier. So in this context, the contribution of case features is noteworthy.

Subsequently, we examined the learned weights of our case sequence features (Table 4) in our best model containing surprisal and all the case marker features. A negative weight is associated with four of the seven identical case marker sequences as well as the *same-seq* feature encoding the overall pattern across all case markers. These negative weights lend support to our hypothesis that Hindi shows a dispreference for placing together constituents whose heads are marked using the same case inflection. Interference due to repetition of phonologically identical case markers may be a plausible explanation for this phenomenon. However, three other case marker sequences have a positive weight and hence indicate a tendency towards adjacency. These three case markers are much lower in frequency in the HUTB compared to the other four and might not represent the dominant tendency. However, future inquiries need to explore the role of case-based facilitation (Logačev and Vasishth, 2012). Since our features are not sensitive to clause boundaries, conclusive evidence for phonological interference will emerge only after controlling for clause boundaries.

The best model (baseline + case marker features) picked the reference sentence (Example 1a) while the baseline model erroneously selected the artificially generated variants (Examples 1b and 1c). The reference sentence has two *ko*-marked constituents separated by intervening constituents. In contrast, the variant sentences have two adjacent *ko*-marked constituents, potentially causing interference. These examples also highlight the ambiguous nature of the *ko*-marker in denoting several functions in Hindi. As noted by Ahmed (2006), *ko* marks both accusative and dative case on objects (*company* in the cited examples) as well as dative subjects. In addition, it also occurs on spatial and temporal adjuncts (as in *28 April 1998*). In these examples, since *ko* marks both dative case and temporality, interference might be purely phonological in nature and not related to the actual grammatical function being marked. Further, we calculated the ranking accuracy of our main models, *i.e.*, the percentage of times a model ranked the reference sentence compared to all its variants. Table 5 (column 3) indicates that introducing case marker features into the baseline model induced significant ranking accuracy gains (McNemar's two-tailed significance $p < 0.001$). So our best model ranked Example 1a as the best sentence among all the other variants. Our classification and ranking results suggest that the PDC *Reduce Interference* principle of production ease is a valid constraint in constituent ordering.

In Hindi sentence comprehension, Vasishth (2003) explored the idea of Positional similarity (Lewis and Nakayama, 2001), whereby the position of otherwise syntactically indiscriminable NPs in the structure contribute to interference at the subsequent verb. So he compared reading times at the innermost verb in the sequences of constituents with heads marked by *ne-se-ko-ko* and *ne-ko-se-ko* inflections. However, there was no significant difference in reading times between these sequences, thus offering no support for positional similarity during comprehension. This is the experimental condition which is most closely linked to our work. Interpreted in conjunction with our findings, case marker interference in Hindi appears to be a constraint on production rather than comprehension.

5 Discussion

Our main findings are broadly in line with two of the production ease principles of the PDC account. Our first experiment shows that the Hindi language orders words to optimize production ease (quantified using surprisal) at both lexical and syntactic levels, consistent with the PDC *Easy First* principle. Our second experiment shows that case markers make a significant contribution towards the predictive accuracy of both syntactic and trigram surprisal in choosing the reference sentence amongst grammatical variants denoting the same meaning. The role of surprisal and case markers in conferring accessibility needs to be investigated more thoroughly in future work. Finally, our third experiment shows that Hindi tends to disprefer constituent sequences with heads case marked by identical case markers, as predicted by the PDC principle of *Reduce Interference*. However, the lack of case marker interference in Hindi comprehension necessitates further inquiries into the PDC account, which conceives the lexico-syntactic statistics of production data (result of biases in utterance planning) as guiding comprehension processes. Thus, overall, we would like to conclude that certain aspects of PDC are validated by our experimental results. Further computational inquiries will be facilitated by formulating an algorithmic sketch of a process model outlining the causes of mismatches between production and comprehension. Finally, the PDC account conceives word order variation in languages of the world as emerging from an interplay of the three PDC production principles. Crucially, PDC conceives learning biases to be production biases, *i.e.*, speakers learn forms which are easier to produce (MacDonald, 2013). Future inquiries can explore whether learning outcomes are indeed consistent with typological patterns described by language universals.

6 Acknowledgements

We are grateful to the anonymous reviewers of this workshop, NAACL-2019 and Sigmorphon-2018 for their feedback. The second author acknowledges support from IISER Bhopal's Faculty Initiation Grant (IISERB/R&D/2018-19/77).

References

Rama Kant Agnihotri. 2007. *Hindi: An Essential Grammar*. Essential Grammars. Routledge.

Arpit Agrawal, Sumeet Agarwal, and Samar Husain. 2017. Role of expectation and working memory constraints in hindi comprehension: An eyetracking corpus analysis. *Journal of Eye Movement Research*, 10(2).

Tafseer Ahmed. 2006. Spatial, temporal and structural uses of urdu ko. In Miriam Butt and Tracy Holloway King, editors, *Proceedings of the 11th International LFG Conference*. CSLI Publications, Stanford.

Jennifer E. Arnold. 2011. Ordering choices in production: For the speaker or for the listener? In Emily M. Bender and Jennifer E. Arnold, editors, *Language From a Cognitive Perspective: Grammar, Usage, and Processing*, pages 199–222. CSLI Publishers.

Paul Baker, Andrew Hardie, Tony McEnery, Hamish Cunningham, and Robert Gaizauskas. 2002. Emille: a 67-million word corpus of indic languages: data collection, mark-up and harmonization. In *Proceedings of LREC 2002*, pages 819–827. Lancaster University.

Alan Bell, Jason M Brenier, Michelle Gregory, Cynthia Girand, and Dan Jurafsky. 2009. Predictability effects on durations of content and function words in conversational English. *Journal of Memory and Language*, 60(1):92–111.

Rajesh Bhatt, Bhuvana Narasimhan, Martha Palmer, Owen Rambow, Dipti Misra Sharma, and Fei Xia. 2009. A multi-representational and multi-layered treebank for hindi/urdu. In *Proceedings of the Third Linguistic Annotation Workshop*, ACL-IJCNLP '09, pages 186–189, Stroudsburg, PA, USA. Association for Computational Linguistics.

Barry J. Blake. 2001. *Case*, 2 edition. Cambridge Textbooks in Linguistics. Cambridge University Press.

Kathryn Bock. 1987. An effect of the accessibility of word forms on sentence structures. *Journal of Memory and Language*, 26(2):119 – 137.

Marisa Ferrara Boston, John T. Hale, Shravan Vasishth, and Reinhold Kliegl. 2011. Parallel processing and sentence comprehension difficulty. *Language and Cognitive Processes*, 26(3):301–349.

Miriam Butt and Tracy Holloway King. 1996. Structural topic and focus without movement. In Miriam Butt and Tracy Holloway King, editors, *Proceedings of the First LFG Conference*. CSLI Publications, Stanford.

Noam Chomsky. 1965. *Aspects of the Theory of Syntax*, volume 11. The MIT press.

Morten H. Christiansen and Nick Chater. 2008. Language as shaped by the brain. *Behavioral and Brain Sciences*, 31(5):489509.

Vera Demberg, Asad B. Sayeed, Philip J. Gorinski, and Nikolaos Engonopoulos. 2012. Syntactic surprisal affects spoken word duration in conversational contexts. In *Proceedings of the 2012 Joint Conference on Empirical Methods in Natural Language Processing and Computational Natural Language Learning*, EMNLP-CoNLL '12, pages 356–367, Stroudsburg, PA, USA. Association for Computational Linguistics.

Ezra Van Everbroeck. 2003. Language type frequency and learnability from a connectionist perspective. *Linguistic Typology*, 7(1):1–50.

Maryia Fedzechkina, T. Florian Jaeger, and Elissa L. Newport. 2012. Language learners restructure their input to facilitate efficient communication. *Proceedings of the National Academy of Sciences*, 109(44):17897–17902.

Maryia Fedzechkina, Elissa L. Newport, and T. Florian Jaeger. 2017. Balancing effort and information transmission during language acquisition: Evidence from word order and case marking. *Cognitive Science*, 41(2):416–446.

Janet Dean Fodor. 2001. Setting syntactic parameters. *The Handbook of Contemporary Syntactic Theory*, pages 730–767.

A. Frank and T.F. Jaeger. 2008. Speaking rationally: Uniform information density as an optimal strategy for language production. *Cogsci. Washington, DC: CogSci*.

Silvia P. Gennari and Maryellen C. MacDonald. 2008. Semantic indeterminacy in object relative clauses. *Journal of Memory and Language*, 58(2):161 – 187.

Silvia P. Gennari and Maryellen C. MacDonald. 2009. Linking production and comprehension processes: The case of relative clauses. *Cognition*, 111(1):1 – 23.

Silvia P. Gennari, Jelena Mirkovi, and Maryellen C. MacDonald. 2012. Animacy and competition in relative clause production: A cross-linguistic investigation. *Cognitive Psychology*, 65(2):141 – 176.

Edward Gibson. 2000. Dependency locality theory: A distance-based theory of linguistic complexity. In Alec Marantz, Yasushi Miyashita, and Wayne O'Neil, editors, *Image, Language, brain: Papers from the First Mind Articulation Project Symposium*. MIT Press, Cambridge, MA.

Joseph H. Greenberg. 1963. Some universals of grammar with particular reference to the order of meaningful elements. In Joseph H. Greenberg, editor, *Universals of Human Language*, pages 73–113. MIT Press, Cambridge, Mass.

Alvin Grissom II, Naho Orita, and Jordan Boyd-Graber. 2016. Incremental prediction of sentence-final verbs: Humans versus machines. In *Proceedings of The 20th SIGNLL Conference on Computational Natural Language Learning*, pages 95–104. Association for Computational Linguistics.

John Hale. 2001. A probabilistic Earley parser as a psycholinguistic model. In *Proceedings of the second meeting of the North American Chapter of the Association for Computational Linguistics on Language technologies*, NAACL '01, pages 1–8, Pittsburgh, Pennsylvania. Association for Computational Linguistics.

John A. Hawkins. 2004. *Efficiency and Complexity in Grammars*. Oxford University Press.

Florian Jaeger, Katrina Furth, and Caitlin Hilliard. 2012. Incremental phonological encoding during unscripted sentence production. *Frontiers in Psychology*, 3:481.

T. Florian Jaeger. 2010. Redundancy and reduction: Speakers manage information density. *Cognitive Psychology*, 61(1):23–62.

T. Florian Jaeger and Harold Tily. 2011. Language processing complexity and communicative efficiency. *WIRE: Cognitive Science*, 2(3):323–335.

Thorsten Joachims. 2002. Optimizing search engines using clickthrough data. In *Proceedings of the Eighth ACM SIGKDD International Conference on Knowledge Discovery and Data Mining*, KDD '02, pages 133–142, New York, NY, USA. ACM.

Y. Kachru. 2006. *Hindi*. London Oriental and African language library. John Benjamins Publishing Company.

Ayesha Kidwai. 2000. *XP-Adjunction in Universal Grammar: Scrambling and Binding in Hindi-Urdu: Scrambling and Binding in Hindi-Urdu*. Oxford studies in comparative syntax. Oxford University Press.

Chigusa Kurumada and T. Florian Jaeger. 2015. Communicative efficiency in language production: Optional case-marking in japanese. *Journal of Memory and Language*, 83(Supplement C):152 – 178.

Sun-Hee Lee, Mineharu Nakayama, and Richard L. Lewis. 2005. Difficulty of processing Japanese and Korean center-embedding constructions. In M. Minami, H. Kobayashi, M. Nakayama, and H.Sirai, editors, *Studies in Language Science*, volume Volume 4, pages 99–118. Kurosio Publishers, Tokyo, Tokyo.

Roger Levy. 2008. Expectation-based syntactic comprehension. *Cognition*, 106(3):1126 – 1177.

Roger Levy and Edward Gibson. 2013. Surprisal, the pdc, and the primary locus of processing difficulty in relative clauses. *Frontiers in Psychology*, 4(229).

Roger P Levy. 2018. Communicative efficiency, uniform information density, and the rational speech act theory.

Roger P. Levy and Frank Keller. 2013. Expectation and locality effects in german verb-final structures. *Journal of Memory and Language*, 68(2):199 – 222.

Richard L. Lewis. 1998. Interference in working memory: Retroactive and proactive interference in parsing. CUNY sentence processing conference.

Richard L. Lewis and Mineharu Nakayama. 2001. Syntactic and positional similarity effects in the processing of Japanese embeddings. In *Sentence Processing in East Asian Languages*, pages 85–113, Stanford, CA. CSLI.

Pavel Logačev and Shravan Vasishth. 2012. Case matching and conflicting bindings interference. In Monique Lamers and Peter de Swart, editors, *Case, Word Order and Prominence: Interacting Cues in Language Production and Comprehension*, pages 187–216. Springer Netherlands, Dordrecht.

Gary Lupyan and Morten H. Christiansen. 2002. Case, word order, and language learnability: Insights from connectionist modeling. In *In Proceedings of the 24th Annual Conference of the Cognitive Science Society*, pages 596–601. Erlbaum.

Maryellen C. MacDonald. 2013. How language production shapes language form and comprehension. *Frontiers in Psychology*, 4(226):1–16. Published with commentaries in Frontiers.

Joakim Nivre. 2008. Algorithms for deterministic incremental dependency parsing. *Comput. Linguist.*, 34(4):513–553.

Umesh Patil, Gerrit Kentner, Anja Gollrad, Frank Kügler, Caroline Féry, and Shravan Vasishth. 2008. Focus, word order and intonation in Hindi. *Journal of South Asian Linguistics*, 1(1):55–72.

Mark Pluymaekers, Mirjam Ernestus, and R Harald Baayen. 2005. Lexical frequency and acoustic reduction in spoken dutch. *The Journal of the Acoustical Society of America*, 118(4):2561–2569.

Rajakrishnan Rajkumar, Marten van Schijndel, Michael White, and William Schuler. 2016. Investigating locality effects and surprisal in written English syntactic choice phenomena. *Cognition*, 155:204–232.

Sidharth Ranjan. 2015. Investigation of locality effects in hindi language production. Master's thesis, Indian Institute of Technology (IIT) Delhi. Unpublished thesis.

Sidharth Ranjan, Rajakrishnan Rajkumar, and Sumeet Agarwal. In Preparation. Locality and surprisal effects in hindi preverbal constituent ordering.

Edward Sapir. 1921. *Language: An Introduction to the Study of Speech*. Harcourt, Brace, New York.

Andreas Stolcke. 2002. SRILM — An extensible language modeling toolkit. In *Proc. ICSLP-02*.

J Vaid and Anshum Gupta. 2002. Exploring word recognition in a semi-alphabetic script: The case of Devanagari. *Brain and Language*, 81:679–90.

Julie A. Van Dyke. 2007. Interference effects from grammatically unavailable constituents during sentence processing. *Journal of Experimental Psychology. Learning, Memory, and Cognition*, 33 2:407–30.

Julie A. Van Dyke and Brian McElree. 2006. Retrieval interference in sentence comprehension. *Journal of Memory and Language*, 55(2):157 – 166.

S. Vasishth. 2003. *Working Memory in Sentence Comprehension: Processing Hindi Center Embeddings*. Outstanding Dissertations in Linguistics. Taylor & Francis.

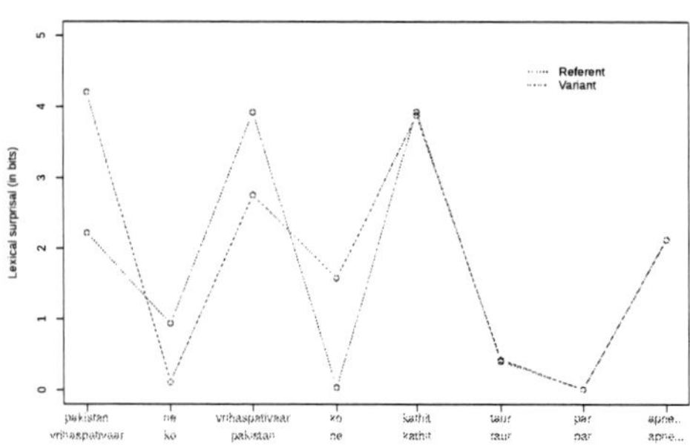

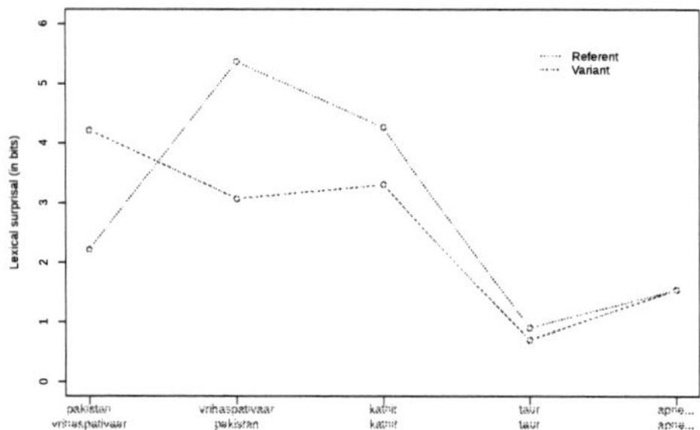

Figure 3: Lexical surprisal profiles of normal and the caseless artificial version of Hindi

Sentence type	Label	Lexical surprisal	Syntactic surprisal
Reference	1	97.45	156.64
Variant$_1$	0	97.69	160.77
Variant$_2$	0	98.25	156.91
Variant$_3$	0	97.97	159.50
Variant$_4$	0	98.16	161.94

Table 6: Original dataset

A Appendix

A.1 Joachims Transformation

Consider the first example in the following Hindi sentences as reference corresponding to *'Jayalalitha has written a letter to the prime minister on this issue'* and remaining as grammatical variants expressing the same idea. Assuming this as a toy dataset, Table 6 denotes their lexical and syntactic surprisal feature values whereas Table 7 represents its Joachims transformation.

Reference [jayalalitha-ne]$_1$ [is mazle par]$_2$ [pradhanmantri-ko]$_3$ [ek patr]$_4$ V ...

Variant$_1$ [is mazle par]$_2$ [jayalalitha-ne]$_1$ [pradhanmantri-ko]$_3$ [ek patr]$_4$ V ...

Variant$_2$ [jayalalitha-ne]$_1$ [pradhanmantri-ko]$_3$ [is mazle par]$_2$ [ek patr]$_4$ V ...

Variant$_3$ [pradhanmantri-ko]$_3$ [is mazle par]$_2$ [jayalalitha-ne]$_1$ [ek patr]$_4$ V ...

Variant$_4$ [is mazle par]$_2$ [pradhanmantri-ko]$_3$ [jayalalitha-ne]$_1$ [ek patr]$_4$ V ...

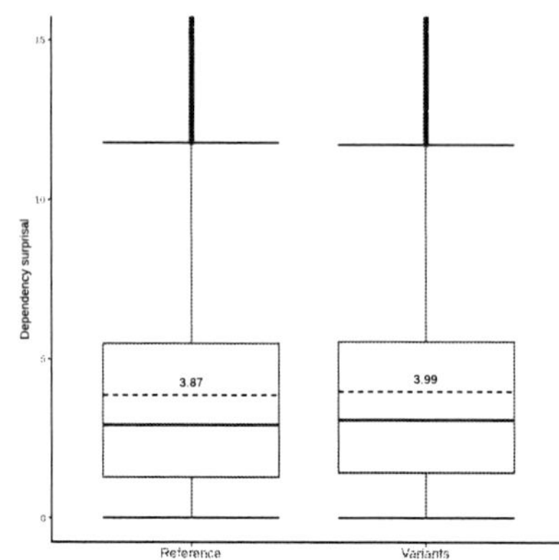

Figure 4: Mean syntactic surprisal per sentence of reference and variant sentences (95% confidence intervals indicated)

New	Label	δ Lexical surprisal	δ Syntactic surprisal
Variant$_1$-Reference	0	0.25	4.13
Reference-Variant$_2$	1	-0.81	-0.28
Variant$_3$-Reference	0	0.53	2.87
Reference-Variant$_4$	1	-0.72	-5.30

Table 7: Transformed dataset

Here are the steps to transform the data set using the Joachims transformation technique.

1. Equal number of ordered pairs of type *(Reference, Variant)* and *(Variant, Reference)* were created.

2. Differences between the feature values of the elements of these ordered pairs were taken (see Table 7).

3. *<Reference-Variant>* pairs were labelled as **1** and *<Variant-Reference>* pairs were labelled as **0**. Here, 1 stands for the correct choice and 0 denotes the incorrect choice.

Label	Dependency relation
Invariant syntactic relations	
k1	subject/agent
k2	object/patient
k4	recipient
k7	location (elsewhere)
k7t	location (in time)
r6	genitive/possessive
Local word group (lwg)	
lwg_psp	postposition
lwg_vaux	auxilliary verb
Symbols	
rsym	symbol relation
Indirect dependency relations	
ccof	co-ordination and sub-ordination
pof	part of units such as conjunct verbs
pof_cn	part of units such as compound noun

Table 8: Glossary of dependency relations

Modeling Hierarchical Syntactic Structures in Morphological Processing

Yohei Oseki
Faculty of Science & Engineering
Waseda University
oseki@aoni.waseda.jp

Charles Yang
Department of Linguistics & Psychology
University of Pennsylvania
charles.yang@ling.upenn.edu

Alec Marantz
Department of Linguistics & Psychology
New York University
marantz@nyu.edu

Abstract

Sentences are represented as hierarchical syntactic structures, which have been successfully modeled in sentence processing. In contrast, despite the theoretical agreement on hierarchical syntactic structures within words, words have been argued to be computationally less complex than sentences and implemented by finite-state models as linear strings of morphemes, and even the psychological reality of morphemes has been denied. In this paper, extending the computational models employed in sentence processing to morphological processing, we performed a computational simulation experiment where, given incremental surprisal as a linking hypothesis, five computational models with different representational assumptions were evaluated against human reaction times in visual lexical decision experiments available from the English Lexicon Project (ELP), a "shared task" in the morphological processing literature. The simulation experiment demonstrated that (i) "amorphous" models without morpheme units underperformed relative to "morphous" models, (ii) a computational model with hierarchical syntactic structures, Probabilistic Context-Free Grammar (PCFG), most accurately explained human reaction times, and (iii) this performance was achieved on top of surface frequency effects. These results strongly suggest that morphological processing tracks morphemes incrementally from left to right and parses them into hierarchical syntactic structures, contrary to "amorphous" and finite-state models of morphological processing.

1 Introduction

Sentences are represented as hierarchical structures, not linear strings of words (Chomsky, 1957; Everaert et al., 2015). The hierarchical representations of sentences have been successfully modeled in sentence processing (Hale 2001; Levy 2008; Boston et al. 2008; Demberg and Keller 2008; Roark et al. 2009; Fossum and Levy 2012; cf. Frank and Bod 2011; Frank et al. 2012). In contrast, despite the theoretical agreement on hierarchical syntactic structures within words, especially derivational morphology, among various linguistic theories (Lieber, 1992; Anderson, 1992; Halle and Marantz, 1993; Aronoff, 1994), words have been argued to be computationally less complex than sentences (Langendoen 1981; Heinz and Idsardi 2011; cf. Carden 1983) and implemented by finite-state models as linear strings of morphemes (Beesley and Karttunen, 2003; Roark and Sproat, 2007; Virpioja et al., 2017), and even the psychological reality of morphemes has been denied by connectionist models (Baayen et al. 2011; Milin et al. 2017; cf. Anderson 1992). Consequently, the hierarchical representations of words have not been sufficiently considered in morphological processing, with a few exceptions (Libben, 2003, 2006; de Almeida and Libben, 2005; Pollatsek et al., 2010; Song et al., 2019).

In this paper, extending the computational models employed in sentence processing to morphological processing, we perform a computational simulation experiment where, given cumulative surprisal as a linking hypothesis (Hale, 2001; Levy, 2008), several computational models with different representational assumptions are evaluated against human reaction times (RTs) in visual lexical decision experiments available from the English Lexicon Project (ELP; Balota et al., 2007), a "shared task" in the morphological processing literature, with special focus on derivational morphology. The goal of this paper is to investigate whether morphological processing tracks morphemes and parses them into hierarchical syntactic structures.

Specifically, we employ five computational models with different representational assump-

Proceedings of the Workshop on Cognitive Modeling and Computational Linguistics, pages 43–52
Minneapolis, USA, June 7, 2019. ©2019 Association for Computational Linguistics

tions from sentence processing: two "amorphous" models, Letter Markov Model and Syllable Markov Model, with transition probabilities among letters and syllables, respectively, without reference to morpheme units and three "morphous" models, Markov Model, Hidden Markov Model, and Probabilistic Context-Free Grammars (PCFG), with conditional probabilities among morphemes, part-of-speech (POS) tags, and nonterminal nodes of hierarchical structures, respectively. Importantly, in the sentence processing literature, Markov Models and PCFGs have been exclusively compared (Frank and Bod, 2011; Fossum and Levy, 2012), but these computational models differ not only in the presence of hierarchical structures but also POS tags. Thus, we included HMM as an important "midpoint" model with POS tags but no hierarchical structures (cf. Lau et al., 2016). The prediction is that, if morphological processing tracks hierarchical syntactic structures, PCFG should outperform the alternative non-hierarchical models. Moreover, if morphological processing tracks morphemes, the "morphous" models should outperform the "amorphous" models.

2 Methods

2.1 Simulation Data

The simulation data was created by intersecting two corpora: CELEX (Baayen et al., 1995) and English Lexicon Project (ELP; Balota et al., 2007). These two corpora were selected because CELEX annotates morphological tree structures on which PCFG can be trained supervisedly, while ELP provides human reaction times (RTs) of visual lexical decision experiments against which computational models can be evaluated. First, every word except structurally ambiguous duplicates was extracted from the revised CELEX (O'Donnell, 2015) that only includes morphologically complex derived and monomorphemic words, hence 22,969 CELEX words.[1] Second, every word except those missing RTs or any control predictors to be included in the baseline model was extracted from the restricted ELP, hence 35,493 ELP words.[2] Finally, those sets of CELEX and

ELP words were intersected, resulting in the simulation data of 13,244 morphologically complex derived and monomorphemic words.[3]

In order to make sure that model performance does not depend on the particular training/testing split, we adopted Monte Carlo cross-validation (MCCV), also known as repeated random subsampling, that repeatedly and randomly samples a subset of the full simulation data as the testing data and assigns the remaining data as the training data.[4] We only sampled bimorphemic words as the testing data, either suffixed (e.g. *teach+er*) or prefixed (e.g. *un+lock*), for the following two reasons. First, among morphologically complex words ($n = 9{,}336$), bimorphemic words account for more than 70% ($n = 6{,}551$), while trimorphemic, tetramorphemic, and super-tetramorphemic words amount to only 24% ($n = 2{,}277$), 5% ($n = 461$), and 1% ($n = 47$), respectively. In other words, super-bimorphemic words can be nothing but outliers in the testing data. Second, given that computational models are multiplicative in nature (Yang, 2017), it is not fair to simultaneously test the words with different numbers of morphemes. That is, shorter words are exponentially more probable than longer ones, but shorter expressions are not necessarily more acceptable or easier to process (Lau et al., 2016; Sprouse et al., 2018). Given these two reasons, for each MCCV iteration, 10% of the bimorphemic words ($n = 655$) was randomly held out as the testing data and the remaining 90% ($n = 13{,}244 - 655 = 12{,}589$) was assigned as the train-

---

(2007) for details.

[3]Another possibility would be that, like Virpioja et al. (2017), CELEX and ELP are independently used as training and testing data, respectively. While it is crucial in our computational simulation for morphemes to be consistent in training and testing data, however, morphological segmentations are not comparable across the two corpora, causing some morphemes to be unknown to computational models during testing, hence poor performance. Therefore, the intersection of the two corpora was necessary to ensure that morphemes are maximally identical in training and testing data.

[4]Another approach would be k-fold cross-validation (kFCV), that splits the full simulation data into k mutually exclusive and equally sized subsets and selects one subset for testing and k–1 subsets for training. kFCV is unbiased in that each word is guaranteed to get tested exactly once, but more variable because the number of iterations is restricted to k, the number of subsets. In contrast, MCCV is more robust than kFCV in that the number of iterations is not limited to the number of pre-split subsets (though biased because each word may be tested different times). That is, there is a general trade-off between variances and biases. Since the purpose here is just to ensure that model performance is robust among different training/testing splits, we adopted MCCV.

---

[1]The revised CELEX cleaned and expanded the original CELEX via hand annotation and heuristic parsing. See O'Donnell (2015, §7.2.2) for details.

[2]The restricted ELP only includes the words for which RT is available and computes paradigmatic lexical statistics like neighborhood density only among them. See Balota et al.

ing data. On the assumption that morphologically complex words are decomposed into component morphemes before morphological parsing, the testing words were represented as morpheme sequences (e.g. ['compute', 'ion', 'al']).[5] The number of iterations was set to 100 and the results presented below are all averaged across those 100 iterations, where the unparsed testing words were excluded (11 words per iteration on average).

2.2 Computational Models

The computational models were implemented with Natural Language Tool Kit (NLTK; Bird et al., 2009) in Python. The architectures of three types of computational models are summarized below: Markov Model, Hidden Markov Model, and Probabilistic Context-Free Grammar.

Markov Model: A Markov Model (also called n-gram model) was implemented with the `model` module. The Markov Model can be defined by an n-order Markov process that computes the transition probabilities of morphemes at position i given the i–n context, e.g. $P(m_i|m_{i-n}, m_{i-1})$. When $i = 1$, the 1st-order Markov Model (i.e. bigram model) computes the transition probabilities of morphemes at position i given the i–1 context, e.g. $P(m_i|m_{i-1})$. When $n = 2$, the 2nd-order Markov Model (i.e. trigram model) computes the transition probabilities of morphemes at position i given the i–2 context, e.g. $P(m_i|m_{i-1}, m_{i-2})$. Given the Markov assumption, the local probabilities of component morphemes in morphologically complex words are merely their transition probabilities.[6]

The transition probabilities are the model parameters empirically estimated from morpheme sequences in the training data via Maximum Likelihood Estimation with token weighting and Lidstone smoothing at $\alpha = 0.1$. The Markov Model is linear and string-oriented in that the transition probabilities merely track morphemes from left to right, which should effectively capture lexically specific dependencies among morphemes.

Hidden Markov Model (HMM): A HMM was implemented with the `hmm` module. A HMM generalizes the Markov Model by hypothesizing "hidden" structures behind visible strings. The HMM computes the transition probabilities of POS tags at position i given the i–1 context, e.g. $P(t_i|t_{i-1})$, and the emission probabilities of morphemes at position i given POS tags at the same position i, e.g. $P(m_i|t_i)$. Although the HMM, like the Markov Model, can be defined by an n-order Markov process over POS tags, only the Bigram HMM is investigated in this paper. The local probabilities of component morphemes in morphologically complex words are the ratio of prefix probabilities at position k to position k–1, where prefix probabilities are the sum of path probabilities compatible with morphemes until position k (Rabinar, 1989).[7]

While the local probabilities of component morphemes in structurally ambiguous words can be computed via a forward algorithm (`sum` of all paths) or a Viterbi algorithm (`max` of all paths), given that most probability mass was allocated to the best path and thus there were no substantial differences between forward and Viterbi algorithms, we adopted the forward algorithm. Both transition and emission probabilities are the model parameters empirically estimated from tagged morpheme sequences in the training data via Maximum Likelihood Estimation with token weighting and Lidstone smoothing at $\alpha = 0.1$. The HMM is structure-oriented in that hidden structures of POS tags are hypothesized behind visible strings, but still linear because the transition probabilities track POS tags from left to right.

Probabilistic Context-Free Grammar (PCFG): A PCFG was implemented with the `grammar` module. A PCFG is most representationally sophisticated among three types of computational models investigated in this paper and, crucially, can model hierarchical structures. The PCFG computes nonterminal production probabilities of right-hand sides given left-hand side nonterminals, e.g. $P(rhs|lhs)$, and terminal production probabilities of right-hand side terminals given left-hand side nonterminals, e.g. $P(m_i|t_i)$, corresponding to HMM emission prob-

---

[5]This is an empirical question whether morphological decomposition and morphological parsing are the same or different morphological computation(s). One possibility would be that top-down morphological parsing generates hierarchical structures while "emitting" morphemes as terminal nodes that provide cues to morphological decomposition.

[6]Bigram Markov Models append one word initial symbol <w> as the necessary context to estimate the probability of the first morpheme. Trigram Markov Models append two word initial symbols <w>, <w> to provide the context for the first morpheme, and so on.

[7]The term "prefix" as in prefix probabilities should not be confused with the term "prefix" in morphology (i.e. a type of affix linearly attached to the left of the base). The term "prefix" here means morpheme sequences that the incremental algorithm has encountered up to the current position.

abilities. The local probabilities of component morphemes in morphologically complex words are the ratio of prefix probabilities at position k to position $k-1$, where prefix probabilities are the sum of tree probabilities compatible with morphemes until position k (Earley, 1970; Stolcke, 1995). Note that HMMs and PCFGs make different predictions even for bimorphemic words because derivational affixes are head-lexicalized in PCFGs (e.g. N $\rightarrow$ V er), while "emitted" from POS tags in HMMs.

Just like HMMs, while the local probabilities of component morphemes in structurally ambiguous words can be computed via an Earley algorithm (`sum` of all trees) or a Viterbi algorithm (`max` of all trees), we employed the Earley algorithm which may have interesting consequences for the incremental nature of morphological processing. Both nonterminal and terminal production probabilities are the model parameters empirically estimated from morphological tree structures in the training data via Maximum Likelihood Estimation with token weighting and Lidstone smoothing at $\alpha = 0.1$. The PCFG is hierarchical and structure-oriented in that the probabilities are defined over hierarchical structures permitted by the grammar.

2.3 Linking Hypothesis

The information-theoretic complexity metric, *surprisal* (i.e. self-information), was employed as a linking hypothesis that bridges between representation and processing (Hale, 2001; Levy, 2008). The surprisal of morpheme m, $I(m)$, is defined as Equation (1):

$$I(m) = \log_2 \frac{1}{P(m)} = -\log_2 P(m) \quad (1)$$

The surprisal estimated by computational models has been demonstrated to explain self-paced reading times or eye-fixation durations in sentence processing (Boston et al., 2008; Demberg and Keller, 2008; Roark et al., 2009; Frank and Bod, 2011; Fossum and Levy, 2012) and remains to be extended to morphological processing (cf. Virpioja et al., 2017). Surprisal is a theory-neutral complexity metric in that computational models with different representational assumptions can be compared on the same probabilistic ground, unlike node counting (Miller and Chomsky, 1963) which only applies to the models with hierarchical structures. Thus, despite different representational as-

sumptions, Markov Model, HMM, and PCFG can be equally evaluated through a lens of surprisal. Interestingly, Levy (2008) and Smith and Levy (2013) dubbed surprisal as a causal bottleneck: "surprisal serves as a causal bottleneck between the linguistic representations constructed during sentence comprehension and the processing difficulty incurred at a given word within a sentence" (Levy, 2008, p.1128). That is, various representational hypotheses assumed by different computational models can be evaluated via only one complexity metric ("the bottleneck"). See Hale (2016) for a review of information-theoretic complexity metrics.

On the assumption that morphological processing proceeds incrementally from left to right, we propose that processing costs of morphologically complex words are proportional to *cumulative surprisal* of their component morphemes. The cumulative surprisal of word w, $CI(w)$, is defined as Equation (2):[8]

$$CI(w) = CI(m_1, ..., m_n) = \sum_{i=1}^{n} I(m_i) \quad (2)$$

where $I(m)$ is the surprisal of morpheme m defined as Equation (1). In fact, the mathematical equivalence of the cumulative surprisal of word w, $CI(w)$, and the vanilla surprisal of word w, $I(w)$ can be proved simply via the combination of the chain rule and the Markov assumption.

2.4 Statistical Analyses

Ordinary linear regression models were fitted with the `lm` function in R.[9] The baseline regression model was first fitted with log-transformed by-item average RTs as the dependent variable and control predictors as independent variables. For each computational model, the target regression model was then fitted with cumulative surprisal as the independent variable of interest on top of control predictors in the baseline regression model.

---

[8]In sentence processing, the processing costs of words within sentences can be easily measured with self-paced reading or eye-tracking experiments, but the processing costs of morphemes within words cannot, so that cumulative surprisal should be computed to transform processing costs from morphemes to words.

[9]Another approach would be linear mixed-effects regression (Baayen et al., 2008) with by-iteration random effects without averaging across 100 MCCV iterations. However, because of methodological uncertainties and convergence failures, we followed the standard practice of cross-validation and averaged the results across 100 MCCV iterations.

That is, the target and baseline regression models minimally differ only in the presence of cumulative surprisal. Therefore, the cumulative surprisal estimated by computational models was evaluated with nested model comparisons via log-likelihood ratio tests based on the χ^2-distribution with df = 1, the difference in the number of parameters between two nested regression models. Furthermore, the control predictors were evaluated via one-sample t-tests on beta regression coefficients based on the z-distribution, given that t-statistics approximately follow the z-distribution with 500 > observations.

Following Lignos and Gorman (2012), four control predictors were included in the baseline regression model relative to which cumulative surprisal was evaluated: squared length, number of syllables, orthographic neighborhood density, and surface frequency. All control predictors were obtained from the ELP.

Squared length: Length (i.e. number of letters) has inhibitory effects on visual word recognition: longer words are recognized more slowly. Since New et al. (2006) found that the quadratic term of length (i.e. number of letters squared) was closely correlated with RTs in the ELP (i.e. "U-shaped curve" of RTs as a function of length), we adopted squared length.

Number of syllables: New et al. (2006) also observed that number of syllables had "robust linear inhibitory effects" on visual word recognition independent of squared length and thus we adopted number of syllables.

Orthographic neighborhood density: Orthographic neighborhood density has been recognized to have inhibitory effects on visual word recognition: words in denser neighborhood are recognized more slowly. Yarkoni et al. (2008) proposed a new measure of orthographic neighborhood density called Orthographic Levenshtein Distance (OLD) which was shown to predict RTs in the ELP better than the classic measure known as Coltheart's N (Coltheart et al., 1977). Thus, we included a version of OLD computed based on 20 closest orthographic neighbors (OLD20).

Surface frequency: Frequency has facilitatory effects on visual word recognition and probably is the most important predictor in the psycholinguistics literature: more frequent words are recognized more quickly. In morphologically complex visual word recognition, theoretical interpre-

tations of frequency crucially depend on the linguistic units over which frequency is computed. For example, surface frequency has been interpreted as an index of storage of morphologically complex words as unanalyzed wholes, whereas base frequency as a "litmus paper" of computation of morphologically complex words from component morphemes. Among various frequency norms such as the Brown Corpus (Kucera and Francis, 1967), the CELEX (Baayen et al., 1995), and the HAL (Burgess and Livesay, 1998), we used the SUBTLEX frequency norm (Brysbaert and New, 2009) which was demonstrated to predict RTs in the ELP better than the previous frequency norms. Specifically, we log-transformed a version of SUBTLEX frequency scaled per million, because frequency is known to follow the nonlinear Zipfian distribution (Zipf, 1949). Note that surface frequency is proportional to unigram probability estimated by "word unigram model", the model of storage discussed by Virpioja et al. (2017), simply because unigram probabilities are computed by dividing surface frequencies by the corpus size.

2.5 Evaluation Metrics

Two evaluation metrics are derived from surprisal: linguistic accuracy and psychological accuracy (Frank and Bod, 2011; Fossum and Levy, 2012).[10] The linguistic accuracy of model M, $LA(M)$, is defined as Equation (3):

$$LA(M) = -\frac{1}{n}\sum_{i=1}^{n} I(m_i) \qquad (3)$$

where $I(m)$ is the surprisal of morpheme m defined as Equation (1). That is, the linguistic accuracy is the negative average surprisal over morphemes of morphologically complex words in the testing data. Note also that the linguistic accuracy is just the negative of the NLP evaluation metric *cross-entropy*. The linguistic accuracy may be cognitively interpreted as offline grammaticality judgment (Keller, 2000; Lau et al., 2016; Sprouse et al., 2018): the higher the linguistic accuracy is, the more grammatical the model "judges" the testing data never seen before. Note that the linguistic accuracy is completely independent of human be-

---

[10]Virpioja et al. (2017) call variants of linguistic and psychological accuracies as text prediction and cognitive prediction accuracies, respectively.

havior (i.e. human RTs), in contrast with the psychological accuracy introduced below.

The psychological accuracy of model M, $PA(M)$, is defined as Equation (4):

$$PA(M) = \Delta D_B - \Delta D_M \tag{4}$$

where ΔD is the delta deviance defined as –2 times log-likelihood and B is the baseline model without cumulative surprisal included. That is, the psychological accuracy is the decrease in delta deviance between the baseline model and the target model fitted to the testing data. The psychological accuracy may be cognitively interpreted as online morphological processing: the higher psychological accuracy is, the less costly the model "processes" the testing data never seen before. For example, suppose that the grammatical sentence *Colorless green ideas sleep furiously* (Chomsky, 1957) empirically turned out to be less costly. The most "human-like" model must assign the high probability, hence the less surprisal, to this sentence. Interestingly, Frank and Bod (2011) and Fossum and Levy (2012) inductively observed that linguistic and psychological accuracies are positively correlated (cf. Virpioja et al., 2017), suggesting that the relationship between representation and processing is transparent (Chomsky, 1965; Hale, 2001).

3   Results

3.1   Linguistic and Psychological Accuracies

Linguistic and psychological accuracies of computational models are summarized in Figure 1, where the x-axis is linguistic accuracy (negative average surprisal) and the y-axis is psychological accuracy (decrease in delta deviance). The accuracies are averaged across 100 MCCV iterations. Points represent computational models and vertical bars on the points are 95% confidence intervals of the psychological accuracy.[11] The horizontal dashed line is $\chi^2 = 3.84$, the critical χ^2-statistic at $p = 0.05$ with $df = 1$.

First, "morphous" models were psychologically more accurate than "amorphous" models. Nested model comparisons via log-likelihood ratio tests revealed that all "morphous" models were statistically significant ($p < 0.01$), but one of two "amor-

---

[11]Thanks to the central limit theorem, while the test statistic itself is χ^2-statistic, the samples of χ^2-statistic follow the Gaussian distribution, based on which 95% confidence intervals can be computed.

phous" models (i.e. Letter Markov Model) did not reached statistical significance. Second, the PCFG was psychologically most accurate among the five computational models: PCFG ($\chi^2 = 14.57$) > HMM ($\chi^2 = 13.83$) > Morpheme Markov Model ($\chi^2 = 13.65$) > Syllable Markov Model ($\chi^2 = 12.84$) < Letter Markov Model ($\chi^2 = 3.52$). Third, the PCFG was also linguistically most accurate, where the correlation between linguistic and psychological accuracies among five computational models was high ($r = 0.81$).

3.2   Control Predictors

Effects of control predictors are summarized in Figure 2, where the x-axis is t-statistic and the y-axis is control predictors. The t-statistics are averaged across 100 MCCV iterations. Points represent computational models and horizontal bars on the points are 95% confidence intervals of the t-statistic. Vertical dashed lines are $t = \pm1.96$, the critical t-statistic at $p = 0.05$ with $df = \infty$.

All control predictors except visual predictors like squared length and number of syllables were statistically significant ($p < 0.05$). The surface frequency effects were most robustly observed among the four control predictors: Letter Markov Model ($t = -17.34$), Syllable Markov Model ($t = -16.71$), Morpheme Markov Model ($t = -16.19$), HMM ($t = -16.49$), and PCFG ($t = -16.58$). Note that surface frequency was most pronounced in combination with the PCFG among three "morphous" models, suggesting that cumulative surprisal estimated by the PCFG explains unique variances not covered by surface frequency.

4   Discussion

In summary, the results of the simulation experiment demonstrated that "morphous" models were more psychologically accurate than "amorphous" models, contrary to "amorphous" models of morphological processing (Baayen et al., 2011; Milin et al., 2017). Among three computational models with morpheme units, the PCFG was most accurate both linguistically and psychologically, suggesting that morphological processing tracks hierarchical syntactic structures, contrary to finite-state models of morphological processing (Beesley and Karttunen, 2003; Roark and Sproat, 2007; Virpioja et al., 2017). Interestingly, syntactic granularity was transparently mapped to psychological accuracy: PCFG with hierarchical

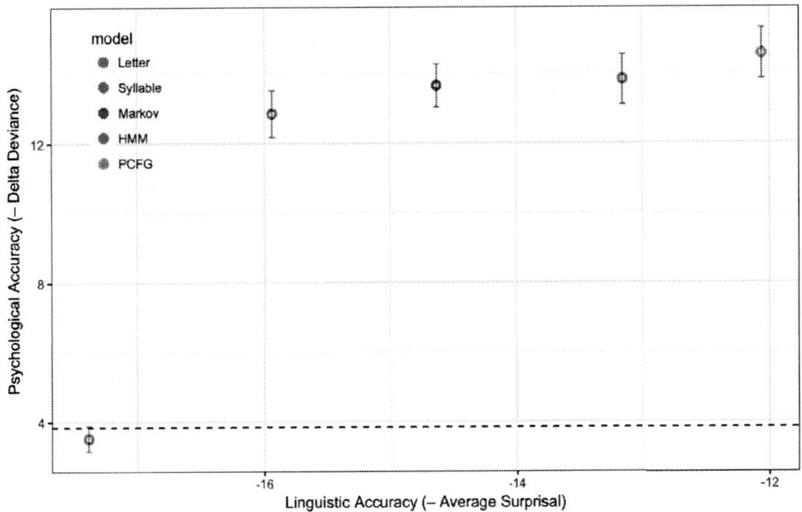

Figure 1: Linguistic and psychological accuracies of computational models, averaged across 100 MCCV iterations. The x-axis is linguistic accuracy (negative average surprisal), while the y-axis is psychological accuracy (decrease in delta deviance). Points represent computational models. Vertical bars on the points are 95% confidence intervals of the psychological accuracy. The horizontal dashed line is $\chi^2 = 3.84$, the critical χ^2-statistic at $p = 0.05$ with $df = 1$. All computational models except Letter Markov Model were statistically significant ($p < 0.01$).

structures was more accurate than HMM with POS tags but no hierarchical structures, which in turn was more accurate than Markov Model with neither hierarchical structures nor POS tags, meaning that hierarchical structures and POS tags made independent contributions for predicting human RTs in visual word recognition. In addition, given that the cumulative surprisal was computed by the PCFG via a probabilistic Earley parser (Earley, 1970; Stolcke, 1995), a top-down parser that incrementally computes probabilities morpheme by morpheme in morphologically complex words, this result may also indicate that morphological processing proceeds incrementally from left to right, despite the inherently non-incremental nature of visual word recognition.[12]

Moreover, the effects of surface frequency and cumulative surprisal were simultaneously observed, theoretically reflecting storage and computation, respectively. The simultaneous effects of surface frequency and cumulative surprisal were not surprising under either the single-route decomposition model of morphological processing (Taft, 1979, 2004; Taft and Forster, 1975), where

storage and computation are indexed at functionally different stages of morphological processing (cf. Solomyak and Marantz, 2010; Fruchter and Marantz, 2015) or the dual-route model of morphological processing (Pinker and Prince, 1988; Pinker and Ullman, 2002), where storage and computation "routes" work in parallel. While Virpioja et al. (2017) interpreted the simultaneous effects of storage and computation as evidence in favor of the dual-route model of morphological processing, however, since RTs are an "endpoint" measure of morphological processing, the two competing models cannot be conclusively dissociated. In fact, Virpioja et al. (2017, p.29) admits that "As the present study used simple RTs which provide an end-point measure of the entire recognition process, either or both of these alternatives about the word recognition process could be correct". Remember that surface frequency was most pronounced with the PCFG among three "morphous" models, indicating that the PCFG can explain unique uncorrelated variances not covered by surface frequency. Additionally, the recent conclusion reached by Virpioja et al. (2017) that derived words are primarily stored in the mental lexicon, not computed from their component morphemes, does not harmonize with the simultaneous effects of surface frequency and cumulative

---

[12]An anonymous reviewer insightfully pointed out that the Cohort Model (Marslen-Wilson, 1987) may harmonize with the present idea that a probabilistic parser applied to morphological processing incrementally contracts the mental lexicon from left to right, which remained to be investigated in future.

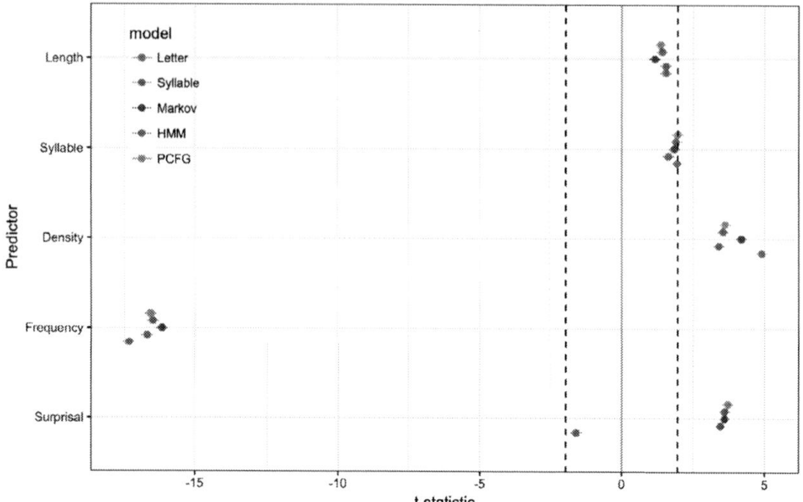

Figure 2: Effects of control predictors, averaged across 100 MCCV iterations. The *x*-axis is *t*-statistic, while the *y*-axis is control predictors. Points represent computational models. Horizontal bars on the points are 95% confidence intervals of the *t*-statistic. Vertical dashed lines are $t = \pm 1.96$, the critical *t*-statistic at $p = 0.05$ with *df* $= \infty$. All control predictors except visual predictors were statistically significant ($p < 0.05$).

surprisal, either.

Nevertheless, remember that we only sampled bimorphemic words as the testing data. However, as Libben (2003, 2006) pointed out, bimorphemic words are not sufficient to distinguish hierarchical structures and linear strings, and trimorphemic words are minimally required. In future, the computational models must be evaluated against trimorphemic words to make sure that the results will generalize beyond bimorphemic words.

5 Conclusion

In this paper, we performed a computational simulation experiment with human RTs in visual lexical decision experiments available from the ELP (Balota et al., 2007), a "shared task" in the morphological processing literature, and evaluated computational models with different representational assumptions via cumulative surprisal as a linking hypothesis (Hale, 2001; Levy, 2008), in order to investigate whether morphological processing tracks morphemes and parses them into hierarchical syntactic structures. Consequently, the results of the simulation experiment demonstrated that "morphous" models were psychologically more accurate than "amorphous" models and, importantly, a computational model with hierarchical syntactic structures, PCFG, was most psychologically accurate among five computa-

tional models, contrary to "amorphous" (Baayen et al., 2011) and finite-state (Beesley and Karttunen, 2003) models of morphological processing.

Acknowledgments

We would like to thank Tal Linzen and CMCL anonymous reviewers for valuable suggestions. This work was supported by JSPS KAKENHI Grant Number JP18H05589.

References

Roberto de Almeida and Gary Libben. 2005. Changing morphological structures: The effect of sentence context on the interpretation of structurally ambiguous English trimorphemic words. *Language and Cognitive Processes*, 20:373–394.

Stephen Anderson. 1992. *A-morphous morphology*. Cambridge University Press, Cambridge.

Mark Aronoff. 1994. *Morphology by Itself*. MIT Press, Cambridge, MA.

Harald Baayen, Douglas Davidson, and Douglas Bates. 2008. Mixed-effects modeling with crossed random effects for subjects and items. *Journal of Memory and Language*, 59:390–412.

Harald Baayen, Petar Milin, Dusica Filipovic Durdevic, Peter Hendrix, and Marco Marelli. 2011. An Amorphous Model for Morphological Processing in Visual Comprehension Based on Naive Discriminative Learning. *Psychological Review*, 118:438–481.

R. H. Baayen, R. Piepenbrock, and L. Gulikers. 1995. *The CELEX Lexical Database (CD-ROM)*. Linguistic Data Consortium, University of Pennsylvania, Philadelphia, PA.

D.A. Balota, M.J. Yap, M.J. Cortese, K.A. Hutchison, B. Kessler, B. Loftis, J.H. Neely, D.L. Nelson, G.B. Simpson, and R. Treiman. 2007. The English Lexicon Project. *Behavior Research Methods*, 39:445–459.

Kenneth Beesley and Lauri Karttunen. 2003. *Finite State Morphology*. CSLI Publications, University of Chicago Press.

Steven Bird, Ewan Klein, and Edward Loper. 2009. *Natural Language Processing with Python*. O'Reilly Media.

Marisa Boston, John Hale, Reinhold Kliegl, Umesh Patil, and Shravan Vasishht. 2008. Parsing costs as predictors of reading difficulty: An evaluation using the Potsdam Sentence Corpus. *Journal of Eye Movement Research*, 2:1–12.

Marc Brysbaert and Boris New. 2009. Moving beyond Kučera and Francis: A critical evaluation of current word frequency norms and the introduction of a new and improved word frequency measure for American English. *Behavior Research Methods*, 41:977–990.

Curt Burgess and Kay Livesay. 1998. The effect of corpus size in predicting reaction time in a basic word recognition task: Moving on from Kučera and Francis. *Behavior Research Methods*, 30:272–277.

Guy Carden. 1983. The Non-Finite = State-Ness of the Word Formation Component. *Linguistic Inquiry*, 14:537–541.

Noam Chomsky. 1957. *Syntactic Structures*. Mouton, The Hague.

Noam Chomsky. 1965. *Aspects of the Theory of Syntax*. MIT Press, Cambridge, MA.

Max Coltheart, Eileen Davelaar, Jon Torfi Jonasson, and Derek Besner. 1977. Access to the internal lexicon. In Stanislav Dornic, editor, *Attention and Performance*, pages 535–555. Erlbaum, Hillsdale, NJ.

Vera Demberg and Frank Keller. 2008. Data from eye-tracking corpora as evidence for theories of syntactic processing complexity. *Cognition*, 109:193–210.

Jay Earley. 1970. An ecient context-free parsing algorithm. *Communications of the Association for Computing Machinery*, 13:94–102.

Martin Everaert, Marinus Huybregts, Noam Chomsky, Robert Berwick, and Johan Bolhuis. 2015. Structures, Not Strings: Linguistics as Part of the Cognitive Sciences. *Trends in Cognitive Sciences*, 19:729–743.

Victoria Fossum and Roger Levy. 2012. Sequential vs. hierarchical syntactic models of human incremental sentence processing. *Proceedings of the 3rd Workshop on Cognitive Modeling and Computational Linguistics*, pages 61–69.

Stefan Frank and Rens Bod. 2011. Insensitivity of the human sentence-processing system to hierarchical structure. *Psychological Science*, 22:829–834.

Stefan Frank, Rens Bod, and Morten Christiansen. 2012. How hierarchical is language use? *Proceedings of the Royal Society B*, 279:4522–4531.

Joseph Fruchter and Alec Marantz. 2015. Decomposition, lookup, and recombination: MEG evidence for the Full Decomposition model of complex visual work recognition. *Brain and Language*, 143:81–96.

John Hale. 2001. A Probabilistic Earley Parser as a Psycholinguistic Model. *Proceedings of NAACL-2001*, pages 159–166.

John Hale. 2016. Information-theoretical Complexity Metrics. *Language and Linguistics Compass*, 10:397–412.

Morris Halle and Alec Marantz. 1993. Distributed Morphology and the Pieces of Inflection. In Ken Hale and Samuel Keyser, editors, *The View from from Building 20: Essays in Linguistics in Honor of Sylvain Bromberger*, pages 111–176. MIT Press, Cambridge, MA.

Jeffrey Heinz and William Idsardi. 2011. Sentence and Word Complexity. *Science*, 333:295–297.

Frank Keller. 2000. *Gradience in grammar: Experimental and computational aspects of degrees of grammaticality*. Ph.D. thesis, University of Edinburgh.

Henry Kucera and Nelson Francis. 1967. *Computational analysis of present-day American English*. Brown University Press, Providence.

Terence Langendoen. 1981. The Generative Capacity of Word-Formation Components. *Linguistic Inquiry*, 12:320–322.

Jey Han Lau, Alexander Clark, and Shalom Lappin. 2016. Grammaticality, acceptability, and probability: a probabilistic view of linguistic knowledge. *Cognitive Science*, pages 1–40.

Roger Levy. 2008. Expectation-based syntactic comprehension. *Cognition*, 106:1126–1177.

Gary Libben. 2003. Morphological parsing and morphological structure. In Egbert Assink and Dominiek Sandra, editors, *Reading Complex Words*, pages 221–239. Kluwer, New York.

Gary Libben. 2006. Getting at psychological reality: On- and off-line tasks in the investigation of hierarchical morphological structure. In G. Wiebe,

G. Libben, T. Priestly, R. Smyth, and S. Wang, editors, *Phonology, Morphology, and the Empirical Imperative*, pages 349–369. Crane, Taipei.

Rochelle Lieber. 1992. *Deconstructing Morphology.* University of Chicago Press, Chicago.

Constantine Lignos and Kyle Gorman. 2012. Revisiting frequency and storage in morphological processing. *Proceedings of CLS*, 48:447–461.

William Marslen-Wilson. 1987. Functional parallelism in spoken word recognition. *Cognition*, 25:71–102.

Petar Milin, Laurie Feldman, Michael Ramscar, Peter Hendrix, and Harald Baayen. 2017. Discrimination in lexical decision. *PLoS ONE*, 12.

George Miller and Noam Chomsky. 1963. Finitary models of language users. In Duncan Luce, Robert Bush, and Eugene Galanter, editors, *Handbook of Mathematical Psychology*, volume 2, pages 419–491. Wiley, New York.

Boris New, Ludovic Ferrand, Christophe Pallier, and Marc Brysbaert. 2006. Reexamining the word length effect in visual word recognition: New evidence from the English Lexicon Project. *Psychonomic Bulletion and Review*, 13:45–52.

Timothy O'Donnell. 2015. *Productivity and Reuse in Language*. MIT Press, Cambridge, MA.

Steven Pinker and Alan Prince. 1988. On language and connectionism. *Cognition*, 28:73–193.

Steven Pinker and Michael Ullman. 2002. The past and future of the past tense. *Trends in Cognitive Sciences*, 6:456–462.

Alexander Pollatsek, Denis Drieghe, Linnaea Stockall, and Roberto de Almeida. 2010. The interpretation of ambiguous trimorphemic words in sentence context. *Psychonomic Bulletion and Review*, 17:88–94.

Lawrence Rabinar. 1989. A Tutorial on Hidden Markov Models and Selected Applications in Speech Recognition. *Proceedings of the IEEE*, 77:257–286.

Brian Roark, Asaf Bachrach, Carlos Cardenas, and Christophe Pallier. 2009. Deriving lexical and syntactic expectation-based measures for psycholinguistic modeling via incremental top-down parsing. *Proceedings of the Conference on Empirical Methods in Natural Language Processing*, pages 324–333.

Brian Roark and Richard Sproat. 2007. *Computational Approaches to Morphology and Syntax*. Oxford University Press, Oxford.

Nathaniel Smith and Roger Levy. 2013. The effect of word predictability on reading time is logarithmic. *Cognition*, 128:302–319.

Olla Solomyak and Alec Marantz. 2010. Evidence for Early Morphological Decomposition in Visual Word Recognition: A Single-Trial Correlational MEG Study. *Journal of Cognitive Neuroscience*, 22:2042–2057.

Yoonsang Song, Youngah Do, Jongbong Lee, Arthur Thompson, and Eileen Waegemaekers. 2019. The reality of hierarchical morphological structure in multimorphemic words. *Cognition*, 183:269–276.

Jon Sprouse, Sagar Indurkhya, Beracah Yankama, Sandiway Fong, and Robert C. Berwick. 2018. Colorless green ideas do sleep furiously: gradient acceptability and the nature of the grammar. *Linguistic Review*, 35:575–599.

Andreas Stolcke. 1995. An ecient probabilistic context-free parsing algorithm that computes prefix probabilities. *Computational Linguistics*, 21:165–201.

M. Taft. 1979. Recognition of affixed words and the word frequency effect. *Memory and Cognition*, 7:263–272.

M. Taft. 2004. Morphological decomposition and the reverse base frequency effect. *The Quarterly Journal of Experimental Psychology*, 57:745–765.

M. Taft and K. I. Forster. 1975. Lexical storage and retrieval of prefixed words. *Journal of Verbal Learning and Verbal Behavior*, 14:638–647.

Sami Virpioja, Minna Lehtonen, Annika Hulten, Henna Kivikari, Riitta Salmelin, and Krista Lagus. 2017. Using Statistical Models of Morphology in the Search for Optimal Units of Representation in the Human Mental Lexicon. *Cognitive Science*, pages 1–35.

Charles Yang. 2017. Rage against the machine: Evaluation metrics in the 21st century. *Language Acquisition*, 24:100–125.

Tal Yarkoni, David Balota, and Melvin Yap. 2008. Moving beyond Coltheart's N: A new measure of orthographic similarity. *Psychonomic Bulletion and Review*, 15:971–979.

George Zipf. 1949. *Human behavior and the principle of least effort: An introduction to human ecology.* Addison-Wesley, Cambridge, MA.

A Modeling Study of the Effects of Surprisal and Entropy in Perceptual Decision Making of an Adaptive Agent

Pyeong Whan Cho
Department of Psychology
University of Michigan
Ann Arbor, MI 48109
pyeongwc@umich.edu

Richard L. Lewis
Department of Psychology
University of Michigan
Ann Arbor, MI 48109
rickl@umich.edu

Abstract

Processing difficulty in online language comprehension has been explained in terms of surprisal and entropy reduction. Although both hypotheses have been supported by experimental data, we do not fully understand their relative contributions on processing difficulty. To develop a better understanding, we propose a mechanistic model of perceptual decision making that interacts with a simulated task environment with temporal dynamics. The proposed model collects noisy bottom-up evidence over multiple timesteps, integrates it with its top-down expectation, and makes perceptual decisions, producing processing time data directly without relying on any linking hypothesis. Temporal dynamics in the task environment was determined by a simple finite-state grammar, which was designed to create the situations where the surprisal and entropy reduction hypotheses predict different patterns. After the model was trained to maximize rewards, the model developed an adaptive policy and both surprisal and entropy effects were observed especially in a measure reflecting earlier processing.

1 Introduction

Over the past decades, computational models of sentence comprehension have improved our understanding of processing difficulty arising in online language comprehension. It has been discovered that information-theoretic complexity metrics can predict processing difficulty (for review, see Hale, 2016).

The surprisal hypothesis (Hale, 2001; Levy, 2008) proposes processing difficulty of a word w_k in a context $w_{1:k-1}$ is proportional to its surprisal, $-\log p(w_k|w_{1:k-1})$. Levy (2008) proved that surprisal is equivalent to Kullback-Leibler divergence between the probability distributions over parse trees T before and after observing the word w_k, $D_{\mathrm{KL}}(P(T|w_{1:k})\|P(T|w_{1:k-1}))$.

On the other hand, the entropy reduction hypothesis (Hale, 2003) claims that processing difficulty is proportional to a non-negative amount of entropy reduced after observing a word w_k: $\max(H(S|w_{1:k-1}) - H(S|w_{1:k}), 0)$ where S is a random variable of sentences. It is not clear why the language processing system works insensitive to negative entropy changes.

Both hypotheses have been supported by experimental data (for surprisal, see Demberg and Keller, 2008; Smith and Levy, 2013; for entropy reduction, see Frank, 2013; Linzen and Jaeger, 2016). Some behavioral studies reported both effects of surprisal and entropy reduction (Linzen and Jaeger, 2016; Lowder et al., 2018) and in such cases, the surprisal effect was much stronger than the entropy reduction effect.

However, we do not have comprehensive understanding of their relative contribution to processing load. Empirically, the estimation of surprisal and entropy values requires a language model, the quality of which depends on many factors (e.g., the corpus size, the model type) (c.f., Goodkind and Bicknell, 2018 argued the effect of surprisal was robust when the measures were estimated using a wide range of language models with different qualities). Also surprisal and entropy values tend to be highly correlated in natural languages, which makes it difficult to tease apart their relative roles in online language processing.

To avoid these empirical problems, we introduce a simple experimental paradigm, which combines two well-established paradigms: saccade target selection (OReilly et al., 2013) and artificial language paradigm (Harrison et al., 2006), both of which have been used to answer related questions. In the artificial language paradigm, we design a language such that it has some distributional

Proceedings of the Workshop on Cognitive Modeling and Computational Linguistics, pages 53–61
Minneapolis, USA, June 7, 2019. ©2019 Association for Computational Linguistics

properties of interest. For example, we can design a grammar in which the surprisal and the entropy reduction hypotheses make different predictions. For example, Linzen and Jaeger (2014) used a simple finite-state grammar to create such situation and discussed alternative accounts of processing difficulty. In the present study, we used a variant of their grammar (see Figure 3). Due to the simplicity of the grammar, entropy and entropy reduction measures are perfectly correlated. When we discuss the effect of those measures, we will refer to it as the entropy effect but we are neutral in whether it should be interpreted as the effect of entropy or the effect of entropy reduction; we reserve the question for future work.

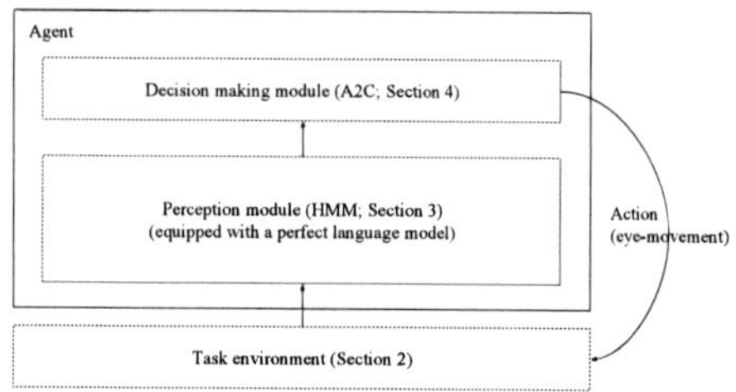

Figure 1: Model architecture. The model consists of two modules: perception module and decision making module. Equipped with a perfect language model, the perception module (implemented as a Hidden Markov Model) integrates noisy inputs from environment with its top-down expectation. The decision making module (implemented as a neural network with the Actor Critic architecture) makes an action based on the output of the perception module.

To develop a better understanding, we propose a mechanistic model of perceptual decision making and investigate its behavior in a simulated task environment with temporal dynamics, focusing on the effects of surprisal and/or entropy. Figure 1 presents the architecture of the model and how it interacts with the task environment. It consists of two components: the perception module at the bottom collects noisy bottom-up evidence from the task environment and updates its state (expressed in [posterior] probability distributions). The decision making module at the top monitors the state of the perception module and makes an action (i.e., decision), which will update the state of the task environment. The design of the perception module was inspired by Bicknell and Levy (2010) that investigated a related research question. Unlike their model, we used reinforcement

learning to let the agent develop an optimal policy.

The main contribution of the present study is that we propose a full cognitive architecture that performs perceptual decision making, which we argue shares a core computational problem of uncertainty management with online language comprehension tasks (e.g., self-paced reading) and investigate the optimal behavior by exploring an unrestricted decision policy space.

In the following sections, we will present each component in Figure 1 in detail. In Discussion, we conclude.

2 Task Environment

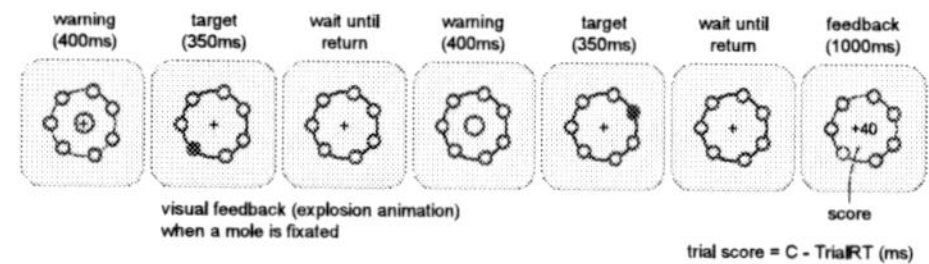

Figure 2: Task environment. The events occurring at two sample trials are shown. The agent is asked to "look at" the target (color dot) as quickly and accurately as possible.

We created a simulated saccade target selection task environment (e.g., OReilly et al., 2013) (see Figure 2). In each trial, a target appears at one of 7 positions and the agent is asked to "look at" the target as quickly and accurately as possible and look back at the center. The returning fixation terminates the trial and initiates the next trial.

In the simulated task environment, each of 7 locations was represented as an angle (in radian) in a circular space $[0, 2\pi)$ and associated with a symbol. The center location was associated with an empty symbol ϵ, representing the absence of a target. A selection of a symbol was treated as the fixation on its associated location.[1] Following OReilly et al. (2013), we measured the number of timesteps that the agent took to select the target (*target arrival*) and the number of timesteps that the agent took to make the first "meaningful" decision, by which we mean the first selection of a non-center location which may or may not be correct (*first saccade onset*).[2]

The locations of the targets changed following a simple finite-state grammar (see Figure 3 so

---

[1] For modeling convenience, we ignored eye-movement details (e.g., the minimal duration of a saccade).

[2] The proposed model selects a symbol at every timestep. When the model selects the symbol that it previously selected, we treat it as a continuation of the previous fixation.

Sample space	Description
$\mathcal{V} = \{a, b, c, d, e, f, g\}$	the set of input symbols
$\mathcal{U} = \{\epsilon\}$	the set of the empty symbol
$\mathcal{W} = [0, 2\pi)$	a circular space of angles
$\mathcal{S} = (\mathcal{V} \times \mathcal{U}) \cup (\mathcal{U} \times \mathcal{V})$	the set of states
$\mathcal{X} = \mathcal{V} \cup \mathcal{U}$	the set of input symbols
$\mathcal{Y} = \mathcal{W} \cup \mathcal{U}$	the set of observations

Table 1: Sample spaces

were partially predictable. We were interested in whether the onset and arrival measures are dependent on the amount of uncertainty.

3 Agent: Perception Module

For discussion, we introduce some notational conventions. We use the uppercase (e.g., X), lowercase (e.g., x), and calligraphic font (e.g., $\mathcal{X}$) to denote a random variable, a particular sample, and its sample space. We use the superscript to denote the position of a symbol in a sequence of symbols and the subscript to denote a particular element in a sample space.

Let S, X, and Y be a discrete random variable of states, a discrete random variable of input symbols, and a mixed random variable of observations. A probability distribution over states $P(S)$ will be referred to as a "parser state", which should be distinguished from simple states. The sample spaces of those variables are $\mathcal{S}$, $\mathcal{X}$, and $\mathcal{Y}$, respectively (see Table 1).

The perception module was implemented as a Hidden Markov Model (HMM), where the hidden variable $S^{(k)}$ represents states after processing the k-th symbol $x^{*(k)}$ in a sequence of symbols, assuming the agent is equipped with a perfect language model. $X^{(k)}$ representing symbol identities is conditioned on $S^{(k)}$. $Y^{(k)}$ represents the observations of the input symbol (i.e., a particular location in the task environment [see Figure 4]).

3.1 Language Model

Let us begin with the agent's language model. We used a Markov chain (See Figure 3) to implement a language model but other types of models can be used if they can emulate the environmental dynamics. For convenience, unique bigrams were used as states: $s^{(k)} = x^{(k)}x^{(k+1)}$. In this simple language, each state $s^{(k)}$ uniquely specifies the present input symbol $x^{(k)}$; $p(x_j|s_i) = 1$ if $s_i = x_j x_k$ and 0 otherwise. An example sequence of two sentences is $c\,\epsilon\,f\,\epsilon\,|\,a\,\epsilon\,d\,\epsilon$ where $|$ indicates a hidden sentence boundary; the underlying state

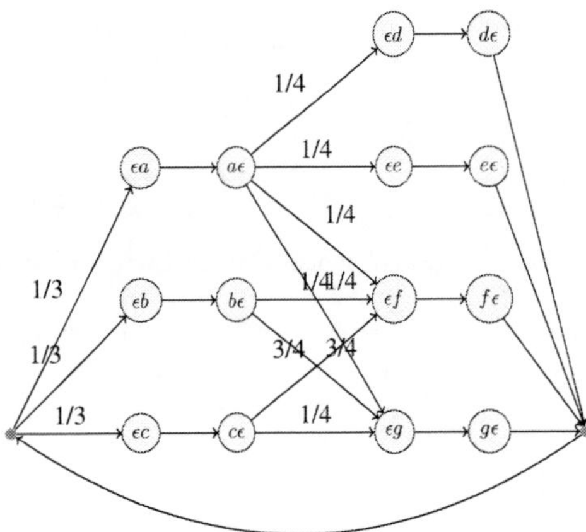

Figure 3: Grammar G specifies probabilistic transitions from a state s_i to another state s_j between symbols. The transition probability $p(s_j|s_i)$ is shown on an edge from node i to node j. The edges with no labels have the transition probability of 1.

change is as follows: $c\epsilon$-ϵf-$f\epsilon$-ϵa-$a\epsilon$-ϵd-$d\epsilon$-ϵb.

Some distributional information of the language is given in Table 2. In the present study, we will focus on three conditions where f is presented in different contexts $a\epsilon$, $b\epsilon$, and $c\epsilon$ at which surprisal and entropy reduction hypotheses predict different patterns.[3] We will refer to the three conditions as HiE/HiS (HighEntropy/HighSurprisal), LoE/HiS, and LoE/LoS. Let RT($\cdot$) be a decision making time (in onset or arrival) at a certain condition. The surprisal hypothesis predicts: RT(LoE/LoS) < RT(LoE/HiS) = RT(HiE/HiS). The entropy reduction hypothesis predicts: RT(LoE/LoS) = RT(LoE/HiS) < RT(HiE/HiS). If both surprisal and entropy (reduction) have unique contributions to processing load, assuming the surprisal effect is stronger than the entropy effect, we expect: RT(LoE/LoS) < RT(LoE/HiS) < RT(HiE/HiS).

3.2 Mapping between Symbols and Observations

Figure 4 presents the mapping of symbols to the locations on the task environment. The empty symbol, representing the absence of target, is mapped to the center location. The other symbols

---

[3]The target g in the same three contexts was designed to be a mirror case of f and introduced (1) for counterbalancing and (2) to increase the number of data points in the planned human experiment. However, due to the difference in their closest neighbors, processing f and g in the same three contexts can be different.

context	target	p_{targ}	surprisal	entropy
$a\epsilon$	d, e	0.083	1.386	1.386
$a\epsilon$	f, g	0.417	1.386	1.386
$b\epsilon$	f	0.417	1.386	0.562
$b\epsilon$	g	0.417	0.288	0.562
$c\epsilon$	f	0.417	0.288	0.562
$c\epsilon$	g	0.417	1.386	0.562

Table 2: Distributional information for unique context-target combinations. p_{targ} represents the unigram target probability. Entropy measures the amount of uncertainty after processing context but before receiving target: $H(P(X|\text{context})) = -\sum_x p(x|\text{context}) \log p(x|\text{context})$. Surprisal and entropy were calculated with e as base.

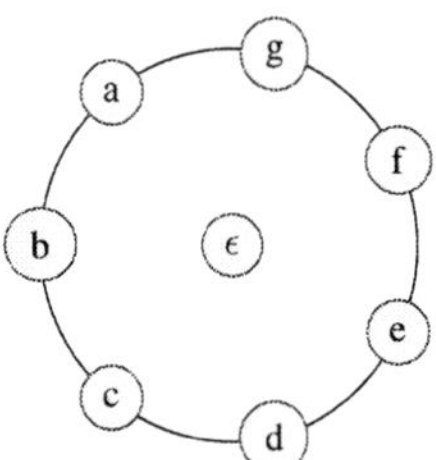

Figure 4: Screen configuration. Each of 7 symbols (a - g) is mapped to a unique location on the ring. At the center, there is a fixation cross, corresponding to a null symbol ϵ.

in $\mathcal{V}$ are mapped to 7 equally-distributed real numbers in $\mathcal{W}$ via a bijective function A; the image of $\mathcal{V}$ is $\{(2\pi)(i/7) + j | i \in \{0, \cdots, 6\}\}$ where j can take any arbitrary number in $[0, 2\pi)$. In the following example, we consider a simple mapping: $A(b) = 0$, $A(c) = (2\pi)(1/7)$, $A(d) = (2\pi)(2/7)$, $A(e) = (2\pi)(3/7)$, $A(f) = (2\pi)(4/7)$, $A(g) = (2\pi)(5/7)$, $A(a) = (2\pi)(6/7)$.

3.3 Noisy Input Channel

Let y^* be the noise-free observation of the target symbol x^*. Note that x^* is chosen by the task environment dynamics. We assume that the perception module samples an observation y via a noisy input channel at every timestep. The conditional probability of y given x, $p(y|x)$, is presented in Table 3. Observations y's over multiple timesteps are assumed to be independent from each other given target x^*.[4] We will use the same conditional prob-

ability distribution when the module updates the posterior probability of symbol x given noisy observation y. Parameters α and β are false positive and false negative rates, respectively. In the false positive case, we assume every value in the circular space $\mathcal{W}$ is equally likely. In the true positive case (i.e., $x^* \in \mathcal{V}$, we assume $p(y|x^*)$ is higher as y is closer to $y^* = A(x^*)$. This intuition is implemented by introducing a von Mises distribution (with parameters μ and κ), which is a Gaussian-like distribution applied to a circular space.

	sample a location on the ring $y \in \mathcal{W}$	sample the center $y \in \mathcal{U}$
target present ($x \in \mathcal{V}$)	$(1 - \beta)F(y; \mu = A(x), \kappa)$	β
target absent ($x \in \mathcal{U}$)	$\alpha/(2\pi)$	$1 - \alpha$

Table 3: $p(y|x)$, a conditional probability of a noisy sample y given a symbol x where α and β are the rates of false positive and false negative, F is the probability density function of the von Mises distribution with location and scale parameters μ and κ. As κ increases, larger probability mass is placed near the mean μ

3.4 Noisy Memory

In addition to noisy input, we consider noise in memory. More specifically, we assume the memory of the parser state is noisy such that a state s can be replaced with another state s'. Noisy memory is implemented by applying the confusion matrix to the parser state $P(S)$: $P(S') = P(S) \cdot \mathbf{P}'_{S \to S'}$ where $P(S)$ is a row vector of probabilities over possible states and $\mathbf{P}'_{S \to S'}$ is the transition probability matrix in which the (i, j)-th component represents $p(s'_j | s_i)$.

We consider three types of confusion: (1: rand) purely random noise which allows every transition $s_i \to s_j$ for all pairs of i and j, (2) similarity-based interference allows transitions between two states similar to each other. Two types of similarities were considered. (2a: sim1) symbol-type similarity; e.g., a, b, c are similar because they occur at the same position in a sequence (i.e., as the first word of a two-word sentence) so $a\epsilon$ can be recalled as $a\epsilon$, $b\epsilon$, or $c\epsilon$. (2b: sim2) transposition

---

[4]The likelihood of observation y is also conditioned on the present fixation location, which is modeled as the symbol chosen by the decision making module at the previous timestep (see Section 4). The likelihood function in the target present condition (see Table 3) assumes that the present fixation is on the center, which is true at the beginning of each target-present trial; the measure of *first saccade onset* is accu-

rate. However, the likelihood function would not be ideal for modeling the belief update from noisy observations after the first saccade to a non-target location. Although not accurate, the measure of *target arrival* can still be informative because it contains information about whether the target was chosen at the first try or not.

+ symbol-type similarity; for example, $a\epsilon$ can be confused as ϵa, ϵb, and ϵc.

More specifically, we consider $p(s_j|s_i) = (1 - \eta_{noise})\delta_{ij} + \eta_{noise}\{\eta_{rand}\, p_{rand}(s_j|s_i) + (1 - \eta_{rand})((1 - \eta_{trans})\, p_{sim1}(s_j|s_i) + \eta_{trans} p_{sim2}(s_j|s_i))\}$; $p_{type}(s_j|s_i)$ (where $type \in \{\text{rand, sim1, sim2}\}$) was set to the reciprocal of the number of transitions corresponding to the type of confusion if $s_i \rightarrow s_j$ is allowed and 0 otherwise. We aggregate the conditional probabilities into a transition probability matrix $\mathbf{P}'_{S\rightarrow S'}$ such that $p_{i,j} = p(s_j|s_i)$. In the present study, $\eta_{noise} = 0.001$, $\eta_{rand} = 0.1$, $\eta_{trans} = 0.1$.

3.5 Belief Update

The module updates posterior probabilities of target locations over multiple timesteps by accumulating bottom-up noisy evidence (likelihood) and integrating it with top-down expectation (prior probabilities) $p(x^{(k)}|s^{(k-1,T_{k-1})})$ where T_k is the last timestep at the previous trial $k - 1$. More detailed processes are presented in the below.

Step 1: Each trial begins with the instantaneous update of input symbol from $x^{*(k-1)}$ to $x^{*(k)}$. The model uses the last parser state $P(S^{(k-1,T_{k-1})})$ to set log priors for $X^{(k)}$ and $S^{(k)}$. $\mathrm{LP}_S(k) = \log\{P(S^{(k-1,T_{k-1})}) \cdot \mathbf{P}'_{S\rightarrow S'} \cdot \mathbf{P}_{S\rightarrow S}\}$ ($\mathbf{P}'_{S\rightarrow S'}$ adds noise to the past parser state and $\mathbf{P}_{S\rightarrow S}$ [from the language model] uses the noisy past parser state to predict the following parser state); $\mathrm{LP}_X(k) = \log\{P(S_k) \cdot \mathbf{P}_{S\rightarrow X}\}$.

Step 2: At every timestep t, the module collects a noisy observation $y^{(k,t)}$ and updates log-likelihoods of $X^{(k)}$ and $S^{(k)}$: the i-th component of a row vector $\mathrm{LL}_X(k,t)$ is $\sum_{t'=1}^{t} \log p(y^{(k,t')}|x_i)$; $\mathrm{LL}_S(k,t) = \mathbf{P}_{S\rightarrow X} \exp\{\mathrm{LL}_X(k,t)\}^{\top}$.

Step 3. Posteriors of X_k and S_k given $y_k^{(1:t)}$ are as follows: $P(X^{(k)}|y^{(k,1:t)}) = \sigma(\mathrm{LL}_X(k,t) + \mathrm{LP}_X(k))$; $P(S_k|y^{(k,1:t)}) = \sigma(\mathrm{LL}_S(k,t) + \mathrm{LP}_S(k))$ where σ is the standard softmax function.

Step 2 and Step 3 are iterated until (1) the decision making module (see the next section) selects the target symbol x^* correctly or (2) the maximum number of timesteps (= 100) has passed.

3.6 The Module Behavior

We created multiple instances of the perception module by setting some module parameters to different values (see Table 4) and investigated how the posterior probabilities changed in the three

conditions of our interest. Each of 3 modules processed 200 blocks of 8 different sentence types. In each block, the presentation order of the sentences was randomized. For each sentence, the model processed each symbol over 50 timesteps.

Module	memory noise η_{noise}	perception noise ($1/\kappa$)
M1	0.001	1
M2	0.001	1/3
M3	0.2	1

Table 4: Different module settings. η_{noise} determines the amount of memory noise while $1/\kappa$ determines the amount of input noise. We fixed α (false negative rate) and β (false positive rate) to 0.05 in this study.

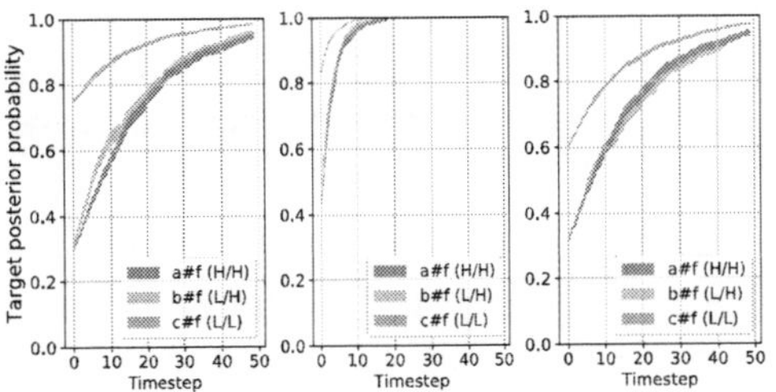

Figure 5: Plots of target posterior probabilities in different conditions. Each ribbon presents mean $\pm$ one standard error calculated from 200 trials.

Figure 5 presents the target posterior probability change as the modules processed f in three different contexts $a\epsilon$ (HiE/HiS), $b\epsilon$ (LoE/HiS), and $c\epsilon$ (LoE/LoS). The effect of surprisal is clear in all three modules. This is expected from our belief update process. When a new symbol (i.e., f) is presented, the perception module uses the last parser state to reset log priors, which determine different starting points before evidence integration. When the race begins, the symbol candidate with a low surprisal value is many steps ahead of its competitors with high surprisal values.

On the other hand, the effect of entropy (reduction) was weakly suggested only in Module 1 (see panel A in Figure 5). The target posterior probability increased slightly faster in context $b\epsilon$ (LoE/HiS) than in context $c\epsilon$ (HiE/HiS).

Based on the observed patterns, we chose Module 1 as the perception module of the agent.

4 Agent: Decision Making Module

Instead of searching a restricted policy space (e.g., static decision boundary such as $\max_x p(x) > .9$, or as in Bicknell and Levy, 2010), we use reinforcement learning to search a huge policy space with no restriction to discover a (near-)optimal decision policy in the task environment.

4.1 Advantageous Actor-Critic

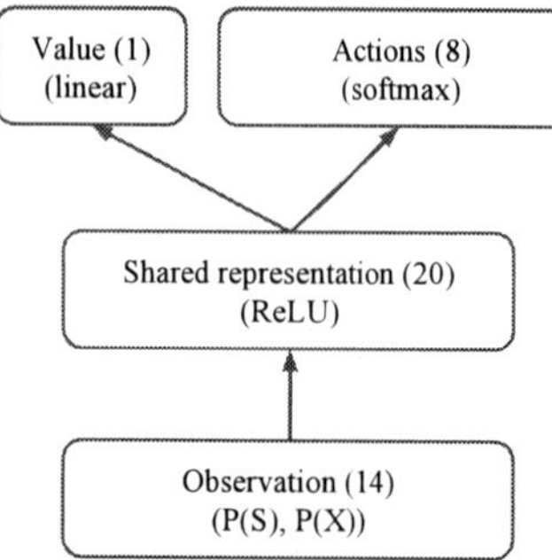

Figure 6: Actor-critic architecture of the decision making module. The number in parentheses indicates the number of units in each layer.

The decision making module has an Advantageous Actor-Critic (A2C) architecture (c.f., for the asynchronous version A3C, see Mnih et al., 2016) (see Figure 6) in which each of 8 actions was mapped to a unique location in the task environment. Let $\mathbf{s}_t$ be the state of the perception module at timestep t. Let $V(\mathbf{s}_t)$ and $\pi(a_i|\mathbf{s}_t)$ be the value output and the probability of choosing an action a_i given input $\mathbf{s}_t$. For the input, an action a_t is sampled from the action probability distribution. The *advantage* of the action is defined as follows:

$$\mathrm{Adv}(\mathbf{s}_t, a_t; \theta) = \sum_{i=0}^{k-1} \gamma^i r_{t+i} + \gamma^k V(\mathbf{s}_{t+k}; \theta) - V(\mathbf{s}_t; \theta)$$

where $\gamma(= 0.99)$ is the discount factor for future rewards, r_t is the acquired reward at timestep t by making an action a_t, and θ is the vector of the model parameters. The module makes actions under the current policy over $k(= 5)$ steps and uses the rewards collected over k steps to improve the value estimate.

4.2 Reward in the Task

We constructed 4 instances of the task environment in which the perception module (Module1, see Table 4) was exposed to different sequences of symbols (that were generated by the same grammar). The decision making module interacted with all four environments simultaneously to collect tuples (state, action, reward, next state). This is motivated to collect relatively independent training samples. At every step, the perception mod-

ule collects a new observation and updates its posterior probabilities over symbols and over states. The decision making module takes both distributions as input and outputs its value and an action sampled from the action probability distribution. When the action chosen at timestep $t(\leq 100)$ corresponds to the target symbol, it terminates the present trial and the new target symbol is presented in the task environment. In this case, the module receives a reward $(100 - t)/100$; faster responses are rewarded more than slower responses. If the module selects a non-target symbol (which is different from its previous selection), the model receives a penalty (= -1). If the model selects the same wrong symbol as in the previous timestep (i.e., $a_t = a_{t-1}$), the model is not penalized; the reward is 0 in this case. For example, let us suppose the decision making module made a sequence of choices $\epsilon, \epsilon, a, a, \epsilon, b, \epsilon, c$ when the target symbol was c, assuming the previous trial ended at the selection of the previous target ϵ. Then, the module would receive a sequence of rewards $0, 0, -1, 0, -1, 0, (100 - 8)/100$. If the model fails to choose the target symbol for 100 timesteps, the task environment is updated to present a new target symbol. Thus, the decision making module has an option not to select any new symbol; technically, the model can keep choosing the previous target symbol over 100 timesteps. This suboptimal policy is better than choosing a non-target symbol; while the maximum reward per trial is 0.99 (if the model chooses the correct target at the first timestep after the task environment update), the model is given -1 for a single wrong selection.

4.3 Training

Over the course of training, the model parameters are updated to minimize the following loss function:

$$L(\mathbf{s}_t, a_t; \theta) = - \log \pi(a_t|\mathbf{s}_t, \theta) \mathrm{Adv}(\mathbf{s}_t, a_t; \theta)$$
$$- \lambda_H H(\mathbf{s}_t)$$
$$+ \lambda_C \mathrm{Adv}(\mathbf{s}_t, a_t; \theta)^2$$

where $H(\mathbf{s}_t)$ is the entropy of action probabilities $\pi(a|\mathbf{s}_t)$. Hyperparameter λ_H determines the strength of entropy regularization, which is intended to encourage the module to explore the policy space without converging to a suboptimal policy too early. In our case, the model developed suboptimal policies when λ_H was fixed at a small value from the beginning; the model never chose target symbols d and e that have lower unigram frequencies than f and g. When d and e were presented in context $a\epsilon$, the module waited until the trial ended after the deadline (100 timesteps) without choosing any non-center location.

We used the ADAM optimizer (Kingma and Ba, 2014) (learning rate = 0.0003) to update the decision making module's parameters. The coefficient of value prediction cost (λ_C) was fixed at 0.5 but the coefficient of entropy regularization (λ_H) started at 0.01 and reduced to 0.001 after $400,000$ timesteps and 0.0001 after $1,000,000$ timesteps. We stopped training after $1,200,000$ timesteps after observing the performance did not improve. Figure 7 presents the average reward acquired on a randomly generated grammatical sequence of 10 symbols during test.[5]

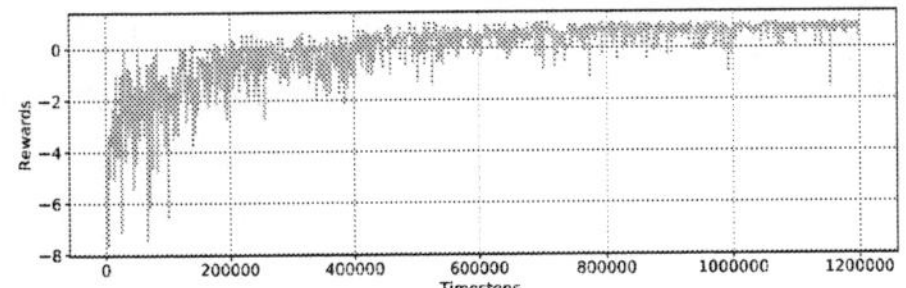

Figure 7: Trajectory of average reward acquired during model evaluation.

4.4 The Model Behaviors

The model consisted of the perception module (Module 1) and the trained decision making module. It was given a long sequence of symbols, a concatenation of 200 blocks of 12 sentences (of 8 sentence types); $b\epsilon g\epsilon$ and $c\epsilon f\epsilon$ were three times more frequent than other sentence types (see Figure 3). We focus on the model's behaviors when f was presented in three different contexts $a\epsilon$ (HiE/HiS), $b\epsilon$ (LoE/HiS), and $c\epsilon$ (LoE/LoS).

Figure 8 presents the distributions of log(onset) and log(arrival) as well as their means, standard errors (thick lines), and standard deviations (thin lines), suggesting the effects of both surprisal and entropy. The entropy effect was more salient in log(onset), which reflects the perception module's states earlier in processing.

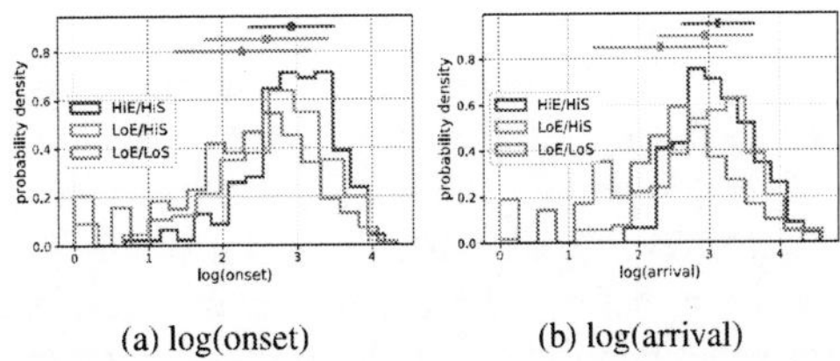

(a) log(onset) (b) log(arrival)

Figure 8: Histograms of (a) log onset time and (b) log arrival time in timesteps. The mean $\pm$ one standard error (thick line) or one standard deviation (thin line) in each condition was presented at the top.

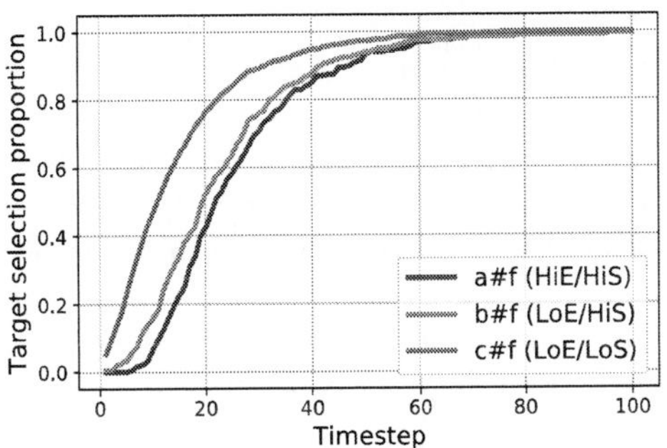

Figure 9: Timecourses of target selection proportions.

Figure 9 presents the proportion of target selection as a function of timesteps and contexts.[6] Both surprisal and entropy effects are clear.

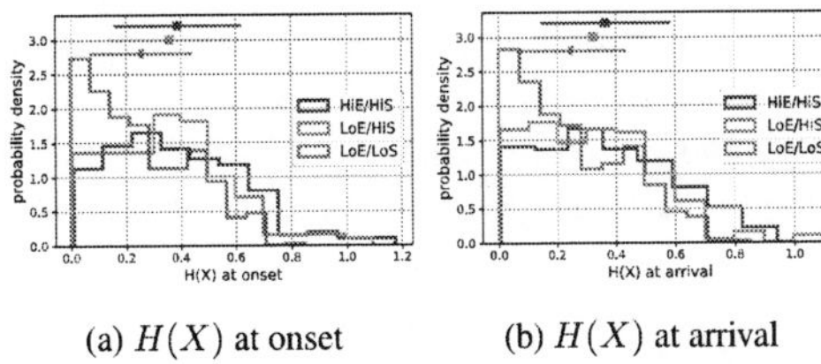

(a) $H(X)$ at onset (b) $H(X)$ at arrival

Figure 10: Histograms of entropy values of posterior probability distributions at (a) onset and (b) arrival. The mean $\pm$ one standard error (thick line) or one standard deviation (thin line) is presented for each condition at the top.

Figure 10 presents the distribution of the entropy values of X in the perception module when the decision making module chose the first non-center location (onset) and the target location (ar-

---

[5]We trained three instances of the model with different random seeds. Their behaviors were not identical but similar. In the text, we report the behavior of the best model that achieved the highest reward over 2400 four-symbol sentences because we are interested in the optimal agent's behavior. When the trials with a trivial target ϵ were excluded, the best model achieved average reward of 0.591. Other two models acquired average rewards of 0.566 and 0.485.

[6]Different trials ended at different timesteps, typically much earlier than the maximum timesteps (= 100). For the purpose of calculating the proportion, we extended the final choice to the maximum timestep; for example, if the last action (i.e., selection of symbol f) was made at timestep 30 in a trial, we treated the module chose the same symbol for the next 70 timesteps.

rival). Distributions in the conditions HiE/HiS and LoE/HiS are largely overlapped but can be distinguished. Note that in all three conditions, the ideal target posterior probability is 1 and the entropy is 0. However, the decision making module made decisions before the perception module developed its belief on the target to the ideal level. This was true especially in HiE/HiS and LoE/HiS conditions. This is because the target posterior probability increased slowly either because the target has many competitors (HiE/HiS) or because the target has a very strong competitor (LoE/HiS). Instead of waiting until the target posterior probability increased enough, the module seemed to take a more risky approach (i.e., making a choice in a more uncertain situation) to obtain more rewards. It makes sense that the model took a safer approach for the target f in the LoS context $c\epsilon$ given that symbol f in the LoS context was three times more frequent than f in each HiS context. Developing a risky policy for such case will be harmful.

5 Discussion

In this study, we introduced a simple task that combines the saccade target selection task (e.g., OReilly et al., 2013) with the artificial language paradigm (e.g., Harrison et al., 2006), both of which have been used to investigate how the human cognitive system deals with uncertainty. Inspired by Linzen and Jaeger (2014), we designed a simple artificial language in which the surprisal hypothesis and the entropy reduction hypothesis predict different patterns. When a perceptual decision making model was trained to maximize rewards in the simulated task environment, both surprisal and entropy effects were observed in the model's behavior; consistent with the literature (Linzen and Jaeger, 2016; Lowder et al., 2018), the surprisal effect was stronger than the entropy effect.

The model developed a flexible decision policy such that it made more risky decisions in the HiE/HiS and LoE/HiS conditions than in the LoE/LoS condition. It was interpreted as the model pursuing a good balance between speed and accuracy because the model could obtain higher rewards from faster responses. The investigation of decision policy reveals the adaptive nature of the system which is not clear from pure rational models.

Our modeling study was intended to explore design-related issues and predict results in human eye-tracking experiments that we plan to run. In human experiments, participants need to learn the grammar hidden in a sequence of symbols. To make learning easier, we chose a simple grammar which made it hard to interpret the effect of entropy; it could be the effect of entropy or the effect of entropy reduction. However, the proposed model is general enough to cover more complex grammars and diverse situations (e.g., self-paced reading). We chose the Hidden Markov Model and the A2C architecture for the perception the decision making modules mainly for modeling convenience. The HMM can be replaced with a more elaborated neural language model when dealing with more complex grammars. The emphasis should be given to our architectual choice. The addition of the decision making module that has the ability to develop a policy on its own provides the system to control the amount of uncertainty flexibly in response to the task situations.

Bicknell and Levy (2010) took the same approach similar to explain reading eye movement patterns, which influenced our work. Our work is different from theirs in that (1) we considered noisy memory more directly and (2) we used reinforcement learning to let the model discover a good decision policy; we believe both additions can lead us to interesting research questions.

References

Klinton Bicknell and Roger Levy. 2010. A rational model of eye movement control in reading. In *Proceedings of the 48th annual meeting of the Association for Computational Linguistics*, pages 1168–1178. Association for Computational Linguistics.

Vera Demberg and Frank Keller. 2008. Data from eye-tracking corpora as evidence for theories of syntactic processing complexity. *Cognition*, 109(2):193–210.

Stefan L. Frank. 2013. Uncertainty reduction as a measure of cognitive load in sentence comprehension. *Topics in Cognitive Science*, 5(3):475–494.

Adam Goodkind and Klinton Bicknell. 2018. Predictive power of word surprisal for reading times is a linear function of language model quality. *Proceedings of the 8th Workshop on Cognitive Modeling and Computational Linguistics (CMCL 2018)*, pages 10–18.

John Hale. 2001. A probabilistic Earley parser as a psycholinguistic model. In *Proceedings of the Second Meeting of the North American Chapter of the Association for Computational Linguistics on*

Language Technologies, NAACL '01, pages 1–8, Stroudsburg, PA, USA. Association for Computational Linguistics.

John Hale. 2003. The information conveyed by words in sentences. *Journal of Psycholinguistic Research*, 32(2):101–123.

John Hale. 2016. Information-theoretical complexity metrics. *Language and Linguistics Compass*, 10(9):397–412.

L. M. Harrison, A. Duggins, and K. J. Friston. 2006. Encoding uncertainty in the hippocampus. *Neural Networks*, 19(5):535–546.

Diederik P. Kingma and Jimmy Ba. 2014. Adam: A method for stochastic optimization. *arXiv:1412.6980 [cs]*. ArXiv: 1412.6980.

Roger Levy. 2008. Expectation-based syntactic comprehension. *Cognition*, 106(3):1126–1177.

Tal Linzen and T. Florian Jaeger. 2014. Investigating the role of entropy in sentence processing. In *Proceedings of the Fifth Workshop on Cognitive Modeling and Computational Linguistics*, pages 10–18.

Tal Linzen and T. Florian Jaeger. 2016. Uncertainty and expectation in sentence processing: Evidence from subcategorization distributions. *Cognitive Science*, 40(6):1382–1411.

Matthew W. Lowder, Wonil Choi, Fernanda Ferreira, and John M. Henderson. 2018. Lexical predictability during natural reading: Effects of surprisal and entropy reduction. *Cognitive Science*, 42(S4):1166–1183.

Volodymyr Mnih, Adri Puigdomnech Badia, Mehdi Mirza, Alex Graves, Timothy P. Lillicrap, Tim Harley, David Silver, and Koray Kavukcuoglu. 2016. Asynchronous methods for deep reinforcement learning. *arXiv:1602.01783 [cs]*. ArXiv: 1602.01783.

Jill X. OReilly, Urs Schffelgen, Steven F. Cuell, Timothy E. J. Behrens, Rogier B. Mars, and Matthew F. S. Rushworth. 2013. Dissociable effects of surprise and model update in parietal and anterior cingulate cortex. *Proceedings of the National Academy of Sciences*, 110(38):E3660–E3669.

Nathaniel J. Smith and Roger Levy. 2013. The effect of word predictability on reading time is logarithmic. *Cognition*, 128(3):302–319.

Modeling Long-Distance Cue Integration in Spoken Word Recognition

Wednesday Bushong
Brain & Cognitive Sciences Department
University of Rochester
wbushong@ur.rochester.edu

T. Florian Jaeger
Brain & Cognitive Sciences Department
University of Rochester
fjaeger@ur.rochester.edu

Abstract

Cues to linguistic categories are distributed across the speech signal. Optimal categorization thus requires that listeners maintain gradient representations of incoming input in order to integrate that information with later cues. There is now evidence that listeners can and do integrate cues that occur far apart in time. Computational models of this integration have however been lacking. We take a first step at addressing this gap by mathematically formalizing four models of how listeners may maintain and use cue information during spoken language understanding and test them on two perception experiments. In one experiment, we find support for rational integration of cues at long distances. In a second, more memory and attention-taxing experiment, we find evidence in favor of a switching model that avoids maintaining detailed representations of cues in memory. These results are a first step in understanding what kinds of mechanisms listeners use for cue integration under different memory and attentional constraints.

1 Introduction

Language is a fast, temporally unfolding signal. Humans must quickly compress large amounts of information into abstract linguistic representations and meanings that contain more manageable amounts of information. However, cues to linguistic categories often do not temporallly co-occur, but are distributed quite broadly across the signal. Rational information integration thus requires maintenance of gradient subcategorical information so as to integrate cues that occur at different points in time. For example, one of the primary cues to the voicing of a syllable-final stop consonant in English is the duration of the *preceding* vowel (Klatt, 1976). Thus, in order to obtain a good estimate of the voicing of a syllable-final stop, listeners must retain some subcategorical information about the preceding vowel in memory. This is typical across languages and occurs at multiple timescales: cues to sound categories can come not only from proximate acoustic properties, but also from, e.g., later semantic context that could potentially occur an unlimited distance away from the target. This poses a memory challenge for language comprehenders: how can one possibly maintain subcategorical information for later use when such maintenance should overload working memory?

This challenge has motivated theories of language processing that contend that listeners compress input into abstract representations as quickly as possible and discard all gradient information after a categorical perceptual decision has been reached (Just and Carpenter, 1980; Christiansen and Chater, 2016). According to these accounts, listeners cannot maintain gradient sub-categorical information for cue integration at any significant timescale, at certainly not beyond word boundaries. However, a growing body of literature has suggested that listeners are in principle capable of maintaining subcategorical representations (McMurray et al., 2009), including at timescales beyond the word boundary (Connine et al., 1991; Brown-Schmidt and Toscano, 2017; Gwilliams et al., 2018). For example, Connine et al. (1991) exposed participants to sentences that contained two cues about a target word, "tent" or "dent" in the sentence. The first cue was the voice-onset time (VOT) of the first sound in the word, which was varied to form a continuum from more /t/-like to more /d/-like. The second cue was a subsequent word that contextually biased toward either the "tent" interpretation (e.g., "campground") or the "dent" interpretation (e.g., "teapot"). Participants heard sentences like "When the ?ent Sue had found in the [campground/teapot]...", and were asked to categorize whether they heard the word

Proceedings of the Workshop on Cognitive Modeling and Computational Linguistics, pages 62–70
Minneapolis, USA, June 7, 2019. ©2019 Association for Computational Linguistics

"tent" or "dent" in the sentence. They found that participants' categorizations were influenced *both* by the VOT of the sound *and* by subsequent context, suggesting that listeners maintained a gradient representation of the initial sound for later use in cue integration and categorization. Subsequent studies have confirmed that listeners can maintain subcategorical representations well beyond word boundaries (Szostak and Pitt, 2013; Bushong and Jaeger, 2017).

Despite recent interest in this phenomenon, to date there has been no comprehensive effort to spell out and quantitatively compare different models of long-distance cue integration under different memory/information constraints. This paper is a first attempt to explore this space, driven largely by previous conceptual proposals. We consider four different models that vary in the extent to which they maintain sub-categorical information and utilize multiple time-distant cues. Two of the models maintain subcategorical information about cues over time, and two do not.

These four models make distinct quantitative and qualitative predictions about how human categorization judgments should be affected by two cues. We first present the mathematical models along with their predictions. We then evaluate the models against human data from two behavioral experiments. In these experiments, participants hear sentences like those in Connine et al. paradigm. We manipulated the same two types of cues as in the Connine et al. paradigm (i.e., VOT and subsequent semantic context).

2 Models

We first describe how an ideal observer would categorize stimuli based on the first cue alone (VOT). Then we describe the four potential models of cue integration, along with their predictions. Figures 2 and 3 illustrate these predictions. Predictions are shown with regard to log-odds (of a "t"-response), since the predictions of all four models look (misleadingly) similar in proportion space. The prediction plots are meant as qualitative demonstrations. For example, the predicted slope of the VOT effect depends on listeners' beliefs about the means and variances of the /t/ and /d/ categories along the VOT continuum. Similarly, the specific magnitude of the context effect depends on the bias (or information) provided by context and the perceptual uncertainty about the VOT cue. Regardless

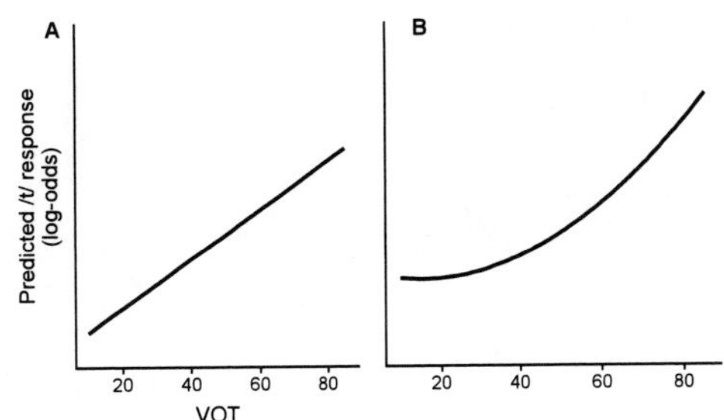

Figure 1: Linear (**A**) vs. quadratic (**B**) effect of VOT on log-odds of "t"-responses.

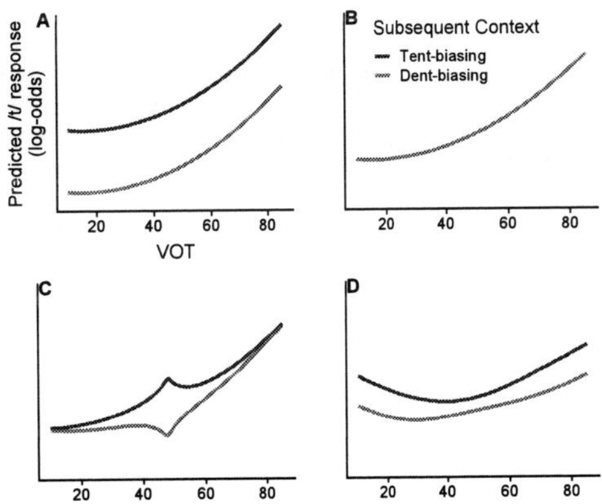

Figure 2: Qualitative predictions of each model in log-odds of "t"-responses (for a context bias of 0.95). (**A**): ideal integration model, (**B**): categorize-&-discard model, (**C**): ambiguity-only model, (**D**): categorize-discard-&-switch model. Shown predictions assume a quadratic effect of VOT (but predicted context effects are identical even if VOT has a linear effect).

of these details, however, some qualitative differences in the context effect emerge across the four different models (see Figure 3). It is these predicted shapes of the context effect that we later compare against human responses from perception experiments.

For all predictions, we assume Luce's choice rule for the link between models' posterior probability of /t/ and the predicted decision to respond "t" or "d"—i.e., $p_{model}(\text{respond "t"}) = p_{model}(/t/|context, VOT)$

2.1 Ideal Observers: Predicting VOT Effects

Before we introduce our models of *cue integration*, we first spell out an ideal observer's predictions for the effect of VOT in the absence of any

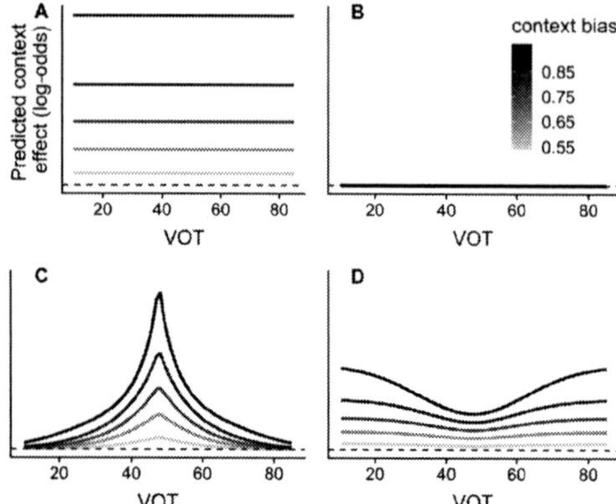

Figure 3: Predicted context effect (difference between blue and red line in Figure 3) for different possible context biases. **(A):** ideal integration model, **(B):** categorize-&-discard model, **(C):** ambiguity-only model, **(D):** categorize-discard-&-switch model. Dashed line represents 0.

second cue. If two Gaussian categories (/t/ and /d/) along VOT have equal variance, an ideal observer will exhibit linear effects of VOT on the log-odds of "t"-responses (Figure 1). However, it is well established that voicing contrasts (including /t/ vs. /d/) exhibit unequal variances along the VOT continuum (Lisker and Abramson, 1967). A standard ideal-observer model thus predicts quadratic effects of VOT on the log-odds of "t"-responses. We thus will visualize all of our model predictions with an assumed quadratic effect of VOT. Next, we turn to the four models of cue integration. We emphasize, however, that the predicted effect of context—the effect we test below—does not depend on this assumption.

2.2 Ideal Integration

The *ideal integration model* holds that listeners maintain subcategorical information about the temporally first cue (here, VOT) in memory for subsequent integration with a later cue (here, context). Note that we use the term 'ideal' in the sense of rational cue integration frameworks proposed across the literature (Ernst and Banks, 2002). These normative models, like the ideal integration model, provide an optimal baseline against which to compare human behavior. The ideal integration model always maintains subcategorical (gradient) information about VOT because optimal categorization requires access to at least $P(category|VOT)$ (or richer information about

VOT) during integration with context. Specifically, ideal integration predicts *additive* effects of the two cues on the log-odds of categorization (Bicknell et al., under review).

If humans have no memory constraints and perfectly integrate all cues available to them, their behavior should resemble predictions of the ideal observer; that is, "t"-responses should be conditioned on both VOT and context:

$$p_{ideal}(\text{respond "t"}) = p(/t/|VOT, context) \quad (1)$$

We can apply Bayes' Theorem to arrive at the following:

$$p(/t/|VOT, context) = \\ \frac{p(VOT|context, /t/)p(context, /t/)}{p(VOT, context)} = \\ \frac{p(VOT|context, /t/)p(/t/|context)}{p(VOT|context)} \quad (2)$$

Under the plausible assumption that VOT and context are conditionally independent (as in Bicknell et al., under review)[1]:

$$p_{ideal}(\text{respond "t"}) \propto p(VOT|/t/)p(/t/|context) \quad (3)$$

As shown in Figure 2A and 3A, the ideal integration model predicts additive effects of VOT and subsequent context in log-odds space.

2.3 Ambiguity-Only

In contrast to the ideal integration model, the *ambiguity-only* model stores information about VOT to the extent to which VOT is perceptually ambiguous: the more ambiguous VOT is, the more likely listeners should be to maintain information about VOT for subsequent integration with context. The ambiguity-only hypothesis—first proposed by Connine et al. (1991)—thus sees maintenance of subcategorical information as a special case: if the signal is relatively clear then listeners immediately categorize and discard low-level information; only when the perceptual input is ambiguous is information about it maintained in memory so as to facilitate robust integration with

---

[1] In our descriptions of the remaining models, we will use $p(/t/|VOT, context)$ and $p(/t/|VOT)$ as shorthand rather than fully expanding them using Bayes' Theorem as in this initial example.

subsequent cues. This can be seen as serving memory economy (for related proposals, see also Dahan, 2010).

There are several ways of operationalizing the idea that information about VOT is only maintained if VOT is perceptually ambiguous. Here, we evaluate a gradient version of this hypothesis: with increasingly unambiguous VOT evidence—i.e., for $p(/t/|VOT)$ closer to 0 or 1—, listeners are assumed to be less likely to maintain gradient representations of VOT to integrate with later context, instead categorizing on the basis of VOT alone. As VOT becomes more ambiguous—$p(/t/|VOT)$ closer to 0.5—, listeners are assumed to be more likely to maintain gradient representations for later integration. We can quantify the degree of perceptual ambiguity as:

$$\lambda = 2|p(/t/|VOT) - 0.5| \qquad (4)$$

We note that λ is determined by the perceptual ambiguity of the stimulus and does not constitute a free parameter for this model. We can then use λ as a weight in a mixture model that describes the relative probability of using VOT only or integrating VOT and context:

$$p_{ambiguity}(\text{respond "t"}) = \lambda p(/t/|VOT) +$$
$$(1 - \lambda)p(/t/|VOT, context) \quad (5)$$

Intuitively, we can think of this as listeners *not* maintaining gradient representations of VOT on λ proportion of trials, and maintaining gradient representations on the remaining proportion.

2.4 Categorize-&-Discard

The other two models we consider do *not* maintain information about VOT in memory, but rather immediately categorize based on the first cue and then discard all subcategorical information about that cue. These *categorize-&-discard* models maximize memory economy at the cost of integration accuracy. Categorize-discard models thus capture the influential view that prolonged maintenance of subcategorical information about the speech signal is not feasible given the bounds of the relevant memory systems (see, e.g., Christiansen and Chater, 2016). The most simple *categorize-&-discard model* categorizes based on VOT, discards all subcategorical information about VOT, and then never revisits the categorization decision. As this model never considers the

second source of information (VOT), its categorization accuracy will necessarily be suboptimal. We formalize this model as simply making decisions on the basis of VOT alone:

$$p_{cat\_discard}(\text{respond "t"}) = p(/t/|VOT) \quad (6)$$

2.5 Categorize-Discard-&-Switch

The final model we consider also discards all subcategorical information about VOT immediately after having used it to categorize. However, unlike the category-discard model, the *categorize-discard-&-switch* model has a mechanism to take into account context: if context conflicts with the initial categorization decision, the model will change its categorization response in proportion to the evidence from context. Concretely, if the model initially categorizes a segment as /d/, but later evidence from context is more consistent with /t/, the model will switch to /t/ in proportion (over trials) to how strongly context points toward the alternative categorization. While the categorization accuracy achieved by the categorize-discard-&-switch model is better than that of the simpler categorize-&-discard model, it is still suboptimal (i.e., underperforms compared to the ideal integration model).

$$p_{cat\_switch}(\text{respond "t"}) \propto p(/t/|VOT) +$$
$$(1 - p(/t/|VOT))p(/t/|context) \quad (7)$$

Like the ambiguity-only model, w can think of this as a cross-trial description of the outcomes of categorization. On some proportion of trials $p(/t/|VOT)$, listeners would have categorized a stimulus as /t/ based on VOT alone. On the remaining trials where listeners would have made a /d/ categorization based on VOT alone, they sometimes switch, proportional to the evidence from context.

The categorize-discard-&-switch model is of particular relevance in light of the recent findings of Bicknell et al. (under review). In their comparison of the ideal integration model with the ambiguity-only model, Bicknell et al. (under review) found no evidence that perceptually less ambiguous VOTs were associated with smaller effects of subsequent context. Rather, the human data seemed to support a constant effect of subsequent context across the entire VOT spectrum. If anything, some of the behavioral data considered by Bicknell et al. (under review) contained numerical trends towards *larger* effects of subsequent context for perceptually less ambiguous VOTs. As can be seen in Figures 2D and 3D, such a pattern would be predicted by the categorize-discard-&-switch model. In order to put the hypothesis of ideal integration to a stronger test, it is thus necessary to compare the ideal integration model also against the new plausible competitor we have identified, the categorize-discard-&-switch model. Next, we describe the two perception experiments that we use to model human responses.

3 Behavioral Experiments

The human data we analyze here stem from two experiments originally reported in Bushong and Jaeger (under review). In both experiments, participants are exposed to sentences and have to make categorization judgments about a target word in the sentence. We varied a critical word in the sentence to vary acoustically between "tent" and "dent", and a subsequent word in the sentence provides a contextual bias relevant to the critical target word (e.g., "campgrounds" biases towards a "tent" interpretation over a "dent" interpretation). The critical difference between the two experiments is which words participants needed to categorize. In Experiment 1, participants always were asked to make categorization decisions about our critical target words, "tent" and "dent". In Experiment 2, this was only their task on half of the trials; on the other half, they were asked to categorize a different word in the sentence that was neither our critical target word nor the subsequent contextually biasing word (see Figure 4). The basic conceptual difference here is that in Experiment 1, it is relatively easy for participants to ideally integrate cues: they always know which cue they need to maintain a gradient representation of (i.e., the initial sound of the target word). Experiment 2 increases the memory and attentional burden of maintaining gradient representations, however: now participants have several possible words they could be asked about and thus cannot perfectly predict which parts of the signal will be relevant for the task. We hypothesized that structure of Experiment 2 might bias participants towards discarding subcategorical information about the speech input (like the categorize-&-discard and categorize-discard-&-switch models).

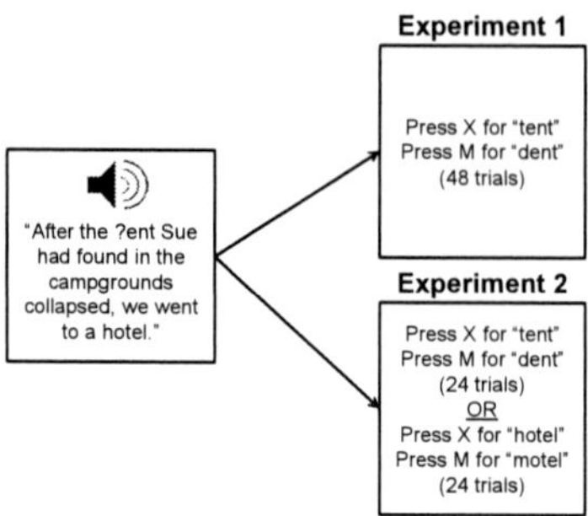

Figure 4: Visualization of an example trial.

3.1 Participants

We recruited 128 native English-speaking participants from Amazon Mechanical Turk for each experiment who were rewarded $3.00 for their participation in the experiment. No participants completed both Experiment 1 and Experiment 2.

3.2 Materials

We take the paradigm from Bushong and Jaeger (2017) as a starting point for our experiments. We constructed 12 sentence pairs like the following:

(1) After the ?ent Sue had found in the campgrounds collapsed, we went to a hotel. (tent-biasing context)

(2) After the ?ent Sue had found in the teapot was noticed, we threw it away. (dent-biasing context)

We manipulated two aspects of the sentence stimuli. First, we acoustically manipulated the "?" to range between /d/ and /t/ by changing the value of its voice-onset time (VOT), the primary cue distinguishing voiced from voiceless consonants. Based on norming and previous experiments, we chose to test VOT values of 10, 40, 50, 60, 70, and 85ms to cover a perceptual range from unambiguous /d/ to unambiguous /t/ with ambiguous points in between. Second, we manipulated whether later context biased toward a /t/-interpretation, /d/-interpretation, or neither. The onset of informative context words were between 6-9 syllables after target word offset.

3.3 Procedure

Both experiments were split into two phases: Exposure (72 trials) and Test (48 trials). The original purpose of these experiments was to test a

Experiment 1	Likelihood Ratio Test		Bayesian Analysis	
Comparison	χ^2	p	Bayes Factor	Posterior Probability
Analysis 2 vs. Analysis 1	38.78	< 0.001	3.5×10^6	> 0.999
Analysis 3 vs. **Analysis 2**	3.76	0.15	0.001	0.001
Experiment 2	Likelihood Ratio Test		Bayesian Analysis	
Comparison	χ^2	p	Bayes Factor	Posterior Probability
Analysis 2 vs. Analysis 1	71.23	< 0.001	5.66×10^{13}	> 0.999
Analysis 3 vs. Analysis 2	40.07	< 0.001	1.9×10^5	> 0.999
Analysis 3 vs. Analysis 3 control	39.27	< 0.001	6.5×10^6	> 0.999

Table 1: Model comparisons for Experiments 1 and 2, both in terms of likelihood ratio tests and Bayes Factor. Best-fitting model is bolded for each experiment.

particular relationship between exposure and test in a between-subjects manipulation (see Bushong and Jaeger, under review). The difference between the experimental groups is that one group of subjects heard sentences with no subsequent biasing context in the exposure phase, while the other group always heard sentences with subsequent context. Because of this imbalance between groups, we only analyze data from the test phase which was identical across participants[2]. What is important here is that in the test phase, all participants heard sentences that contained the full range of our VOT manipulation (evenly split between all values) and informative later context (split evenly between /t/-biasing and /d/-biasing contexts). Test sentences crossed all 6 steps of our VOT continuum with the two context conditions (/t/-biasing and /d/-biasing). All 12 combinations of VOT and context occurred equally often, so as to allow us to reliably estimate the effect of context across the VOT continuum.

Participants' task was simply to categorize whether they heard the word "tent" or "dent" after they heard the full sentence. In Experiment 1, this task was constant across all trials. In Experiment 2, on half of all trials, participants instead had to categorize another word in the sentence (e.g., for sentence (2) above they were asked whether they heard "hotel" or "motel"). Figure 4 shows the structure of the two experiments.

4 Analysis

Following previous work (Bushong and Jaeger, 2017), we excluded participants whose categorization responses were not modulated by VOT, sug-

gesting that they did not understand the task. This resulted in the exclusion of 11 participants from Experiment 1 (8.6%) and 16 participants from Experiment 2 (12.5%).

We fit mixed-effects logistic regression analyses predicting the log-odds of /t/ responses in the test phase from predictors of interest. Regressions were fit using the lme4 package in R (Bates et al., 2014). Each analysis contained the maximal random effects structure that resulted in successful model convergence. We fit four different types of analyses to each of the two experiments in order to assess each of the models outlined above:

Analysis 1: /t/ response $\sim$ VOT + VOT^2. This analysis represents the categorize-&-discard model, where participants only categorize based on VOT then immediately discard information (and thus do not integrate the subsequent context cue).

Analysis 2: /t/ response $\sim$ VOT + context + VOT^2. This analysis represents the ideal integration model, where participants optimally integrate VOT and context (i.e., use both with no interaction).

Analysis 3: /t/ response $\sim$ VOT*context + VOT^2*context. This analysis represents both the ambiguity-only and categorize-discard-&-switch models. Both models predict that there is a quadratic interaction between VOT and context. A negative quadratic coefficient supports the ambiguity-only model, and a positive coefficient supports the categorize-discard-&-switch model.

Analysis 3 control: /t/ response $\sim$ VOT*context + VOT^2. Since both a linear and squared interaction between VOT and context are necessary to support the ambiguity-only and categorize-discard-&-switch models, we fit an additional control model with only a linear

---

[2]Additionally, not all combinations of VOT and context were tested in the exposure phase for the group that did hear subsequent context.

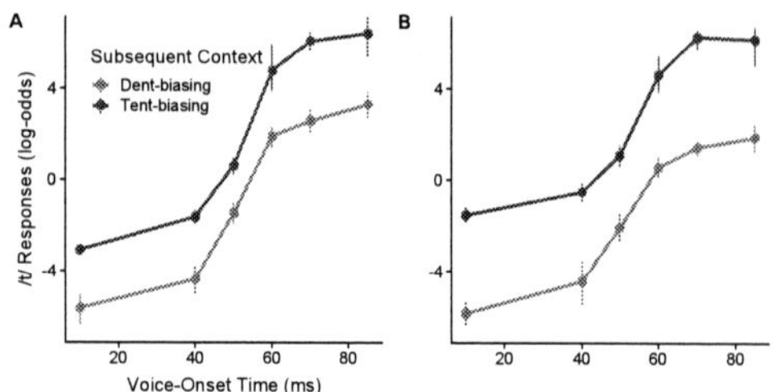

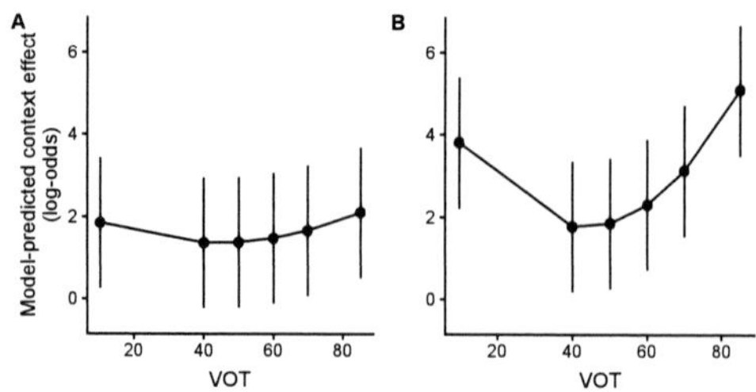

Figure 5: Log-odds of /t/-categorizations in Experiments 1 (**A**) and 2 (**B**) by VOT and subsequent context. Error bars are 95% confidence intervals over item means.

Figure 6: Model-predicted context effect (in log-odds) from Analysis 3 for Experiment 1 (**A**) and Experiment 2 (**B**). Error bars are 95% confidence intervals.

interaction between VOT and context. Thus, for us to conclude that the ambiguity-only or ategorize-discard-&-switch models have support, Analysis 3 must be a better fit compared to Analysis 2 *and* Analysis 3 must be a better fit compared to Analysis 3 control.

Note that both the ambiguity-only and categorize-discard-&-switch models also predict an overall smaller context effect, compared to the ideal integration model (see Figure 3). Additionally, the categorize-discard-&-switch model also predicts a more shallow slope for the VOT effect, compared to all other models (see Figure 2). However, the test of these more specific predictions would require precise knowledge of listeners' beliefs about both a) the distribution of VOT for /t/ and /d/, and b) the exact strength of the context cue. Since we do not have access to this information, we instead take advantage of the qualitative differences in predictions captured by Analyses 1-3.

To determine which models were the best fit for each experiment, we conducted two kinds of model comparisons between the analyses. First, we conducted standard likelihood ratio tests between each pair of models. We additionally derived Bayes Factor (BF) and posterior probability estimates by comparing the BICs of pairs of models (see Wagenmakers, 2007).

Table 1 shows the results for Experiments 1 and 2. The results of the likelihood ratio tests and the Bayesian analysis support the same conclusions.

5 Results

5.1 Experiment 1

Analysis 2 (corresponding to the ideal-integration model) was the best fit both by standard likeli-

hood ratio tests and Bayes Factor. Within Analysis 2, we found significant effects of z-scored VOT ($\hat{\beta} = 1.43, z = 5.72, p < 0.001$), z-scored squared VOT ($\hat{\beta} = 2.43, z = 6.62, p < 0.001$), and subsequent context ($\hat{\beta} = 0.8, z = 6.67, p < 0.001$).

5.2 Experiment 2

Analysis 3 was the best fit to the Experiment 2 data both by standard likelihood ratio tests and Bayes Factor. Within Analysis 3, we found effects of z-scored VOT ($\hat{\beta} = 0.73, z = 2.5, p = 0.01$), z-scored squared VOT ($\hat{\beta} = 1.67, z = 4.873, p < 0.001$), subsequent context ($\hat{\beta} = 1.28, z = 9.75, p < 0.001$), and an interaction between z-scored squared VOT and susbequent context ($\hat{\beta} = 0.23, z = 2.494, p = 0.01$).

5.3 Discussion

Both experiments return clearly significant effects of squared VOT. This is predicted by an ideal observer model, since the /t/ and /d/ categories have unequal variance along the VOT continuum (Lisker and Abramson, 1967). With regard to the question of ideal *integration*, the results differ between the two experiments.

In Experiment 1, we found strong evidence for the ideal integration model: participants displayed effects of VOT and context, with no interaction between these factors. This suggests that participants were able to maintain gradient representations of VOT to later integrate with our contextual cue.

In Experiment 2, we found strong evidence for the categorize-discard-&-switch model: participants showed effects of VOT and context, but also showed a positive interaction between squared VOT and context such that the context effect was largest at the endpoints and smallest at the most ambiguous points. These results suggest that participants in Experiment 2 took a more memory-efficient strategy where they did not maintain gradient information about VOT but were still able to use both relevant cues in categorization.

6 General Discussion

Language is a signal that carries thousands of bits of acoustic information per second that listeners need to somehow compress into categorical abstract representations. However, maintaining some sub-categorical detail about the original signal in memory in order to integrate it with later potentially relevant cues is beneficial for achieving optimal categorization. Several lines of work have suggested either that this kind of integration is severely limited by time (Christiansen and Chater, 2016), the ambiguity of the initial signal (Connine et al., 1991), or is actually optimal and not very constrained by time or ambiguity (Bicknell et al., under review). However, these proposals have not been formalized and tested in a rigorous way (but see Bicknell et al., under review, for a discussion of ideal observers and one formalization of the ambiguity hypothesis). Here, we took a first step toward understanding and testing these three proposals.

We enumerated four possible models for the integration of cues that occur at different points in the speech signal. Two of these models involve maintaining gradient representations of the initial speech cue in memory for later integration with the subsequent cue, either being fully optimal (the ideal integration model), or partially restricted by ambiguity of the first cue (the ambiguity-only model). The other two models reduce the burden on memory by not maintaining gradient information about the initial speech cue, either by immediately categorizing and ignoring later cues (the categorize-&-discard model), or potentially changing categorization if later information conflicts with the initial binary categorization (the categorize-discard-&-switch model).

In Experiment 1, we found strong evidence for the ideal integration model, in line with previous work (Bicknell et al., under review; Szostak and Pitt, 2013). Experiment 2 added a manipulation that made it more difficult for participants to predict which words they would need to attend to in our sentences. When we introduced this manipulation, we interestingly found strong support

for the categorize-discard-&-switch model, suggesting that listeners were not maintaining subcategorical information about initial speech cues in memory. This finding is particularly noteworthy since the categorize-discard-&-switch model has not been previously considered in the literature as a possibility for cue integration during language processing. Significantly, in neither experiment did we find any evidence for the ambiguity-only model, which has been the primary proposal for how subcategorical information is maintained (Connine et al., 1991; Dahan, 2010).

Our results here suggest that listeners behave like ideal integrators under the task demands of typical right-context studies in the literature (Connine et al., 1991; Szostak and Pitt, 2013; Bushong and Jaeger, 2017; Bicknell et al., under review). However, those task demands are quite far from those of everyday language processing where listeners need to attend to many different parts of the signal and topics change rapidly. To the extent that Experiment 2 more closely reflects the task demands of natural language understanding—which strikes us as likely—our results suggest that listeners may not ideally integrate long-distance cues. Future work should continue to investigate the limits of subcategorical maintenance: what do listeners do when confronted with the typical demands of natural language use?

7 Future Work

One question not addressed in the current work is the extent to which different participants engage in different integration strategies or may change strategy over time. Our data are likely a mix of participants who show ideal integrator-like behavior and categorize-discard-&-switch behavior—what drives these differences? One possibility could be differences in working memory and attention. In addition, it is plausible that strategies could change over time as a sort of adaptation to task demands. It is possible that listeners under naturalistic demands tend to take a memory-saving suboptimal strategy for the memory benefits (like in our Experiment 2), but with a more constrained, easier-to-predict task become more inclined to switch to a more optimal strategy. Future work should investigate whether and why these changes may occur.

By making models of cue integration explicit, we inform future theoretical and experimental work. For example, we can analyze these models to understand how well each model performs word recognition: we can directly quantify how much word identification accuracy is expected to decline for the non-optimal models compared to ideal integration. Paired with experiments that emphasize different task demands of typical language use, we can then begin to investigate (i) under what circumstances listeners are (sub)optimal and (ii) whether listeners maximize accuracy given task demands. It may be the case, for example, that in some contexts non-optimal integration is preferred to ideal integration if the expected gain in accuracy does not justify the expected memory demand of maintaining subcategorical information for ideal integration. Equipped with these formal models, we can begin to address such questions.

References

Douglas Bates, Martin Maechler, Ben Bolker, Steven Walker, et al. 2014. lme4: Linear mixed-effects models using eigen and s4. *R package version*, 1(7):1–23.

Klinton Bicknell, Wednesday Bushong, Michael K Tanenhaus, and T Florian Jaeger. under review. Listeners can maintain and rationally update uncertainty about prior words.

Sarah Brown-Schmidt and Joseph C Toscano. 2017. Gradient acoustic information induces long-lasting referential uncertainty in short discourses. *Language, Cognition and Neuroscience*, 32(10):1211–1228.

Wednesday Bushong and T Florian Jaeger. 2017. Maintenance of perceptual information in speech perception. Thirty-Ninth Annual Conference of the Cognitive Science Society.

Wednesday Bushong and T Florian Jaeger. under review. Memory maintenance of gradient speech representations is mediated by their expected utility.

Morten H Christiansen and Nick Chater. 2016. The now-or-never bottleneck: A fundamental constraint on language. *Behavioral and Brain Sciences*, 39.

Cynthia M Connine, Dawn G Blasko, and Michael Hall. 1991. Effects of subsequent sentence context in auditory word recognition: Temporal and linguistic constraints. *Journal of Memory and Language*, 30(1):234.

Delphine Dahan. 2010. The time course of interpretation in speech comprehension. *Current Directions in Psychological Science*, 19(2):121–126.

Marc O Ernst and Martin S Banks. 2002. Humans integrate visual and haptic information in a statistically optimal fashion. *Nature*, 415(6870):429.

Laura Gwilliams, Tal Linzen, David Poeppel, and Alec Marantz. 2018. In spoken word recognition, the future predicts the past. *Journal of Neuroscience*, 38(35):7585–7599.

Marcel A Just and Patricia A Carpenter. 1980. A theory of reading: From eye fixations to comprehension. *Psychological review*, 87(4):329.

Dennis H Klatt. 1976. Linguistic uses of segmental duration in english: Acoustic and perceptual evidence. *The Journal of the Acoustical Society of America*, 59(5):1208–1221.

Leigh Lisker and Arthur S Abramson. 1967. Some effects of context on voice onset time in english stops. *Language and speech*, 10(1):1–28.

Bob McMurray, Michael K Tanenhaus, and Richard N Aslin. 2009. Within-category vot affects recovery from lexical garden-paths: Evidence against phoneme-level inhibition. *Journal of memory and language*, 60(1):65–91.

Christine M Szostak and Mark A Pitt. 2013. The prolonged influence of subsequent context on spoken word recognition. *Attention, Perception, & Psychophysics*, 75(7):1533–1546.

Eric-Jan Wagenmakers. 2007. A practical solution to the pervasive problems of p values. *Psychonomic bulletin & review*, 14(5):779–804.

Toward a Computational Multidimensional Lexical Similarity Measure for Modeling Word Association Tasks in Psycholinguistics

Bruno Gaume[1], Lydia-Mai Ho-Dac[1], Ludovic Tanguy[1], Cécile Fabre[1],
Bénédicte Pierrejean[1], Nabil Hathout[1], Jérôme Farinas[2], Julien Pinquier[2]
Lola Danet[3], Patrice Péran[4], Xavier De Boissezon[3], Mélanie Jucla[5]

1 CLLE-ERSS: CNRS and University of Toulouse, Toulouse, France
`bruno.gaume, lydia-mai.ho-dac, ludovic.tanguy,`
`cecile.fabre, benedicte.pierrejean, nabil.hathout}@univ-tlse2.fr`

2 IRIT: University of Toulouse and CNRS, Toulouse, France
`{jerome.farinas, julien.pinquier}@irit.fr`

3 CHU de Toulouse & ToNIC: University of Toulouse, Inserm, UPS, Toulouse, France
`lola.danet@inserm.fr, deboissezon.xavier@chu-toulouse.fr`

4 ToNIC: University of Toulouse, Inserm, UPS, Toulouse, France
`patrice.peran@inserm.fr`

5 URI Octogone-Lordat: Universit de Toulouse, Toulouse, France
`melanie.jucla@univ-tlse2.fr`

Abstract

This paper presents the first results of a multidisciplinary project, the "Evolex" project, gathering researchers in Psycholinguistics, Neuropsychology, Computer Science, Natural Language Processing and Linguistics. The Evolex project aims at proposing a new data-based inductive method for automatically characterising the relation between pairs of french words collected in psycholinguistics experiments on lexical access. This method takes advantage of several complementary computational measures of semantic similarity. We show that some measures are more correlated than others with the frequency of lexical associations, and that they also differ in the way they capture different semantic relations. This allows us to consider building a multidimensional lexical similarity to automate the classification of lexical associations.

1 Introduction

The Evolex project[1] brings together researchers in Psycholinguistics and Natural Language Processing (NLP) and focuses on lexical access and lexical relations by pursuing a threefold objective: (1) to propose a new computerised tool for assessing lexical access in population with or without language deficits; (2) to complement and reinforce the neuropsychological characterisation of lexical access using both qualitative and quantitative analyses; (3) to develop and train appropriated

NLP tools to automatically measure and identify lexical relations. From a neuropsychology's perspective, assessing and characterising lexical access involves answering basic questions such as: How close two words can be in someone's mental lexicon? What are the nearest neighbours of a specific word? Are there more or less "typical" relations between words and do age (Burke and Peters, 1986), gender, sociodemographic status and language deficits (Péran et al., 2004) have an impact on those relations? The traditional method for tackling such issues is to use word association tasks where a participant has to produce a word in response to a stimulus, i.e. a word that is read out loud or written (*e.g.* answering *dog* after hearing the stimulus *cat*). The variables typically analysed are latencies, error rate, length of the response and its lexical frequency obtained from the analysis of large corpora (see for instance lexical frequency measures (New et al., 2004)). There are two main problems with such a method. First, we lack benchmarks about the typical answers produced by a large sample of participants and thus cannot reliably know whether a stimulus/response pair is more or less plausible for a large number of words (see for French norms Ferrand and Alario (1998) based on 300 words for young adults, de La Haye (2003) based on 200 words for children and young adults and Tarrago et al. (2005) based on 150 words for elderly people). Secondly, a qualitative subject-by-subject and item-by-item analysis is time consuming and prone to subjective interpretation. An answer to these challenges

---

[1]Evolex.1 was funded by the FHU HoPES (Federation for Cognitive, Psychiatric and Sensory Disabilities) of the Toulouse University Hospital (CHU de Toulouse).

71

Proceedings of the Workshop on Cognitive Modeling and Computational Linguistics, pages 71–76
Minneapolis, USA, June 7, 2019. ©2019 Association for Computational Linguistics

is to obtain such data through the analysis of reference language data with NLP techniques. The use of data-based inductive methods for automatically measuring the similarity between words is one of the key task in computational semantics. If the first methods were based on the collocation frequency of words in large corpora (Church and Hanks, 1990; Evert, 2009), newer techniques rely on the principles of distributional semantics (Lenci, 2008; Mikolov et al., 2013). Even if the performance of these systems is impressive for some specific tasks (analogy resolution, lexical substitution, etc.), they usually fail to provide a fine grained characterisation of the relation between two words. Current distributional semantic models tend to aggregate all the classical lexical relations (e.g. synonymy, hypo/hypernymy, meronymy) and to confuse relations between similar words (e.g. *couch - sofa*) and relations between associated words (e.g. *couch - nap*). There is also a need for evaluation data when comparing and assessing these techniques (Hill et al., 2015; Baroni and Lenci, 2010). This paper proposes a step toward the satisfaction of both needs. We use data gathered in psycholinguistics experiments to compare different similarity measures and at the same time investigate how using complementary computational semantic techniques can help characterising lexical relations between stimuli and responses provided by subjects in a word association task. Section 2 describes the Evolex protocol from which data was collected as well as the manual annotation of the lexical relations in the collected dataset. We present the computational measures of semantic similarity in Section 3. Section 4 contains the quantitative analyses and results.

2 Data Collection Process in Evolex and Qualitative Analysis of Dataset

The Evolex protocol includes different tasks to assess lexical access: a semantic fluency test (Benton, 1968), a phonemic fluency test (Newcombe, 1969), a classical Picture Naming task and a Word Association task. In addition to these 4 tasks, participants undergo 5 Cognitive Assessment Tests (MoCA, reading aloud, Trail Making Test, Digit Span, Stroop). This paper focuses mainly on the Word Association task which consists in vocalising the first word coming to mind after listening to a simple item (e.g. *fruit, painting, igloo*). The items used as audio stimuli were selected according to their grammatical category (nouns), num-

co-hyponym:balanoire(swing)/toboggan(slide)	73(13.1%)
hypernym:balancoire(swing)/jeu(game)	52 (9.3%)
meronym:balancoire(swing)/corde(rope)	49 (8.8%)
hyponym:animal(animal)/chat(cat	45 (8.1%)
holonym:doigt(finger)/main(hand)	29 (5.2%)
synonym:canap(couch)/sofa(sofa)	21 (3.8%)
antonym:aube(dawn)/crpuscule(dusk)	2 (0.4%)
classical relations:	**271(48.5%)**
associated:balancoire(swing)/enfant(child)	202(36.1%)
syntagmatic:fleur(flower)/peau(skin)	47 (8.4%)
none found:perroquet(parrot)/placard(closet)	28 (5.0%)
instance:magicien(wizard)/Merlin(Merlin)	6 (1.1%)
phonology:chapiteau(circus tent)/chateau(castle)	5 (0.9%)
non classical relations:	**288(51.5%)**

Table 1: Breakdown of the semantic relations used to categorise the 559 distinct stimulus-response word pairs.

ber of syllables (same number of occurrences of words of 1, 2 and 3 syllables) as well as their frequency in generic corpora (as given by the Lexique resource, (New et al., 2004)). This paper exploits a first dataset of pairs of words collected from a pilot study with 60 stimuli and conducted with 30 participants presenting no language disorders, that are native French speaker aged between 15 and 58 (mean age 31 $\pm$ 13.06), with various levels of education (from 10 to 20 years of schooling, mean 15.4 $\pm$ 2.97). The following instructions were given to participants: *You will hear French common nouns. You will have to pronounce the first word which comes to your mind related to the one you just heard as fast as possible. For instance, when you hear TABLE, you may answer CHAIR.*

After cleaning up and normalising the 1800 (60 $\times$ 30) individual collected responses, we obtained 559 distinct stimulus-response pairs. Independent double annotation was performed and followed by adjudication. The tagset is composed of 12 tags including 7 classical relations. Table 1 gives the number and % of distinct pairs annotated according to these 12 relations.

3 Computational Measures of Semantic Similarity

In this section we describe the different techniques used in order to compute the similarity measures that we apply to the stimulus-response word pairs collected from the Word Association task. The six techniques we tested differ according to (1) the linguistic resources they used and (2) the use of either a first or second order similarity. Three resources reflecting three points of view on language were distinguished: a large corpus, giving access to word usage; a dictionary, reflecting expert point of view on word meaning; crowdsourced lexical resource resulting from a GWAP (Game With A Purpose) proposing a Word Association Task very similar to ours that offers the advantage of having access to many more participants. The corpus used is *FrWaC* (Baroni et al., 2009), a collection of Web pages from the .fr domain and consisting of 1.6 billion words. The dictionary is the *TLF* (Trésor de la Langue Française, see (Dendien and JM., 2003)). The crowdsourced lexical resource is part of the GWAP *JDM* (Jeux De Mots [2]) where players have to find as many words as possible and as fast as possible in response to a term displayed on the screen, according to several instructions involving different type of lexical relations (semantic association, synonymy, etc., see (Lafourcade, 2007)). The potential atypicality of answers is partially controlled by the the game where two anonymous and asynchronous players earn points each time they give the same answer. If an answer is rarely given by other players it gets more points. Several instructions are proposed including a Word Association task ("As-W" task) very similar to ours with the following instruction: *"You are being asked to enumerate terms most closely associated with the target word... What does this word make you think about?"*. The three resources have been POS-tagged and lemmatised with the Talismane toolkit (Urieli, 2013). The second dimension on which these techniques contrasts opposes 1st order similarity (cooccurrences or direct relation between two words in the dictionary or the lexical relation) to 2nd order similarity, also known as distributional similarity, considering that words sharing first-order similar words show a possibly different degree of similarity. 2nd order similarity measures require more complex algorithms such as word embeddings for processing corpus similarity and random walk approach (Bollobas, 2002) for dictionary and lexical resources. Each measure is described in the next subsections.

3.1 Corpus-Based Similarity

FrWaC.1st similarity considers collocation: two words are considered similar if they frequently and systematically collocate in the FrWaC corpus. This measure has a large number of uses in NLP and corpus linguistics, and is known to capture a large variety of semantic relations (Evert, 2009; Wettler et al., 2005). We computed this similarity using Positive Pairwise Mutual Information (Evert, 2009). Each word was considered using its POS-tag and lemma, and its collocations were extracted in a symmetrical rectangular (unweighted) window of 3 words in both directions.

FrWac.2nd similarity relies on the principle of distributional semantics, which considers that words appearing in the same contexts have similar meanings. 2nd-order similarity can be computed in a number of ways (Baroni and Lenci, 2010; Baroni et al., 2009), and for a few years most of the work and research has focused on word embeddings. For this experiment, we used Word2vec (Mikolov et al., 2013) on the same FrWac corpus to obtain a dense matrix in which each word is represented by a numeric vector. The cosine distance was then computed to measure the similarity between two words. In the absence of benchmark test sets for French (while many exist for English, including BLESS that can be used to tune a model for specific semantic relations (Baroni and Lenci, 2011), we relied on the default parameters[3].

3.2 Dictionary-Based Similarity

TLF.1st similarity is based on the principle that two words are considered similar if one appears in the definition of the other. We computed this similarity by building an undirected and unweighted graph with words as vertices (V) and relations between words as edges (E). The TLF.1st measure relies on the graph $G_{TLF} = (V_{TLF}, E_{TLF})$ where $\forall x, y \in V_{TLF}, \{x, y\} \in E_{TLF}$ iff x appears in the TLF's definition of y or vice-versa (or both). This similarity measure is therefore binary: the similarity between x and y is 1 if x and y are neighbors in G_{TLF} and 0 otherwise.

TLF.2nd similarity used a graph traversal technique. We adopted a random walk approach (Bollobas, 2002) that is known to provide a broader and more "robust" measure of similarity between the nodes of a graph (Gaume et al., 2016). By applying this technique to the G_{TLF} graph, TLF.2nd corresponds to $P^t_{G_{TLF}}(x, y) \in [0, 1]$ i.e. the probability of a walker crossing the links of G_{TLF}, starting on vertex x, to reach the vertex y, after t steps. In this study, the length of the random walks is $t = 3$.

---

[2] http://www.lirmm.fr/jeuxdemots/jdm-accueil.php

[3] Skipgram algorithm with negative sampling (rate 5), window size 5, 500 dimensions, subsampling rate 10−3 , 5 iterations, minimum frequency 100

Similarity measure	Spearman's ρ	p-value
FrWac.1st	0.25	2.06e-09
FrWaC.2nd	0.22	6.86e-08
TLF.1st	0.23	3.44e-08
TLF.2nd	0.38	8.48e-21
JDM.1st	0.47	2.30e-32
JDM.2nd	0.51	1.44e-38

Table 2: Spearman correlation.

3.3 Crowdsourced Resource-Based Similarity

JDM.1st similarity also relies on graph techniques with the principle that words are more or less similar according to the number of pairs collected through the "As-W" task. We built a directed and weighted graph $G_{JDM} = (V_{JDM}, E_{JDM}, W_{JDM})$ where W_{JDM} are the weights of the links: $x \rightarrow y$ = the number of times the word y has been associated with x. The similarity between x and y is the weight of the link $x \rightarrow y$ in the graph G_{JDM}.

JDM.2nd similarity is computed by applying the technique used for TLF.2nd to the graph G_{JDM}, but where the probability of jumping in a step from a vertex x to a vertex y is then proportional to the weight of the edge $x \rightarrow y$ relative to the sum of the weights of the arcs coming out of x. As for TLF.2nd, the length of the random walks is $t = 3$.

4 Quantitative Analysis and Results

We performed two kinds of analysis on this data. First, we computed the correlation between the six similarity measures presented in Section 4 and the response frequency, i.e. the number of subjects that gave the same response for a given stimulus. We computed the Spearman correlation coefficient over all distinct pairs and obtained the scores presented in Table 2. We can see that all correlation values are positive and statistically significant. The highest value (0.51) is obtained with JDM.2nd. Using a random walk approach (2nd order) increases the Spearman correlation from 0.23 to 0.38, (up to 65%) for TLF-based methods and from 0.47 to 0.51 (up to 8%) for JDM-based methods. In order to get a more detailed view of the complementarity of these measures and to examine the behaviour of these measures regarding the semantic relations between stimulus and response, we performed a multidimensional analysis. We ran a standard Principal Component Analysis on the matrix with Stimulus/Response pairs (559) as rows and 19 columns i.e. 1 for pair frequency, 1 per similarity measure and 1 per tagged relation

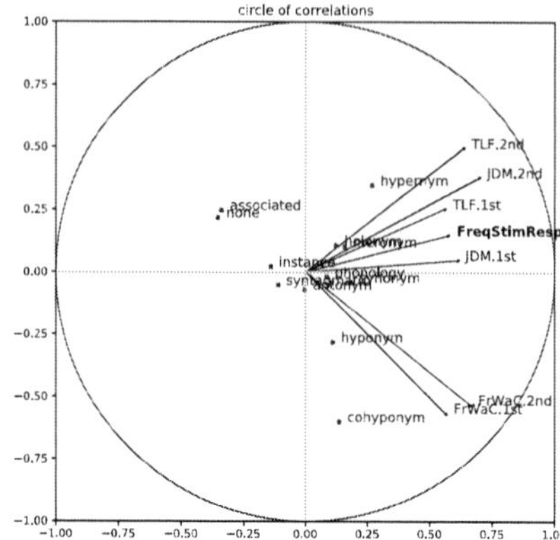

Figure 1: Circle of correlations in the first factor map of PCA.

(e.g. synonymy, see Table 1) converted to a binary value. The main factor map represents 33% of the global variance (see Fig. 1). Several elements can be learned from this analysis. It clearly shows that the three resources provide different aspects of lexical similarity, and that the shifting from 1st to 2nd order preserves these differences. When looking at the categorised semantic relations, several phenomena can be identified. First, it appears that all measures are positively correlated to classical semantic relations, although we observed some variation: measures based on lexical resources (TLF or JDM) capture the hypernymy relation more easily, while corpus-based similarity favour co-hyponymy. Other classical semantic relations are positively correlated with all measures, without a clear advantage for any of them. In contrast, all similarity measures are negatively correlated to non classical relations (none cases and associated word pairs). Instance, syntagmatic, antonym and phonology relations appear in the centre of the factor map, indicating that no clear trend can be identified for these relations. This is somewhat surprising that even corpus-based first order similarity (FrWac.1st) does not capture the pairs in syntagmatic relations.

5 Beyond Semantic Relations: Clustering Responses

Although the reliable identification of specific semantic relations between a stimulus and responses provided by the subjects is currently out of reach, some of the NLP techniques used to compute similarity can be used to provide a structure for the set of responses. This is especially the case for word embeddings, which are known to provide vector representation of words that are suitable for a number of semantic tasks. For example, we can

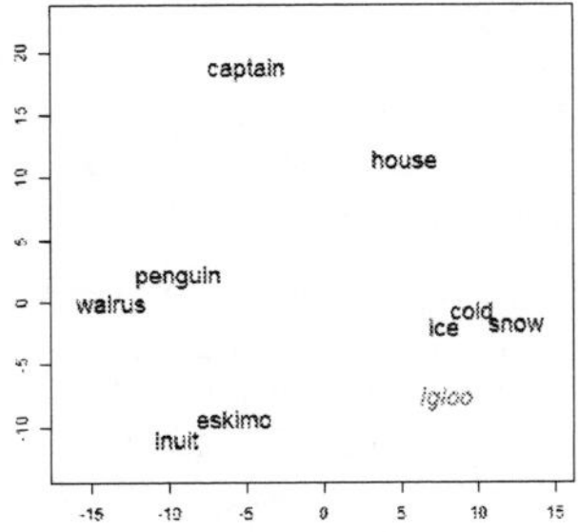

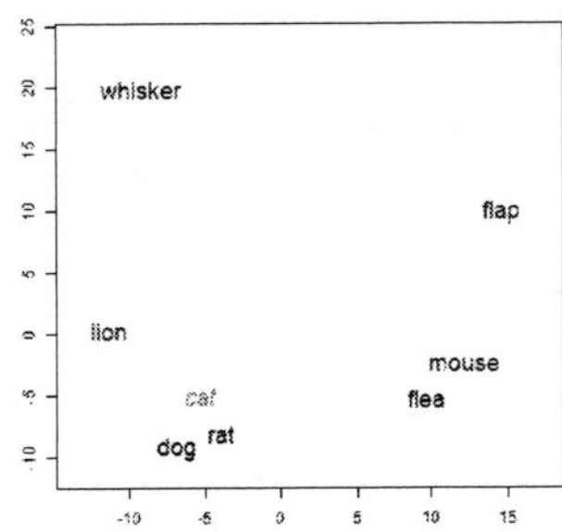

Figure 2: PCA maps of the responses to the stimuli (in red) igloo (left) and cat (right), based on word embeddings.

use these representations to identify clusters of responses based on their position in the vector space (vector space computed from the distribution of words in a corpus). We show here two examples of such an analysis. Focusing on the stimuli *igloo* and *cat*, we extracted the word embeddings for all responses (as well as the stimulus) and represented them in a two-dimensional space by the means of a PCA on the initial 500-dimension vectors. The results can be seen in Figure 2. While the dimensions themselves cannot be interpreted, it appears that interesting clustering can be identified in the responses. For *igloo*, we can see that all words related to an igloos typical climate and environment are gathered close to the stimulus (*cold, ice, snow*), while the prototypical inhabitants (*Eskimo, Inuit*) and fauna (*penguin, walrus*) are farther on the left. The hypernym *house* is located in another area, closer to the top. Another interesting case in this example is the presence of *captain* in the responses: it refers to a fictional character named Captain Igloo who used to appear in TV commercials for frozen fish sticks. Its position in the figure is understandably the most extremely afar from the stimulus. It is important to note that the semantic relations of most of the responses with this stimulus fall under the associated category, with the exception of the meronym *ice*, the hypernym *house* and the syntagmatically-related noun *captain*. However, it appears that word embeddings are able to separate them efficiently in relevant subsets. The results for *cat* are more self-explanatory, with the interesting case of *mouse* which is not considered as a close co-hyponym (as are *dog, rat* and *lion*) but more as an association because of the cat and mouse topoi.

6   Conclusion

This paper exploits a first dataset of pairs of words collected from the pilot study of the Evolex project. We proposed six techniques to compute lexical similarities of pairs of words. These six techniques are based on three kind of resources (large corpus, dictionary and crowdsourced lexical resource) with the computation of either first or second order similarity. First we computed the correlation between these six similarity measures and the response frequency. All correlation values are positive and statistically significant. The highest value (0.51) is obtained with JDM.2nd i.e. the method based on second order similarity using a short random walk approach over the crowdsourced lexical resource, collected with a protocol fairly similar to Evolex. From the experiments conducted, it appears that exceeding 0.51 might be challenging. This needs to be investigated with further experiments. Secondly, we show that the three resources provide different aspects of lexical similarity and that shifting from 1st to 2nd order preserves these differences. This conclusion will be very useful for the future of Evolex as a diagnostic tool in clinical studies. We are able to position each pair in a multidimensional space (one dimension by similarity) and to identify clusters of pairs with the final objective of defining region i.e. profiles for characterising an incoming answer to a stimulus. Such profiles may be then used for evaluating if a given phenomenon (context, age, sex, level of education, cognitive profile, language deficit, ...) favours the production of stimulus/response pairs positioned in a particular region of this multidimensional space, this can then help to identify the phenomenon as a hidden variable.

Other factors made available by the Evolex protocol have now to be taken into account, as for example the reaction time of each response and the results obtained by the participants to the other tasks of the Evolex protocol.

References

Baroni, M., Bernardini, S., Ferraresi, A., and Zanchetta, E. (2009). The wacky wide web: a collection of very large linguistically processed web-crawled corpora. *Language Resources and Evaluation*, 43:209–226.

Baroni, M. and Lenci, A. (2010). Distributional memory: A general framework for corpus-based semantics. *Computational Linguistics*, 36:673–721.

Baroni, M. and Lenci, A. (2011). How we blessed distributional semantic evaluation. In *Proceedings of the GEMS 2011 Workshop on GEometrical Models of Natural Language Semantics*, pages 1–10. Association for Computational Linguistics.

Benton, A. L. (1968). Differential behavioral effects in frontal lobe disease. *Neuropsychologia*, 6(1):53–60.

Bollobas, B. (2002). *Modern Graph Theory*. Springer-Verlag New York Inc.

Burke, D. M. and Peters, L. (1986). Word associations in old age: Evidence for consistency in semantic encoding during adulthood. *Psychology and Aging*, 1(4):283.

Church, K. W. and Hanks, P. (1990). Word association norms, mutual information, and lexicography. *Computational linguistics*, 16(1):22–29.

de La Haye, F. (2003). Normes d'associations verbales chez des enfants de 9, 10 et 11 ans et des adultes. *L'Année psychologique*, 103(1):109–130.

Dendien, J. and JM., P. (2003). Le trésor de la langue française informatisé : un exemple d'informatisation d'un dictionnaire de langue de référence. *TAL*, 44(2).

Evert, S. (2009). Corpora and collocations. *Corpus Linguistics: An International Handbook*, 2:1212–1248.

Ferrand, L. and Alario, F.-X. (1998). Normes d'associations verbales pour 366 noms d'objets concrets. *L'Année psychologique*, 98(4):659–709.

Gaume, B., Duvignau, K., Navarro, E., Desalle, Y., Cheung, H., Hsieh, S., Magistry, P., and Prévot, L. (2016). Skillex: a graph-based lexical score for measuring the semantic efficiency of used verbs by human subjects describing actions. *TAL*, 55, Numéro spécial sur Traitement Automatique des Langues et Sciences Cognitives(3):97 – 121.

Hill, F., Reichart, R., and Korhonen, A. (2015). Simlex-999: Evaluating semantic models with (genuine) similarity estimation. *Computational Linguistics*, 41(4):665–695.

Lafourcade, M. (2007). Making People Play for Lexical Acquisition with the JeuxDeMots prototype. In *SNLP'07: 7th Int. Symposium on NLP*, Pattaya, Thailand.

Lenci, A. (2008). Distributional semantics in linguistic and cognitive research. *Italian journal of linguistics*, 20(1):1–31.

Mikolov, T., Chen, K., Corrado, G., and Dean, J. (2013). Efficient estimation of word representations in vector space. *arXiv preprint arXiv:1301.3781*.

New, B., Pallier, C., Brysbaert, M., and Ferrand, L. (2004). Lexique 2: A new french lexical database. *Behavior Research Methods, Instruments, & Computers*, 36(3):516–524.

Newcombe, F. (1969). *Missile wounds of the brain: A study of psychological deficits*. Oxford University Press.

Péran, P., Démonet, J.-F., Pernet, C., and Cardebat, D. (2004). Verb and noun generation tasks in huntington's disease. *Movement disorders: official journal of the Movement Disorder Society*, 19(5):565–571.

Tarrago, R., Martin, S., De La Haye, F., and Brouillet, D. (2005). Normes d'associations verbales chez des sujets âgés. *Revue Européenne de Psychologie Appliquée/European Review of Applied Psychology*, 55(4):245–253.

Urieli, A. (2013). *Robust French syntax analysis: reconciling statistical methods and linguistic knowledge in the Talismane toolkit*. PhD thesis, Université Toulouse le Mirail-Toulouse II.

Wettler, M., Rapp, R., and Sedlmeier, P. (2005). Free word associations correspond to contiguities between words in texts. *Journal of Quantitative Linguistics*, 12(2-3):111–122.

Dependency Parsing with your Eyes:
Dependency Structure Predicts Eye Regressions During Reading

Alessandro Lopopolo
Center for Language Studies
Radboud University
Nijmegen, the Netherlands.
`a.lopopolo@let.ru.nl`

Stefan L. Frank
Center for Language Studies
Radboud University
Nijmegen, the Netherlands.
`s.frank@let.ru.nl`

Antal van den Bosch
Meertens Institute - KNAW
Amsterdam, the Netherlands.
Center for Language Studies
Radboud University
Nijmegen, the Netherlands.
`a.vandenbosch@let.ru.nl`

Roel M. Willems
Center for Language Studies & Donders Institute
Radboud University
Nijmegen, the Netherlands.
MPI for Psycholinguistics
Nijmegen, The Netherlands.
`r.willems@donders.ru.nl`

Abstract

Backward saccades during reading have been hypothesized to be involved in structural re-analysis, or to be related to the level of text difficulty. We test the hypothesis that backward saccades are involved in online syntactic analysis. If this is the case we expect that saccades will coincide, at least partially, with the edges of the relations computed by a dependency parser. In order to test this, we analyzed a large eye-tracking dataset collected while 102 participants read three short narrative texts. Our results show a relation between backward saccades and the syntactic structure of sentences.

1 Introduction

Written language consists of a sequence of graphic signs. While most eye movements during reading indeed follow this sequential order, they are also occasionally interleaved with jumps back to words in preceding portions of the text. We refer to these backward saccades as regressions throughout this paper. There are at least two competing hypotheses concerning the nature and function of this phenomenon.

The first main line of hypotheses on the role of regressions emphasizes their active role in computing linguistic representations (Kennedy, 1992), the second stresses their function as a reanalysis tool in the event of detected parsing errors (Rayner and Sereno, 1994). In this paper we start from the former; in particular, we aim to investigate the relation between regressions and the structure of sentences as computed by a dependency parser.

We take dependency structures as a valid approximation of syntactic properties of the sentences, and we investigate whether these are reflected in eye movement regressions during naturalistic text reading.

We consider regressions from each word in the text, and relate those to dependency relations that link pairs of words in the sentence. In this way we can represent syntactic properties of the sentences as shallow structural information at the word level, by focusing on the number and direction of the syntactic relations that each word in a sentence is engaged in.

The aim of this paper is two-fold: on the one hand we want to investigate whether regressions might play a role in online sentence parsing; on the other hand – as an implication of the previous goal – we are interested in finding traces of syntactic parsing during reading. We report the results of a mixed-effect regression analysis showing a relation between the pattern of eye regressions and the syntactic structure of sentences.

2 Theoretical Background

2.1 The Role of Regressions in Text Comprehension

Regressions (backward saccades) are relatively rare, occurring usually only with 15 to 25% of the words (Rayner & Pollatsek, 1989). They do not seem to be random, however. Regressions typically aim at specific word locations, moving fixation from the current word back to one of the previously encountered words (Vitu, 2005). Nonethe-

Proceedings of the Workshop on Cognitive Modeling and Computational Linguistics, pages 77–85
Minneapolis, USA, June 7, 2019. ©2019 Association for Computational Linguistics

less their function in language comprehension is still debated. Here we will review two proposed explanations: the first links regressions to the difficulty of text processing; the second instead sees them as tools for language processing, not necessarily linked to processing difficulties or errors. According to the first proposal regressions only start to play a role in reading once difficulties are encountered; according to the second proposal they are part and parcel of regular reading.

2.1.1 Regression as a Response to Comprehension Difficulty

The first hypothesis interprets regressions as part of the reanalysis of textual input due to encountered comprehension problems. In a milestone study, Altmann et al. (1992) introduced the notion of regression-contingent analysis, based on the assumption that regressive eye movements are a necessary consequence of subjects being garden-pathed. A garden-path effect occurs when readers incrementally construct an incorrect interpretation of a sentence as a consequence of its locally ambiguous syntactic structure. This does not necessarily mean that the presence of a difficult structure, leading for instance to the reader being garden-pathed, triggers a regression. Rayner and colleagues reported data showing that strong garden path effects can occur sometimes without triggering any regressions (Rayner and Sereno, 1994; Castelhano and Rayner, 2008). Nonetheless, other studies have given support to the idea that regressions are linked to textual ambiguity and contextual difficulties. Readers make more regressions when the text is complex (Rayner and Pollatsek, 1995), when the topic changes (Hyn, 1995), when the text contains grammatical errors or ambiguities (Reichle et al., 2013), or when they encounter information that disambiguates the preceding text (Blanchard and IranNejad, 1987; Frazier and Rayner, 1982). The general hypothesis holds that the probability of regressions and their span might depend on the difficulty of the text. Therefore these regressions might allow the reader to reread information that has been missed, forgotten, or wrongly interpreted (Rayner, 1998).

2.1.2 Regression as a Tool for Comprehension

The alternative explanation focuses instead on the role of eye movements as a tool in language processing, used independently from the structural difficulty of the input. The idea is that regressions help the reader reactivate cognitive information that is associated with the regressed-to location. Kennedy (1992) refers to this as the Spatial Code Hypothesis. The hypothesis is that readers use the position of words on the page as a support to their working memory by reactivating previously read words associated with information relevant for the processing of the word from which the regression originated (O'Regan, 1992; Spivey et al., 2004). This hypothesis has been criticized by Booth and Weger (2013). They presented three experiments showing that reader comprehension is not hindered when reading conditions inhibit or discourage visual access to already read material. In their Experiment 1, readers knew that candidate targets for regression were no longer available for rereading. Experiment 2 discouraged regressions by forcing readers to follow a visual placeholder on the stimulus while it was also presented in auditory form. Finally, in Experiment 3, candidate targets for regression were manipulated after reading. In all these three experiments, readers showed no hindered comprehension of the presented stimulus sentences. As an entailment of these results, Booth and Weger suggested that readers do not use regressions to cue their memory for previously read words.

Our hypothesis is that readers might make use of regressions to reactivate previously read information in the context of naturalistic language comprehension, in order to help compute linguistic information.

We want to examine whether there is an alignment between patterns of regressions and word-to-word syntactic relations as described by the dependency structure of the stimulus. We hypothesize that regressions play a role in syntactic parsing that may go beyond the reanalysis of ambiguous material. We do not deny their role in reanalysis and repair, but we rather stand with the hypothesis that they allow re-reading and cueing of previous words, as an aid to memory, when this is required for a successful construction of a syntactic representation of the text.

In order to test this hypothesis we rely on an eye-tracker dataset that was collected during normal text reading of unmodified literary narratives. We assess whether there is a relation between the number of eye regressions from the words and the number of syntactic relations that those words entertain with their preceding text. These syntactic relations are derived from the dependency structures (described in Section 4) of the sentences composing the stimuli of the eye-tracker dataset.

2.2 Regressions and Sequence Processing

The hypothesized relation between dependency structure and eye movement taps into a broader debate on whether language processing relies mainly on the sequential structure of the input or whether it involves the computation of non-sequential syntactic parses (Jackendoff and Wittenberg, 2014). Undeniably, the linguistic stimulus is presented as a string of symbols, nonetheless regressions seem to counter the notion that it is processed strictly in a sequential order. If these eye movements are involved only in re-analysis, then their existence does not necessarily contradict sequential processing accounts. They can be explained as an "emergency recovery" operation that takes place only in cases of processing difficulties. On the other hand, if we find evidence of a relation between saccades and syntactic dependency structures independent from processing difficulty, then we might conclude that saccades offer behavioral evidence that processing involves the computation of non-sequential structures.

This question is related to the line of research in psycholinguistics and neuroscience investigating the computation of syntactic structures in the mind/brain during language processing. In this context, sequential structures are usually contrasted with hierarchical ones, where input items are grouped into larger units, which in turn are (possibly recursively) grouped in even larger units. These larger units are commonly referred to as syntactic constituents or phrases and have a central position in theoretical linguistics (Chomsky, 1965; Jackendoff, 2002, 2007). An increasing amount of evidence against a strictly hierarchical processing of language has emerged over the past decades. Psycholinguistic studies have supplied evidence suggesting that the mere sequential properties of the stimulus are sufficient to explain aspects of human behavior during reading and listening. Frank et al. (2012) provide a review of evidence from cognitive neuroscience, psycholinguistics and computational modeling studies supporting the hypothesis that hierarchical structure may not play a central role in language processing and acquisition, and that sequential structure instead has a significant explanatory power. They argue that hierarchical structure is rarely needed to explain behavioral and neural correlates of language processing in vivo. In contrast with these findings, recent neuroimaging studies have delineated a slightly more complex landscape in which both hierarchical and sequential processing may be carried out simultaneously by the human brain during language processing (Brennan et al., 2016; Nelson et al., 2017).

Dependency parses are different from constituency parses as they lack the non-terminal nodes characteristic of constituency parses. Nonetheless they still constitute a non-sequential type of structure. Demonstrating a relation between eye movement and such structure will provide evidence for the non-sequentiality of language processing, at least in the context of text reading.

3 Related Work

The present work studies the relation between eye movements during reading and the dependency structure as produced by a dependency parser (see Section 5.2 for more details). Several other studies tested language processing hypotheses by using computational models as predictors of eye movements during sentence reading.

Boston et al. (2008) demonstrates the importance of including parsing costs implemented as surprisal as a predictor of comprehension difficulty in models of reading. They showed that surprisal of grammatical structures has an effect on fixation durations and regression probabilities.

Demberg and Keller (2008) compared linguistic integration cost computed as a function of dependency relations distances and word surprisal as predictors of gaze duration. They showed that distance is not a significant predictor of reading times except for nouns. On the other hand, they demonstrate that surprisal can predict reading times for arbitrary words in the corpus, concluding that the two predictors may capture distinct aspects of naturalistic language processing.

In the context of Natural Language Processing, Klerke et al. (2015) used eye-tracker data as a metric for the quality of automatic text simplification and compression, which are operations used in machine translation and automatic summarization. Their proposal is grounded in the hypothesis that eye movements are related to perceived text diffi-

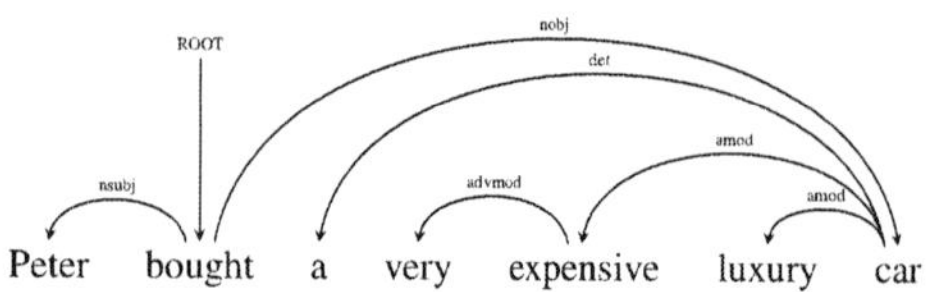

Figure 1: Dependency Parse of Sentence 1

culty (Rayner and Pollatsek, 1995), one of the two hypothesis we have introduced in Section 2 above.

4 Dependency Structure

We chose dependency grammar as the formalism of non-sequential syntactic structure. Dependency grammar describes a sentence as a set of relations between words (heads) and their dependents. These relations are called dependencies and correspond to grammatical functions and – together with the words they link – are the only descriptive elements composing the structure, which has the form and properties of a directed graph (Tesnière et al., 2015; Mel'čuk, 1988; Nivre and Kübler, 2009).

(1) Peter bought a very expensive luxury car.

Take for instance Sentence 1 above. Figure 1 contains the dependency graph representing the dependency structure of the sentence in terms of typified head-dependent relations. The main verb (*bought*) acts as head for *Peter* and *car*, with which it is in **subject** and **object** relations, respectively. A dependent of one dependency relation can in turn be the head of another one. For instance *car* is head of *luxury* and of *expensive* with which it is linked by **modifier** relations, and also head of the article *a* via a **determiner** relation.

This structure lacks phrasal non-terminal constituents. In addition, it is not strictly sequential, or put differently, it is not isomorphic to the sequence of items that makes up the stimulus. This is based on the fact that the dependency relations can hold between words that are non-consecutive or possibly even far apart in the sentence. There is the assumption that during reading, these links are created once a suitable candidate for the second term of the dependency is introduced. Therefore, online dependency parsing proceeds by introducing one word at a time, and by looking back at the prefix in order to assess whether this novel input is a suitable candidate for a dependency link with a preceding word that has not yet been matched.

5 Materials and Methods

5.1 Eye-tracker data

The eye tracker data used in this study was originally collected for a study on mental stimulation during literary reading by Mak and Willems (2018) at Radboud University, Nijmegen, the Netherlands. For more details on data acquisition and preprocessing we refer to the original publication.

5.1.1 Participants and Stimuli

Data was collected from 102 participants (82 females, mean age 23.27, range 18–40), all of whom were native speakers of Dutch, with normal or corrected-to-normal vision. All participants gave written informed consent in accordance with the Declaration of Helsinki.

Stimuli consisted of three published short stories in Dutch. Stories 1 and 2 were written by contemporary Dutch writers, and Story 3 was translated from American English to Dutch. Their lengths were 2143, 2659, and 2988 words respectively, and they required around 10-15 minutes each to be read.

5.1.2 Data Acquisition and Pre-processing

For eye-movement data collection, a monocular desktop-mounted EyeLink1000+ eye-tracking system was used (500 Hz sampling rate). Head movements were minimized using a head stabilizer, ensuring that all participants were seated at 108 cm from the screen.

The stimuli were presented using SR Research Experiment Builder software (SR Research, Ottawa, Canada). The stories were divided into 30 sections each. The stories were presented in counterbalanced order. After data collection, participants were presented with a comprehension questionnaire.

All fixations were checked to make sure that they did not drift off and enter a different interest area. If correction of the drifts was not possible, individual sections were excluded. Data for at least one section was removed for 40 participants. For four participants, the number of excluded sections exceeded six, resulting in the exclusion of one story for these participants.

Eight participants answered more than one comprehension question incorrectly for one of the three stories (four times for Story 2 and four times for Story 3), resulting in the exclusion of the data for one story reading for eight participants.

The dataset contains a total of 582,807 words across all participants and narratives.

5.1.3 Eye Tracker Measures

For the present study we focus on the number of eye regressions. A regression consists of a fast eye movement from a word back to a previous word.

5.2 Dependency Parsing

The text of the three stories presented to the participants were fed to the ALPINO toolbox for Dutch natural language processing (Noord, 2006) to generate a dependency parse for each of their sentences. The parser creates a structure composed of dependency triples consisting of a head word, the type of dependency relation and its dependent word. A parse is produced for each sentence independently, therefore no relation can be assigned between words belonging to different sentences. The output of the parser was manually checked in order to prevent tokenization and sentence segmentation errors.

5.2.1 Number of Dependency Relations

As described in Section 4, every word in a sentence entertains at least one relation with another word in the same sentence. Every non-final and non-initial word can have relations with a variable number of other words on its right and its left. Because we are interested in eye regressions, we decided to focus our attention only on relations between a word w and its preceding context. Therefore only relations with a head and possible dependents on the words preceding w are counted.

From the dependency structure of a sentence, we derived the following count measures:

- **N_head** indicates the presence of a syntactic relation between w_i and a word in $w_{1:i-1}$ that is head of w_i;

- **N_dependents** counts the number of syntactic relations between w_i and words in $w_{1:i-1}$ that are dependents of w_i.

Measure **N_head** is a binary variable indicating whether word w has a head in its left context $w_{1:t-1}$. This is because every word has one, and only one, head.

For example, the word *expensive* in Sentence 1 has one head relation with a word on its right

	Peter	bought	a	very	expensive	luxury	car
N_head	0	0	0	0	0	0	1
N_dependents	0	1	0	0	1	0	3

Table 1: Number of dependency relations per word w that correspond to words in w's own preceding context.

(*car*), no dependents on its right, and one on its left (*very*). On the other hand, the word *car*, being sentence-final, does not have any links on its right, but it has 1 head (*bought*) and 3 dependents (*a, expensive, luxury*) on its left. Table 1 contains the count measures (*N_head* and *N_dependents*) for Sentence 1.

5.3 Descriptors not Related to Dependencies

We are interested in the effect of syntactic structure, implemented as dependency relations, on the pattern of regressions. For this reason it is necessary to control for other possible quantifiable factors affecting these eye movements. We chose to use log-transformed lexical frequency and surprisal.

Base-2 log-transformed lexical frequency per word was computed using the Subtlex NL corpus (Keuleers et al., 2010). Surprisal was computed from a second-order Markov model, also known as trigram model, trained on a random selection of 10 million sentences (comprising 197 million word tokens; 2.1 million types) from the Dutch section of Corpora from the Web (NLCOW2012; Schäfer and Bildhauer, 2012). Surprisal of word w_t is the negative logarithm of the conditional probability of encountering w_t after having read sequence w_{t-2}, w_{t-1}, or: $-\log P(w_t|w_{t-2}, w_{t-1})$. The computation was performed by the SRILM toolbox (Stolcke, 2002).

Frequency and surprisal are computed in order to control for processing difficulties. Intuitively, infrequent words and words with high surprisal are more difficult to retrieve (and possibly to integrate) with their preceding context. Controlling for processing difficulty is motivated by the alternative hypothesis regarding the role of regressions as depending on the level of complexity posed by a linguistic input.

In addition to frequency and surprisal, we also use word position in the sentence. Intuitively, the probability of regressing from a word to its previous context increases linearly with the position of the word in a sequence. By controlling for it, we ensure that the eye movements are not due simply to the opportunity given by the larger target pool to regress to.

5.4 Analyses

We fitted two logistic mixed-effect models predicting eye regressions. The first model (**null**, Eq. (1) below) contains as predictors only the position of the words in their sentences (*word_order*), and probabilistic information consisting of the above-mentioned log-transformed frequency (*freq*) and surprisal (*surp*). The second model (**full**, Eq. (2) below) contains as predictors of interest also the number of left-hand side dependency relations (i.e. *N_head* and *N_dependents*) of each word. In addition, we included by-participant and by-word random intercepts, as well as by-participant random slopes for *word_order* in the **null** model and for *word_order*, *N_head* and *N_dependents* in the **full** models.

We expect the model's fit to improve significantly after inclusion of the measures derived from the dependency parse as regressors. The increase in model fit is quantified by the χ^2-statistic of a likelihood-ratio test for significance between the **null** and **full** models and is taken as the measure of the fit of *N_head* and *N_dependents* measures at each word to the probability of a regression being generated at each word.

$$\textbf{null} : eye\_regressions$$
$$\sim word\_order + surp + freq + (1|word)$$
$$+ (1 + word\_order|participant)$$
$$(1)$$

$$\textbf{full} : eye\_regressions$$
$$\sim word\_order + surp + freq$$
$$+ N\_head + N\_dependents$$
$$+ (1|word) + (1 + word\_order + N\_head$$
$$+ N\_dependents|participant)$$
$$(2)$$

The models are fit by maximum likelihood (Laplace Approximation) and with a binomial distribution.

6 Results

6.1 Regression Model Analysis

In the results below we first describe the fit of each of the two models (**null** and **full**) separately, then we report the results of the model comparison analysis using the χ^2-statistic.

Table 2 presents the fitted **null** model. Table 3 shows the fitted **full** model. The head and dependent regressors have significant effects on the number of regressions (*eye_regressions*) - N_head: $\beta = 0.242, p < .0001$; N_dependents: $\beta = 0.046, p < .0005$.

In addition, both word frequency (*freq*) and surprisal (*surp*) have a significant negative effect. The negative effect of frequency might be due to less frequent words being more difficult to retrieve from memory, therefore triggering a regression to gather more contextual information to help word processing. The negative effect of surprisal indicates that the larger the surprisal of a word – therefore more difficult its integration into the context – the less probable the reader is to regress to the word's previous context. Mak and Willems (2018) reported a positive effect of surprisal on the number of incoming saccades, that is, eye movements into a word back from subsequent parts of the text.

	Estimate	Std. Error	z value	$\Pr(> |z|)$
(Intercept)	−1.616	0.049	−32.9	< .0001
word_order	0.035	0.007	5.2	< .0001
surp	−0.140	0.013	−11.1	< .0001
freq	−0.165	0.028	−6.0	< .0001

Table 2: Fixed effects for the **null** model

	Estimate	Std. Error	z value	$\Pr(> |z|)$
(Intercept)	−1.798	0.049	−36.6	< .0001
word_order	0.019	0.006	3.0	< .003
surp	−0.102	0.012	−8.0	< .0001
freq	−0.125	0.027	−4.6	< .0001
N_head	0.242	0.016	14.8	< .0001
N_dependents	0.046	0.013	3.6	< .0005

Table 3: Fixed effects for the **full** model

In order to test whether the introduction of head and dependent measures improves the fit of the logistic mixed effect model to outgoing saccades, we computed the χ^2-statistic of a likelihood-ratio test for the difference between the **null** and **full** models above. The χ^2 is taken as the measure of the fit of the dependency measures to the probability of a regression being initiated at each word. Table 4 reports the results of the test, showing the difference in model fit to be significant ($\chi^2 = 738.87$, $p < .0001$).

6.2 Analysis of Regression Counts

The results of the regression model comparison indicate that regressions are partially driven by

model	df	AIC	BIC	deviance	χ^2	χ^2df	Pr
null	8	401023	401111	401007			
full	17	400302	400489	400268	738.87	9	< .0001

Table 4: Results of log-likelihood comparison between **null** and **full** model.

the presence of left-hand side dependency relations. In order to corroborate these observations, we counted the number of times regressions generated from each word do actually land on preceding words that are heads or dependents of that word. As reported in Table 5, it turns out that of the 110,336 regressions, about 40% do actually land on a head or dependent of the words they originate from. These are referred to as matches. The analyses were limited only to regressions landing within sentence boundaries. In the table, "misses" refers to the regressions that land on targets that are neither head nor dependent of the the word they originated from.

tot nr of regressions:	110336
tot nr of matches:	46378
tot nr of misses:	63958

Table 5: Total numbers of regressions, matches (i.e. regressions that land on heads or dependents), and misses (i.e. regressions do not land on heads or dependents of the word they originated from).

A χ^2-test of independence was performed to assess the relation between having a dependency relation with a word and generating a regression to that word. The test was computed independently for 10 separate left-hand side distances $d = [-10 : -1]$. In other words, for $d = -1$, we want to assess whether there is a relation between having a dependency relation with the preceding word and looking back at that word; for $d = -2$, we want to assess whether there is a relation between having a dependency relation with the preceding word at position -2 and looking back at that word, and so on for the other considered distances.

Table 6 contains the per-distance results of the χ^2 analyses. An association between presence of a dependency relation at position d and the generation of a regression to that position is significant for distances -1 ($\chi^2 = 132.52, p < 0.001$), -2 ($\chi^2 = 678.14, p < 0.001$), -3 ($\chi^2 = 8.05, p < 0.005$), and -4 ($\chi^2 = 13.68, p < 0.001$). For all other tested distances (between -5 and -10) the association was not significant (see Figure 2). For

$d = \{-1, -2, -3, -4\}$:

- The fraction of words w_i in a dependency relation with w_{i-d} that originate a regression of length $-d$ is significantly higher than the fraction of w_i not in a dependency relation with w_{i-d} originating a regression of length $-d$;

- The fraction of words w_i with a regression of length $-d$ that are in a dependency relation with w_{i-d} is significantly higher than the fraction of w_i without a regression of length $-d$ that are in a dependency relation with w_{i-d}.

dist	+dp+reg	-dp+reg	+dp-reg	-dp-reg	χ^2
-1	29245	19520	305931	228111	**132.52****
-2	5711	14798	113028	449270	**678.14****
-3	937	6239	68785	506846	**8.05***
-4	309	2641	49324	530533	**13.68****
-5	76	1370	33153	548208	0.55
-6	35	850	29823	552099	2.69
-7	17	530	23728	558532	1.42
-8	13	355	17687	564752	0.29
-9	5	261	16774	565767	1.08
-10	3	263	13785	568756	2.18

Table 6: χ^2 analyses for distances $-10 : -1$. **+dp+reg** indicates the number of words in the corpus having a relation and a regression at $-d$; **+dp-reg** the number of words having a relation but not a regression at $-d$; **-dp+reg** number of words not having a relation but having a regression at $-d$; **-dp-reg** not having nor relation nor regression at $-d$ (** $= p < 0.001$, * $= p < 0.01$).

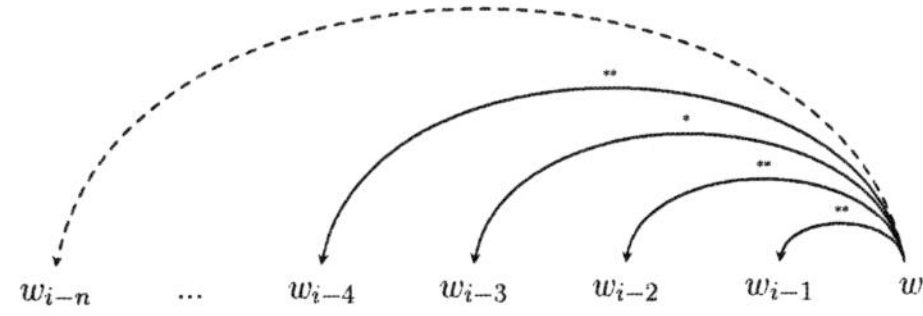

Figure 2: The effect of dependency relations on regressions from w_i is significant only for the preceding four words - further away saccades might not be influenced by a possible relation with w_i (** $= p < 0.001$, * $= p < 0.01$).

This seems to indicate that the effect of the dependency structure of a sentence on the pattern of outgoing eye-movements from a word is present only for short-distance relations (between a word and its four preceding words).

It is important to keep in mind however that the number of dependency relations found by the parser is much higher than the actual number of matches. This is simply because the parser does assign at least a head to each and every word in the text (even words in isolation are assigned a root head), whereas a regression is a relatively rare event (under normal conditions, using naturalistic language). The present work aims at demonstrating that regressions are related (also) to the structure of the dependency graph. The results we have produced so far point in that direction. In other words, it is possible to affirm that if a regression takes place, it might be triggered by the presence of a dependency relation between the word it is generated from and the word it lands on.

7 Conclusion

In this paper we have presented an analysis investigating whether eye movements of readers may be influenced directly by the syntactic structure of the sentence. We tested this using shallow non-hierarchical structures computed by a dependency parser. The hypothesis was that the path of regressions from a word to an earlier word coincide, at least partially, with the edges of dependency relations between these words. We used a substantially large eye-tracking dataset collected while 102 participants were engaged in reading three short narrative texts.

The results of a mixed-effect regression analysis indicate that there is a significant effect of the number of left-hand side dependency relations on the number of backward saccades. This effect is well above chance even after correcting for word position in the sentence and word frequency and surprisal – measures held to explain a large part of natural language processing behavioral and neural correlates. These results are corroborated by the observation that about 40% of backward saccades do indeed land on target words engaged in dependency relations according to the syntactic structure of the sentences composing our stimuli.

The length of the regressions seems to be relatively short: the vast majority being shorter than three words, with a predominance of regressions one position backwards. The results of a series of χ^2 tests for independence shows that there is a significant association between presence of a dependency link and backward saccading between two words holds only for pairs which are not further apart than four positions. This might indicate that the eye regressions are involved predominantly in dependency parsing at the local level, rather than at long distance.

Altogether these results converge on the idea that eye movements reflect, among other things, the shallow syntactic structure of language. Moreover these results seems also to corroborate the idea that humans do engage in online syntactic analysis of the input – at least in the form of local dependency parsing.

Acknowledgments

The work presented here was funded by the Netherlands Organisation for Scientific Research (NWO) Gravitation Grant 024.001.006 to the Language in Interaction Consortium. The authors thank Marloes Mak for providing the eye-tracker data and help in the analyses.

References

Gerry T.M Altmann, Alan Garnham, and Yvette Dennis. 1992. Avoiding the garden path: Eye movements in context. *Journal of Memory and Language*, 31(5):685 – 712.

Harry E. Blanchard and Asghar IranNejad. 1987. Comprehension processes and eye movement patterns in the reading of surpriseending stories. *Discourse Processes*, 10(1):127–138.

Robert W. Booth and Ulrich W. Weger. 2013. The function of regressions in reading: Backward eye movements allow rereading. *Memory & Cognition*, 41(1):82–97.

Marisa Ferrara Boston, John Hale, Reinhold Kliegl, Umesh Patil, and Shravan Vasishth. 2008. Parsing costs as predictors of reading difficulty: An evaluation using the potsdam sentence corpus. *Journal of Eye Movement Research*, 2(1):1–12.

Jonathan R. Brennan, Edward P. Stabler, Sarah E. Van Wagenen, Wen-Ming Luh, and John T. Hale. 2016. Abstract linguistic structure correlates with temporal activity during naturalistic comprehension. *Brain and Language*, 157–158:81–94.

Monica Castelhano and Keith Rayner. 2008. Eye movements during reading, visual search, and scene perception: An overview. In *Cognitive and Cultural Influences on Eye Movements*, pages 175 – 195. Tianjin People's Publishing House.

Noam Chomsky. 1965. *Aspects of the Theory of Syntax*. The MIT Press, Cambridge.

Vera Demberg and Frank Keller. 2008. Data from eye-tracking corpora as evidence for theories of syntactic processing complexity. *Cognition*, 109(2):193 – 210.

Stefan L. Frank, Rens Bod, and Morten H.. Christiansen. 2012. How hierarchical is language use? *Proceedings of the Royal Society B: Biological Sciences*, 279:4522–4531.

Lyn Frazier and Keith Rayner. 1982. Making and correcting errors during sentence comprehension: Eye movements in the analysis of structurally ambiguous sentences. *Cognitive Psychology*, 14(2):178 – 210.

Jukka Hyn. 1995. An eye movement analysis of topic-shift effect during repeated reading. *Journal of Experimental Psychology Learning Memory and Cognition*, 21:1365–1373.

Ray Jackendoff. 2002. *Foundations of language: brain, meaning, grammar, evolution*. Oxford University Press.

Ray Jackendoff. 2007. A parallel architecture perspective on language processing. *Brain Research*, 1146:222.

Ray Jackendoff and Eva Wittenberg. 2014. What you can say without syntax: A hierarchy of grammatical complexity. In *Measuring grammatical complexity*, pages 65 – 82. Oxford: Oxford University Press.

Alan Kennedy. 1992. The spatial code hypothesis. In K. Rayner, editor, *Eye Movements and Visual Cognition. Springer Series in Neuropsychology*. New York: Springer.

Emmanuel Keuleers, Marc Brysbaert, and Boris New. 2010. SUBTLEX-NL: A new measure for Dutch word frequency based on film subtitles. *Behavior Research Methods*, 42(3):643–650.

Sigrid Klerke, Maria Jung Barrett, Sheila Castilho, and Anders Søgaard. 2015. Reading metrics for estimating task efficiency with SMT output. In *Proceedings of the Sixth Workshop on Cognitive Aspects of Computational Language Learning*, pages 6–13. Association for Computational Linguistics.

Marloes Mak and Roel M. Willems. 2018. Mental simulation during literary reading: Individual differences revealed with eye-tracking. *Language, Cognition and Neuroscience*, 34(4):511–535.

Igor Mel'čuk. 1988. *Dependency Syntax: Theory and Practice*. State University of New York Press.

Matthew J. Nelson, Imen El Karoui, Kristof Giber, Xiaofang Yang, Laurent Cohen, Hilda Koopman, Sydney S. Cash, Lionel Naccache, John T. Hale, Christophe Pallier, and Stanislas Dehaene. 2017. Neurophysiological dynamics of phrase-structure building during sentence processing. *Proceedings of the National Academy of Sciences*, 114(18):E3669–E3678.

Joakim Nivre and Sandra Kübler. 2009. Dependency parsing. *Synthesis Lectures on Human Language Technologies*, 2.

Gertjan Van Noord. 2006. At last parsing is now operational. In *In TALN 2006*, pages 20–42.

John Kevin O'Regan. 1992. Solving the "real" mysteries of visual perception: The world as an outside memory. *Canadian Journal of Psychology*, 463:461–488.

Keith Rayner. 1998. Eye movements in reading and information processing: 20 years of research. *Psychological Bulletin*, 124:372–422.

Keith Rayner and Alexander Pollatsek. 1995. *The Psychology of Reading*. Lawrence Erlbaum Associates, Hillsdale.

Keith Rayner and Sara C. Sereno. 1994. Regressive eye movements and sentence parsing: On the use of regression-contingent analyses. *Memory & Cognition*, 22(3):281–285.

Erik D. Reichle, Simon P. Liversedge, Denis Drieghe, Hazel I. Blythe, Holly S.S.L. Joseph, Sarah J. White, and Keith Rayner. 2013. Using E–Z Reader to examine the concurrent development of eye-movement control and reading skill. *Developmental Review*, 33(2):110 – 149.

Roland Schäfer and Felix Bildhauer. 2012. Building large corpora from the web using a new efficient tool chain. In *LREC*, pages 486–493. European Language Resources Association (ELRA).

Michael Spivey, Daniel Richardson, and Stanka A. Fitneva. 2004. Thinking outside the brain: Spatial indices to visual and linguistic information. In J. Henderson and F. Ferreira, editors, *Interfacing Language, Vision, and Action*, pages 161–190. CA: Academic Press, San Diego.

Andreas Stolcke. 2002. SRILM - An Extensible Language Modeling Toolkit. In *Proceedings of the International Conference on Spoken Language Processing*, pages 901–904.

Lucien Tesnière, Timothy J. Osborne, and Sylvain Kahane. 2015. *Elements of Structural Syntax*. John Benjamins Publishing Company.

Françoise Vitu. 2005. Visual extraction processes and regressive saccades in reading. *Cognitive Processes in Eye Guidance*, pages 1–32.

A Framework for Decoding Event-Related Potentials from Text

Shaorong Yan
Department of Brain and Cognitive Sciences
University of Rochester
Rochester, NY 14627, USA
`syan13@ur.rochester.edu`

Aaron Steven White
Deparment of Linguistics
University of Rochester
Rochester, NY 14627, USA
`aaron.white@rochester.edu`

Abstract

We propose a novel framework for modeling event-related potentials (ERPs) collected during reading that couples pre-trained convolutional decoders with a language model. Using this framework, we compare the abilities of a variety of existing and novel sentence processing models to reconstruct ERPs. We find that modern contextual word embeddings underperform surprisal-based models but that, combined, the two outperform either on its own.

1 Introduction

Understanding the mechanisms by which comprehenders incrementally process linguistic input in real time has been a key endeavor of cognitive scientists and psycholinguists. Due to its fine time resolution, event-related potentials (ERPs) are an effective tool in probing the rapid, online cognitive processes underlying language comprehension. Traditionally, ERP research has focused on how the properties of the language input affect different ERP components (see Van Petten and Luka, 2012; Kuperberg, 2016, for reviews).[1]

While this approach has been fruitful, researchers have also long been aware of the potential drawbacks to this *component-centric* approach: a predictor's effects can be too transient to detect when averaging ERP amplitudes over a wide time window—as is typical in component-based approaches (see Hauk et al., 2006, for discussion). Different predictors can affect ERP in the same time window as an established component but have slightly different temporal (Frank and Willems, 2017) or spatial (DeLong et al.,

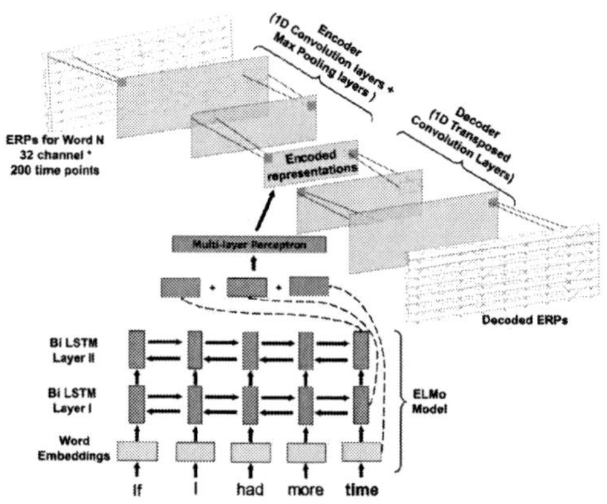

Figure 1: An instance of our framework using a bidirectional language model as the text encoder.

2005) profiles. This means that the definition of a component strongly affects interpretation.

There are two typical approaches to resolving these issues. The first is to plot the data and use visual inspection to select an analysis plan, introducing uncontrollable researcher degrees of freedom (Gelman and Loken, 2014). Another approach is to run separate models for each time point (or even each electrode) to look for the emergence of an effect. This necessitates complex statistical tests to monitor for inflated Type I error (see, e.g., Blair and Karniski, 1993; Laszlo and Federmeier, 2014, for discussion) and to control for autocorrelation across time points (Smith and Kutas, 2015a,b).

We explore an alternative approach to the analysis of ERP data in language studies that substantially reduces such researcher degrees of freedom: directly decoding the raw electroencephalography (EEG) measurements by which ERPs are collected. Inspired by multimodal tasks like image captioning (see Hossain et al., 2019, for a review) and visual question answering (Antol et al., 2015), we propose to model EEG using standard convolutional neural networks (CNNs) pre-trained

---

[1] Examples of such components include the N1/P2 (Sereno et al., 1998; Dambacher et al., 2006); N250 (Grainger et al., 2006); N400 (Kutas and Hillyard, 1980; Hagoort et al., 2004; Lau et al., 2008); and P600 (Osterhout and Holcomb, 1992; Kuperberg et al., 2003; Kim and Osterhout, 2005)

Proceedings of the Workshop on Cognitive Modeling and Computational Linguistics, pages 86–92
Minneapolis, USA, June 7, 2019. ©2019 Association for Computational Linguistics

under an autoencoding objective. The decoder CNN can then be decoupled from its encoder and recoupled with any language processing model, thus enabling explicit quantitative comparison of such models. We demonstrate the efficacy of this framework by using it to compare existing sentence processing models based on surprisal and/or static word embeddings with novel models based on contextual word embeddings. We find that surprisal-based models actually outperform contextual word embeddings on their own, but when combined, the two outperform either model alone.

2 Models

All of the models we present have two components: (i) a pre-trained CNN for decoding raw EEG measurements time-locked to each word in a sentence; and (ii) a language model from which features can be extracted for each word—e.g. the surprisal of that word given previous words or its contextual word embedding. An example model structure using ELMo embeddings (Peters et al., 2018) is illustrated in Figure 1.

Convolutional decoder   For all models, we use a convolutional decoder pre-trained as a component of an autoencoder. To reduce researcher degrees of freedom, the decoder architecture is selected from a set of possible architectures by cross-validation of the containing autoencoder.

The autoencoder consists of two parts: (a) a convolutional encoder that finds a way to best compress the ERP signals; and (b) a convolutional decoder with a homomorphic architecture that reconstructs the ERP data from the compressed representation. ERPs were organized into a 2D matrix (channel $\times$ time points). For the encoder, we pass the ERPs through multiple interleaved 1D convolutional and max pooling layers with receptive fields along the time dimension, shrinking the number of latent channels at each step. Correspondingly, for the decoder part, we use a homomorphic series of 1D transposed convolutional layers to reconstruct the ERP data.

At train time, the decoder weights are frozen, and the encoder is replaced by one of the language models described below. This entails fitting an *interface mapping*—a linear transformation for each channel produced by the encoder—from the features extracted from the language model into the representation space output by the encoder.

Language models   We consider a variety of features that can be extracted from a language model.

Surprisal   We use the lexical surprisal $-\log p(w_i \mid w_1, \ldots, w_{i-1})$ obtained from a RNN trained by Frank et al. (2015).

Semantic distance   Following Frank and Willems (2017), we point-wise average the GloVe embedding (Pennington et al., 2014) of each word prior to a particular word to obtain a context embedding and then calculate the cosine distance between the context embedding and the word embedding for that word. We use the GloVe embeddings trained on Wikipedia 2014 and Gigaword 5 (6B tokens, 400K vocabulary size).

Static word embeddings   We also consider the GloVe embedding dimensions as features. We do not tune the GloVe embeddings using an additional recurrent neural network (RNN), instead just passing the them through a multi-layer perceptron with one hidden layer of tanh nonlinearities. The idea here is that the GloVe-only model tells us how much the distributional properties of a word, outside of the current context, contribute to ERPs.

Contextual word embeddings   We consider contextual word embeddings generated from ELMo (Peters et al., 2018) using the `allennlp` package (Gardner et al., 2017). ELMo produces contextual word embeddings using a combination of character-level CNNs and bidirectional RNNs trained against a language modeling objective, and thus it is a useful contrast to GloVe, since it captures not only a word's distributional properties, but how they interact with the current context.

We take all three layers of the hidden layer output in the ELMo model and concatenate them. To ensure a fair comparison with the surprisal- and GloVe-based models, we use the same tuning procedure employed for the static word embeddings. Further, because sentences are presented incrementally in ERP experiments and because ELMo is bidirectional and thus later words in the sentence will affect the word embeddings of previous words, we do not obtain an embedding for a particular word on the basis of the entire sentence, instead using only the portion of the sentence up to and including that word to obtain its embedding.

Combined models   We also consider models that combine either static or contextual word embedding features with frequency, surprisal, and se-

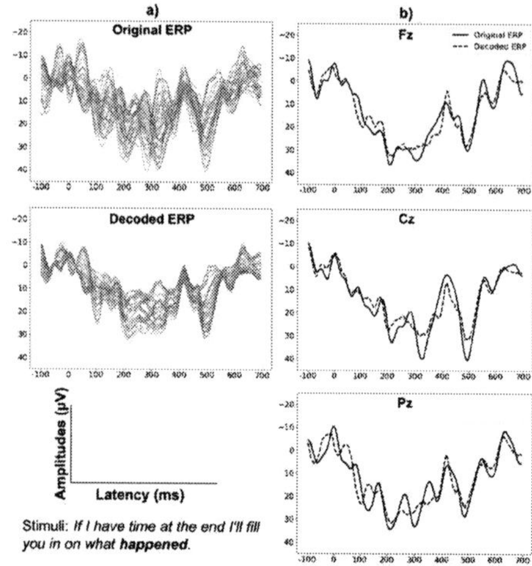

Figure 2: Original ERPs and ERPs decoded from the trained autoencoder of an example trial. a) ERPs from all 32 channels (denoted by color). b) Original (solid) and decoded ERPs (dashed) for example electrodes.

mantic distance. The latter features were concatenated onto the tuned word embeddings before being passed to the interface mapping.

3 Experiments

We use the EEG recordings collected and modeled by Frank and Willems (2017). In their study, 24 subjects read sentences drawn from natural text. Sentences were presented word-by-word using a rapid serial visual presentation paradigm. We use the ERPs of each word epoched from -100 to 700ms and time-locked to word onset from all the 32 recorded scalp channels. After artifact rejection (provided by Frank and Willems with the data), this dataset contains 41,009 training instances.

Pre-training To select which decoder to use, we compare the performance of two CNN architectures motivated by well-known properties of EEG. The first architecture has 5 latent channels and 9 time steps. Given the sampling rate and size of the input (250Hz, 200 time steps), this roughly corresponds to filtering the EEG data with alpha band frequency ($\sim$ 10Hz). The other has 10 latent channels and 20 time steps, thus lying within the range of beta band activity ($\sim$ 25Hz). In addition to these two architectures, we also examine whether including subject- and electrode-specific random intercepts improves model performance.

We conduct a 5-fold cross-validation for each architecture to find the one that has the best performance in reconstructing ERP data. As shown in Table 1, the beta models perform better overall than alpha models, since they likely capture both alpha and beta band activities. Adding subject-specific intercept, on the other hand, did not greatly improve the model performance.

Model	No Intercept	Intercept
alpha	49.9 (0.532)	49.7 (0.533)
beta	33.5 (0.686)	32.7 (0.692)

Table 1: Mean MSE and R^2 (in parentheses).

Figure 2 shows the reconstructed ERPs of the beta model on one trial. The autoencoder can reconstruct the ERP signal very well. The selected channels are illustrative of the reconstruction accuracy across all channels. We thus selected the beta model without subject-specific intercept as the decoder for our consequent models.

Training The interface mapping and (where applicable) word embedding tuner are trained under an MSE loss using mini-batch gradient descent (batch size = 128) with the Adam optimizer (`learning rate=0.001` and default settings for `beta1`, `beta2`, and `epsilon`) implemented in `pytorch` (Paszke et al., 2017). Each model is trained for 200 epochs. Since we need at least one preceding word to compute contextual word embeddings, we do not include the first word of the sentence. This left ERPs for 1,618 word tokens per subject (638 word types). After excluding trials containing artifacts, a total of 37,112 training instances remain.

Development To avoid overfitting, we use early stopping and report the models with the best performance on the development set. We did a parameter search over three different weight decays: `1e-5, 1e-3, 1e-1`. For each model, we chose the weight decay that produced the best mean performance on held-out data in a 5-fold cross-validation.

Baselines As a baseline we train an intercept-only model that passes a constant input (optimized to best predict the data) to the decoder. In addition, we fit a baseline model that only has word frequency as a feature. Frequency is also included as an additional feature in all models.

Metrics To account for the fact that our model performance is bounded by the performance of the autoencoder, we report a modified form of R^2 to evaluate the overall model performance.

$$R^2_{\mathrm{mod}} = 1 - \frac{\mathrm{MSE}_{\mathrm{model}} - \mathrm{MSE}_{\mathrm{autoencoder}}}{\mathrm{MSE}_{\mathrm{intercept}} - \mathrm{MSE}_{\mathrm{autoencoder}}}$$

Model	R^2_{mod}	95% CI
Frequency	19.5	$[18.5, 20.7]$
F + Surp	37.4	$[36.5, 38.3]$
F + SemDis	36.1	$[32.3, 38.4]$
F + GLoVE	35.0	$[31.8, 38.2]$
F + ELMo	35.2	$[34.3, 36.2]$
F + S + SD	46.6	$[43.5, 49.7]$
F + S + SD + GloVe	47.1	$[43.2, 49.4]$
F + S + SD + ELMo	49.5	$[48.9, 50.1]$

Table 2: Proportion variance explained by each model ($\times 100$) and confidence interval across folds computed by a nonparametric bootstrap. F = frequency, S(urp) = surprisal, S(em)D(is) = semantic distance.

4 Results

Table 2 shows the R^2_{mod} metric for each model. We see that both surprisal and semantic distance outperform both types of word embedding features, all of which outperform frequency alone. When combined, surprisal and semantic distance outperform either alone, and further gains can be made with the addition of either static (GloVe) or contextual (ELMo) embedding features. The addition of contextual embedding features increases performance more than the addition of static word embedding features, such that there is some benefit to capturing context over and above that provided by surprisal and semantic distance.

Time course analysis To understand where in time each predictor improved model performance, we examine the increase in correlation over the intercept model at each time point (Figure 3). There are roughly three regions where the language models outperform the intercept model. The first is right after 100ms post word onset: corresponding to the N1 component, which is typically considered to reflect perceptual processing; the second is between 200 and 350ms: corresponding to the N250 component, which correlates with lexical access (Grainger et al., 2006; Laszlo and Federmeier, 2014); and the third is between 300ms and 500ms: corresponding to the N400, which is typically associated with semantic processing.

Consistent with previous findings (Hauk et al., 2006; Laszlo and Federmeier, 2014; Yan and Jaeger, 2019), adding frequency into the model improved model performance in all three time windows. Also consistent with the literature, adding surprisal and semantic distance improved model performance in the N400 time window

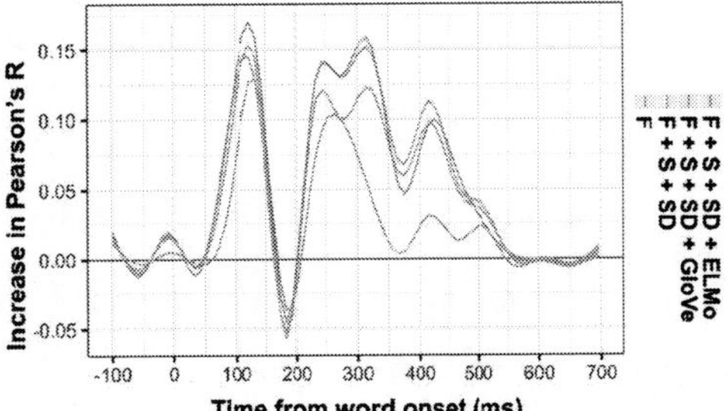

Figure 3: Increase in Pearson's R between predicted and actual ERPs. Lines show GAM smooth over time.

(Frank and Willems, 2017; Yan and Jaeger, 2019).

Models with word embeddings do not differ much from the models containing only frequency, surprisal, and semantic distance, with the biggest difference around 300ms post word onset. This might indicate an effect in the early N400 time window. This could also indicate that processes commonly associated with the N250 may be better captured by the models containing word embeddings. If so, it is less expected and potentially interesting, since most of our models have no access to perceptual properties of the input—with the possible exception of ELMo, whose charCNN may capture orthographic regularities. These effects could reflect our models' ability to capture top-down lexical processing (see, e.g., Penolazzi et al., 2007; Yan and Jaeger, 2019) or possibly systematic correlations between higher-level features and perceptual features.

Part-of-speech analysis Prior work on ERP during reading distinguishes function word—such as determiners, conjunctions, pronouns, prepositions, numerals, particles—from content words—such as (proper) nouns, verbs, adjectives, adverbs (Nobre and McCarthy, 1994; Frank et al., 2015). As such, we also examine whether each model's performance differs for content words and function words. We calculate the Pearson's correlation between the predicted and actual ERPs for each word of each model and used linear mixed-effects model to examine the influence on model fit with the inclusion of different information. If a model included a specific type of information, the corresponding predictor is coded as 1, otherwise it was coded as -1. For example, the surprisal model was trained with surprisal but not semantic distance, so the surprisal predictor is 1 for this model and the semantic distance predictor is -1. We further included the interaction between models and word

Predictor	$\hat{\beta}$	t	
Intercept	-0.0013	-0.225	
Word Type (Content)	0.0030	2.01	*
Frequency	0.0110	21.2	**
Surprisal	0.0050	13.0	**
Semantic Distance	0.0040	11.60	**
GloVe Embeddings	0.0040	10.3	**
ELMo Embeddings	0.0040	10.1	**
Freq : Word Type	-0.0010	-2.43	*
Surp : Word Type	0.0001	0.24	
SemDis : Word Type	-0.0003	-0.70	
GloVe : Word Type	0.0002	0.55	
ELMo : Word Type	0.0007	-1.85	+

Table 3: Model estimates and t statistics from mixed-effects model. $^{**} : p < 0.01$; $^{*} : p < 0.05$; $^{+} : p < 0.1$

types (function=-1, content=1).

Table 3 shows the resulting coefficients. Overall, models display better performance for content words than for function words ($\hat{\beta} = 0.003, t = 2.01, p < 0.05$), consistent with previous findings (Frank et al., 2015). Including each type of information also significantly increased model fit (ts $> 10.1, p < 0.01$). There was a significant interaction between frequency and word type ($\hat{\beta} = -0.001, t = -2.43, p < 0.02$): including frequency increased model performance for function words more than for content words. There was also a marginally significant interaction between ELMo and word type ($\hat{\beta} = 0.0007, t = -1.85, p < 0.064$), suggesting that including ELMo embeddings increased model performance for content words more than for function words.

We also examine the interaction between each type of information and each part-of-speech. Overall, the models had worse performance for particles ($\hat{\beta} = -0.017, t = -3.37, p < 0.01$), nouns ($\hat{\beta} = -0.007, t = -1.95, p < 0.051$) and pronouns ($\hat{\beta} = -0.012, t = -1.76, p < 0.08$). Including each type of information increased overall model fit (ts $> 6.05, p < 0.01$). While including frequency increased overall model fit, it increased the model fit for verbs less ($\hat{\beta} = -0.003, t = -2.04, p < 0.05$). No other effects reached significance.

5   Related Work

Traditionally, ERP studies of language processing use coarse-grained predictors like cloze rates, which often lack the precision to differentiate different neural computational models (for discussion, see Yan et al., 2017; Rabovsky et al., 2018). To overcome such limitations, a main line of attack has been to extract measures from probabilistic language models and evaluate them against ERP amplitudes (Frank et al., 2015; Brouwer et al., 2017; Rabovsky et al., 2018; Delaney-Busch et al., 2019; Fitz and Chang, 2018; Szewczyk and Wodniecka, 2018; Biemann et al., 2015).

While prior studies have also predicted ERPs from language model-based features (Broderick et al., 2018; Frank and Willems, 2017; Hale et al., 2018), they fit to aspects of the EEG signals that are unlikely to be related to language processing. Our approach threads the needle by first finding abstract structure in the ERPs with a CNN, then using that knowledge in predicting that structure from linguistic features. We are not the first to use CNNs to model EEG/ERPs (Lawhern et al., 2016; Schirrmeister et al., 2017; Seeliger et al., 2018; Acharya et al., 2018; Moon et al., 2018), but to our knowledge, no other work has yet used CNNs for modeling ERPs during reading.

6   Conclusion

We proposed a novel framework for modeling ERPs collected during reading. Using this framework, we compared the abilities of a variety of existing and novel sentence processing models to reconstruct ERPs, finding that modern contextual word embeddings underperform surprisal-based models but that, combined, the two outperform either on its own.

ERP data provides a rich testbed not only for comparing models of language processing, but potentially also for probing and improving the representations constructed by natural language processing (NLP) systems. We provided one example of how such probing might be carried out by analyzing the differences among models as a function of processing time, but this analysis only scratches the surface of what is possible using our framework, especially for understanding the more complex neural models used in NLP.

Acknowledgments

We are grateful to Dr. Stefan Frank for sharing the EEG data, sentence materials, and language model predictors. We would also like to thank three anonymous CMCL reviewers as well as the the FACTS.lab and HLP lab at UR for providing valuable feedback on the draft.

References

U Rajendra Acharya, Shu Lih Oh, Yuki Hagiwara, Jen Hong Tan, and Hojjat Adeli. 2018. Deep convolutional neural network for the automated detection and diagnosis of seizure using EEG signals. *Computers in biology and medicine*, 100:270–278.

Stanislaw Antol, Aishwarya Agrawal, Jiasen Lu, Margaret Mitchell, Dhruv Batra, C Lawrence Zitnick, and Devi Parikh. 2015. VQA: Visual Question Answering. In *Proceedings of the IEEE international conference on computer vision*, pages 2425–2433.

Chris Biemann, Steffen Remus, and Markus J Hofmann. 2015. Predicting word 'predictability' in cloze completion, electroencephalographic and eye movement data. In *Proceedings of natural language processing and cognitive science*, pages 83–93. Libreria Editrice Cafoscarina.

R Clifford Blair and Walt Karniski. 1993. An alternative method for significance testing of waveform difference potentials. *Psychophysiology*, 30(5):518–524.

Michael P Broderick, Andrew J Anderson, Giovanni M Di Liberto, Michael J Crosse, and Edmund C Lalor. 2018. Electrophysiological correlates of semantic dissimilarity reflect the comprehension of natural, narrative speech. *Current Biology*, 28(5):803–809.

Harm Brouwer, Matthew W Crocker, Noortje J Venhuizen, and John CJ Hoeks. 2017. A neurocomputational model of the N400 and the P600 in language processing. *Cognitive Science*, 41:1318–1352.

Michael Dambacher, Reinhold Kliegl, Markus Hofmann, and Arthur M Jacobs. 2006. Frequency and predictability effects on event-related potentials during reading. *Brain Research*, 1084(1):89–103.

Nathaniel Delaney-Busch, Emily Morgan, Ellen Lau, and Gina R Kuperberg. 2019. Neural evidence for bayesian trial-by-trial adaptation on the N400 during semantic priming. *Cognition*, 187:10–20.

Katherine A DeLong, Thomas P Urbach, and Marta Kutas. 2005. Probabilistic word pre-activation during language comprehension inferred from electrical brain activity. *Nature Neuroscience*, 8(8):1117–1121.

Hartmut Fitz and Franklin Chang. 2018. Sentence-level erp effects as error propagation: A neurocomputational model. *PsyArXiv*.

Stefan L Frank, Leun J Otten, Giulia Galli, and Gabriella Vigliocco. 2015. The ERP response to the amount of information conveyed by words in sentences. *Brain and Language*, 140:1–11.

Stefan L Frank and Roel M Willems. 2017. Word predictability and semantic similarity show distinct patterns of brain activity during language comprehension. *Language, Cognition and Neuroscience*, 32(9):1192–1203.

Matt Gardner, Joel Grus, Mark Neumann, Oyvind Tafjord, Pradeep Dasigi, Nelson F. Liu, Matthew Peters, Michael Schmitz, and Luke S. Zettlemoyer. 2017. AllenNLP: A Deep Semantic Natural Language Processing Platform.

Andrew Gelman and Eric Loken. 2014. The statistical crisis in science. *The best writing on mathematics*, 102(6):460–465.

Jonathan Grainger, Kristi Kiyonaga, and Phillip J Holcomb. 2006. The time course of orthographic and phonological code activation. *Psychological Science*, 17(12):1021–1026.

Peter Hagoort, Lea Hald, Marcel Bastiaansen, and Karl Magnus Petersson. 2004. Integration of word meaning and world knowledge in language comprehension. *Science*, 304(5669):438–441.

John Hale, Chris Dyer, Adhiguna Kuncoro, and Jonathan Brennan. 2018. Finding syntax in human encephalography with beam search. In *Proceedings of the 56th Annual Meeting of the Association for Computational Linguistics (Volume 1: Long Papers)*, pages 2727–2736. Association for Computational Linguistics.

Olaf Hauk, Matthew H Davis, M Ford, Friedemann Pulvermüller, and William D Marslen-Wilson. 2006. The time course of visual word recognition as revealed by linear regression analysis of ERP data. *Neuroimage*, 30(4):1383–1400.

MD. Zakir Hossain, Ferdous Sohel, Mohd Fairuz Shiratuddin, and Hamid Laga. 2019. A comprehensive survey of Deep Learning for Image Captioning. *ACM Comput. Surv.*, 51(6):118:1–118:36.

Albert Kim and Lee Osterhout. 2005. The independence of combinatory semantic processing: Evidence from event-related potentials. *Journal of Memory and Language*, 52(2):205–225.

Gina R Kuperberg. 2016. Separate streams or probabilistic inference? what the N400 can tell us about the comprehension of events. *Language, Cognition and Neuroscience*, 31(5):602–616.

Gina R Kuperberg, Tatiana Sitnikova, David Caplan, and Phillip J Holcomb. 2003. Electrophysiological distinctions in processing conceptual relationships within simple sentences. *Cognitive Brain Research*, 17(1):117–129.

Marta Kutas and Steven A Hillyard. 1980. Reading senseless sentences: Brain potentials reflect semantic incongruity. *Science*, 207(4427):203–205.

Sarah Laszlo and Kara D Federmeier. 2014. Never seem to find the time: evaluating the physiological time course of visual word recognition with regression analysis of single-item event-related potentials. *Language, Cognition and Neuroscience*, 29(5):642–661.

Ellen F Lau, Colin Phillips, and David Poeppel. 2008. A cortical network for semantics:(de) constructing the N400. *Nature Reviews Neuroscience*, 9(12):920–933.

Vernon J Lawhern, Amelia J Solon, Nicholas R Waytowich, Stephen M Gordon, Chou P Hung, and Brent J Lance. 2016. EEGnet: A compact convolutional network for EEG-based brain-computer interfaces. *arXiv preprint arXiv:1611.08024.*

Seong-Eun Moon, Soobeom Jang, and Jong-Seok Lee. 2018. Convolutional neural network approach for EEG-based emotion recognition using brain connectivity and its spatial information. In *2018 IEEE International Conference on Acoustics, Speech and Signal Processing (ICASSP)*, pages 2556–2560. IEEE.

Anna C Nobre and Gregory McCarthy. 1994. Language-related erps: Scalp distributions and modulation by word type and semantic priming. *Journal of Cognitive Neuroscience*, 6(3):233–255.

Lee Osterhout and Phillip J Holcomb. 1992. Event-related brain potentials elicited by syntactic anomaly. *Journal of Memory and Language*, 31(6):785–806.

Adam Paszke, Sam Gross, Soumith Chintala, Gregory Chanan, Edward Yang, Zachary DeVito, Zeming Lin, Alban Desmaison, Luca Antiga, and Adam Lerer. 2017. Automatic differentiation in pytorch.

Jeffrey Pennington, Richard Socher, and Christopher Manning. 2014. Glove: Global vectors for word representation. In *Proceedings of the 2014 conference on empirical methods in natural language processing (EMNLP)*, pages 1532–1543.

Barbara Penolazzi, Olaf Hauk, and Friedemann Pulvermüller. 2007. Early semantic context integration and lexical access as revealed by event-related brain potentials. *Biological Psychology*, 74(3):374–388.

Matthew Peters, Mark Neumann, Mohit Iyyer, Matt Gardner, Christopher Clark, Kenton Lee, and Luke Zettlemoyer. 2018. Deep contextualized word representations. In *Proceedings of the 2018 Conference of the North American Chapter of the Association for Computational Linguistics: Human Language Technologies, Volume 1 (Long Papers)*, volume 1, pages 2227–2237.

Milena Rabovsky, Steven S Hansen, and James L McClelland. 2018. Modelling the N400 brain potential as change in a probabilistic representation of meaning. *Nature Human Behaviour*, 2(9):693–705.

Robin Tibor Schirrmeister, Jost Tobias Springenberg, Lukas Dominique Josef Fiederer, Martin Glasstetter, Katharina Eggensperger, Michael Tangermann, Frank Hutter, Wolfram Burgard, and Tonio Ball. 2017. Deep learning with convolutional neural networks for EEG decoding and visualization. *Human Brain Mapping*, 38(11):5391–5420.

Katja Seeliger, Matthias Fritsche, Umut Güçlü, Sanne Schoenmakers, Jan-Mathijs Schoffelen, Sander Bosch, and Marcel van Gerven. 2018. Convolutional neural network-based encoding and decoding of visual object recognition in space and time. *NeuroImage*, 180:253–266.

Sara C Sereno, Keith Rayner, and Michael I Posner. 1998. Establishing a time-line of word recognition: evidence from eye movements and event-related potentials. *Neuroreport*, 9(10):2195–2200.

Nathaniel J Smith and Marta Kutas. 2015a. Regression-based estimation of ERP waveforms: I. the rERP framework. *Psychophysiology*, 52(2):157–168.

Nathaniel J Smith and Marta Kutas. 2015b. Regression-based estimation of ERP waveforms: Ii. nonlinear effects, overlap correction, and practical considerations. *Psychophysiology*, 52(2):169–181.

Jakub M Szewczyk and Zofia Wodniecka. 2018. The mechanisms of prediction updating that impact processing of upcoming words – an event-related study on sentence comprehension. *PsyArXiv*.

Cyma Van Petten and Barbara J Luka. 2012. Prediction during language comprehension: Benefits, costs, and ERP components. *International Journal of Psychophysiology*, 83(2):176–190.

Shaorong Yan and T. Florian Jaeger. 2019. (Early) context effects on event-related potentials over natural inputs. *Language, Cognition and Neuroscience*, pages 1–22.

Shaorong Yan, Gina R Kuperberg, and T Florian Jaeger. 2017. Prediction (or not) during language processing. a commentary on Nieuwland et al.(2017) and Delong et al.(2005). *bioRxiv*.

Testing a Minimalist Grammar Parser
on Italian Relative Clause Asymmetries

Aniello De Santo
Department of Linguistics
Stony Brook University
`aniello.desanto@stonybrook.edu`

Abstract

Stabler's (2013) top-down parser for Minimalist grammars has been used to account for off-line processing preferences across a variety of seemingly unrelated phenomena cross-linguistically, via complexity metrics measuring "memory burden". This paper extends the empirical coverage of the model by looking at the processing asymmetries of Italian relative clauses, as I discuss the relevance of these constructions in evaluating plausible structure-driven models of processing difficulty.

1 Introduction

Recent studies have shown that a top-down parser for Minimalist grammars (MGs; Stabler, 1996, 2013)) can be combined with complexity metrics to relate parsing behavior to memory usage, and successfully used to model sentence processing preferences across a variety of phenomena cross-linguistically (Kobele et al., 2013; Gerth, 2015; Graf et al., 2017). This kind of work follows a line of research on syntactic processing that sees computational models provide a transparent, interpretable linking theory between syntactic assumptions and processing behavior (Joshi, 1990; Rambow and Joshi, 1994; Hale, 2011). Importantly, at the core of the particular approach adopted here is a theory of grammatical structure driving off-line processing cost, thus connecting longstanding ideas about memory resources with explicit syntactic analyses in rigorous ways. Extending the range of phenomena correctly modeled by the parser is then going to be crucial to confirm the empirical feasibility of the approach.

Here, I adopt Kobele *et al.*'s (2013) implementation of Stabler's (2013) top-down traversal algorithm, coupled with the set of complexity metrics defined by Graf et al. (2017). We test the MG parser's performance on the processing asymmetries reported for Italian relative clauses, which have been object of extensive study in the psycholinguistic literature. Apart from conforming to a well-attested cross-linguistic preference for subject over object relatives, Italian speakers also show increased processing difficulties when encountering relative clauses with subjects in postverbal position. This difficulty gradient has often been accounted for in the literature in terms of the cost of local ambiguity resolution. Since in the particular formulation of Kobele et al. (2013) the MG parser acts as an oracle and deliberately ignores structural ambiguity, these constructions thus make for a challenging testing ground for a model attempting to account for processing contrasts *just* in terms of *structural complexity*.

The paper is structured as follows. Section 2 presents an informal introduction to MGs and Stabler's (2013) top-down parser, and an overview of previous work on combining the MG parser with complexity metrics measuring memory burden. Section 3 discusses Italian relative clause asymmetries and our modeling assumptions. Section 4 looks at the modeling results, and shows how the MG parser succeeds in predicting the correct processing preferences. Section 5 concludes with a brief discussion of possible limits of the model, and promising future work.

2 Preliminaries

2.1 Minimalist Grammars

MGs (Stabler, 1996, 2011) are a highly lexicalized, mildly context-sensitive formalism incorporating the structurally rich analyses of Minimalist syntax — the most recent version of Chomsky's transformational grammar framework. Therefore, they have proven to be a fruitful grammar formalism in investigating how ideas from theoretical syntax weight on sentence processing. While

Proceedings of the Workshop on Cognitive Modeling and Computational Linguistics, pages 93–104
Minneapolis, USA, June 7, 2019. ©2019 Association for Computational Linguistics

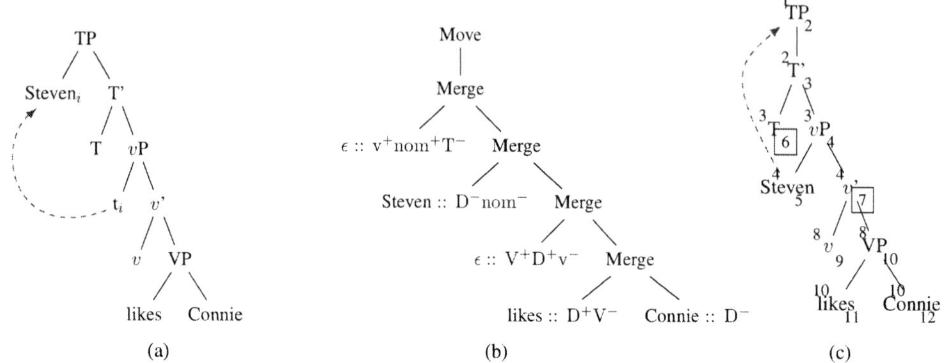

Figure 1: Phrase structure tree (a), MG derivation tree (b), and annotated derivation tree (c) for *Steven likes Connie*. Boxed nodes in (c) are those with tenure value greater than 2, following (Graf and Marcinek, 2014).

much work has been done on the formal properties of MGs, the fine-grained details of the formalism are unnecessary given the focus of this paper. Thus, I introduce MGs in a mostly informal way, as my main goal is to provide the reader with an intuitive understanding of the core data structure the parser is going to operate on: derivation trees.

An MG grammar is a set of of lexical items (LIs) consisting of a phonetic form and a finite, non-empty string of features. They distinguish two types on features, each with either *positive* or *negative* polarity: *Merge* features (written here in upper caps, with the exception of little v), and *Move* features (in lower caps). LIs are assembled via two feature checking operations: *Merge* and *Move*. Informally, Merge combines two LIs if their respective first unchecked features are Merge features of opposite polarity. Move removes a phrase from an already assembled tree and displaces it to a different position (Stabler, 2011). Intuitively, Merge encodes subcategorization, while Move long-distance movement dependencies.

MGs succinctly encode the sequence of Merge and Move operations required to build the phrase structure tree for a specific sentence into *derivation trees* (Michaelis, 1998; Harkema, 2001; Kobele et al., 2007). For instance, Fig. 1a and Fig. 1b compare these two kind of trees for a simplified analysis of the sentence *Steven likes Connie*. In the derivation tree (Fig. 1b), all leaf nodes are labeled by LIs, while unary and binary branching nodes are labeled as Move or Merge, respectively. Crucially, the main difference between the phrase structure tree and the derivation tree is that in the latter, moving phrases remain in their base po-

sition, and their landing site can be fully reconstructed via the feature calculus. Thus, the final word order of a sentence is not directly reflected in the order of the leaf nodes in a derivation tree.

Importantly, MG derivation trees form a regular tree language, and thus — modulo a more complex mapping from trees to strings — can be regarded as a simple variant of context-free grammars (CFG), which have been studied extensively in the computational parsing literature. This is the crucial insight behind Stabler's top-down parser.

2.2 MG Parsing

Stabler's (2013) parser for MGs is a variant of a standard depth-first, top-down parser for CFGs: it takes as input a sentence represented as string of words, hypothesizes the structure top-down, verifies that the words in the structure match the input string, and outputs a tree encoding of the sentence structure. Basically, the parser scans the nodes from top to bottom and from left to right; but since the surface order of lexical items in the derivation tree is not the phrase structure tree's surface order, simple left-to-right scanning of the leaf nodes yields the wrong word order. Thus, while scanning the nodes, the MG parser must also keep tracking the derivational operations which affect the linear word order.

Without delving too much in technical details, the parsing procedure can be outlined slightly more clearly as follows: I) hypothesize the top of structure and add nodes downward (toward words) and left-to-right; II) if *move* is predicted, it triggers the search for mover ⇒ build the shortest path towards predicted mover; III) once the mover has been found, continue from the point where it was predicted (Kobele et al., 2013).

Essential to this procedure is the role of memory: if a node is hypothesized at step i, but cannot be worked on until step j, it must be stored for $j - i$ steps in a priority queue. To make the traversal strategy easy to follow, I adopt Kobele *et al.*'s (2013) notation, in which each node in the tree is annotated with an *index* (superscript) and an *outdex* (subscript). Intuitively, the annotation indicates for each node in the tree when it is first conjectured by the parser (index) and placed in the memory queue, and at what point it is considered completed and flushed from memory (outdex). In the rest of the paper I adopt an annotated, simplified version of derivation trees, with internal nodes explicitly labelled and dashed arrows indicating movement relations (as shown in Fig. 1c).[1]

Finally, note that in Stabler's original formulation the parser is equipped with a search beam discarding the most unlikely predictions. In this paper though, I follow Kobele et al. (2013) in ignoring the beam and assuming that the parser is equipped with a perfect oracle, which always makes the right choices when constructing a tree. This idealization is clearly implausible from a psycholinguistic point of view. However, it is made with a precise purpose in mind: to ignore the cost of choosing among several possible predictions and, by assuming a deterministic parse, to focus on the specific contribution of syntactic complexity to processing difficulty. In Sec. 3 I will discuss how assuming an idealized parser is exactly what makes Italian RCs an interesting test case.

2.3 Complexity Metrics

In order to allow for psycholinguistic predictions, the behavior of the parser must be related to processing difficulty via a linking theory, which here takes the form of complexity metrics. Specifically, I employ complexity metrics that predict processing difficulty based on how the geometry of the trees built by the parser affects memory usage.

Extending previous work on MG parsing (Kobele et al., 2013; Graf and Marcinek, 2014; Gerth, 2015), Graf et al. (2017) distinguish three cognitive notions of memory usage: I) how long a node is kept in memory (*tenure*); II) how many nodes must be kept in memory (*payload*); or III)

how many bits a node consumes in memory (*size*). Tenure and payload for each node n in the tree can be easily computed via the node annotation scheme of Kobele *et al.*: a node's tenure is equal to the difference between its index and its outdex; the payload of a derivation tree is computed as the number of nodes with a tenure strictly greater than 2. Defining size in an informal way is slightly trickier, as its original conception was based on how information about movers is stored by Stabler's top-down parser (for a technical discussion, see Graf et al., 2015). Procedurally, the size of the parse item corresponding to each node n can be simply computed by exploiting our simplified representation of derivation trees: it corresponds to the number of nodes below n that have a movement arrow pointing to somewhere above n.[2] For example, referring to the annotated tree in Fig. 1c, the size of vP is 1, while the size of VP is 0. In practice, size encodes how many nodes in a derivation consume more memory because a certain phrase m moves across them.

With the exception of payload, these concepts are not exactly metrics we can use to directly compare derivations. What we are missing is a way for them to be applied to a given derivation as measures of overall processing difficulty. In order to do so, these notions of memory have been used to define a vast set of complexity metrics measuring processing difficulty over a full derivation tree. In this paper, we look at Italian relative clause asymmetries using the full set of 1600 metrics as defined in Graf et al. (2017). However, in what follows we only give a general intuition of how such metrics can be defined, and we refer the reader to Graf *et al.* for the detailed formal definitions. Importantly, just a few of these metrics are enough to account for the contrasts we are interested in.

Kobele et al. (2013) show that tenure can be associated to quantitative values by defining metrics like MAXT $:= max(\{tenure\text{-}of(n)\})$ and SUMT $:= \sum_n tenure\text{-}of(n)$. MAXT measures the maximum amount of time any node stays in memory during processing, while SUMT measures the overall amount of memory usage for all nodes whose tenure is not trivial (i.e., > 2). It thus captures total memory usage over the course of a parse. Building on these findings, Graf and Marcinek (2014) show that MAXT (restricted to

---

[1]Note that, due to the fact that intermediate landing sites for moved phrases do not affect the traversal strategy, they not explicitly marked by movement arrows.

[2]Thus, as a reviewer correctly notes, size is sensitive to the hierarchical distance between the filler and the gap.

pronounced nodes) makes the right difficulty predictions for several phenomena, such as right embedding vs. center embedding, nested dependencies vs. crossing dependencies, as well as a set of contrasts involving relative clauses.

Extending Graf & Marcinek's (2014) analysis of relative clause constructions, Graf et al. (2015) argue for the insufficiency of MAXT as a single, reliable metric. They then introduce several new metrics, inspired by those defined for tenure. For example, they define an the equivalent of SUMT for size, which measures the overall cost of maintaining long-distance filler-gap dependencies over a derivation. Let M be the set of all nodes of derivation tree t that are the root of a subtree undergoing movement. For each $m \in M$, $i(m)$ is the index of m and $f(m)$ is the index of the highest Move node that m's subtree is moved to. Then SUMS is defined as $\sum_{m \in M} i(m) - f(m)$.

Graf et al. (2015) also introduce the idea of ranked metrics of the type $\langle M_1, M_2, \ldots, M_n \rangle$, similar to constraint ranking in Optimality Theory (Prince and Smolensky, 2008): a lower ranked metric matters only if all higher ranked metric have failed to pick out a unique winner (e.g., if two constructions result in a *tie* over MAXT). This suggestion is fully explored in Graf et al. (2017), which show that when complexity metrics are allowed to be ranked in such a way the total number of possible metrics quickly reaches an astronomical size. However, surveying the variety of previously modeled phenomena, the authors also suggest that the number of metrics truly needed to account for human processing contrasts can be reduced to a small number of core metrics (particularly, they point toward a combination of MAXT and SUMS), an hypothesis that seems supported by recent work on several different constructions (Liu, 2018; Lee, 2018).

3 Modeling Italian RCs

3.1 Processing Asymmetries

Restrictive relative clauses (RCs) in Italian have been the focus of extensive experimental studies from the perspective of comprehension (Volpato and Adani, 2009), production (Belletti and Contemori, 2009), and acquisition (Volpato, 2010; Friedmann et al., 2009). Italian speakers conform to the general cross-linguistic preference for subject over object RCs (Frauenfelder et al., 1980; King and Kutas, 1995; Schriefers et al., 1995,

a.o.), so that (1) is easier to process than (2):

(1)   Il cavallo che ha inseguito i leoni
       The horse that has chased the lions
       "The horse that chased the lions"   **SRC**

(2)   Il cavallo che i leoni hanno inseguito
       The horse that the lions have chased
       "The horse that the lions chased"   **ORC**

Interestingly, Italian also allows for sentences like (3), ambiguous between a SRC interpretation (3a) and an ORC interpretation (3a) with the embedded subject expressed postverbally:

(3)   Il cavallo che ha inseguito il leone
       The horse that has chased the lion

    a. "The horse that chased the lion" **SRC**

    b. "The horse that the lion chased" **ORCp**

Although postverbal subject constructions are very common in Italian, in such cases native speakers show a marked preference for the SRC interpretation over the ORCp one. Sentences like (3) can be disambiguated by grammatical cues like subject-verb agreement:

(4)   Il cavallo che hanno inseguito i leoni **ORCp**
       The horse that have chased the lions
       "The horse that the lions chased"

However, even in unambiguous cases like (4), studies report increased efforts with ORCp, leading to the following difficulty gradient: SRC < ORC < ORCp (Utzeri, 2007, a.o.).

The contrast between SRCs and ORCs has been well studied in the past, and it is compatible with a variety of models, such as surprisal (Levy, 2013), cue-based memory retrieval (Lewis and Vasishth, 2005), the active filler strategy (Frazier, 1987), the Dependency Locality Theory (Gibson, 1998, 2000), the Competition Model (Bates and MacWhinney, 1987), the Minimal Chain Principle (De Vincenzi, 1991), among many. The increased complexity reported for ORCs with postverbal subjects comes as a challenge to some of these models (e.g., for the Competition model and Dependency Locality Theory; Arosio et al., 2009). However, their processing profile can be explained in terms of economy of gap prediction and cost of structural re-analysis, due to the possible ambiguity in ORCps at the embedded subject site — where the parser has the choice of either postulating a null pronominal subject or establishing a filler-gap dependency. Importantly though, the

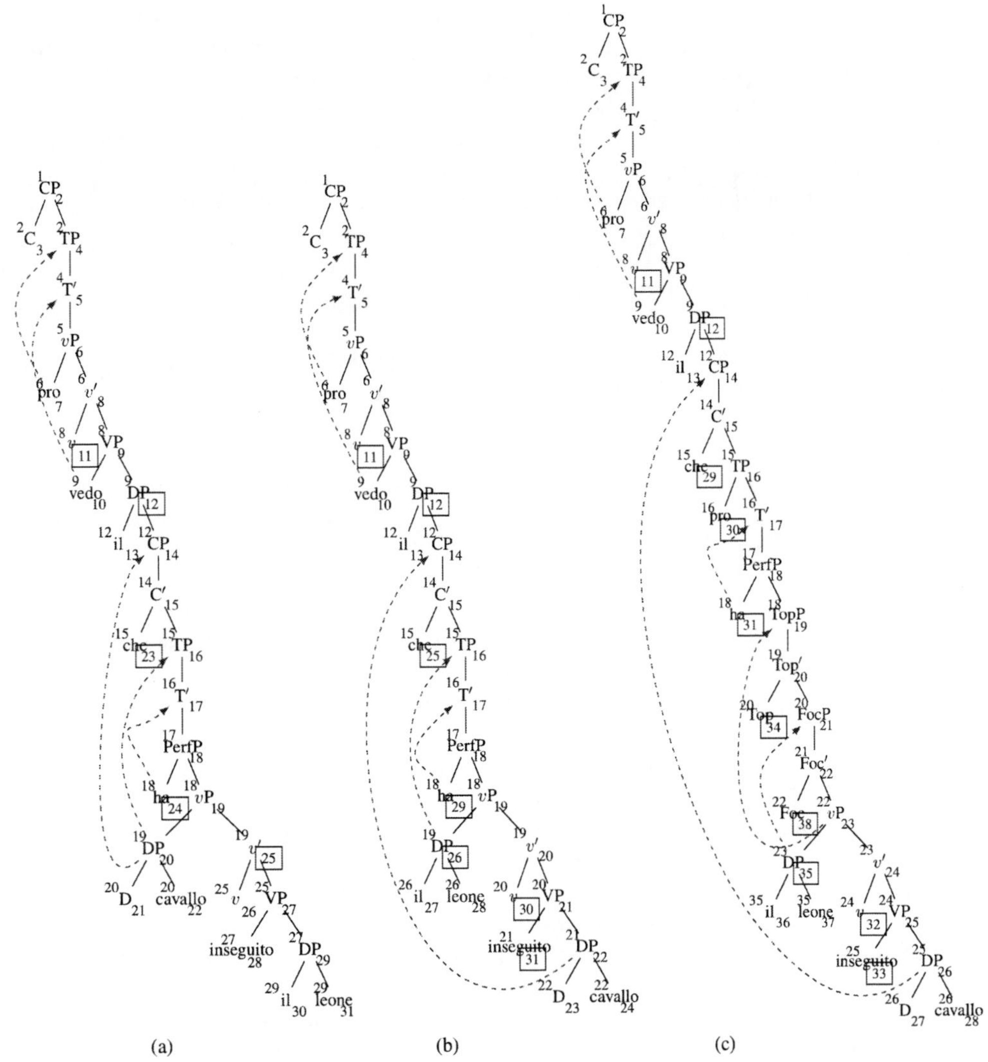

Figure 2: Annotated derivation trees for right-embedding (a) SRC, (b) ORC, and (c) ORCp.

aim of this paper is not to argue for the correctness (or lack thereof) of these accounts. Our purpose is to extend previous evaluations of memory metrics for a top-down MG parser as a reliable model of processing difficulty.

As discussed above, the MG parser has already been successful in accounting for RC asymmetries cross-linguistically (Graf et al., 2017; Zhang, 2017). Thus, Italian RCs are the perfect next step in understanding the plausibility of the model, allowing us to build on the insights provided by previous work while incrementally exploring new structural configurations. In particular, the fact that by assumption the MG parser ignores structural ambiguity (thus potential costs associated to reanalysis) and deterministically builds only the correct parse, makes ORCs with postverbal subjects an intriguing test case.

3.2 Syntactic Assumptions

The central tenant of the MG model is to take syntactic commitments seriously, so to explore how different aspects of sentence structure drive processing cost. The choice of a syntactic analysis is then particularly important. In line with most of the psycholinguistic literature on Italian RCs, this paper's analysis of postverbal subjects follows Belletti and Leonini (2004, a.o.). Specifically, I assume that in ORCp constructions the subject DP *[i leoni]* is merged in preverbal subject position Spec,*v*P, and then raised to a Spec,Focus position in the clause-internal *v*P periphery. The whole verbal cluster is raised to a clause-internal Spec,Topic position; and an expletive *pro* is base generated in Spec,TP and co-indexed with the postverbal subject (Fig. 2c).[3] Furthermore, again consistently with the Italian psycholinguistic literature (Arosio et al., 2017, a.o.), we adopt a promotion analysis of relative clauses (Kayne, 1994). That is to say, the head noun starts out as an argument of the embedded verb and undergoes movement into the specifier of the RC. The RC itself is treated as an NP, and selected by the determiner that would normally select the head noun in more traditional, head-external accounts (Chomsky, 1977).

4 Modeling Results

4.1 Core Results

I tested the parser performance on right-branching restrictive RCs of the form *(pro) vedo il cavallo [$_{RC}$ che ...]* (*I see the horse [$_{RC}$ that ...]*) — the RC head raising to the matrix object position, and the embedded relative clause either an SRC (1), an ORC (2), or an ORCp (4). The corresponding derivation trees, annotated by the MG parser with index and outdex values at each node, are shown in Fig. 2a, Fig. 2b, and Fig. 2c respectively. Recall that by assumption the parser is equipped with a perfect oracle, and that the complexity metrics are *only* sensitive to structural differences (i.e., the MG model is blind to agreement relationships). Contrasting (1) and (4) is then equivalent to contrasting (3a) and (3b). Thus, to reiterate the central tenents of the approach, these comparisons aim to model both the preference for SRC in ambiguous cases, and the overall increased processing difficulty of ORCps, just in terms of structural differences.

Modeling results show that the parser correctly predicts the gradient of difficulty observed for Italian RCs (SRC < ORC < ORCp), across a variety of complexity metrics.[4] In fact, the increased difficulty of ORCps over both SRCs and ORCs is predicted by *every* base (i.e., non ranked) metrics defined in (Graf et al., 2017). However, since the relationship between complexity metrics and the structure of a specific derivation tree is subtle, a detailed discussion of why each metric fares the way it does is not feasible within the scope of this paper. In what follows, I focus on two metrics that have been noted in previous studies as consistent predictors of processing difficulty: MAXT and SUMS.

The fact that MAXT (SRC: 8/*che*; ORC: 11/*ha*; ORCp:16/*Foc*) succeeds in predicting the reported processing preferences is encouraging, given the past success of this metric on many different constructions.[5] In particular, observe how the string-driven traversal strategy of the MG parser makes tenure sensitive to minor structural differences. In the SRC, *che* is introduced at step 15. Since, based on information in the input string, the parser is looking for the the subject DP *il cavallo*, *che* has to be kept in memory until the latter is found. Thus, it is flushed from memory at step 23. In the ORC, *che* is also put in memory at step 15. However, since the head of the relative clause is the embedded object, the parser will discard the standard CFG top-down strategy, ignore the subject DP, and keep expanding nodes until *il cavallo* is found. Thus, *che* cannot be flushed from memory until step 25.

The difference between SRC and ORC also highlights how tenure interacts with movement. Once *che* has been found in the SRC tree, the next node in the stack is *ha*, which can be discharged from memory immediately after. In the ORC however, the parser still has to find the subject DP. Thus, *ha* has to be kept in memory for the three additional steps that are required to conjecture and scan *il leone*.

Similarly, the maximum tenure recorded on the Foc head in ORCp highlights the cost of the additional movement steps postulated for this construction. The Foc node needs to wait until both the RC object *and* subject are built and scanned, before being itself discharged from the memory

---

[3]Technically, Belletti & Leonini (2004) assume that VP, not *v*P, raises to Spec,Topic. This follows from the authors adopting Collins (2005)'s smuggling analysis of passives directly. However, if we follow the traditional view of active verbs moving out of their base position to adjoin to little *v*, this analysis cannot hold as it would derive the wrong word order. Thus, I raise the whole *v*P cluster to Topic. This also seems to be in the spirit of what suggested by Belletti and Contemori (2009). But note that the modeling results in the following section would remain mostly unchanged even if we were to leave the *v*P shell in its base position, while both verb and object raise above.

[4]https://github.com/CompLab-StonyBrook/mgproc.

[5]These predictions hold even if we ignore tenure on unpronounced nodes — as suggested by Graf et al. (2017) — since we would obtain (SRC: 8/*that*; ORC: 11/*has*; ORCp:14/*that*.

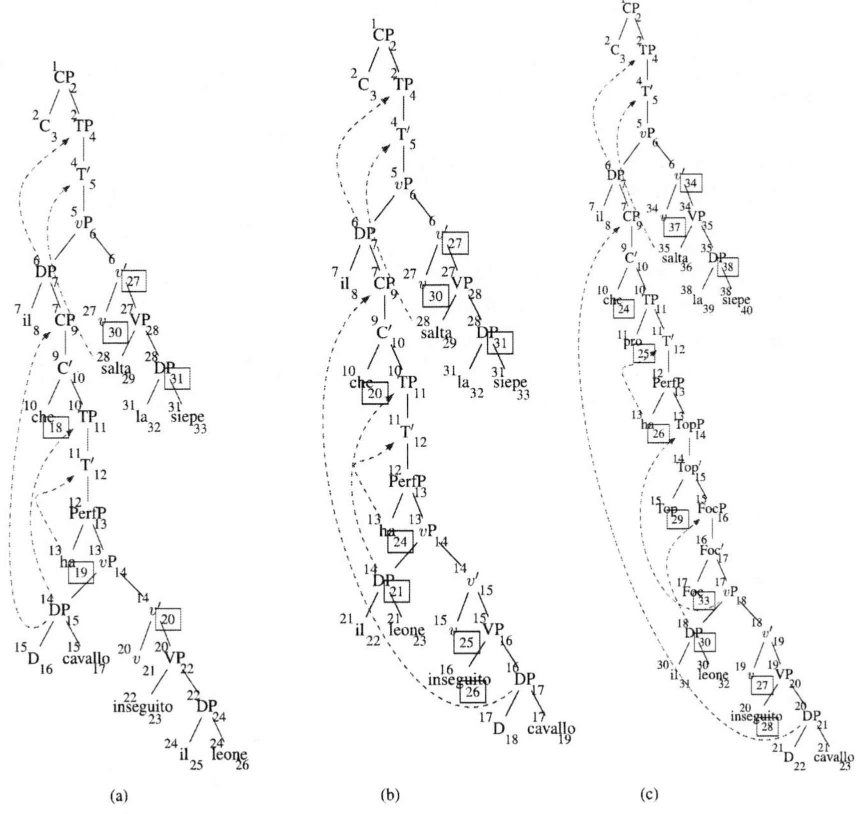

Figure 3: Annotated derivation trees for left-embedding (a) SRC (b) ORC and (c) ORCp.

queue.

4.2 Additional Simulations

From one side, the successful predictions made by MAXT are a welcome result, as they confirm the sensitivity of tenure-based metrics to fine-grained structural details. From the other though, one might wonder exactly how much these differences depend on the specific case study we are modeling. In this section, I partially address this issue by looking at variations in the construction of the RCs, and at two more processing asymmetries involving Italian post-verbal subjects.[6] I return to the general issue of the sensitivity of the MG results to syntactic choices in Sec. 5.

4.2.1 Left-Embedding RCs

Due to the string-driven nature of its traversal strategy, the MG parser is peculiarly sensitive to the depth of left- vs. right-embedding constructions. To control for this, I tested the parser pre-

dictions on sentences of the form *Il cavallo [RC che ...] salta la siepe* (*The horse [RC that ...] jumps the fence*, Fig. 3), with the head noun raising to the *subject* position in the matrix clause. Here, MAXT predicts that SRC and ORC should have the same processing complexity (they *tie*), since their memory differences are flattened by the increased tenure on the matrix *v'* (the Merge node expanding the matrix *v*P). The tenure of this node depends on the size of the matrix subject — thus, on the size of the relative clause. Since the size of the SRC and of the ORC is the same (the only thing changing being the site of extraction), MAXT for the whole sentence will never vary between the two constructions. This issue is solved by SUMS, which correctly predicts SRC < ORC, as well as the SRC/ORC < ORCp contrast.

Interestingly, MAXT also correctly predicts the increased difficulty of ORCps in these left-embedding cases. As seen above, MAXT flattens the differences in clauses with subject-modifying SRC/ORCs because the size of the RCs in subject

---

[6]Trees for these simulations can be found in Appendix A.

position is identical. This is not the case for OR-Cps, due the sequence of projections and movement steps involved in deriving postverbal subjects from the base SVO order. Thus, while MAXT in these sentences in still measured on the matrix v' (28), this value is also picking up on the additional steps required to derive the internal structure of the ORCp construction.

4.2.2 Postverbal Subjects in Matrix Clauses

In order to understand the complexity of the grammatical assumptions made for the postverbal subjects, we can look at processing asymmetries of postverbal constructions outside of RC environments. Consider Italian declarative sentences with a lexically empty subject position, like in (5).

(5) Ha chiamato Gio
Has called Giovanni

    a. "He/she/it called Gio"   **SVO**

    b. "Gio called"   **VS**

Without contextual/discourse cues, sentences like (5) are structurally ambiguous between a null-subject interpretation (5a) and a postverbal subject one (5b), with a marked processing preference for (5a) as compared to (5b) (De Vincenzi, 1991).

As summarized in Tbl. 1, both MAXT and SUMS predict the correct preferences under Belletti and Leonini (2004)'s analysis, as the Top and Foc heads have to wait for the whole vP to be found, before they can be discharged from memory themselves (cf. Fig. 4 and Fig. 5).

4.2.3 Unaccusatives vs. Unergatives

Finally, it is interesting to look at declarative sentences containing intransitive verbs of two classes: unaccusatives (6) and unergatives (7).

(6) È arrivato Gio
Is arrived Gio
"Gio arrived"   **Unaccusative**

(7) Ha corso Gio
Has ran Gio
"Gio ran"   **Unergative**

While on the surface these sentences look very similar, they differ in that the subject originates in postverbal position for unaccusatives but in preverbal position for unergatives (Belletti, 1988). Importantly, De Vincenzi (1991) reports faster reading times and higher comprehension accuracy for (6) over (7), a preference that is again correctly captured both by MAXT and SUMS (cf. Fig. 6

Clause Type	MaxT	SumS
obj. SRC	8/*che*	18
obj. ORC	11/*ha*	24
obj. ORCp	16/*Foc*	31
subj. SRC	21/*v'*	37
subj. ORC	21/*v'*	44
subj. ORCp	28/*v'*	56
matrix SVO	3/*ha*/*v'*	7
matrix VOS	7/*Top*/*Foc*	11
VS unacc	2/*v*P	3
VS unerg	7/*Top*/*Foc*	11

Table 1: Summary of MAXT (*value/node*) and SUMS by construction. Obj. and subj. indicate the landing site of the RC head in the matrix clause.

and Fig. 7). In particular, due to unaccusative subjects being base-generated postverbally, MAXT for these constructions is the lowest it can be (2, the tenure of any right sibling which is predicted and immediately discharged).

5 Discussion

The success of a top-down parser in modeling the processing difficulties of Italian RCs adds support to the MG model as a valuable theory of how processing cost is tied to structure.

As some reviewers point out though, one potential concern with the plausibility of the approach is in the degrees of freedom that are left to the model. In particular, the processing predictions depend on the interaction of three factors: the parsing strategy, the syntactic analysis, and the complexity metrics. Here, I put aside the choice of parsing strategy (but see Hunter, 2018; Stanojević and Stabler, 2018), and briefly address concerns about the remaining two factors.

Due the large number of existing metrics, it is conceivable that some combination of syntactic analysis and metric could have explained any other processing ranking among sentences. Similarly, it is possible that any syntactic analysis would make the right (i.e., empirically supported) predictions with some metric. Both these possibilities would undermine the relevance of this kind of modeling. Luckily, this does not seem to be the case. In fact, previous work has ruled out the vast majority of the existing metrics, by showing their insufficiency in accounting for some crucial constructions across a variety of possible grammatical analyses (Graf et al., 2017). Thus, it seems that underspecification is not an issue in practice.

The results in this paper are indeed consistent with these observations, as they show SUMS as a reliable complexity metric. Importantly, as subject-modifying SRCs and ORCs only *tie* on MAXT, these findings are also consistent with Graf et al. (2017)'s hypothesis that SUMS should be used a secondary metric to adjudicate between constructions, after they tie on MAXT.[7]

A second, reasonable concern is how much the correct predictions depend on the specific syntactic analysis of choice. Due to the richness of existing analyses and to space constraints, in this paper I only considered an analysis of Italian RCs and postverbal constructions which had been extensively referred to in the psycholinguistic literature. To partially address this concern though, I showed how SUMS and MAXT not only make the right predictions for RC constructions under a few different syntactic configurations, but they also correctly account for postverbal subject asymmetries in different kind of sentences. Nonetheless, an important future enterprise will be to look at alternative approaches to postverbal subject configurations, such as *right dislocation* (Antinucci and Cinque, 1977; Cardinaletti, 1998), or *leftward scrambling* (Ordóñez, 1998). Note though that these analyses all assume additional movement dependencies in the structure of ORCps compared to clauses with preverbal subjects. Given what this paper taught us about SUMS and MAXT, it seems probable that such dependencies would also be picked up by these metrics.

Independently on the specific predictions of the parser for alternative analyses though, the contributions of this line of inquiry would be twofold. From one side, it will improve our understanding of the MG model, by clarifying which aspects of sentence structure drive the parser's performance, and how they weight on the recruitment of memory resources as measured by different metrics. Secondly, grounded in the discriminative power given to MAXT and SUMS by their success across empirical phenomena, comparing the predictions made by the parser for different analyses of the same construction might help adjudicate between competing theoretical assumptions, as was the original goal of Kobele et al. (2013).

Clearly, the fact that the parser relies on an ide-

alized deterministic search strategy is one of the (potentially) most contentious assumption of the MG model, and could thus be used as yet another objection to the plausibility of the linking theory. As already mentioned, the goal is not to claim this as a comprehensive model of processing difficulty, as a cognitively realistic theory would see multiple factors interact with each other to derive the correct contrasts (Demberg and Keller, 2008; Brennan et al., 2016, a.o.). In principle though, the MG parser can be integrated with several of these additional factors (e.g., uncertainty; Hunter and Dyer, 2013; Yun et al., 2015). Crucially, the main advantage of the MG model is its transparent specification of the parser's behavior, which clarifies the effects of structural complexity on memory burden and would allow us to separate them from other effects contributing to processing load.

Moreover, while uncertainty is clearly a fundamental component of the human sentence processing system, the fact that an account deliberately abstracting away from all ambiguity can explain effects that would usually be attributed to it is an intriguing result. A fascinating open question is then whether we can characterize those phenomena where ambiguity really is the decisive factor, and cannot be "eliminated" from the model.

Finally, another advantage of having a computational model which provides a testable link between syntactic theory and behavioral data, is that it allows us to formally integrate structural hypotheses in existing psycholinguistic theories in a way that leads to precise quantitative predictions. However, as one reviewer observes, the complexity metrics exploited by the MG parser rely on very weak assumptions about the nature of human memory. In a sense, this could be considered a perk, as it leaves the model open to connections with a variety of sentence processing theories. In another sense though, this lack of cognitive plausibility weakens the impact of the approach, as it is often difficult to connect its results to more general concerns in the sentence processing literature. An important future research direction will thus be to re-evaluate the existing complexity metrics in light of psychological insights about human memory mechanisms (cf. Zhang, 2017).

Acknowledgments

I am extremely grateful to four anonymous reviewers for their insightful feedback.

---

[7] SUMS by itself does not seem to be enough, as it fails to predict the right preferences for contrasts like English right vs. center embedding (Graf et al., 2017).

References

Francesco Antinucci and Guglielmo Cinque. 1977. Sull'ordine delle parole in italiano: l'emarginazione. *Studi di grammatica italiana VI, pp. 121-146.*

Fabrizio Arosio, Flavia Adani, and Maria Teresa Guasti. 2009. Grammatical features in the comprehension of Italian Relative Clauses by children. *Merging Features: Computation, Interpretation, and Acquisition*, pages 138–158.

Fabrizio Arosio, Francesca Panzeri, Bruna Molteni, Santina Magazù, and Maria Teresa Guasti. 2017. The comprehension of Italian relative clauses in poor readers and in children with specific language impairment. *Glossa: a journal of general linguistics*, 2(1).

Elizabeth Bates and Brian MacWhinney. 1987. Competition, variation, and language leaning. *Mechanisms of language acquisition.*

Adriana Belletti. 1988. The case of unaccusatives. *Linguistic inquiry*, 19(1):1–34.

Adriana Belletti and Carla Contemori. 2009. Intervention and attraction. on the production of subject and object relatives by Italian (young) children and adults. In *Language acquisition and development, 3. Proceedings of Gala*, pages 39–52.

Adriana Belletti and Chiara Leonini. 2004. Subject inversion in L2 Italian. *EUROSLA yearbook*, 4:95–118.

Jonathan R Brennan, Edward P Stabler, Sarah E Van Wagenen, Wen-Ming Luh, and John T Hale. 2016. Abstract linguistic structure correlates with temporal activity during naturalistic comprehension. *Brain and Language*, 157:81–94.

Anna Cardinaletti. 1998. A second thought on" emarginazione": Destressing vs." right dislocation". *Working Papers in Linguistics, 8.2, 1998, pp. 1-28.*

Noam Chomsky. 1977. On wh-movement. *Formal syntax*, pages 71–132.

Chris Collins. 2005. A smuggling approach to the passive in english. *Syntax*, 8(2):81–120.

Marica De Vincenzi. 1991. *Syntactic parsing strategies in Italian: The minimal chain principle*, volume 12. Springer Science & Business Media.

Vera Demberg and Frank Keller. 2008. Data from eye-tracking corpora as evidence for theories of syntactic processing complexity. *Cognition*, 109(2):193 – 210.

Ulrich Hans Frauenfelder, Juan Segui, and Jacques Mehler. 1980. Monitoring around the relative clause. *Journal of Verbal Learning and Verbal Behavior*, 19(3):328–337.

Lyn Frazier. 1987. Syntactic processing: evidence from Dutch. *Natural Language & Linguistic Theory*, 5(4):519–559.

Naama Friedmann, Adriana Belletti, and Luigi Rizzi. 2009. Relativized relatives: Types of intervention in the acquisition of a-bar dependencies. *Lingua*, 119(1):67–88.

Sabrina Gerth. 2015. *Memory Limitations in Sentence Comprehension: A Structural-based Complexity Metric of Processing Difficulty*, volume 6. Universitätsverlag Potsdam.

Edward Gibson. 1998. Linguistic complexity: Locality of syntactic dependencies. *Cognition*, 68(1):1–76.

Edward Gibson. 2000. The dependency locality theory: A distance-based theory of linguistic complexity. *Image, language, brain*, pages 95–126.

Thomas Graf, Brigitta Fodor, James Monette, Gianpaul Rachiele, Aunika Warren, and Chong Zhang. 2015. A refined notion of memory usage for minimalist parsing. In *Proceedings of the 14th Meeting on the Mathematics of Language (MoL 2015)*, pages 1–14, Chicago, USA. Association for Computational Linguistics.

Thomas Graf and Bradley Marcinek. 2014. Evaluating evaluation metrics for minimalist parsing. In *Proceedings of the 2014 ACL Workshop on Cognitive Modeling and Computational Linguistics*, pages 28–36.

Thomas Graf, James Monette, and Chong Zhang. 2017. Relative clauses as a benchmark for Minimalist parsing. *Journal of Language Modelling*, 5:57–106.

John T Hale. 2011. What a rational parser would do. *Cognitive Science*, 35(3):399–443.

Henk Harkema. 2001. A characterization of minimalist languages. In *International Conference on Logical Aspects of Computational Linguistics*, pages 193–211. Springer.

Tim Hunter. 2018. Formal methods in experimental syntax. *The Oxford Handbook of Experimental Syntax.*

Tim Hunter and Chris Dyer. 2013. Distributions on minimalist grammar derivations. In *Proceedings of the 13th Meeting on the Mathematics of Language (MoL 13)*, pages 1–11.

Aravind K Joshi. 1990. Processing crossed and nested dependencies: An automation perspective on the psycholinguistic results. *Language and cognitive processes*, 5(1):1–27.

Richard S Kayne. 1994. *The antisymmetry of syntax.* 25. MIT Press.

Jonathan W King and Marta Kutas. 1995. Who did what and when? using word-and clause-level erps to monitor working memory usage in reading. *Journal of cognitive neuroscience*, 7(3):376–395.

Gregory Kobele, Christian Retoré, and Sylvain Salvati. 2007. An automata-theoretic approach to minimalism. In *Model Theoretic Syntax at 10*, pages 73–82. J. Rogers and S. Kepser.

Gregory M Kobele, Sabrina Gerth, and John Hale. 2013. Memory resource allocation in top-down minimalist parsing. In *Formal Grammar*, pages 32–51. Springer.

So Young Lee. 2018. A minimalist parsing account of attachment ambiguity in English and Korean. *Journal of Cognitive Science*, 19(3):291–329.

Roger Levy. 2013. Memory and surprisal in human sentence comprehension. In *Sentence processing*, pages 90–126. Psychology Press.

Richard L Lewis and Shravan Vasishth. 2005. An activation-based model of sentence processing as skilled memory retrieval. *Cognitive science*, 29(3):375–419.

Lei Liu. 2018. Minimalist Parsing of Heavy NP Shift. In *Proceedings of PACLIC 32 The 32nd Pacific Asia Conference on Language, Information and Computation*, The Hong Kong Polytechnic University, Hong Kong SAR.

Jens Michaelis. 1998. Derivational minimalism is mildly context–sensitive. In *International Conference on Logical Aspects of Computational Linguistics*, pages 179–198. Springer.

Francisco Ordóñez. 1998. Post-verbal asymmetries in Spanish. *Natural Language & Linguistic Theory*, 16(2):313–345.

Alan Prince and Paul Smolensky. 2008. *Optimality Theory: Constraint interaction in generative grammar*. John Wiley & Sons.

Owen Rambow and Aravind K Joshi. 1994. A processing model for free word order languages. *Perspectives on Sentence Processing*.

Herbert Schriefers, Angela D Friederici, and Katja Kuhn. 1995. The processing of locally ambiguous relative clauses in german. *Journal of Memory and Language*, 34(4):499.

Edward P Stabler. 1996. Derivational minimalism. In *International Conference on Logical Aspects of Computational Linguistics*, pages 68–95. Springer.

Edward P Stabler. 2011. Computational perspectives on minimalism. In *The Oxford Handbook of Linguistic Minimalism*.

Edward P Stabler. 2013. Two models of minimalist, incremental syntactic analysis. *Topics in cognitive science*, 5(3):611–633.

Miloš Stanojević and Edward Stabler. 2018. A sound and complete left-corner parsing for minimalist grammars. In *Proceedings of the Eight Workshop on Cognitive Aspects of Computational Language Learning and Processing*, pages 65–74.

Irene Utzeri. 2007. The production and acquisition of subject and object relative clauses in Italian: a comparative experimental study. *Nanzan Linguistics*, 2.

Francesca Volpato. 2010. *The acquisition of relative clauses and phi-features: evidence from hearing and hearing-impaired populations*. Ph.D. thesis, Università Ca'Foscari di Venezia.

Francesca Volpato and Flavia Adani. 2009. The subject/object relative clause asymmetry in Italian hearing-impaired children: evidence from a comprehension task. *Studies in Linguistics*, 3:269–281.

Jiwon Yun, Zhong Chen, Tim Hunter, John Whitman, and John Hale. 2015. Uncertainty in processing relative clauses across East Asian languages. *Journal of East Asian Linguistics*, 24(2):113–148.

Chong Zhang. 2017. *Stacked Relatives: Their Structure, Processing and Computation*. Ph.D. thesis, State University of New York at Stony Brook.

A Appendix

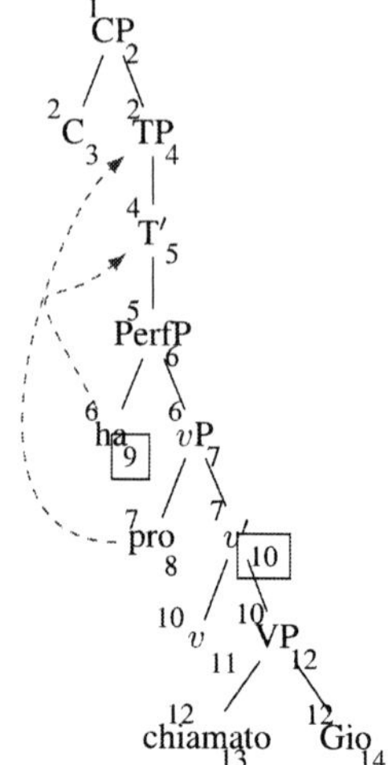

Figure 4: Annotated derivation tree for the SVO sentence in (5a)

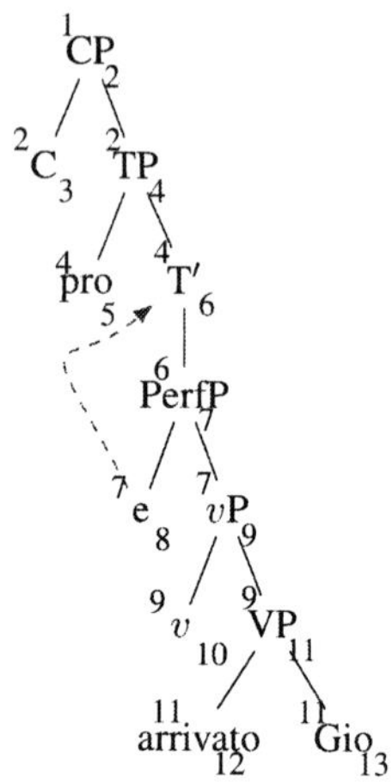

Figure 6: Annotated derivation trees for the unaccusative sentence in (6)

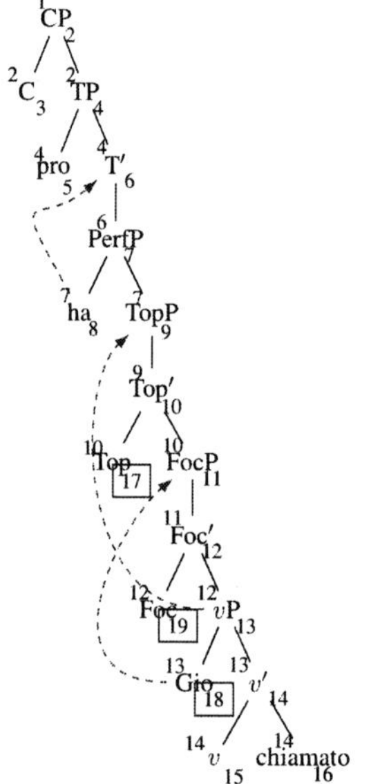

Figure 5: Annotated derivation trees for the VS sentences in (5b)

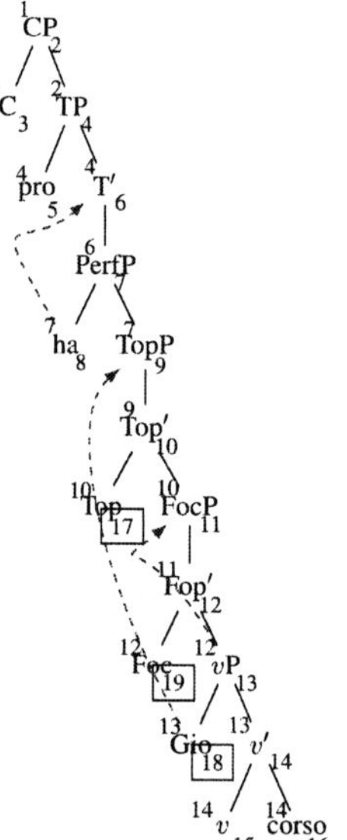

Figure 7: Annotated derivation trees for the unergative sentence in (7)

Quantifiers in a Multimodal World:
Hallucinating Vision with Language and Sound

Alberto Testoni
CIMeC - University of Trento
alberto.testoni@studenti.unitn.it

Sandro Pezzelle
ILLC - University of Amsterdam
s.pezzelle@uva.nl

Raffaella Bernardi
CIMeC, DISI - University of Trento
raffaella.bernardi@unitn.it

Abstract

Inspired by the literature on multisensory integration, we develop a computational model to ground quantifiers in perception. The model learns to pick out of nine quantifiers ('few', 'many', 'all', etc.) the one that is more likely to describe the percent of animals in a visual-auditory input containing both animals and artifacts. We show that relying on concurrent sensory inputs increases model performance on the quantification task. Moreover, we evaluate the model in a situation in which only the auditory modality is given, while the visual one is 'hallucinanted' either from the auditory input itself or from a linguistic caption describing the quantity of entities in the auditory input. This way, the model exploits *prior* associations between modalities. We show that the model profits from the prior knowledge and outperforms the auditory-only setting.

1 Introduction

Quantifiers (words like 'some', 'most', 'all') have long been the *holy grail* of formal semanticists (see Peters et al. (2006) for an overview). More recently, they have caught the attention of cognitive scientists, who showed that these expressions are handled by children quite early in life (Halberda et al., 2008), even before developing the ability to count (Hurewitz et al., 2006). Though some effort has been paid to model these high-frequency expressions from their use in big *corpora* of texts (Baroni et al., 2012; Herbelot and Vecchi, 2015), relatively little work has focused on the models' ability to quantify using these words.

In computer vision, some focus to the task of extracting quantities from images has been expressed through visual question answering, whose benchmark dataset (Antol et al., 2015) contains 'count questions' (e.g., 'How many Xs have the property Y?') that repeatedly turned out to be

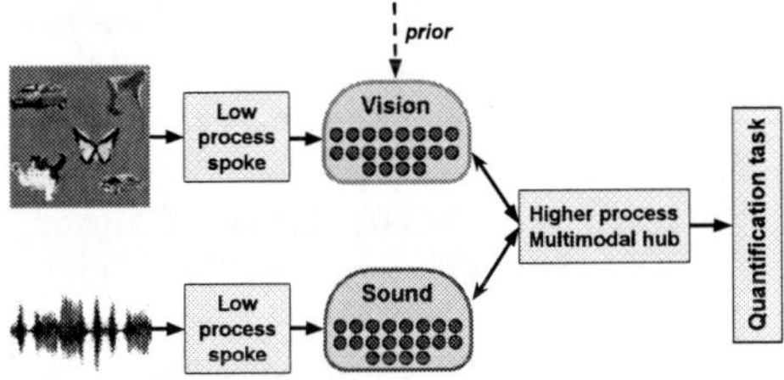

Figure 1: Learning to quantify through a 'Hub and Spoke' model enhanced with prior knowledge. The Hub learns to integrate multisensory inputs, whose representations (Spokes) are affected by such integration and can be 'hallucinated' by prior knowledge. We focus on how this prior knowledge hallucinates the visual representation (signalled by the dotted arrow).

rather challenging (Malinowski et al., 2015; Fukui et al., 2016). While this work paid little attention to quantifiers, a few recent studies specifically investigated their computational learning from visual inputs (Sorodoc et al., 2016; Pezzelle et al., 2017). These works built on the evidence that (part of) the meaning of quantifiers is *grounded* in perception. However, they only experimented with the visual modality, though the numerical representations humans derive from sensory inputs have been shown to be shared across modalities, e.g., vision and sound (Feigenson et al., 2004).

In the literature on multisensory integration it is well established that redundant information conveyed through different sensory inputs leads to a better performance on semantic tasks (McGurk and MacDonald, 1976). These findings have brought researchers to propose the 'Hub and Spoke' model (hence, H&S): concepts are learned by mutual interaction of the representation produced by sensory specific processors, the 'spokes', with a transmodal 'hub' (Patterson et al., 2007;

Proceedings of the Workshop on Cognitive Modeling and Computational Linguistics, pages 105–116
Minneapolis, USA, June 7, 2019. ©2019 Association for Computational Linguistics

Ralph et al., 2017). The role of the cross-modal hub is to take each of the spokes' output and to reproduce the correct information across the others by back-propagation (Ralph et al., 2017). There is evidence that memory recall is affected by the multisensory context in which the concept was learned. In particular, it has been shown that a congruent pair of audiovisual inputs may facilitate subsequent recall. In other words, we learn to process a sound (e.g., 'meow' or 'woof') and to associate it to the visual representation of the entity we see making it, and this facilitates the recall of the corresponding concept (i.e., 'cat' or 'dog').

In this work, we apply the H&S model to the conceptual learning of quantifiers and study how the hub learns to integrate the visual and auditory spoke representations (as illustrated in Figure 1) to perform the quantification task. That is, the model has to learn to say that 'none', 'few', 'most', etc. of the objects in the visual and auditory inputs belong to a given category, that of animals. We focus on 9 common quantifiers and experiment with visual and auditory inputs strongly aligned (viz., aligned at the entity level). We show that

- Using congruent audio visual inputs increases the performance of the model in learning quantifiers within single-sensory models;

- The H&S model can generalize to unseen data quite well. In particular, it generalizes better when trained on small combinations and tested on large ones than *vice versa*.

Furthermore, a second part of our work is based on an ongoing debate in multisensory integration, namely whether the processing of sensory inputs is passive or rather influenced by previous experience that creates cross-sensory associations. Within this debate, one of the most influential frameworks is the Predictive Coding Model (hence, PCM), according to which prior knowledge affects the representation of perceptual inputs (Friston, 2010). There is a general agreement on the *predictive* effects between visual and auditory inputs, whereas the role of language in priming visual perception is still under debate (see Simanova et al. (2016) for an overview).

Inspired by this work, we compare a single auditory sensory model with a model in which the processing of the auditory stimuli is facilitated by prior expectation elicited by either the visual spoke (implemented as a mapping from the experienced auditory input to its corresponding visual representation) or the language input (again implemented as a mapping from language to visual representations). In Figure 1, the 'prior' arrow illustrates this predictive factor. Simplifying somewhat, we simulate a setting where a model, trained to quantify from co-occurring synchronous audio visual inputs, is tested on a situation where (a) it *hears* but does not *see* the entities (audio-vision association prior) or (b) it *reads* a description of the entities and *hears* their sounds but does not *see* them (language-vision association prior). We show that

- Using priors hallucinating the visual representation improves the performance of the model compared to when it receives only auditory inputs;

- Language prior is slightly more effective than sound prior to hallucinate concurring vision.

2 Related Work

2.1 Multimodal Models

Fueled by the explosion of deep learning, much effort has been paid in recent years to develop models that exploit information from various modalities. Attention has been mostly on language and vision, for which various tasks have been proposed, i.e. image captioning (Hodosh et al., 2013), visual question answering (Antol et al., 2015; Goyal et al., 2017), visual reasoning (Andreas et al., 2016; Johnson et al., 2017; Suhr et al., 2017), visual storytelling (Huang et al., 2016; Gonzalez-Rico and Fuentes-Pineda, 2018), and visual dialogue (De Vries et al., 2017). While all this work combines images with *written* text, some other studies employed *spoken* language to perform various tasks, such as image-audio retrieval (Chrupała et al., 2017; Harwath et al., 2018). Overall, these works repeatedly showed that combining information from language and vision leads to representations that are beneficial in virtually any task.

A relatively recent strand of research focused on the integration of visual and *sound* information, where the latter is, e.g., the 'roar' of a fast car (Owens et al., 2016, 2018; Zhao et al., 2018).

More akin to our work is Aytar et al. (2017), who jointly investigated language, vision, and sound. By training a deep convolutional network for aligned representation learning across the three modalities, they showed that the emerging alignment improved both retrieval and classification performance. Interestingly, their results also suggested that, even though the network was never exposed to pairs of sounds and text inputs during training, an alignment between these two modalities was learned, possibly due to the use of images as an internal 'bridge'. We explore the same three modalities studied by Aytar et al. (2017). However, we use different models and evaluation settings (to mimic the PCM) and tackle a different task, namely quantification.

2.2 Computational Models of Quantification

The task of quantification (in the broad sense of providing some quantitative information), has been largely explored in computer vision (Seguí et al., 2015; Zhang et al., 2015a; Arteta et al., 2016). In these works, the focus is to provide the exact *number* of objects in a scene, and only rarely it is inspired by cognitive abilities (Zhang et al., 2015b; Chattopadhyay et al., 2017). Similarly, in the visual question answering community, the so called 'number' questions are almost exclusively about cardinals, with some exceptions including generalized quantifiers like *every* or *more than half* (Suhr et al., 2017; Kuhnle et al., 2018).

Inspired by the cognitive skill of Approximate Number Sense (ANS) is instead Stoianov and Zorzi (2012), which tested hierarchical generative networks and showed that they learn ANS as a statistical property of images. Practically speaking, the model was able to compare one approximate 'numerosity' against another and to perform a more/less task. Similar high-level cognitive abilities are required to humans to use *vague* quantifiers such as *few*, *many*, or *most*, whose meaning is heavily dependent on contextual factors. Using visual scenes as *context*, a recent strand of work has focused on the computational learning of quantifiers with neural networks. One approach tackled the task in a visual question answering fashion (Sorodoc et al., 2018), while another aimed at learning to apply the *correct* quantifier to a given scene (Sorodoc et al., 2016; Pezzelle et al., 2017).

More related to our work is Pezzelle et al. (2018b), which tested a model in the task of predicting the *probability* of each quantifier to be used in a given scene. The network was trained with probabilities from human participants by Pezzelle

et al. (2018a). We use the same human annotation but make two steps further: First, we also experiment with auditory inputs; second, we experiment with different settings inspired by the literature on multisensory integration.

3 Task and Datasets

3.1 Task

Given an input (a scene) consisting of entities that are either animals (targets) or artifacts (distractors), the model has to quantify the former. For instance, given the image in Figure 2 on the left, it should assign a high probability to 'most', whereas for the image on the right it should assign a high probability to 'few'. The inputs are either unimodal (sound, vision) or multimodal (sound+*real* vision, sound+*hallucinated* vision). We inherit and adapt to our multimodal datasets the gold standard annotation collected by Pezzelle et al. (2018a): Human participants were asked to select, out of nine quantifiers ('none', 'almost none', 'few', 'the smaller part', 'some', 'many', 'most', 'almost all', 'all'), the one that best referred to the set of animals depicted in a briefly-presented visual scene (these scenes were similar, but not identical to those in Figure 2). Each quantifier turned out to be used to refer to various proportions of animals. For instance, 'most' could apply when animals corresponded to 57%, 60%, 67%, 75% and 80% of the objects. At the same time, various proportions had different probabilities to be referred by a given quantifier. With a proportion of 60% animals, for example, the probability to choose 'most', 'many' and 'some' is 0.52, 0.20 and 0.18, respectively. The models have to learn the probability distribution associated with each proportion. Intuitively, 'none' and 'all' are almost exclusively used with, respectively, 0% and 100% animals.

3.2 Datasets

Following Pezzelle et al. (2018a), our datasets consist of scenes containing animals and artifacts with a minimum of 3 and a maximum of 20 entities in total. There are in total 17 proportions, out of which 8 contain more animals than artifacts, 8 contain more artifacts than animals, and 1 contains an equal number of them.[1] For each proportion

---

[1] The proportions obtained by having min. 3 max 20 objects are: 0%, 10%, 17%, 20%, 25%, 33%, 40%, 43%, 50%, 57%, 60%, 67%, 75%, 80%, 83%, 90%, 100%.

Figure 2: Visual dataset. Left: 'most' (60%) of the objects are animals, viz. 3:2. Right: 'few' (20%) of the objects are animals, viz. 1:4.

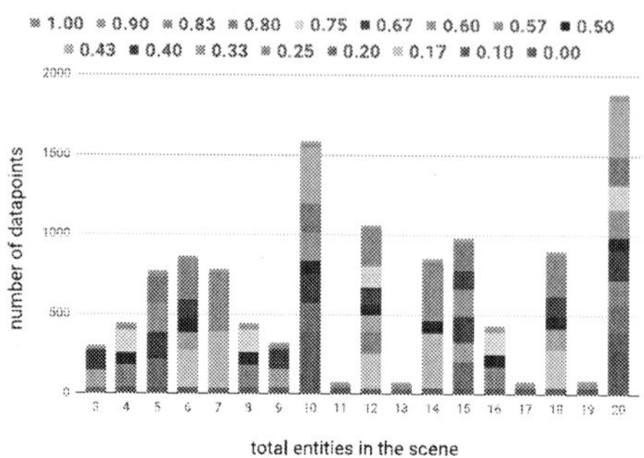

Figure 3: Histogram representing the number of total objects in the scene for the 17 different proportions (training set). On top the 17 proportions.

we generated scenes containing all possible combinations of cardinalities: For the proportion 0%, for example, 17 combinations were built, ranging from 0:3 (0 animals, 3 artifacts) to 0:20.

We built visual and auditory datasets aligned at the entity level: For each image, we created the corresponding auditory datapoint containing the sound of each entity in the image. By so doing, using the terminology of (Aytar et al., 2018), we obtained strongly aligned visual and auditory datasets. In total, we used 55 unique animals and 55 unique artifacts. We only used those entities for which we could have whole-depicting images (not just parts) and for which we had a corresponding sound. Furthermore, for each audio-visual input we created a corresponding linguistic caption describing the quantities of the entities in it. Details on the three datasets are provided below.

Visual Dataset Similarly to Pezzelle et al. (2018b), we built a large dataset of synthetic visual scenes depicting a variable number of animals and artifacts on top of a neutral grey background (see Figure 2). The scenes were automatically generated using the following pipeline: (a) Natural images depicting target objects (e.g., a dog) or distractors (e.g., a car) were randomly picked up from the 110 entities pre-selected from the dataset by Kiani et al. (2007). As opposed to the synthetic dataset of Pezzelle et al. (2018a), where multiple copies of the same animal/artifact were reproduced in the scene, we have different target/distractor instances in each scenario (e.g, different instances of 'car' as in Figure 2 (right)). However, we do not vary the size and orientation of entities; (b) The proportion of targets in the scene was chosen by selecting only those matching the 17 pre-defined proportions mentioned above. We generated 17K scenes balanced

per proportion (1K scenes/proportion), and split them into train (70%), validation (10%), and test (20%) sets. The distribution of proportions per total number of objects in the training set is illustrated in Figure 3.

Auditory Dataset We followed a similar procedure to build the auditory scenes. We took Audioset (Gemmeke et al., 2017) as our starting point to obtain sounds corresponding to the entities since it contains a huge collection of human-labeled 10-sec sound clips. It is organized as a hierarchical graph of event categories, covering a wide range of human and animal sounds, musical instruments and genres, and common everyday environmental sounds. We took sounds belonging to the categories of 'animals' and 'tools'. We built our auditory dataset starting from the visual one described above and obtained the strongly aligned auditory version. Hence, as in the case of the visual datapoint, an auditory datapoint can contain different instances of the same type of animal/artifact. The auditory dataset consists of 17K scenes again balanced per proportion (1K scenes/proportion), with the same split as the visual one and each 'scene' containing min 3 max 20 entities out of 110 entities.

Linguistic Dataset For each aligned visual and auditory input pair, we built a linguistic caption describing the exact quantities of the entities present in it (for instance, for the image in Figure 2 (left), we obtain 'There are one butterfly, two automobiles and two mammals'). The procedure, illustrated in Figure 4, is as following: (a) We manually annotated each of the 110 entities used to

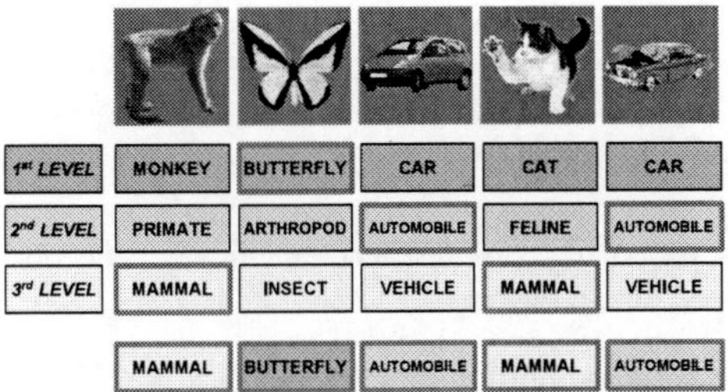

Figure 4: Linguistic dataset construction. In red: randomly selected nouns for each entity. Bottom: generated caption.

build the dataset (55 animals and 55 artifacts) with 3 nouns expressing different levels of an ontological hierarchy (e.g., 'cat', 'feline', 'mammal').[2] (b) For each entity present in the audio-visual scene, we randomly picked one of the three nouns. (c) For each noun, we counted the number of entities present in the audio-visual input, assigned that number to the noun and pluralized it, if necessary. (d) In order to account for more variability, we started the linguistic caption by choosing one of six possible starting phrases.[3] We obtained captions with on average 10.5 nouns (standard deviation: 4.53).

Sensory Representations The vector representation of the *visual* scene is extracted using Inception v3 CNN (Szegedy et al., 2016) pretrained on ImageNet (Deng et al., 2009) from the last average pooling layer which consists of 2048-d visual vectors.

For the *auditory* dataset, we built the representation of each entity and the scenes containing them as following. We started from the audio features computed with the VGG-inspired auditory model described in Hershey et al. (2017) which has been trained on a preliminary version of YouTube-8M.[4] For each second of a sound clip, the model produces a 128-d vector; hence each 10-sec sound clip of the Audioset dataset (Gemmeke et al., 2017) would be represented by a 1280-d vector. To work with smaller and more representative vectors, we selected the two central seconds of each 10-sec audio clip (the 5th and 6th) and used the resulting 256-d vector as the representation of the corresponding entity. Out of these entity representations we built the representation of the scene by concatenating the entity vectors. Scenes can contain min 3 and max 20 entities, hence we use vectors of 20 'cells'. When there are less than 20 entities, there are 'empty cells' which are visually represented by the grey background. We represented their auditory counterpart with a 'silent sound' computed as following: we recorded a 10-sec sound clip of silence, picked the 5th and 6th seconds and obtained the 256-d auditory vector using the model of Hershey et al. (2017). The 20 total 'cells' are then shuffled, resulting in a 5120-d auditory vector.

As for the *linguistic* scenes, for each caption we extracted the features through the Universal Sentence Encoder (USE) (Cer et al., 2018) producing 512 dimensional vectors for each sentence. Alternatively, we could have used LSTM modules to process from scratch both the linguistic and acoustic inputs exploiting their sequential nature. We rejected this alternative mainly to avoid that, during the training process, the neural network learns task-dependent representations and arbitrary associations. It has been shown (e.g., in Cer et al. (2018)) that USE provides sentence-level embeddings with strong transfer performance on several NLP tasks. We consider this point as a strong motivation for our choice: in this way, we get more consistent representations across different modalities and the overall architecture turns out to be easier, more scalable and less prone to learn task-specific representations.

The semantic spaces containing the entity representations of the three modalities are rather different. It is interesting to note that the auditory dataset is much more dense than either the visual or the linguistic one: The average cosine similarity between entity pairs is 0.73 for sound vs. 0.44 for vision and 0.43 for language. In other words, entities are visually and linguistically much more distinct than auditorily. This could be possibly due to the fact that, as highlighted by Owens et al. (2018), sound undergoes less transformations than vision, which is affected by, for instance, lighting, scene composition, and viewing angle. In other words, sound could be denser than vision since it

---

[2] Note that in the case of animals, this hierarchy is much more easier to build (e.g. Linnaean taxonomy) while for the artifacts the 3 nouns are generally more often synonyms and often do not represent a real hierarchy/taxonomy.

[3] 'There are …' , 'It seems to me that there are …', 'I'm thinking of …', 'I can spot …', 'There exists …', 'I can spot …').

[4] https://research.google.com/youtube8m/

'abstracts' from all the possible visual transformations that we encounter in the other modality. It follows that integrating these modalities requires some degree of generalization over a variety of transformations, which is intuitively not trivial.

4 Models and Test Settings

Below we describe the 'Hub and Spoke' model (H&S) that takes as input strongly aligned auditory and visual inputs, and the 'Predictive Code Model' (PCM) which differs from the former only at testing time, when it takes as input the vector processed by the auditory spoke and the visual representation obtained by prior knowledge, viz. through an external mapping. We take as baselines the single-modality (visual, auditory inputs) versions of the model.

Hub and Spoke model (H&S)   As illustrated in Figure 5 (up), this model takes the 2048-d and 5120-d visual and auditory vectors, reduces them to vectors of the same dimensions (512-d) and merges them in the Hub through multiplication. The multimodal output is reduced to 128-d via a ReLU hidden layer, then a softmax layer is applied to output a 9-d vector with the probabilities to assign each of the 9 quantifiers.

Unimodal model   The three layers of the hub described above are trained to perform the quantification task from either the visual or auditory representations alone.

Predictive Code Model (PCM)   We take the hub trained using the representations produced by the visual and auditory spokes (namely the hub of the H&S) and evaluate it on new types of audio-visual inputs: the auditory vectors are produced by the auditory spoke as for the H&S, while the visual vectors are obtained via a linear mapping function that simulates *prior knowledge* which 'hallucinates' the visual perception. The mapping function takes as input either (a) the auditory input itself (auditory prior) or (b) the corresponding linguistic caption (language prior), as illustrated in Figure 5 (bottom, (a) left vs. (b) right). For sake of simplicity, the mapping function is trained outside the model. It is implemented as a linear neural network which is exposed to the aligned data of the training and validation sets used for the H&S. Hence, when used in the PCM setting it is applied to data that was never seen before. The mapping is trained using Mean Squared Error (MSE).

We only experimented with hallucinated visual representations and left for the future the other direction – a visual experience facilitated by the corresponding imagined auditory. Since the semantic space of the auditory input is rather dense, we expect that a non-linear mapping might be necessary to obtain the latter.

Implementation details   We used ReLU activation function for all the hidden layers, and Adam optimizer (Kingma and Ba, 2015) with learning rate = 0.0001 and default weight decay. All models were trained for no more than 150 epochs (using early stopping) by minimizing the Kullback-Leibler (KL) divergence loss between the activations by softmax and the probability distribution of human responses for each proportion by Pezzelle et al. (2018a). All models were implemented in PyTorch v0.4.

5 Experiments and Results

Evaluation   All models are evaluated by computing the Pearson product-moment correlation coefficient between the Softmax probabilities and the 9-d vectors from Pezzelle et al. (2018a), which encode the probability of each quantifier to be used with respect to a given proportion based on human choices.

5.1 Experiments

Unimodal vs. multimodal models   Testing the models on the unimodal and multimodal data might lead to results that are influenced by the different sizes of data seen during training. To rule out this possibility, we use unimodal and multimodal datasets of equal size. We take 11,900 datapoints for each single modality; and in the multimodal model, we use 5950 instances for each modality which sum up to 11,900 datapoints.

Incongruent visual-auditory inputs   In order to test the effectiveness of the integration of the two modalities, we take the H&S trained on aligned (congruent) visual-auditory data and we test it with incongruent data, viz. inputs that do not have the same proportion of animals. Given a visual input containing, e.g., 3 animals and 2 artifacts (as in Figure 2 left), we pair it with an auditory input having 3 artifacts and 2 animals. This way, the corresponding probability distributions are different, hence we refer to these pairs as *incongruent auditory* input. Similarly, we generate *incongruent vi-*

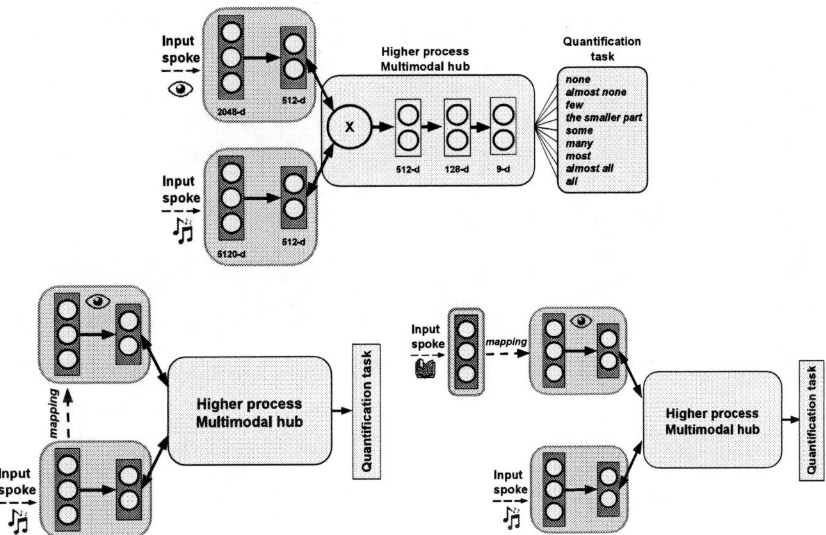

Figure 5: Up: **H&S** To learn quantifiers, the hub learns to integrate the auditory and visual sensory inputs; Bottom: **PCM** The hub trained to perform audio-visual integration can quantify the animals present in the auditory inputs by exploiting the 'hallucinated' visual representation obtained either from (a) the auditory input it self (left corner) or (b) the the language input (right corner).

sual inputs by pairing an auditory input with, e.g, a 3:2 proportion with a visual input with a proportion of 2:3, and consider as the correct probability distribution the one corresponding to the 3:2 proportion encoded by the auditory input. To ensure that the difference between the two modalities is high, we avoid pairing proportions with extremely similar probability distributions. Rather, we focus on a subset of proportion pairs, namely 0-100%, 10-90%, and 17-83%. If the hub exploits the alignment between the modalities, we expect the model to perform poorly in this setting (lower is better).

Unseen combinations We evaluate the generalization power of the models by testing them on unseen data. We want to study how well the model generalizes from (a) small cardinalities to larger ones and (b) vice versa. To this end, we divide the training and test sets as following: For each of the 17 proportions, we use as the test set the scenes containing (a) the largest possible number of objects (e.g., for proportion 0%, we test on 0:20 and train on all the other combinations); (b) the smallest possible number of objects (e.g., for proportion 0%, we test on 0:3 and train on all the other combinations).

	Pearson's r
Sound	0.68
Vision	0.72
H&S	0.86
PCM: auditory prior	0.78
PCM: language prior	0.81
H&S on incongruent visual inputs	-0.25
H&S on incongruent auditory inputs	0.02

Table 1: Pearson's r correlation results - human judgments used as target results. Unimodal vs. multimodal model trained and tested on datasets of equal size.

5.2 Quantitative Results

Unimodal vs. multimodal models Table 1 reports the Pearson's r correlation results comparing the unimodal and multimodal models. As we can see, the visual data is slightly more informative than the auditory one for learning the quantification task (0.68 vs. 0.72). The first main result is that the multimodal model outperforms the unimodal ones to a large extent. The H&S obtains 0.18 and 0.14 higher correlation than the auditory and visual model, respectively. This result shows that the multimodal data provide complementary information that the model manages to exploit. Regarding the effect of prior knowledge,

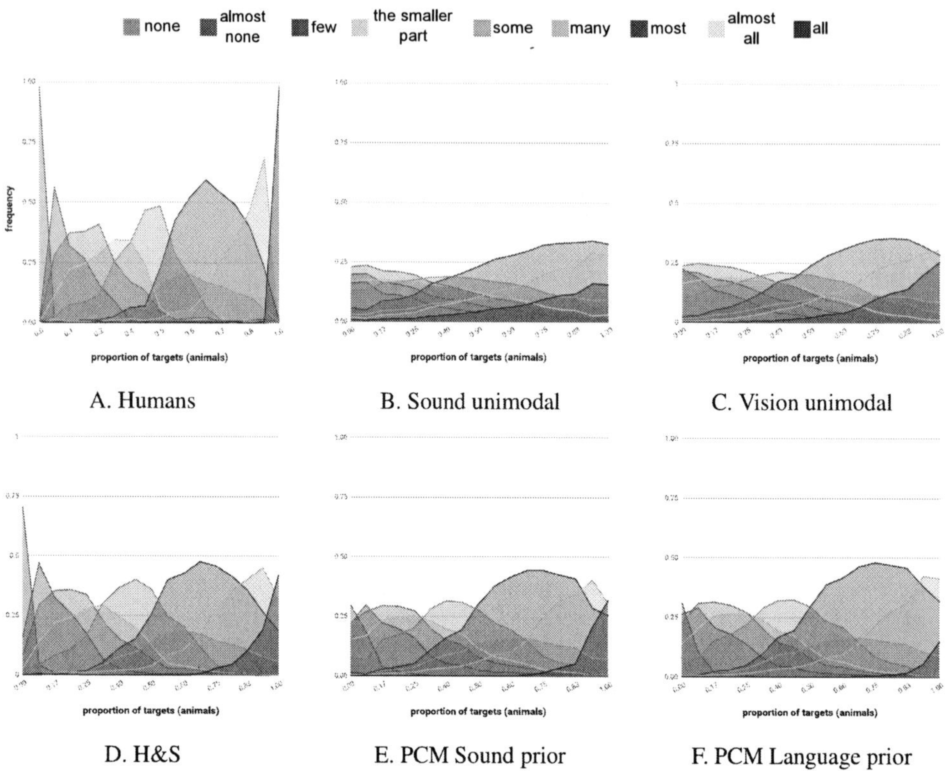

Figure 6: A: Density plot reporting the frequency of human responses for the 9 quantifiers (y-axis) against the proportion of targets in the scene (x-axis). B-F: Average probabilities predicted by models in test set (same axes).

	Pearson's r	
	large $\rightarrow$ small	small $\rightarrow$ large
Sound	0.55	0.73
Vision	0.64	0.76
H&S	0.74	0.85

Table 2: Unimodal vs. multimodal models tested on unseen combinations which have smaller or larger number of entities than the seen data.

we see that hallucinating the visual representations improves over processing only the auditory input. Using the latter to hallucinate the visual scene leads to an increase of 0.10 in correlation, and an even higher increase (+0.13) is obtained when the hallucination is induced by a linguistic description of the scene. It is worth noticing, however, that the correlation values obtained by the PCMs are slightly lower than the one obtained by the H&S. This is intuitive since the latter can capitalize on *first-hand* information from both modalities.

To better understand the behavior of the multimodal model, we scrutinize its results by investigating whether the absolute difference between the animals and artifacts sets has an impact on the performance of the model. Figure 7 reports Pearson's r obtained by the H&S model for the smallest and highest combination of each proportion (we do not plot proportion 0.5 since the distance is 0 for all its combinations). For instance, for proportion 67%, the smallest combination is 2/3 (2 targets, 1 non-targets), the largest combination is 12/18 (12, 6), and their absolute difference is equal to 1 and 6, respectively. As can be seen from the plot, smaller absolute differences are always harder than higher ones.

Incongruent sensory pairs As the results in Table 1 show, the model is strongly sensitive to these incongruent data, suggesting that cross-modal integration is actually part of the models.

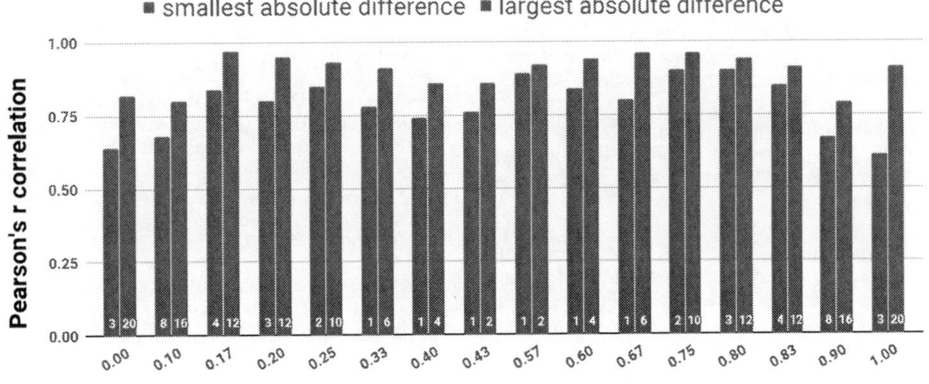

Figure 7: H&S Pearson's r obtained for the smallest (blue) and biggest (red) combination of each proportion. Note that numbers in white at the bottom of each bar refer to the absolute difference between animals and artifacts sets.

Unseen combinations Table 2 shows that models are able to generalize to unseen combinations quite well. In particular, they turn out to be *always* better in generalization when they learn from small combinations and are tested on large ones. This pattern of results reflects the findings illustrated in Figure 7, assuming that a model trained on hard cases and tested on easier ones would lead to higher results compared to the opposite 'direction'.

5.3   Qualitative Results

Figure 6 compares the probability distributions learned by the tested models (panels B-F) against the distribution of responses by humans (panel A) from Pezzelle et al. (2018a). As can be clearly seen, both unimodal models (B-C) show a much lower correlation with human data compared to either H&S (D) or PCMs (E-F). In particular, the unimodal models tend to produce very similar curves for all quantifiers, thus predicting them with a similar probability at any proportion (i.e., there are no clear 'peaks'). Both the H&S and the PCMs, in contrast, output a distribution that is very similar to that by humans (mirrored in the results of Table 1). While plots D-F are almost identical, it can be noted that the H&S is slightly better than both PCMs at the 'extreme' proportions, particularly 0% and 100%. We conjecture this ability is responsible of the slightly higher correlation obtained by this model compared to the PCMs.

6   Conclusion

In this paper, we show that concurrent multisensory information bootstraps models performance in a semantic task, namely grounding quantifiers, in line with the results on human perception. Also, we provide computational evidence that the predicting code hypothesis advocated in the cognitive literature is an interesting and useful source of inspiration for computational models. We plan to further investigate how predictions from prior knowledge can be compared with those obtained through sensory experience to further improve the performance on semantic tasks.

Acknowledgements

We kindly acknowledge the support of NVIDIA Corporation with the donation to the University of Trento of the GPUs used in our research. We thank Aurélie Herbelot, Manuela Piazza, and Marco Marelli for their valuable comments. The second author is funded by the Netherlands Organisation for Scientific Research (NWO) under VIDI grant no. 276-89-008, *Asymmetry in Conversation*.

References

Jacob Andreas, Marcus Rohrbach, Trevor Darrell, and Dan Klein. 2016. Neural module networks. In *Proceedings of the IEEE Conference on Computer Vision and Pattern Recognition*, pages 39–48.

Stanislaw Antol, Aishwarya Agrawal, Jiasen Lu, Margaret Mitchell, Dhruv Batra, C Lawrence Zitnick, and Devi Parikh. 2015. Vqa: Visual question answering. In *Proceedings of the IEEE international conference on computer vision*, pages 2425–2433.

Carlos Arteta, Victor Lempitsky, and Andrew Zisserman. 2016. Counting in the wild. In *European Conference on Computer Vision*, pages 483–498. Springer.

Yusuf Aytar, Lluis Castrejon, Carl Vondrick, Hamed Pirsiavash, and Antonio Torralba. 2018. Cross-modal scene networks. *IEEE transactions on pattern analysis and machine intelligence*, 40(10):2303–2314.

Yusuf Aytar, Carl Vondrick, and Antonio Torralba. 2017. See, hear, and read: Deep aligned representations. *arXiv preprint arXiv:1706.00932*.

Marco Baroni, Raffaella Bernardi, Ngoc-Quynh Do, and Chung-chieh Shan. 2012. Entailment above the word level in distributional semantics. In *Proceedings of the 13th Conference of the European Chapter of the Association for Computational Linguistics*, pages 23–32. Association for Computational Linguistics.

Daniel Cer, Yinfei Yang, Sheng-yi Kong, Nan Hua, Nicole Limtiaco, Rhomni St John, Noah Constant, Mario Guajardo-Cespedes, Steve Yuan, Chris Tar, et al. 2018. Universal sentence encoder. *arXiv preprint arXiv:1803.11175*.

Prithvijit Chattopadhyay, Ramakrishna Vedantam, Ramprasaath R. Selvaraju, Dhruv Batra, and Devi Parikh. 2017. Counting everyday objects in everyday scenes. In *The IEEE Conference on Computer Vision and Pattern Recognition (CVPR)*.

Grzegorz Chrupała, Lieke Gelderloos, and Afra Alishahi. 2017. Representations of language in a model of visually grounded speech signal. In *Proceedings of the 55th Annual Meeting of the Association for Computational Linguistics (Volume 1: Long Papers)*, volume 1, pages 613–622.

Harm De Vries, Florian Strub, Sarath Chandar, Olivier Pietquin, Hugo Larochelle, and Aaron C Courville. 2017. GuessWhat?! Visual object discovery through multi-modal dialogue. In *CVPR*, volume 1, page 3.

Jia Deng, Wei Dong, Richard Socher, Li-Jia Li, Kai Li, and Li Fei-Fei. 2009. Imagenet: A large-scale hierarchical image database. In *Computer Vision and Pattern Recognition, 2009. CVPR 2009. IEEE Conference on*, pages 248–255. Ieee.

Lisa Feigenson, Stanislas Dehaene, and Elizabeth Spelke. 2004. Core systems of number. *Trends in cognitive sciences*, 8(7):307–314.

K. Friston. 2010. The free-energy principle: an unified brain theory? *Thefree-energyprinciple:aunifiedbraintheory?*, 11:127–138. Doi:10.1038/nrn2787.

Akira Fukui, Dong Huk Park, Daylen Yang, Anna Rohrbach, Trevor Darrell, and Marcus Rohrbach. 2016. Multimodal compact bilinear pooling for visual question answering and visual grounding. In *Proceedings of the 2016 Conference on Empirical Methods in Natural Language Processing*, pages 457–468.

Jort F Gemmeke, Daniel PW Ellis, Dylan Freedman, Aren Jansen, Wade Lawrence, R Channing Moore, Manoj Plakal, and Marvin Ritter. 2017. Audio set: An ontology and human-labeled dataset for audio events. In *Acoustics, Speech and Signal Processing (ICASSP), 2017 IEEE International Conference on*, pages 776–780. IEEE.

Diana Gonzalez-Rico and Gibran Fuentes-Pineda. 2018. Contextualize, Show and Tell: A Neural Visual Storyteller. *arXiv preprint arXiv:1806.00738*.

Yash Goyal, Tejas Khot, Douglas Summers-Stay, Dhruv Batra, and Devi Parikh. 2017. Making the V in VQA matter: Elevating the role of image understanding in Visual Question Answering. In *CVPR*, volume 1, page 3.

Justin Halberda, Len Taing, and Jeffrey Lidz. 2008. The development of "most" comprehension and its potential dependence on counting ability in preschoolers. *Language Learning and Development*, 4(2):99–121.

David Harwath, Adrià Recasens, Dídac Surís, Galen Chuang, Antonio Torralba, and James Glass. 2018. Jointly discovering visual objects and spoken words from raw sensory input. In *Proceedings of the European Conference on Computer Vision (ECCV)*, pages 649–665.

Aurélie Herbelot and Eva Maria Vecchi. 2015. Building a shared world: Mapping distributional to model-theoretic semantic spaces. In *Proceedings of the 2015 Conference on Empirical Methods in Natural Language Processing*, pages 22–32.

Shawn Hershey, Sourish Chaudhuri, Daniel PW Ellis, Jort F Gemmeke, Aren Jansen, R Channing Moore, Manoj Plakal, Devin Platt, Rif A Saurous, Bryan Seybold, et al. 2017. Cnn architectures for large-scale audio classification. In *Acoustics, Speech and Signal Processing (ICASSP), 2017 IEEE International Conference on*, pages 131–135. IEEE.

Micah Hodosh, Peter Young, and Julia Hockenmaier. 2013. Framing image description as a ranking task: Data, models and evaluation metrics. *Journal of Artificial Intelligence Research*, 47:853–899.

Ting-Hao Kenneth Huang, Francis Ferraro, Nasrin Mostafazadeh, Ishan Misra, Aishwarya Agrawal, Jacob Devlin, Ross Girshick, Xiaodong He, Pushmeet

Kohli, Dhruv Batra, et al. 2016. Visual storytelling. In *Proceedings of the 2016 Conference of the North American Chapter of the Association for Computational Linguistics: Human Language Technologies*, pages 1233–1239.

Felicia Hurewitz, Anna Papafragou, Lila Gleitman, and Rochel Gelman. 2006. Asymmetries in the acquisition of numbers and quantifiers. *Language learning and development*, 2(2):77–96.

Justin Johnson, Bharath Hariharan, Laurens van der Maaten, Li Fei-Fei, C Lawrence Zitnick, and Ross Girshick. 2017. CLEVR: A diagnostic dataset for compositional language and elementary visual reasoning. In *Computer Vision and Pattern Recognition (CVPR), 2017 IEEE Conference on*, pages 1988–1997. IEEE.

Roozbeh Kiani, Hossein Esteky, Koorosh Mirpour, and Keiji Tanaka. 2007. Object category structure in response patterns of neuronal population in monkey inferior temporal cortex. *Journal of neurophysiology*, 97(6):4296–4309.

Diederick P Kingma and Jimmy Ba. 2015. Adam: A method for stochastic optimization. In *International Conference on Learning Representations (ICLR)*.

Alexander Kuhnle, Huiyuan Xie, and Ann Copestake. 2018. How clever is the FiLM model, and how clever can it be? In *European Conference on Computer Vision*, pages 162–172. Springer.

Mateusz Malinowski, Marcus Rohrbach, and Mario Fritz. 2015. Ask your neurons: A neural-based approach to answering questions about images. In *Proceedings of the IEEE international conference on computer vision*, pages 1–9.

H. McGurk and J. MacDonald. 1976. Hearing lips and seeing voices. *Nature*, 264:746–748. Doi:10.1038/264746a0.

Andrew Owens, Jiajun Wu, Josh H McDermott, William T Freeman, and Antonio Torralba. 2016. Ambient sound provides supervision for visual learning. In *European Conference on Computer Vision*, pages 801–816. Springer.

Andrew Owens, Jiajun Wu, Josh H McDermott, William T Freeman, and Antonio Torralba. 2018. Learning sight from sound: Ambient sound provides supervision for visual learning. *International Journal of Computer Vision*, 126(10):1120–1137.

Karalyn Patterson, Peter J Nestor, and Timothy T Rogers. 2007. Where do you know what you know? the representation of semantic knowledge in the human brain. *Nature Reviews Neuroscience*, 8(12):976.

Stanley Peters, , and Dag Westerståhl. 2006. *Quantifiers in language and logic*. Oxford University Press.

Sandro Pezzelle, Raffaella Bernardi, and Manuela Piazza. 2018a. Probing the mental representation of quantifiers. *Cognition*, 181:117–126.

Sandro Pezzelle, Marco Marelli, and Raffaella Bernardi. 2017. Be precise or fuzzy: Learning the meaning of cardinals and quantifiers from vision. In *Proceedings of the 15th Conference of the European Chapter of the Association for Computational Linguistics: Volume 2, Short Papers*, pages 337–342, Valencia, Spain. Association for Computational Linguistics.

Sandro Pezzelle, Ionut-Teodor Sorodoc, and Raffaella Bernardi. 2018b. Comparatives, quantifiers, proportions: a multi-task model for the learning of quantities from vision. In *Proceedings of the 2018 Conference of the North American Chapter of the Association for Computational Linguistics: Human Language Technologies, Volume 1 (Long Papers)*, pages 419–430. Association for Computational Linguistics.

Matthew A Lambon Ralph, Elizabeth Jefferies, Karalyn Patterson, and Timothy T Rogers. 2017. The neural and computational bases of semantic cognition. *Nature Reviews Neuroscience*, 18(1):42.

Santi Seguí, Oriol Pujol, and Jordi Vitria. 2015. Learning to count with deep object features. In *Proceedings of the IEEE Conference on Computer Vision and Pattern Recognition Workshops*, pages 90–96.

Irina Simanova, Jolien C Francken, Floris P de Lange, and Harold Bekkering. 2016. Linguistic priors shape categorical perception. *Language, Cognition and Neuroscience*, 31(1):159–165.

Ionut Sorodoc, Angeliki Lazaridou, Gemma Boleda, Aurélie Herbelot, Sandro Pezzelle, and Raffaella Bernardi. 2016. "Look, some green circles!": Learning to quantify from images. In *Proceedings of the 5th Workshop on Vision and Language*, pages 75–79.

Ionut Sorodoc, Sandro Pezzelle, Aurélie Herbelot, Mariella Dimiccoli, and Raffaella Bernardi. 2018. Learning quantification from images: A structured neural architecture. *Natural Language Engineering*, page 1–30.

Ivilin Stoianov and Marco Zorzi. 2012. Emergence of a 'visual number sense' in hierarchical generative models. *Nature neuroscience*, 15(2):194–196.

Alane Suhr, Mike Lewis, James Yeh, and Yoav Artzi. 2017. A corpus of natural language for visual reasoning. In *Proceedings of the 55th Annual Meeting of the Association for Computational Linguistics (Volume 2: Short Papers)*, volume 2, pages 217–223.

Christian Szegedy, Vincent Vanhoucke, Sergey Ioffe, Jon Shlens, and Zbigniew Wojna. 2016. Rethinking the inception architecture for computer vision. In *Proceedings of the IEEE conference on computer vision and pattern recognition*, pages 2818–2826.

Cong Zhang, Hongsheng Li, Xiaogang Wang, and Xiaokang Yang. 2015a. Cross-scene crowd counting via deep convolutional neural networks. In *Proceedings of the IEEE Conference on Computer Vision and Pattern Recognition*, pages 833–841.

Jianming Zhang, Shugao Ma, Mehrnoosh Sameki, Stan Sclaroff, Margrit Betke, Zhe Lin, Xiaohui Shen, Brian Price, and Radomir Mech. 2015b. Salient object subitizing. In *Proceedings of the IEEE Conference on Computer Vision and Pattern Recognition*, pages 4045–4054.

Hang Zhao, Chuang Gan, Andrew Rouditchenko, Carl Vondrick, Josh McDermott, and Antonio Torralba. 2018. The sound of pixels. In *Proceedings of the European Conference on Computer Vision (ECCV)*, pages 570–586.

Frequency vs. Association for Constraint Selection in Usage-Based Construction Grammar

Jonathan Dunn

University of Canterbury
Department of Linguistics
`jonathan.dunn@canterbury.ac.nz`

Abstract

A usage-based Construction Grammar (CxG) posits that slot-constraints generalize from common exemplar constructions. But what is the best model of constraint generalization? This paper evaluates competing frequency-based and association-based models across eight languages using a metric derived from the Minimum Description Length paradigm. The experiments show that association-based models produce better generalizations across all languages by a significant margin.

1 Learning Slot-Constraints

The Construction Grammar paradigm (CxG: Langacker, 2008; Goldberg, 2006) represents grammar using a hierarchical inventory of constraint-based *constructions*. In computational terms, a construction is a possibly non-continuous sequence in which each unit satisfies some combination of lexical, syntactic, and semantic constraints (e.g., Chang, et al., 2012; Steels, 2004, 2012, 2017). This paper uses computational modelling to approach the problem of how slot-constraints are learned: do frequency-based or association-based models produce better slot-constraints? How can we evaluate the quality of slot-constraints across an entire grammar in order to make such a comparison possible?

Implementations of CxG such as Fluid Construction Grammar (FCG) and Embodied Construction Grammar (ECG) require the manual specification of constraints using a knowledge representation framework like FrameNet (e.g., Laviola, et al., 2017; Matos, et al., 2017; van Trijp, 2017; Ziem & Boas, 2017; Dodge, et al., 2017). While these approaches can provide high-quality representations, they cannot model the emergence of slot-constraints because their constraints are *defined* rather than *learned*. We instead follow

work that models CxG from a usage-based perspective: first, generating potential constructions given a corpus (Wible & Tsao, 2010; Forsberg, et al., 2014); second, selecting the optimal set of constructions, where optimality is measured against a test corpus (Dunn, 2017, 2018a). This provides a model of how syntactic constraints are learned.

Recent work has used the Minimum Description Length paradigm (MDL: Rissanen, 1978, 1986; Goldsmith, 2001, 2006) to model the interaction between slot-constraints across an entire grammar as a trade-off between memory and computation. The grammar which selects the best constraints will optimize the balance between memory (the encoding size of all constructions) and computation (the encoding size of a test corpus given the grammar). This operationalizes the idea within usage-based theories of grammar that any representation can be stored in memory but that not all representations are worth storing (c.f., Jackendoff, 2002; O'Donnell, et al., 2011). From a different perspective, some constructions prevent the learning of other constructions (Goldberg, 2011; Goldberg, 2016; Perek & Goldberg, 2017).

This paper first considers how constructions and slot-constraints can be represented computationally using a data-driven pipeline (Sections 2 & 3). After describing the data used for the experiments (Section 4), we motivate the contrast between frequency and association (Section 5). The frequency-based and association-based models are described (Sections 6 & 7), along with a construction extraction algorithm (Section 8). Finally, an MDL approach to grammar quality is motivated (Section 9) and used to evaluate the grammars produced by the two extraction algorithms (Section 10). The experiments show that an association-based model produces better generalizatons for each language, although the degree of difference between the two models varies across languages.

117

Proceedings of the Workshop on Cognitive Modeling and Computational Linguistics, pages 117–128
Minneapolis, USA, June 7, 2019. ©2019 Association for Computational Linguistics

(1a) [SYN:NOUN — SEM-SYN:TRANSFER[V] — SEM-SYN:ANIMATE[N] — SYN:NOUN]
(1b) "He gave Bill coffee."
(1c) "He gave Bill trouble."
(1d) "Bill sent him letters."
(2a) [SYN:NOUN — LEX:"give" — SEM-SYN:ANIMATE[N] — LEX:"a hand"]
(2b) "Bill gave me a hand."

Table 1: Construction Notation and Examples

2 Representing Constructions

Following previous work (Dunn, 2017, 2018a), constructions are represented as a sequence of slot-constraints, as in (1a). Slots are separated by dashes and constraints are defined by both type (Syntactic, Joint Semantic-Syntactic, Lexical) and filler (for example: NOUN, a part-of-speech or AN-IMATE, a semantic domain).

The construction in (1a) contains four slots: two with joint semantic-syntactic constraints and two with simple syntactic constraints. The examples in (1b) to (1d) are tokens of the construction in (1a). Lexical constraints, as in (2a), represent idiomatic sentences like (2b). These constructions are context-free because any sequence that satisfies the slot-constraints becomes a token or instance of that construction.

The difficulty of modelling slot-constraints is that constructions can overlap: multiple constructions in the grammar are allowed to represent a single phrase. For example, (2b) is actually a token of both (1a) and (2a). This makes identifying constructions more difficult because reaching the representation in (1a) does not rule out also reaching the representation in (2a). Both could be part of a single speaker's grammar. For this reason we will use the term *extraction* rather than *parsing* to describe the syntactic analysis that is performed by the algorithms described in this paper.

To illustrate the problem of construction extraction, we can view each slot as a node, with the beginning of a construction the root node (c.f., transition parsing for dependency grammars: Zhang & Nivre, 2012; Goldberg, et al., 2013). A construction's root can occur anywhere in a sentence. Each slot-constraint is a state, as visualized in Figure 1 with two forms of the ditransitive. There are four possible transitions: LEX, SYN, SEM-SYN, STOP. In the first example, the slot-constraints are generalized to any transfer verb and any object noun. In the second example, the verb and object slots require idiomatic lexical items. The problem is to find the sequence of slot-constraints that *best* represents the construction. Here, the *best* representation is the most efficient trade-off between memory and computation across an entire grammar.

We first have to develop a pipeline for representing all the possible constraints shown in Figure 1. Such a pipeline provides our hypothesis space: any sequence of constraints that is observed in the training data is a potential construction.

3 Representing Slot-Constraints

This section describes the pipeline that is used to represent the hypothesis space of potential constructions. While it is important to take an empirical approach and evaluate aspects of this representation pipeline, the purpose of this paper is not to provide a counter-factual for each compo-

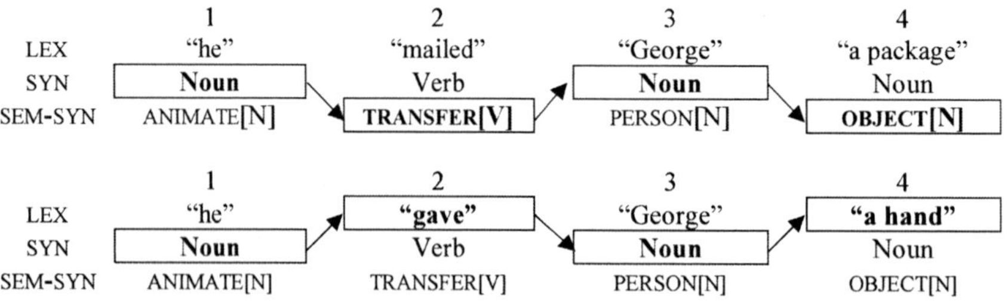

Figure 1: General vs. Idiomatic Ditransitive

nent individually (e.g., what type of embeddings or which part-of-speech tags to use). Instead, the two competing approaches are evaluated using the same representation pipeline in order to put such development decisions in the background. Without a pre-defined ontology of concepts and frames, as in knowledge-based CxG, the representation of slot-constraints becomes a difficult problem.

First, lexical constraints use word-forms separated at whitespace; no morphological analysis is included in the pipeline. The lexicon of allowed word-forms is drawn from a background corpus (Section 4), with a frequency threshold to determine inclusion (500 occurrences in corpora of approximately 1 billion words). An example of a lexical slot-constraint is given in (2a), where this particular construction requires the specific words "give" and "a hand", as in (2b).

Second, syntactic representations are drawn from the part-of-speech categories in the Universal POS tagset using the RDRPOS tagger (Petrov, et al., 2012; Nguyen, et al., 2016); this is a pre-defined syntactic ontology. An unsupervised inventory of syntactic units is outside the scope of this paper, although ideally this would also be part of the representation pipeline. An example of a syntactically-defined slot-constraint is given in (2a), in which any noun can fill the subject position. The problem of recursion within slots is discussed further in Section 11.

Third, semantic constraints are defined using a domain dictionary in which each word-form is assigned to a cluster of word-forms. Clusters are based on word embeddings. First, a background corpus for each language is pos-tagged. No word sense disambiguation is used but word-forms are separated by syntactic category (i.e., *table_verb* is distinct from *table_noun*). A skip-gram embedding with 500 dimensions is trained for each language (Řehůřek & Sojka, 2010). Clusters are then formed by applying x-means to these embeddings (Pelleg & Moore, 2000). While previous work used k-means to create a fixed number of domains across languages (Dunn, 2018a), x-means generalizes the number of clusters per language.

These clusters are heterogenous syntactically. Each output cluster is further divided by syntactic category so that each semantic cluster only contains words from a single part-of-speech, allowing joint semantic-syntactic constraints. The number of clusters for each language, shown in Table 2,

Language	Lexicon Size	N. Clusters
ara	57,216	315
deu	43,080	305
eng	47,723	385
fra	46,876	326
por	65,173	487
rus	49,616	324
spa	51,683	438
zho	59,127	236

Table 2: Semantic Clusters by Language

ranges from 236 (zho) to 487 (por). This variation shows the importance of using x-means for defining semantic constraints instead of k-means with a fixed k across languages.

4   Corpora and Data Divisions

This paper evaluates models on eight languages: Arabic (ara), German (deu), English (eng), French (fra), Portuguese (por), Russian (rus), Spanish (spa), and Chinese (zho). Each language is represented by a large background corpus that is used to (i) train word embeddings, (ii) determine the word-form lexicon, (iii) calculate association measures, and (iv) learn and evaluate CxGs. This section discusses data sources and preparation.

A large portion of the corpus for each language comes from web-crawled data (Baroni, et al., 2009; Majlĭs & Žabokrtský, 2012; Benko, 2014; and data from the CoNLL 2017 Shared Task: Ginter, et al., 2017). Because the goal is to provide a wide representation of each language, this is augmented by legislative texts from the EU and UN (Tiedemann, 2012; Skadiņŝ, et al., 2014), the OpenSubtitles corpus (Tiedemann, 2012), and newspaper texts. The only language-specific pre-processing used is Chinese text segmentation[1].

All punctuation is removed and text converted to lowercase. In order to avoid language-specific assumptions, no sentence splitting is performed. Instead, the corpus is divided into sequences of 100 words that form the main unit of analysis. The corpus is further divided into chunks of 100k samples (for a total of 10 million words per chunk). These chunks are important because the data is randomly divided by chunk as shown in Table 3.

We perform CxG learning across four independent folds. Each fold retains the same lexicon and semantic domains, but every other part of the

---

[1]Jeiba: `https://github.com/fxsjy/jieba`

119

Function	Num. Words
Word embeddings	Entire dataset
Background statistics	200 million words
Generating potentials	50 million words
Optimizing CxGs	10 million words
Evaluation	10 million words (x5)

Table 3: Data Divisions

pipeline is repeated: (i) calculating frequency and association statistics for evaluating potential constructions, (ii) generating potential constructions, (iii) searching through the potential constructions using a tabu search (Dunn, 2018a) to optimize the MDL metric (Section 9).

Each fold produces a single CxG. These CxGs are then merged by concatenation into a single grammar. The idea is that any construction which is productive on a sub-set of the corpus belongs in the final grammar. This final CxG is reduced using horizontal pruning (c.f., Wible & Tsao, 2010) to remove constructions that are wholly or partially contained within larger constructions. The code for this process is provided as an external resource.

5 Frequency and Association

The representation pipeline provides a rich hypothesis space from which to formulate slot-constraints. A usage-based grammar expects that constructions will emerge as common exemplars become entrenched via repeated production and perception. But how do we model *emergence*?

One approach uses frequency: the most common templates (i.e., sequences of constraints) will become a part of the grammar (Bybee, 2006; Arnon & Snider, 2010; Siyanova-Chanturia, et al., 2011). On the other hand, frequency alone will over-represent very common phrases and we know that less common and even rare constructions remain perfectly grammatical. How do learners acquire rare constructions if they learn using frequency information? A second approach uses association: slot-constraints that occur together more frequently than expected indicate an entrenched construction (Wible & Tsao, 2010; Forsberg, et al., 2014; c.f., Ellis & Larsen-Freemen, 2009). An association-based model focuses on frequency relative to specific contexts rather than overall frequency in all contexts.

On the one hand, frequency and association as measures of entrenchment do not need to be mu-

tually exclusive. For example, association measures explicitly depend on frequency information. On the other hand, the purpose of the experiments in this paper is to evaluate competing models of the emergence of slot-constraints against corpus data in order to better understand how CxGs are acquired. It should also be noted that it is not possible to design an association-based algorithm that has no frequency thresholds whatsoever: we need at least a bound on which transitions need to be assigned association values. In the same way, the frequency-based algorithm references some association information; otherwise the number of candidates either will be intractibly large or will include no infrequent forms. Regardless, the algorithms described in Sections 6 and 7 represent implementations of competing hypotheses about the emergence of slot-constraints.

For association, we use the bi-directional ΔP (Gries, 2013; Dunn, 2018b), with both left-to-right and right-to-left variants. For any two slot-fillers, X and Y, X_P indicates that X is present and X_A that X is absent, providing the two direction-specific measures below.

$$\Delta P_{LR} = p(X_P|Y_P) - p(X_P|Y_A)$$

$$\Delta P_{RL} = p(Y_P|X_P) - p(Y_P|X_A)$$

Why not other measures of association? First, the ΔP was developed for precisely this sort of problem (Ellis, 2007). Second, the ΔP is bi-directional while other common measures like pointwise mutual information (PMI) average both directions together, thus disguising directional asymmetries. It has been shown that directional association is necessary to describe many linguistic patterns (Gries, 2013). Here we use the maximum directional ΔP to represent each transition. While a PMI disguises directional differences, this max ΔP allows each possible transition to be represented by its strongest association value.

6 Frequency-Based Constraints

The frequency-based algorithm works in two stages: First, it greedily selects slot-constraints for each sentence by iterating over all adjacent pairs and adding the pair with the highest ΔP (Table 4). Once all slot-constraints are filled, the second stage extracts constraint n-grams from this sequence ($n = 3$–6). This approach posits many different boundaries and uses overall frequency

Variables
$line$ = sequence of units
$unit$ = possible slot-constraints: (lex, syn, sem)
u_i, u_{i+1} = two adjacent units
c_i, c_{i+1} = constraint types for u_i, u_{i+1}
RS = one slot-constraint per unit in line
Algorithm
while RS not complete:
for u_i, u_{i+1} in line:
for all possible transitions c_i, c_{i+1}:
if $\Delta P(c_i, c_{i+1})$ is highest available:
add c_i, c_{i+1} to RS

Table 4: Frequency-Based Selection Algorithm

across the corpus to prune candidates. RS in Table 4 refers to a sequence of slot-constraints that represents the input sentence; this sequence is complete when every slot in the sentence is represented by a hypothesized constraint.

This is similar to a template-based view of CxG: each n-gram of slot-constraints is a template. Only the most frequent templates are considered in the MDL stage. On the other hand, it is not tractable to include every sequence of slot-constraints; past work that took such an approach (Dunn, 2017) had to operate on much less data or enforce a series of intermediate frequency thresholds (i.e., per-chunk thresholds). For practical reasons the algorithm in Table 4 references local association between slot-constraints; at its core, however, this is an operationalization of a frequency-centered model of the emergence of slot-constraints.

This frequency-based algorithm uses a fixed frequency threshold. After all candidates are extracted from a corpus, those candidates with an overall frequency below the threshold are pruned. It is difficult to evaluate different thresholds using a grid search approach (as done below with association) because many thresholds produce candidate sets that are too large to evaluate. For purely practical reasons, then, the frequency threshold is fixed. Along these same lines, horizontal pruning removes any candidate that is entirely contained within another candidate, with the larger candidate always remaining and the smaller candidate always pruned. This type of pruning is essential for a frequency-based model because a frequent sequence $A - B - C - D$ will have frequent subsequences like $A - B - C$ and $B - C - D$. This nesting is not produced by an association-based

model, and so a different pruning strategy is required, as described in Section 7.

7 Association-Based Constraints

The association-based algorithm (Table 5) uses the total directional ΔP (a sum across all transitions) to evaluate potential sequences. To implement this idea, the search follows transitions from one slot-constraint to the next, proceeding left-to-right through the sentence. Any transition below a threshold ΔP stops that line of the search. This algorithm references local association values when choosing a transition from the current state. It also references global (i.e., construction-wide) association for selecting different paths, rather than using the frequency of specific templates.

Any series of constraints identified by this search whose transitions exceed the ΔP threshold is added to the candidate stack. At the end of the search, this stack is scored using each candidate's total ΔP across all transitions. While primarily a transition-based extraction, this approach thus incorporates some global evaluation methods (c.f., Nivre & McDonald, 2008; Zhang & Clark, 2008). A grid search for the best ΔP threshold per language is performed using independent test data.

This association-based algorithm is less influenced by the assumption that co-located slots govern one another's constraints. For example, in reference to Figure 1, the slot filled by a NOUN in 3 and the slot filled by "a hand" in 4 have a local transition that is measured using the association between these two representations. Should we instead ignore the relationship between these two objects and focus on the relationship between each object and the verb slot? This algorithm tries to avoid specifying particular templates like this (i.e., a verb-centered frame) by using the global ΔP evaluation and the thread of associations to draw out these relationships.

But this raises an interesting empirical question: does the entrenchment of the ditransitive construction predict a higher association between the two object slots whether or not the verb itself is included? Is there a shared effect across all double-object constructions? A beam-search dependency parser could resolve this in a practical sense by simply evaluating more non-local relationships. But does CxG itself predict that such local relationships will be more entrenched because they are present within a single construction?

Variables
$node$ = unit (i.e., word) in line
$startingNode$ = start of potential construction
$state$ = type of slot-constraint for node
$path$ = route from root to successor states
$[c]$ = list of immediate successor states
c_i, c_{i+1} = transition to successor constraint
$candidateStack$ = plausible constructions
$evaluate$ = maximize $\sum \Delta P$ for c_i, c_{i+1} in $path$
Main Loop
for each possible startingNode in line:
RecursiveSearch(path = startingNode)
evaluate candidateStack
Recursive Function
RecursiveSearch(path):
for c_i, c_{i+1} in $[c]$ from path:
if ΔP of c_i, c_{i+1} > threshold:
add c_{i+1} to path
RecursiveSearch(path)
else if path is long enough:
add to candidateStack

Table 5: Association-Based Selection Algorithm

8 Extracting Constructions

Given a set of candidates (i.e., a possible CxG), we use an additional algorithm to extract those candidates from a corpus in order to evaluate that grammar. The algorithm proceeds left-to-right across each word in the input. For each word, the extractor checks for constructions whose first slot-constraint is satisfied by the current word. Because there are three types of slot-constraints, the extractor must check each constraint type. If the current word satisfies the first slot-constraint, the extractor looks-ahead and tests each successive word until either (i) all slot-constraints are satisfied and a construction match is identified or (ii) a slot-constraint is not satisfied and this portion of the search is terminated. If there is no match, then a particular construction is not present. This algorithm extracts all candidates identified by the above algorithms so that the competing grammars can be evaluated.

9 Modeling Constraint Quality

We now have frequency-based and association-based models of how slot-constraints emerge from usage. How can we measure the quality of both (i) a set of potential slot-constraints and (ii) an entire CxG? The process of searching over se-

lected slot-constraints using a tabu search (Glover, 1989, 1990) is adopted from previous work (Dunn, 2018a). A tabu search is a meta-level heuristic search that evaluates a number of possible local moves for each turn and then makes the move which produces the best grammar. Importantly, a tabu search allows moves which make the grammar worse in the short-term (with a restricted set of tabu moves) so that the learner can climb out of local optima. Here, each state is a grammar that contains a specific set of constructions. A move changes the current state by adding or removing some constructions. As before, the purpose is not to evaluate counter-factuals for every step in the pipeline because both the frequency-based and association-based models use exactly the same tabu search algorithm.

The MDL metric quantifies the trade-off between memory (operationalized as the encoding size of a grammar) and computation (operationalized as the encoding size of a test corpus given that grammar). A grammar that provides better generalizations will allow the test corpus to be encoded using a smaller number of bits. The metric combines three encoding-based terms: L_1 (the cost of encoding the grammar), $L_2\{C\}$ (the cost of encoding pointers to constructions in the grammar), and $L_2\{R\}$ (the cost of encoding linguistic material that is not in the grammar and thus cannot be encoded using a pointer). A pointer here is a partial parse of an utterance that refers to a construction that is already contained in the grammar.

These terms represent the grammar, the data as described by the grammar, and the data that is not described by the grammar; note that both L_2 terms are combined below. In other words, $L_2(D \mid G)$ is the sum of both $L_2\{C\}$ and $L_2\{R\}$. D in this equation refers to the dataset which is used to evaluate the model. The relationship between these three encoding terms across languages is examined further in Table 7.

$$MDL = \min_{G}\{L_1(G) + L_2(D \mid G)\}$$

Encoding size, in turn, is based on probability: the encoding size of an item, X, is measured in bits, below, using the negative log of its probability. We describe how probabilities are estimated later in this section. The basic idea is that more probable constraints should have smaller encoding sizes.

$$L_C(X) = -log_2 P(X)$$

According to this model, a construction is only worth remembering if its contribution to decreasing the overall encoding size of the test corpus is smaller than its contribution to the encoding size of the grammar. This is important for CxGs because similar constructions overlap, describing the same sentences in the corpus. Each overlapping construction must be individually represented in the grammar, adding to the L_1 term: similar constructions must be encoded separately in L_1 but do not improve the encoding of L_2. For example, the two constructions in (1a) and (2a) describe the same utterance in (2b). Both of these constructions need to be encoded in the grammar, increasing L_1. But encoding only one of them would not increase the regret portion of L_2 because the utterance itself can still be encoded using a pointer to the construction that is in the grammar.

The encoding size of a grammar, L_1, is the sum of the encoding size of all constructions in that grammar. Each construction is a series of slot-constraints that must be satisfied for a linguistic utterance to be an instance of that construction. For each constraint, two items must be encoded: (i) the constraint type (lexical, semantic, syntactic) and (ii) the filler which defines that constraint. As shown in Table 7, this portion of the MDL metric is quite small given a large dataset.

The cost of (i) is fixed because each representation is considered equally probable: the grammar is not explicitly biased towards syntactic constraints. But the cost of (ii) depends on the type of representation: syntactic units come out of a much smaller inventory, so that any given part-of-speech is more probable and thus easier to encode. For example, if there are 14 parts-of-speech, then the probability of observing one of them is $1/14 = 0.0714$ bits. On the other hand, because there are more lexical items, each word is less probable and thus more expensive to encode.

For example, if there are 50k lexical items, then the probability is $1/50,000 = 0.00002$. In this way, the grammar is allowed to employ item-specific slot-constraints, but doing so increases the encoding cost of the grammar. Here, a syntactic constraint contributes 3.8 bits but a lexical constraint contributes 15.6 bits. Future work will evaluate the impact of probability estimation for slot-fillers, currently done only at the contruction level. The total encoding size of a construction is the accumulated bits required to encode each slot-constraint, where N_R represents the number of representation types (here, 3) and T_R represents the number of possible slot-fillers for that type.

$$\sum_i^{N_{SLOTS}} -log_2(\frac{1}{N_{R_i}}) + -log_2(\frac{1}{T_R})$$

The encoding size of the test corpus, L_2, contains two quantities: first, the cost of encoding pointers to constructions in the grammar; second, the cost of encoding on-the-fly any parts of the corpus that cannot be described by the grammar. The cost of encoding pointers is also based on probabilities, so that more probable or common constructions require fewer bits to encode. For example, a construction that occurs 100 times in a corpus of 500k words has a pointer encoding size of 12.28 bits, but a construction that occurs 1,000 times costs only 8.96 bits per use. In this way, the probability of potential constructions influences encoding size. The regret portion of the L_2 term is the cost of words which are not covered by constructions in the current grammar. Each of these is encoded on-the-fly (i.e., not remembered): the more unencoded words accumulate, the more each one costs.

There is a close relationship between MDL and Bayesian inference methods (c.f., Barak, et al., 2016; Barak & Goldberg, 2017; Goldwater, et al., 2009). Information theory describes the relationship between the log probabilities of representations and their encoding size. But it does not estimate the probability of the grammar itself, which here is handled in two ways: First, there is a choice in CxG between different types of representation (LEX, SYN, SEM). This model does not enforce one type, but syntactic constraints are more likely because there are fewer categories. Second, pointers to constructions are assigned probabilities based on their observed frequency; this means that more likely constructions are cheaper to encode and implicitly favored by the model.

The MDL paradigm has previously been applied to phonological structure (Rasin & Katzir, 2016), to morphological structure (Goldsmith, 2001; 2006), to grammar induction in other contexts (c.f., Solomonoff, 1964; Grünwald, 1996; de Marcken, 1996; c.f., Stolcke, 1994), and even to semantics (c.f., Piantadosi, et al., 2016). This application to CxG incorporates two important properties of usage-based constructions (multiple constraint types and overlapping representations) for which an MDL approach is a good fit.

	Frequency	Association	P
ara	44.08%	**29.45%**	0.0001
deu	52.49%	**18.69%**	0.0001
eng	51.80%	**23.11%**	0.0001
fra	43.28%	**40.52%**	0.0037
por	45.13%	**38.91%**	0.0137
rus	54.14%	**13.93%**	0.0001
spa	60.34%	**26.36%**	0.0001
zho	57.01%	**37.96%**	0.0030

Table 6: Compression Rates by Language with Significance of Difference Between Models

10   Does Frequency or Association Produce Better Slot-Constraints?

We evaluate the frequency-based and association-based models on the same test sets, with the same hypothesis spaces derived from the same representation pipeline, using the same implementation of the MDL metric. While we have not evaluated counter-factuals for every development decision made within the pipeline, both competing models rely on the same decisions.[2]

MDL provides a single metric of a grammar's fit relative to a particular dataset. This metric itself is dependent on each dataset; we thus calculate a baseline encoding score that represents the encoding of the dataset without a grammar and use this to derive a compression metric: MDL_{CxG}/MDL_{Base}. The lower this compression metric, the greater the generalizations provided by the CxG. Compression as used in MDL is similar to perplexity within language modelling; the connection is not explored further here except to note that some language models include CxG-like templates (e.g., Gimpel & Smith, 2011).

The evaluation uses all eight languages in order to provide a cross-linguistic counter-factual: do the generalizations agree across languages? Additionally, we evaluate the models against five independent sets of 10 million words for each language. Table 6 shows the average compression by model for each language across these five test sets. We also report the p-values for a paired t-test (paired by dataset) to ensure that the difference in compression between models is significant.

Lower compression scores reflect better generalizations; as shown in Table 6, the association-based model out-performs the frequency-based model for every language. In each case the difference between models is significant. The gap and the significance level, however, vary widely across languages. For Russian, there is a gap of 40.21% compression that is significant below the p = 0.0001 level. But for French and Portuguese that gap is only 2.76% and 6.22%, with much larger p-values to match. Association always provides a better model of the emergence of slot-constraints, but for French and Portuguese the two models are much closer together than for other languages.

The frequency-based model represents what Goldberg calls *conservatism via entrenchment*, the idea that learners are more willing to over-generalize infrequent forms (Goldberg, 2016). In other words, the problem with a frequency-based model is that it does not allow for creative (and thus infrequent) uses of common forms. The more frequent a particular form is, the less likely that form will allow competing representations to emerge. But language is infinitely creative and this model blocks too many emerging constructions.

The association-based model, on the other hand, allows for the emergence of less familiar constructions: a series of transitions between slot-constraints is permitted if it is relatively highly associated, and infrequent forms are more open to forming new associations. This is the advantage of a directional measure like the ΔP. Assume there are two constraints, A and B, in which A is very common but B is rare. The PMI, by averaging, would disguise any association from B to A. But the ΔP allows such new associations to emerge from a limited number of observations. Frequency alone pre-empts less common representations.

We take a closer look at cross-linguistic patterns in Table 7 by breaking down the MDL metric into its three terms: L_1, or the contribution of the complexity of the grammar; $L_2\{C\}$, or the contribution of encoded constructions to the final encoding cost; and $L_2\{R\}$, or the contribution of missing constructions to the final encoding cost. Each term is represented by its percentage of the MDL metric for that dataset. Thus, while the frequency-based models have a higher MDL score overall, Table 7 focuses on how that score is distributed across terms. These percentages are averaged across all five test sets for each language for each model.

---

[2]The exact data used is available for download here: `https://labbcat.canterbury.ac.nz/download/?jonathandunn/CxG_Data_FixedSize`. In addition, the code for the implementation and the grammars themselves are available here: `https://github.com/jonathandunn/c2xg/`.

	L_1 (F)	L_1 (ΔP)	$L_2\{C\}$ (F)	$L_2\{C\}$ (ΔP)	$L_2\{R\}$ (F)	$L_2\{R\}$ (ΔP)
ara	0.43%	1.25%	82.14%	68.65%	17.43%	30.10%
deu	0.50%	1.56%	89.32%	93.42%	10.17%	05.01%
eng	0.57%	1.44%	93.22%	98.04%	06.21%	00.53%
fra	0.44%	0.77%	93.08%	64.09%	06.48%	35.14%
por	0.39%	0.27%	96.72%	25.00%	02.89%	74.73%
rus	0.42%	1.35%	66.37%	94.87%	33.21%	03.78%
spa	0.36%	0.81%	99.59%	82.24%	00.06%	16.95%
zho	0.25%	0.37%	92.24%	96.92%	07.51%	02.71%

Table 7: Break-down of MDL metric by relative proportion of the overall score

First, we see that the grammars themselves (L_1) account for a small percentage of the overall metric. The great majority of the MDL score comes from the encoding of pointers or references of constructions in the grammar in order to represent the dataset. A smaller percentage comes from encoding errors (i.e., parts of the dataset that cannot be represented using known constructions).

Second, however, there are important variations across languages and model-types. For French and Portuguese, the two languages with the least difference between frequency-based and association-based models, the association-based models have significantly higher regret encodings ($L_2\{R\}$). In other words, the overall fit of the association-based models for these languages is not nearly as good: only 64.09% (fra) and 25.00% (por) of the association-based model's MDL score comes from correctly encoded constructions. This suggests that the association-based model provides relatively poor grammars for French and Portuguese, rather than that the frequency-based model provides relatively good grammars. At the same time, this relative distribution of the MDL metric disguises the fact that the overall compression of the association-based model remains better for these two languages than the frequency-based model.

Could we evaluate usage-based grammars without relying on MDL? An alternate approach to evaluating the balance of memory and computation when learning syntactic structures involves psycholinguistically-annotated datasets (c.f., Luong, et al., 2015) or qualitative distinctions such as optional/obligatory arguments (c.f., Bergen, et al., 2013). These approaches are not as comprehensive as the work described in this paper because they cover, in effect, a small sub-set of possible constructions. Yet their interpretation in respect to individual cognition is more straight-forward.

11 Remaining Problems

This section offers a brief discussion of an important remaining challenge: how does a grammar treat non-contiguous constructions? A first option is that a CxG assumes a CFG that provides a notion of constituency: a noun phrase, for example, could be taken as a single slot-filler regardless of its internal structure. From a usage-based perspective, this is potentially problematic: Is there a separate syntactic mechanism for constituents that is based on different capabilities than the mechanism for learning slot-constraints?

A second option is that constituents are a form of purely-syntactic construction that can fill slots within larger constructions. This simpler type of construction would be learned using the same mechanisms as other constructions, but restricted to only syntactic constraints. Two difficulties arise: First, a constituent has a *head* which categorizes it. Thus, if a constituent were categorized as a NOUN, it could fill any slot in a larger construction that was categorized to accept a NOUN. But how do we categorize a construction? Does one single slot in a construction act as the head? The second difficulty is that constructions can overlap within a sentence, as with (1a) and (2a) above. But a constituency grammar cannot allow such ill-defined segmentations.

A third option, taken here implicitly, is to allow partially-filled slots or unfilled slots: rather than posit a constituent with a categorized head as a slot-filler, we could allow a specific head along with unspecified material to fill a slot. For example, assume that the ditransitive in (1a) has "my uncle's wife" in the recipient slot. We could use a constituency grammar to treat this whole phrase as a single *NP*; but we could also allow "wife" to satisfy the slot-constraint on its own and treat its modifiers as under-specified material.

References

Arnon, I. and Snider, N. 2010. More than words: Frequency effects for multi-word phrases. *Journal of Memory and Language*, 62: 67–82.

Barak, L. and Goldberg, A. 2017. Modeling the Partial Productivity of Constructions. *Proceedings of AAAI 2017 Spring Symposium on Computational Construction Grammar and Natural Language Understanding*. 131-138.

Barak, L.; Goldberg, A.; and Stevenson, S. 2017. Comparing Computational Cognitive Models of Generalization in a Language Acquisition Task. In *Proceedings of the Conference on Empirical Methods in NLP*. 96-106.

Baroni, M., Bernardini, S., Ferraresi, A., and Zanchetta, E. 2009. The WaCky Wide Web: A Collection of Very Large Linguistically Processed Web-crawled Corpora. *Language Resources and Evaluation*, 43: 209-226.

Benko, V. 2014. Aranea: Yet Another Family of (Comparable) Web Corpora. In *Proceedings of Text, Speech and Dialogue. 17th International Conference*. 257-264.

Bergen, L.; Gibson, E.; and O'Donnell, T. 2013. Arguments and Modifiers from the Learner's Perspective. In *Proceedings of the Annual Meeting of the Association for Computational Linguistics*, 115-119.

Bybee, J. 2006. From Usage to Grammar: The mind's response to repetition. *Language* 82(4): 711-733.

Chang, N., De Beule, J., and Micelli, V. 2012. Computational construction grammar: Comparing ECG and FCG. In Steels, L. (ed.), *Computational Issues in Fluid Construction Grammar*. Berlin: Springer. 259-288.

Dodge, E., Trott, S., Gilardi, L., and Stickles, E. 2017. Grammar Scaling: Leveraging FrameNet Data to Increase Embodied Construction Grammar Coverage. *Proceedings of AAAI 2017 Spring Symposium on Computational Construction Grammar and Natural Language Understanding*. 154-162.

Dunn, J. 2017. Computational Learning of Construction Grammars. *Language & Cognition*, 9(2): 254-292.

Dunn, J. 2018a. Modeling the Complexity and Descriptive Adequacy of Construction Grammars. In *Proceedings of the Society for Computation in Linguistics (SCiL 2018)*. Stroudsburg, PA: Association for Computational Linguistics. 81-90.

Dunn, J. 2018b. Multi-Unit Directional Measures of Association: Moving Beyond Pairs of Words. *International Journal of Corpus Linguistics*, 23(2): 183-215.

Ellis, N. 2007. Language Acquisition as Rational Contingency Learning. *Applied Linguistics*, 27(1): 1-24.

Ellis, N. and Larsen-Freeman, D. 2009. Constructing a Second Language: Analyses and Computational Simulations of the Emergence of Linguistic Constructions From Usage. *Language Learning: A Journal of Research in Language Studies*, 59(1): 90-125.

Forsberg, M., Johansson, R., Bckstrm, L., Borin, L., Lyngfelt, B., Olofsson, J., and Prentice, J. 2014. From Construction Candidates to Constructicon Entries: An experiment using semi-automatic methods for identifying constructions in corpora. *Constructions and Frames*, 6(1): 114-135.

Gimpel, K. and Smith, N. 2011. Generative Models of Monolingual and Bilingual Gappy Patterns. In *Proceedings of the 6th Workshop on Statistical Machine Translation*, 512-522.

Ginter, F.; Hajiĉ, J.; Luotolahti, J. 2017. CoNLL 2017 Shared Task - Automatically Annotated Raw Texts and Word Embeddings, LINDAT/CLARIN digital library at the Institute of Formal and Applied Linguistics (ÃšFAL), Faculty of Mathematics and Physics, Charles University. http://hdl.handle.net/11234/1-1989.

Glover, F. 1989. Tabu Search, Part 1. *ORSA Journal on Computing*, 1(3): 190-206.

Glover. F. 1990. Tabu Search, Part 2. *ORSA Journal on Computing*, 2(1): 4-32.

Goldberg, A. 2006. *Constructions at Work: The Nature of Generalization in Language*. Oxford: Oxford University Press.

Goldberg, A. 2011. Corpus evidence of the viability of statistical preemption. *Cognitive Linguistics*, 22 1: 131-154.

Goldberg, A. 2016. Partial Productivity of Linguistic Constructions: Dynamic categorization and Statistical preemption. *Language & Cognition*, 8(3): 369-390.

Goldberg, Y., Zhao, K., and Huang, L. 2013. Efficient Implementations of Beam-Search Incremental Parsers *Proceedings of the Annual Meeting of the Association for Computational Linguistics*. 628-633.

Goldsmith, J. 2001. Unsupervised Learning of the Morphology of a Natural Language. *Computational Linguistics*, 27(2): 153-198.

Goldsmith, J. 2006. An Algorithm for the Unsupervised Learning of Morphology. *Natural Language Engineering*, 12(4): 353-371.

Goldwater, S.; Griffiths, T.; and Johnson, M. 2009. A Bayesian framework for word segmentation: Exploring the effects of context. *Cognition*, 112(1): 21–54.

Gries, S. 2013. 50-something years of work on collocations: What is or should be next. *International Journal of Corpus Linguistics*, 18(1): 137-165.

Grünwald, P. 1996. A Minimum Description Length Approach to Grammar Inference. In Wermter, G. S. S. and Riloff, E., (eds.) *Connectionist, Statistical and Symbolic Approaches to Learning for Natural Language Processing*, Springer Lecture Notes in Artificial Intelligence. 203–216.

Jackendoff, R. 2002. *Foundations of Language*. Oxford: Oxford University Press.

Langacker, R. 2008. *Cognitive Grammar: A Basic Introduction*. Oxford: Oxford University Press.

Laviola, A., Lage, L., Marção, N., Tavares, T., Almeida, V., Matos, E., and Torrent, T. 2017. The Brazilian Portuguese Constructicon: Modeling Constructional Inheritance, Frame Evocation and Constraints in FrameNet Brasil. *Proceedings of AAAI 2017 Spring Symposium on Computational Construction Grammar and Natural Language Understanding*. 193-196.

Luong, M.; O'Donnell, T.; and Goodman, N. 2015. Evaluating Models of Computation and Storage in Human Sentence Processing. In *Proceedings of the Sixth Workshop on Cognitive Aspects of Computational Language Learning*, 14–21.

Majliš, M. and Žabokrtský, Z. 2012. Language Richness of the Web. In *Proceedings of the International Conference on Language Resources and Evaluation (LREC 2012)*. https://ufal.mff.cuni.cz/w2c.

de Marcken, C. 1996. *Unsupervised Language Acquisition*. PhD thesis, MIT, Cambridge, MA.

Matos, E., Torrent, T., Almeida, V., Laviola, A., Lage, L., Marção, N., and Tavares, T. 2017. Constructional Analysis Using Constrained Spreading Activation in a FrameNet-Based Structured Connectionist Model. *Proceedings of AAAI 2017 Spring Symposium on Computational Construction Grammar and Natural Language Understanding*. 222-229.

Nguyen, Dat Quoc; Nguyen, Dai Quoc; Pham, Dang Duc; and Pham, Son Bao. 2016. A Robust Transformation-Based Learning Approach Using Ripple Down Rules for Part-Of-Speech Tagging. *AI Communications*, 29(3): 409-422.

Nivre, J. and McDonald, R. 2008. Integrating Graph-Based and Transition-Based Dependency Parsers. *Proceedings of the Annual Meeting of the Association for Computational Linguistics*. 950-958.

O'Donnell, T.; Snedeker, J.; Tenenbaum, J.; and Goodman, N. 2011. Productivity and Reuse in Language. In *Proceedings of the Thirty-Third Annual Conference of the Cognitive Science Society*, 1,613-1,618.

Pelleg, D. and Moore, A. 2000. X-means: Extending K-means with Efficient Estimation of the Number of Clusters. In *Proceedings of the Seventeenth International Conference on Machine Learning*. 727-734.

Perek, F. and Goldberg, A. 2017. Linguistic generalization on the basis of function and constraints on the basis of statistical preemption. *Cognition*, 168, 276-293.

Petrov, S., Das, D., and McDonald, R. 2012. A Universal Part-of-Speech Tagset. In *Proceedings of the Eight International Conference on Language Resources and Evaluation*.

Piantadosi, S. T., Tenenbaum, J. B., and Goodman, N. D. 2016. The Logical Primitives of Thought: Empirical foundations for compositional cognitive models. *Psychological Review*, 123(4):392–424.

Rasin, E. and Katzir, R. 2016. On Evaluation Metrics in Optimality Theory. *Linguistic Inquiry*, 47(2):235–282.

Řehůřek, R. and Sojka, P. 2010. Software Framework for Topic Modelling with Large Corpora. In *Proceedings of the LREC 2010 Workshop on New Challenges for NLP Frameworks*.

Rissanen, J. 1978. Modeling by the Shortest Data Description. *Automatica*, 14: 465-471.

Rissanen, J. 1986. Stochastic Complexity and Modeling. *Annals of Statistics*, 14: 1,080-1,100.

Siyanova-Chanturia, A.; Conklin, K.; and van Heuven, W. 2011. Seeing a phrase "time and again" matters: the role of phrasal frequency in the processing of multiword sequences. *Journal of Experimental Psychology: Learning, Memory and Cognition*, 37(3),776-784.

Skadiņš, R.; Tiedemann, J.; Rozis, R.; & Deksne, D. 2014. Billions of Parallel Words for Free. In *Proceedings of the International Conference on Language Resources and Evaluation (LREC 2014)*. http://opus.lingfil.uu.se/EUbookshop.php

Solomonoff, R. 1964. A Formal Theory of Inductive Inference, Parts I and II. *Information and Control*, 7(1 & 2):1–22, 224–254.

Steels, L. 2004. Constructivist development of grounded construction grammar. In *Proceedings of the 42nd Meeting of the Association for Computational Linguistics*: 9-16.

Steels, L. 2012. Design methods for fluid construction grammar. In Steels, L. (ed), *Computational Issues in Fluid Construction Grammar*. Berlin: Springer. 3-36.

Steels, L. 2017. Requirements for Computational Construction Grammars. *Proceedings of AAAI 2017 Spring Symposium on Computational Construction Grammar and Natural Language Understanding*. 251-257.

Stolcke, A. 1994. *Bayesian Learning of Probabilistic Language Models*. PhD thesis, University of California at Berkeley. Berkeley, California.

Tiedemann, J. 2012. Parallel Data, Tools and Interfaces in OPUS. In *Proceedings of the International Conference on Language Resources and Evaluation (LREC 2012)*. http://opus.lingfil.uu.se

van Trijp, R. 2017. A Computational Construction Grammar for English. *Proceedings of AAAI 2017 Spring Symposium on Computational Construction Grammar and Natural Language Understanding*. 266-273.

Wible, D. and Tsao, N. 2010. StringNet as a Computational Resource for Discovering and Investigating Linguistic Constructions. In *Proceedings of the Workshop on Extracting and Using Constructions in Computational Linguistics (NAACL-HTL)*: 25-31.

Zhang, Y. and Clark, S. 2008. A Tale of Two Parsers: Investigating and Combining Graph-based and Transition-based Dependency Parsing using Beam-search. *Proceedings of the Conference on Empirical Methods in NLP*. 562-571.

Zhang, Y. and Nivre, J. 2012. Analyzing the Effect of Global Learning and Beam-search on Transition-based Dependency Parsing. *Proceedings of COLING*. 1391-1400.

Ziem, A. and Boas, H. 2017. Towards a Constructicon for German. *Proceedings of AAAI 2017 Spring Symposium on Computational Construction Grammar and Natural Language Understanding*. 274-277.

The Development of Abstract Concepts in Children's Early Lexical Networks

Abdellah Fourtassi *   **Isaac L. Scheinfeld ***   **Michael C. Frank**
{afourtas, ischeinfeld, mcfrank}@stanford.edu
Department of Psychology
Stanford University

Abstract

How do children learn abstract concepts such as animal vs. artifact? Previous research has suggested that such concepts can partly be derived using cues from the language children hear around them. Following this suggestion, we propose a model where we represent the children's developing lexicon as an evolving network. The nodes of this network are based on vocabulary knowledge as reported by parents, and the edges between pairs of nodes are based on the probability of their co-occurrence in a corpus of child-directed speech. We found that several abstract categories can be identified as the dense regions in such networks. In addition, our simulations suggest that these categories develop simultaneously, rather than sequentially, thanks to the children's word learning trajectory which favors the exploration of the global conceptual space.

1   Introduction:

One of the central challenges in cognitive development is to understand how concepts develop (Carey, 2009; Keil, 1992; Gopnik and Meltzoff, 1997). Of particular interest is the case of abstract concepts which have non-obvious shared properties such as "animal" and "artifact". For example, a cat and a bird are perceptually quite different but they share some fundamental properties (e.g., breathing, feeding, and reproducing) which make them animals (as opposed to artifacts). In such cases, learning requires in part cultural/linguistic cues which provide information beyond what can be obtained through the senses (Gelman, 2009; Harris, 2012; Csibra and Gergely, 2009).

One way children's conceptual learning can benefit from the language they hear around them is through word co-occurrence. For example, one can learn an abstract concept (e.g., animal) simply by observing how its instances (e.g., "cat" and "bird") go together in speech. Indeed, previous work has shown that the caregiver's input contains rich co-occurrence information about various abstract concepts (Huebner and Willits, 2018). This work, however, has explored the conceptual space from an adult perspective (using the words uttered by the caregivers). Here we explore how abstract concepts may develop from the children's perspective, investigating how their word learning trajectory influences the higher-level organization of their developing lexicon.

We study the real conceptual development (i.e. as induced by the real trajectory of word learning) in comparison to two hypothetical developmental scenarios induced by two possible mechanisms of word learning. On the first mechanism, past lexical knowledge facilitates the future learning of related words, e.g., the word "cat" is more likely to be followed by another animal name than it is to be followed by a food name (Steyvers and Tenenbaum, 2005; Borovsky et al., 2016). On the second mechanism, past lexical knowledge does not influence future learning, e.g., learning the word "cat" does not necessarily increase the odds that the next word will be another animal name (Hills et al., 2009; Sizemore et al., 2018).

The paper is organized as follows. First, we describe the research strategy. In brief, we represented the developing lexicon as an evolving network and we used word co-occurrence in parent speech as a measure of words' relatedness. We operationalized abstract concepts as the highly interconnected regions of the network. Second, we explore how the pattern of children's word learning influences higher-level conceptual development,

Proceedings of the Workshop on Cognitive Modeling and Computational Linguistics, pages 129–133
Minneapolis, USA, June 7, 2019. ©2019 Association for Computational Linguistics

and whether this development corresponds to simultaneous or sequential conceptual growth.

2   Data and Methods

2.1   Constructing Lexical Networks

The networks' nodes were nouns from Wordbank (Frank et al., 2017), an open repository aggregating cross-linguistic developmental data of the MacArthur-Bates Communicative Development Inventory (CDI), Toddler version (Fenson et al., 1994). Pairs of nouns were linked by weighted edges representing their semantic similarity derived based on co-occurrence in the corpus of child-directed speech CHILDES (MacWhinney, 2014), using the Word2Vec algorithm (Mikolov et al., 2013).

First, we constructed the end-state network based on all nouns learned by the last age of acquisition. We used a subset of CDI nouns for which cross-linguistic translations are present, allowing us to explore cross-linguistic variability. We used data from the following ten languages: Croatian, Danish, English, French, Italian, Norwegian, Russian, Spanish, Swedish, and Turkish. The size of this subset varied from 314 in Russian (representing 100% of total nouns present in the CDI data of this language) to 176 in Turkish (representing 59.26% of total nouns). Second, in order to study development towards the end-state, we constructed a different network at each month, based on the nouns that have been learned by that month.

2.2   Identifying Abstract Concepts in a Network

We assume that abstract concepts correspond to clusters of highly interconnected nodes in the networks. We identified such clusters using Walk-Trap (Pons and Latapy, 2006), an unsupervised community detection algorithm based on the fact that a random walker tends to be trapped in dense parts of a network. Figure 1 shows the outcome of cluster identification in the end-state network in English. The algorithm obtained four major clusters corresponding to the categories of clothes, food, animal and artifacts. We refer to this end-state clustering as C^*. To examine developmental change in the conceptual organization, we ran the cluster identification algorithm at each month of acquisition t, and we compared the resulting clustering, noted C_t, to that of the end-state C^*. The method of this comparison is detailed below.

2.3   Measuring Conceptual Development

We measure conceptual development by comparing C_t to C^* across time. We used a standard method in clustering comparison, which is based on word pairs on which the two clusterings agree or disagree (Rand, 1971; Hubert and Arabie, 1985). We quantify clustering comparison using precision $P(C_t)$ and recall $R(C_t)$, defined as follows:

$$P(C_t) = \frac{|tp(C_t)|}{|tp(C_t)| + |fp(C_t)|}$$

$$R(C_t) = \frac{|tp(C_t)|}{|tp(C_t)| + |fn(C_t)|}$$

Where $tp(C_t)$ are the true positives, defined as the word pairs that are placed in the same cluster under C_t and in the same cluster under C^*. $fp(C_t)$ are the false positives, defined as the pairs placed in the same cluster under C_t and in different clusters under C^*. Finally, $fn(C_t)$ are the false negatives, defined as the pairs placed in different clusters under C_t and in the same cluster under C^*.

We made this comparison using different degrees of clustering granularity. More precisely, we fixed the same number of clusters for *both* C_t and C^*, and we varied this number from two to four clusters. We did not use the trivial case of one cluster, nor did we use more than four clusters, since this number was optimal for the largest network (i.e., the end-state network) based on the modularity maximization criterion (Newman, 2006).

2.4   Learning Mechanisms

We examined how abstract concepts develop under an average word learning trajectory derived from real developmental data. To construct this trajectory, we used the normative age of acquisition, that is, the age at which a word is produced by at least 50% of children in each language (Goodman et al., 2008). As mentioned above, we compared this development to the development induced by a first hypothetical trajectory where known words influence future word learning and a second hypothetical trajectory where learning proceeds regardless of what words are already known.

We instantiated the first trajectory through sampling from one conceptual category at a time: the first word is selected randomly from one cluster, subsequent words are sampled from the same cluster. After all words from this cluster are used, a

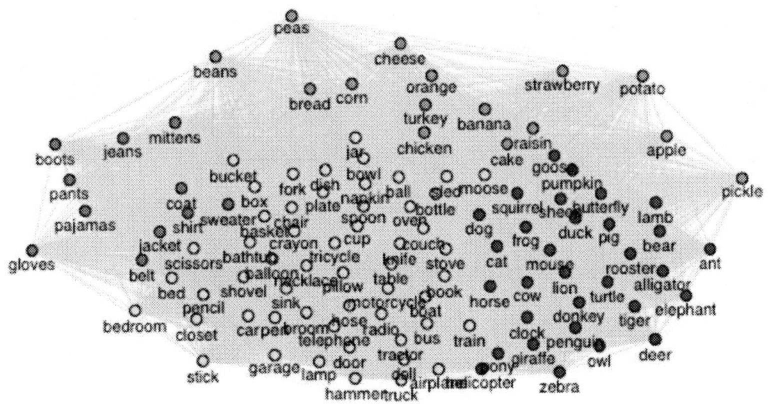

Figure 1: Network obtained using a sample of nouns in CDI data (nodes), and co-occurrence-based similarity from a corpus of child-directed speech (edges). Colors indicate highly interconnected clusters identified using unsupervised network community detection. The clusters correspond, overall, to four higher-level concepts: animal, food, clothes, and artifacts.

word from a different cluster is chosen, and the same process is repeated until all clusters are covered. We call this sampling procedure the *sequential model*. We instantiated the second trajectory through a uniform sampling across time from the end-state vocabulary. We call this sampling procedure the *simultaneous model*.

3 Results

Figure 2 shows the scores obtained through comparing C^* to C_t at different points in time t. For the real word learning trajectory, both precision and recall start relatively low, indicating that the induced conceptual organization is initially quite different from that of the end-state. Both measures converge towards 1 (i.e., perfect score) as C_t becomes more and more similar to C^*.

The simultaneous model mimics closely the patterns of real conceptual development, explaining almost all the variance in mean precision ($R^2 = 0.94$) and recall ($R^2 = 0.99$). In contrast, the sequential model had generally a higher precision, i.e., it induced fewer false positive pairs. This result is due to the fact that we sampled instances from the same category. However, the same model had generally lower recall scores, i.e., it induced more false negative pairs. This second result was due to the fact that sampling from the same category leads to clusterings that are finer in their con-

ceptual granularity than the end-state. As a consequence of this discrepancy with respect to real development, the sequential model explained less variance than the simultaneous model did in both its mean precision ($R^2 = 0.44$) and recall ($R^2 = 0.96$).

4 Discussion

Can children learn abstract concepts based on word co-occurrence in the language they hear around them? Previous work has shown that child-directed speech contains information about several abstract concepts (Huebner and Willits, 2018). Here we investigated when and how this information becomes available to children as their lexical network grows. We found that even with a small lexicon, several high-level concepts such as "animal", "artifact", "food" and "clothes" emerge bottom-up as clusters of highly interconnected nodes in the network. Furthermore, compared with a model that posited sequential learning, we found that these categories tended to emerge in concert with one another.

The development of the higher-level conceptual structure seems to be unaffected by the order with which words are acquired (as long as this order approximates a uniform sampling from the end-state lexicon), suggesting that the process of conceptual development can accommodate a wide range

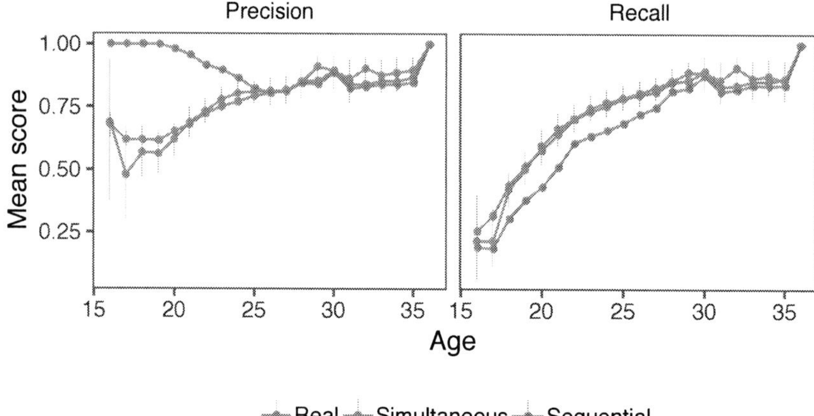

Figure 2: Mean precision and recall scores obtained through comparing the end-state clustering to clusterings at different months of acquisition, averaged across languages and numbers of clusters. Colors indicates real and hypothetical word sampling mechanisms. Errors bars represent 95% confidence intervals.

of word learning trajectories without a qualitative change in the higher-level organization. For example, whether acquisition starts first with the words "cat" and "banana" or with the words "cow" and "potato" does not qualitatively affect the higher-level organization involving "animal" and "food". This property is important as it suggests, for instance, that development is resilient to variability in the children's linguistic input (Slobin, 2014; Hart and Risley, 1995).

Developmental changes were captured by precision and recall. The increase in precision means that false positives decrease over time: some word pairs that are initially lumped together in a same category, are eventually differentiated. Similarly, the increase in recall means that false negatives decrease, that is, some word pairs that are initially distinct, become eventually subsumed by a same category. These patterns suggest a process of conceptual reorganization involving both "differentiation" and "coalescence" as has been suggested in the developmental literature (Carey, 2009).

That said, these developmental changes were not necessarily related to specific concepts (since the patterns were similar in the simultaneous model where we randomized the order of word learning). Instead, this finding suggests that differentiation and coalescence of word pairs in our data are related to the change in the vocabulary size across development: As more words are added to their lexical network, learners may approximate

better the underlying conceptual organization of the mature lexicon and would make fewer categorization errors. Indeed, research in network science indicates that properties of a real network become more distorted as the size of a sampled sub-network decreases (Leskovec and Faloutsos, 2006).

One limitation of this study is that we used the normative age of acquisition, computed using different children at different age groups. This choice was due to the cross-sectional nature of available CDI data. Though such a measure has been widely used to study important aspects of the early lexical networks (Hills et al., 2009; Stella et al., 2017; Storkel, 2009), it only applies at the population level. In our case, though we found that concepts develop simultaneously, individual children may display, at least locally, a sequential-like behavior. For example, prior knowledge about dinosaurs may enable the learning of new dinosaur-related words more easily (Chi and Koeske, 1983).

In sum, this work provided a quantitative account of how abstract concepts can emerge from the interaction of the children's emerging vocabulary and the properties of their linguistic input. One important direction for future work is to investigate the extent to which the correlational findings obtained in this study (e.g., the identity of categories formed across development or the fact that categorization errors decrease with the size of the lexicon) can be corroborated by controlled behavioral experiments.

All data and code are available at
https://github.com/afourtassi/conceptNet

References

Arielle Borovsky, Erica M Ellis, Julia L Evans, and Jeffrey L Elman. 2016. Lexical leverage: Category knowledge boosts real-time novel word recognition in 2-year-olds. *Developmental science*, 19(6).

Susan Carey. 2009. *The origin of concepts*. Oxford University Press.

Michelene TH Chi and Randi Daimon Koeske. 1983. Network representation of a child's dinosaur knowledge. *Developmental psychology*, 19(1).

Gergely Csibra and György Gergely. 2009. Natural pedagogy. *Trends in cognitive sciences*, 13(4).

Larry Fenson, Philip S. Dale, J. Steven Reznick, Elizabeth Bates, Donna J. Thal, Stephen J. Pethick, Michael Tomasello, Carolyn B. Mervis, and Joan Stiles. 1994. Variability in early communicative development. *Monographs of the Society for Research in Child Development*, 59(5).

Michael C. Frank, Mika Braginsky, Daniel Yurovsky, and Virginia A. Marchman. 2017. Wordbank: an open repository for developmental vocabulary data. *Journal of Child Language*, 44(3):677–694.

Susan A Gelman. 2009. Learning from others: Children's construction of concepts. *Annual review of psychology*, 60.

Judith C. Goodman, Philip S. Dale, and Ping Li. 2008. Does frequency count? parental input and the acquisition of vocabulary. *Journal of Child Language*, 35(3):515–531.

Alison Gopnik and Andrew N Meltzoff. 1997. *Words, thoughts, and theories*. MIT Press.

Paul L Harris. 2012. *Trusting what you're told: How children learn from others*. Harvard University Press.

Betty Hart and Todd R Risley. 1995. *Meaningful differences in the everyday experience of young American children*. Paul H Brookes Publishing.

Thomas T. Hills, Mounir Maouene, Josita Maouene, Adam Sheya, and Linda Smith. 2009. Longitudinal analysis of early semantic networks: Preferential attachment or preferential acquisition? *Psychological Science*, 20(6):729–739.

Lawrence Hubert and Phipps Arabie. 1985. Comparing partitions. *Journal of classification*, 2(1).

Philip A Huebner and Jon A Willits. 2018. Structured semantic knowledge can emerge automatically from predicting word sequences in child-directed speech. *Frontiers in Psychology*, 9:133.

Frank C Keil. 1992. *Concepts, kinds, and cognitive development*. MIT Press.

Jure Leskovec and Christos Faloutsos. 2006. Sampling from large graphs. In *Proceedings of the 12th ACM SIGKDD international conference on Knowledge discovery and data mining*. ACM.

Brian MacWhinney. 2014. *The CHILDES project: Tools for analyzing talk, Volume II*. Psychology Press.

Tomas Mikolov, Ilya Sutskever, Kai Chen, Greg S Corrado, and Jeff Dean. 2013. Distributed representations of words and phrases and their compositionality. In *Advances in neural information processing systems*.

Mark EJ Newman. 2006. Modularity and community structure in networks. *Proceedings of the national academy of sciences*, 103(23).

Pascal Pons and Matthieu Latapy. 2006. Computing communities in large networks using random walks. *Journal of Graph Algorithms and Applications*, 10(2).

William M Rand. 1971. Objective criteria for the evaluation of clustering methods. *Journal of the American Statistical association*, 66(336).

Ann E Sizemore, Elisabeth A Karuza, Chad Giusti, and Danielle S Bassett. 2018. Knowledge gaps in the early growth of semantic feature networks. *Nature human behaviour*, 2(9).

Dan Isaac Slobin. 2014. *The crosslinguistic study of language acquisition*, volume 4. Psychology Press.

Massimo Stella, Nicole M Beckage, and Markus Brede. 2017. Multiplex lexical networks reveal patterns in early word acquisition in children. *Scientific Reports*, 7.

Mark Steyvers and Joshua B. Tenenbaum. 2005. The large-scale structure of semantic networks: Statistical analyses and a model of semantic growth. *Cognitive Science*, 29(1):41–78.

Holly L. Storkel. 2009. Developmental differences in the effects of phonological, lexical and semantic variables on word learning by infants. *Journal of Child Language*, 36(2):29–321.

Verb-second Effect on Quantifier Scope Interpretation

Asad Sayeed
Dept. of Philosophy, Linguistics,
and Theory of Science
University of Gothenburg, Sweden
`asad.sayeed@gu.se`

Matthias Lindemann[1], Vera Demberg[1,2]
[1]Dept. of Lang. Sci. and Tech.
[2]Dept. of Math. and CS
Saarland University, Germany
`malinux@t-online.de`
`vera@coli.uni-saarland.de`

Abstract

Sentences like *Every child climbed a tree* have at least two interpretations depending on the precedence order of the universal quantifier and the indefinite. Previous experimental work explores the role that different mechanisms such as semantic reanalysis and world knowledge may have in enabling each interpretation. This paper discusses a web-based task that uses the verb-second characteristic of German main clauses to estimate the influence of word order variation over world knowledge.

1 Introduction

In this paper, we present results from an online cloze (fill-in-the-blank) experiment in German designed to exploit the verb-second syntax of German main clauses in order to understand the relationship between factors involved in quantifier scope ambiguity resolution. An example of quantifier scope ambiguity in English is the sentence "Everybody loves somebody", which has at least two readings: either that (a) every person in the universe of discourse loves some person, but there are possibly different people being loved (linear scope), or (b) that there is exactly one person who is loved by everyone in the universe of discourse[1] (inverse scope).

Humans are both able to perceive scope ambiguities and resolve them in context with relative ease—such that reading (a) is quickly preferred, even though it is a seemingly "out-of-context" example. Potential ambiguities are actually relatively common (Koller et al., 2010), even if example sentences used to understand their formal properties seem rather contrived. Indeed, the

---

[1]Taken in a narrowly logical way, reading (b) permits (a) to be true. Pragmatically speaking, however, reading (a) suggests that there are likely multiple/different people being loved. See Radó and Bott (2018) for an argument that the fine-grained logical implication is important from a processing point of view.

study of the formal properties of scope-ambiguous sentences has a long history in formal semantics (Ruys and Winter, 2011), especially as it pertains to the conditions under which ambiguous readings are available. However, psycholinguistic models of how scope ambiguities are *resolved* (as opposed to merely being made formally available) is a much less developed area of research, but whose development is necessary for, e.g., better computational models of language understanding.

The key issue is the integration of multiple factors: local context, background world-knowledge, "classical" syntax-semantics interface constraints, and so on. For example, in the two readings of *Every child climbed a tree*, common sense generally suggests that the children are climbing multiple trees, which may come from general overall experience of tree-climbing, the affordances (Gibson, 1977) of trees, and so on. Nevertheless, similar sentences have more easily available inverse scope readings, such as *Every jeweler appraised a diamond*. When, if at all, does the human processor "activate" the knowledge that both readings are available (from formal syntactic and semantic structure), and how does this formal knowledge interact with lexical-pragmatic knowledge about trees or diamonds?

2 Background

Early work (e.g., Fodor, 1982) suggested that quantifiers and word order interact, such that when an existential quantifier precedes a universal quantifier, the processor must act to reverse the linear order in order to get a plural reading for the existential quantifier, and *vice versa*. Various psycholinguistic techniques have been brought to bear on the question, especially using the English language as the experimental medium, among them judgement studies, eye-tracking, self-paced read-

Proceedings of the Workshop on Cognitive Modeling and Computational Linguistics, pages 134–139
Minneapolis, USA, June 7, 2019. ©2019 Association for Computational Linguistics

(1) Jeder Spion   hat diesen/einen/diese Auftrag/Aufträge erhalten. [*Der/die Auftrag/Aufträge war(en)*]
    Every spy_{NOM} has this/a/these   order(s)_{ACC}   received. [*The   order(s)   was/were*]
    gefährlich und riskant.
    dangerous and risky.
    'Every spy received this/a/these order(s). [*The order(s) was/were*] dangerous and risky.'

(2) Diesen/Einen/Diese Auftrag/Aufträge hat jeder Spion   erhalten. [*Der/die Auftrag/Aufträge war(en)*]
    This/A/These   order(s)_{ACC}   has every spy_{NOM} received. [*The   order(s)   was/were*]
    gefährlich und riskant.
    dangerous and risky.
    'Every spy received this/a/these order(s). [*The order(s) was/were*] dangerous and risky.'

Figure 1: Stimulus example.

ing, and event-related potentials (ERP). Kurtzman and MacDonald (1993) performed a foundational judgement study in English with a "context-continuation" experimental paradigm, where an ambiguously quantified (universal-existential or existential-universal) sentence (the "context") is followed by another sentence (the "continuation") that contains a singular or plural reference to the existentially quantified noun phrase in the context.

(3) *Context:* Every gardener watered **a plant**.
    Continuation: **The plant** was tall and sturdy.

Example (3) illustrates the context-continuation paradigm. In this case, the singular subject of the continuation requires an inverse scope interpretation of the context.

Testing the acceptability of these sentence pairs is more sensitive to online processing than asking for explicit interpretation outright, and Kurtzman and MacDonald used judgement tasks of this nature and found no single principle under which a preference for particular interpretation could be identified. They tested swapping the linear order of quantifiers (e.g., "A gardener watered every plant"), and found no effect of linear order. One problem with such a study is that the quantifiers are swapped while keeping the semantic roles filled by the same nouns, so that it is not possible to separate the effect of linear order from common-sense interpretation.

Filik et al. (2004) performed judgement and eye-tracking studies on English sentences by using double object constructions where the direct and indirect objects had ambiguous universal and existential quantifier scopes. It is possible to swap these in English. This is under a theory where a grammatical hierarchy of constituents (Ioup, 1975) conflicts with linear order. They found that the linear order effect interacts with the grammatical hierarchy effects in both experimental modalities. However, double object constructions involve either an optional argument or one of a subset of verbs representing events that obligatorily require indirect objects, restricting the ability of this type of study to explore the role of world knowledge[2].

Dwivedi (2013) performed a reading-time study based on stimuli similar to those of Kurtzman and MacDonald, with universal-existential order only for the context sentence and found no significant effects reflecting an online reanalysis process or a competition process in the manner of Kurtzman and MacDonald (1993) or Filik et al. (2004). On the contrary, in a question-answering task after each sentence pair, participants remembered and identified singular continuations at below chance level, being strongly guided by pragmatic intuitions. Dwivedi takes this to reflect a "heuristic first, algorithmic second" theory of scope processing—that the human processor may be *able* to reanalyze ambiguous quantifiers, but does not do so unless very strongly provoked to do so, and instead relies almost entirely on background and contextual knowledge.

Subject-verb-object (SVO) transitive constructions present a greater opportunity to explore the role of semantic events and associated knowledge than double object constructions, but use of the English language presents some limitations. A better exploration of the roles of algorithmic knowledge, linear order, and reanalysis processes in quantifier scope ambiguity processing could be performed in a language that allows for variation of order of the quantifiers without a fundamental change to the semantics of the situation be-

---

[2]See Dwivedi (2013) for further discussion of Filik et al.'s stimuli.

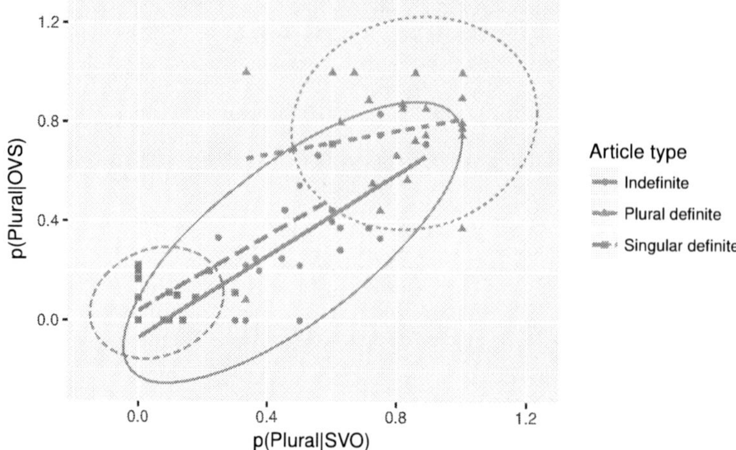

Figure 2: Correlation plot of the probability of plural interpretations given SVO order vs. OVS order, for indefinite, definite singular, and definite plural conditions. Data ellipses illustrate means and standard deviations for each condition in two dimensions (Friendly et al., 2013).

ing represented. Simply swapping object and subject in simple declarative clauses is unacceptable in English, but much less so in verb-second, case-marking languages like German.

Radó and Bott (2018) investigate the role of quantifier distributivity relative to linear order using a series of context-continuation judgement tasks in German. Part of their manipulation is main-clause SVO order vs OSV given German's verb-second characteristic; in German main clauses, quantifier scope ambiguities are possible. However, they use visual aids to explicitly disambiguate the intended interpretation of the sentence, so that the judgement task is about matching the appropriateness of the sentence to the image. Thus, world knowledge effects are factored out of their experiment.

In this work, we instead exploit the SVO/OVS flexibility of German main clauses to better characterise how linear order, formal semantic structure, and world knowledge work together to produce interpretations. We hypothesize that Dwivedi's manipulation yields her result for English because English-speakers rarely, if ever, expect to see linear order variation. The low acceptability of an OVS order in declarative sentences in English means that English users have a much lower expectation of having to reverse the observed linear scope order in order to align their pragmatically-driven interpretation with the observed sentence. Correspondingly, English-

speakers only infrequently invoke "algorithmic" processing mechanisms. German-speakers find OVS order much more acceptable than English-speakers. This means that German-speakers are more likely to confront variation in word order, leading to mismatches between world knowledge and linear order. Since German-speakers expect to confront mismatches more often, syntactic and semantic structure, including word order, will have a more visible effect on number interpretation, providing more visible resistance to the influence of background knowledge. In order to test this, we make use of a web-based cloze task under the context-continuation paradigm, giving participants a free choice of interpretation.

3   Methods and Materials

We translated the English stimuli from Dwivedi (2013) to German, making adjustments or replacements where the syntax or semantics did not work with normal German usage. For the German context sentences, we varied the word order from SVO to OVS order[3] and we had three conditions for the object article: definite singular, indefinite, and definite plural, for six total conditions. The

---

[3] A reviewer points out that our experiment could work, in theory, for any language where the object can optionally precede the subject in a declarative main clause, not merely for verb-second languages. We consider this highly plausible, but we chose not to commit to a more ambitious hypothesis without further analysis of the associated linguistic phenomena beyond Germanic verb-second.

	b	Std. Error	z	$Pr(>|z|)$	
Intercept	-1.1176	0.3732	-2.994	0.00275	**
Linearity(SVO)	0.9260	0.2844	3.256	0.00113	**

Signif. codes: 0 '***' 0.001 '**' 0.01 '*' 0.05 '.' 0.1 ' ' 1

Table 1: Fitted mixed-effects model of word order on plural interpretation for objects with the indefinite article.

continuation sentences were supplied with a blank space for the subject and verb, with a final complement describing the targeted subject. ·

Examples (1) and (2) represent the stimuli we used. The italicized portions are the intended cloze fillers: participants are expected to fill in the subject and the verb, which would thereby reveal their intuitions about number.

The stimuli were randomized into six lists, and 24 fillers were created and added to each list. The stimuli were presented using Lingoturk[4], a workbench for developing and hosting web-based experiments (Pusse et al., 2016), one stimulus per screen, after two training exercises. A mix of participants were recruited, both native-speaker undergraduate students at a university in a German-speaking country and online via Prolific[5], which permits selection by native language.

The collected data (filled blanks) were then coded by a native speaker for whether they represented an unambiguously singular or plural judgement, were ambiguous (e.g., the participant substituted a subject-verb combination that did not refer to the object of the context sentence), or were uninterpretable.

4 Results and Discussion

There were a total of 66 participants, of which 31 were students and 35 were Prolific participants. The student participants were collected first, upon which we discovered that two items had errors. We discarded the data for those items, corrected the errors, and ran the full set with the Prolific participants. This yielded 1546 responses, 1236 of which were unambiguous references to the object of the context sentence with interpretable number[6].

We expected from their semantic interpretations that singular and plural definite articles would produce strong singular and plural interpretations re-

spectively, regardless of any underlying pragmatic bias of the item. We plotted the probability of plural interpretation per item given SVO order vs. OVS order (figure 2). It illustrated that singular and plural interpretations are, as expected, little affected by order when the determiner is definite: they tend to agree with the number of the determiner, and items in the plot cluster near zero probability of plural interpretation for the singular definite condition and high probability of plural interpretation in the plural definite condition. With the indefinite article, however, we obtain nearly the full range of plural biases, with some items having low plural probability with either word order and some high.

We fitted a binomial logit regression model with mixed effects for the indefinite article condition under the hypothesis $Plurality \sim Linearity + (1|Item) + (1 + Linearity|Participant)$; that is, the plural response has a fixed effect of linearity with a random intercept per item (given variation in the overall semantic plural bias of the item) and a correlated random intercept and slope for linearity relative to participant, reflecting overall individual tendencies to give plural interpretations and individual effects of linear order. This was performed in R under the `lme4` package (Bates et al., 2014). The fixed-effects model output is presented in table 1. This model produces a significant effect on plural interpretation in indefinite order sentences, with log-odds ratio $b = 0.926$ in favour of a plural interpretation when the context sentence is in SVO order.

While the plurality of each item is highly preserved in either order, OVS items are indeed less likely to be interpreted as plural, resulting in a slope of the fitted line for the indefinite condition in figure 2 that is visibly less than 1 and reflecting the outcome of the binomial logit regression.

Dwivedi's self-paced reading results in English present a picture of a system that employs reanalysis on ambiguous scopes mostly *in extremis*, but otherwise relies principally on lexical-pragmatic associations in interpretation. Our results do not

---

[4] `https://github.com/FlorianPusse/Lingoturk`

[5] `https://www.prolific.ac`

[6] The data are available upon request to first author.

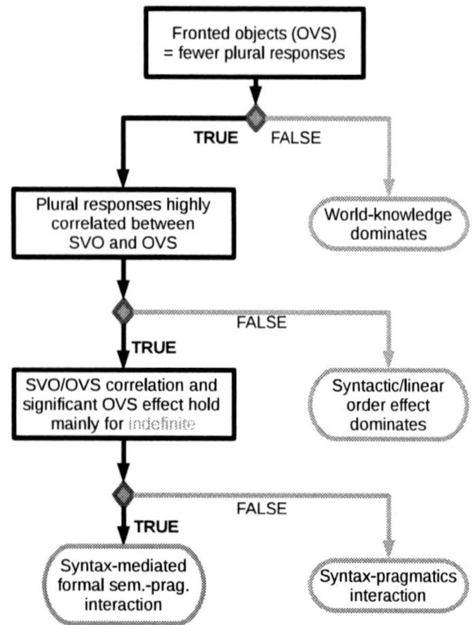

Figure 3: Possible outcomes of the experiment relative to hypothesis over dominant mechanisms of ambiguous quantifier scope processing.

challenge the centrality of background world and lexical knowledge, but instead, reflect a somewhat stronger role for the "algorithmic" component of scope processing. Specifically, German speakers' syntactic expectations admit OVS orders more naturally than English speakers, so that when an OVS order is encountered, it creates a "headwind", triggered by an initial indefinite article, that the powerful force of world knowledge must overcome. This mechanism is specifically invoked by the appearance of an indefinite object noun phrase in the initial position, while singular definite articles totally override world knowledge regardless of order.

Dwivedi measured plural bias for her original 2013 stimuli using a forced choice singular/plural interpretation task. We instead opted for a cloze task, which we believe has higher ecological validity—the task avoids forcing participants to choose among options when they may not feel that any of them are suitable or natural. A potential disadvantage of free completions is that participants sometimes filled the subject/verb field in a manner that would not let us determine whether they intended a singular or a plural reference to the object phrase or with a nonsense response; these responses had to be discarded before analysis. In our case, this happened in 20% of the data, still

leaving us with a sufficient amount of interpretable data. The advantage of this approach in the investigation of quantifier scope processing is that it does not explicitly call on participants to think about and judge plurality as a concept, but rather to come up with a phrase that makes sense to them in context.

5 Conclusions and Future Work

Figure 3 provides a visual description of the hypothesis space we considered for this experiment. To the proposition that world knowledge is overly dominant, we found that our result pushes the needle back in the direction of competition-based hypotheses. The specific role of indefinite articles triggering these ambiguities over word order points once again to a complex interaction at the interface between syntax, semantics, and pragmatics. We also demonstrated the experimental value of free(r) word order languages with case marking.

Our cloze task illustrates an aspect of the role of syntactic variation in quantifier interpretation. In order to investigate its specific time course, the most immediate future work is to take our stimuli to other experimental modalities, including self-paced reading and eyetracking.

In the longer run, we plan to use corpus (Sayeed, 2017) and machine learning investigations to determine the empirical basis of plurality judgements in ambiguously scoped events.

Acknowledgements

This work was supported by funding from the German Research Foundation (DFG) for the Cluster of Excellence "Multimodal Computing and Interaction" (EXC 284) and from the Swedish Research Council (VR) for the Center for Linguistic Theory and Studies in Probability (2014-39).

References

Douglas Bates, Martin Mächler, Ben Bolker, and Steve Walker. 2014. Fitting linear mixed-effects models using lme4. *arXiv preprint arXiv:1406.5823*.

Veena D Dwivedi. 2013. Interpreting quantifier scope ambiguity: Evidence of heuristic first, algorithmic second processing. *PloS one*, 8(11):e81461.

Ruth Filik, Kevin B. Paterson, and Simon P. Liversedge. 2004. Processing doubly quantified sentences: Evidence from eye movements. *Psychonomic Bulletin & Review*, 11(5):953–959.

Janet Dean Fodor. 1982. The mental representation of quantifiers. In *Processes, beliefs, and questions*, pages 129–164. Springer.

Michael Friendly, Georges Monette, and John Fox. 2013. Elliptical insights: Understanding statistical methods through elliptical geometry. *Statist. Sci.*, 28(1):1–39.

James J. Gibson. 1977. The theory of affordances. In John Bransford Robert E Shaw, editor, *Perceiving, acting, and knowing: toward an ecological psychology*, pages pp.67–82. Hillsdale, N.J. : Lawrence Erlbaum Associates.

Georgette Ioup. 1975. Some universals for quantifier scope. *Syntax and semantics*, 4:37–58.

Alexander Koller, Stefan Thater, and Manfred Pinkal. 2010. Scope underspecification with tree descriptions: Theory and practice. In Matthew W. Crocker and Jrg Siekmann, editors, *Resource-Adaptive Cognitive Processes*, Cognitive Technologies, pages 337–364. Springer.

Howard S Kurtzman and Maryellen C MacDonald. 1993. Resolution of quantifier scope ambiguities. *Cognition*, 48(3):243–279.

Florian Pusse, Asad Sayeed, and Vera Demberg. 2016. Lingoturk: managing crowdsourced tasks for psycholinguistics. In *Proceedings of the 2016 Conference of the North American Chapter of the Association for Computational Linguistics: Demonstrations*, pages 57–61, San Diego, California. Association for Computational Linguistics.

Janina Radó and Oliver Bott. 2018. What do speaker judgments tell us about theories of quantifier scope in German? *Glossa: a journal of general linguistics*, 3(1).

EG Ruys and Yoad Winter. 2011. Quantifier scope in formal linguistics. In *Handbook of philosophical logic*, pages 159–225. Springer.

Asad Sayeed. 2017. Towards an annotation framework for incremental scope specification update. In *Proceedings of the conference on logic and machine learning in natural language (LaML 2017)*, Gothenburg.

Neural Models of the Psychosemantics of 'Most'

Lewis O'Sullivan
Brain and Cognitive Sciences
Universiteit van Amsterdam
lewis.osullivan@student.uva.nl

Shane Steinert-Threlkeld
Institute for Logic, Language and Computation
Universiteit van Amsterdam
S.N.M.Steinert-Threlkeld@uva.nl

Abstract

How are the meanings of linguistic expressions related to their use in concrete cognitive tasks? Visual identification tasks show human speakers can exhibit considerable variation in their understanding, representation and verification of certain quantifiers. This paper initiates an investigation into neural models of these psycho-semantic tasks. We trained two types of network – a convolutional neural network (CNN) model and a recurrent model of visual attention (RAM) – on the "most" verification task from Pietroski et al. (2009), manipulating the visual scene and novel notions of task duration. Our results qualitatively mirror certain features of human performance (such as sensitivity to the ratio of set sizes, indicating a reliance on approximate number) while differing in interesting ways (such as exhibiting a subtly different pattern for the effect of image type). We conclude by discussing the prospects for using neural models as cognitive models of this and other psychosemantic tasks.

1 Introduction

Semantics – the scientific study of meaning – has traditionally studied the truth-conditions of sentences and how the meanings of sub-sentential expressions combine to generate them. How exactly truth-conditions are represented and then deployed in concrete acts of production and comprehension has often not been seen as belonging to the purview of semantics properly.

A recent line of work, however, has argued that the mental representation of the meanings of expressions bias behavior in cognitive tasks in ways that allow us to adjudicate between truth-conditionally equivalent but representationally distinct semantic theories. In particular, Pietroski et al. (2009) considered the verification of the sentence "Most of the dots are yellow". The meaning of 'most' can be expressed in distinct, but truth-conditionally equivalent ways. For instance (where, in the running example, A is the set of dots, and B the set of yellow things):

- $[\![\text{most}]\!](A)(B) = 1$ iff $|A \cap B| > |A \setminus B|$

- $[\![\text{most}]\!](A)(B) = 1$ iff there is $f : A \setminus B \to A \cap B$ that is one-to-one, but not onto

The former says that the number of dots which are yellow is larger than the number of non-yellow dots, while the latter says that the former can be paired off with the latter, with some yellow dots remaining. Whilst these representations are truth conditionally equivalent, each is associated with a distinct *verification strategy* to evaluate those truth conditions. When deciding whether most of the dots are yellow: the former representation is associated with an algorithm for computing and comparing two cardinalities, while the latter representation is associated with an algorithm for checking whether a certain correspondence between yellow and non-yellow dots exists. Whilst a speaker may be capable of implementing many possible strategies, Pietroski et al. (2009)'s claim is that, all other things being equal, speakers are biased towards using the default strategy associated with their representation.

Pietroski et al. (2009) sought to determine whether speakers prefer one of the above representations by testing which verification strategy they typically use. By manipulating the arrangement of the dots in images against which 'most' was verified, they created conditions which should ease the implementation of one of the strategies (e.g. dots arranged in pairs should favour correspondence). They found no difference in verification accuracy between three of the four image types used. Participants were significantly more accurate on the remaining image type, which consisted of two paired columns of colour sorted dots.

Proceedings of the Workshop on Cognitive Modeling and Computational Linguistics, pages 140–151
Minneapolis, USA, June 7, 2019. ©2019 Association for Computational Linguistics

Their analysis suggested that the participants used the columns' lengths as a proxy for set cardinality, rather than using a correspondence strategy. The results of the remaining three image types were explaind very well by a psychophyiscal model of approximate number. Given that this system cannot be used to implement a correspondence strategy, they concluded that the meaning of 'most' is best represented in the former way.[1]

In this paper, we begin to develop robust mechanistic *cognitive models* of their sentence verification task to help elucidate the factors underlying the psychosemantics of 'most'. In particular, we are interested in the following question: do various neural models show the potential to be developed into good cognitive models of the meaning of 'most'? A good cognitive model does at least two things: (i) fits human data well and (ii) has movable parameters that enable new predictions to be made. To address this question, we subjected two different classes of models – convolutional networks and recurrent models of visual attention – to the experimental design from Pietroski et al. (2009), together with an additional and novel manipulation for 'task duration' (inspired by Register et al. (2018)). This allows us to assess the models along both dimensions (i) and (ii). Our key contributions are:

- Subjecting neural models to prominent tasks from the psychosemantics literature.

- Operationalizing 'task duration' in two distinct ways: depth of a convolutional network, and the number of glimpses in a model of visual attention.

The key findings from our experiments are:

- Both models exhibit patterns of behavior qualitatively similar to humans, including sensitivity to dot ratio.

- The psychophysical model of approximate number fits model data well, with parameters not too far from human participants.

- Model performance is effected by the image type in a subtly different way than human performance.

---

[1] See Lidz et al. (2011) for further research in this direction, distinguishing between more candidate representations.

- The effect of task duration is more robust for the convolutional networks than for visual attention.

After discussing related work in the next section, we outline the hypotheses of our experiment, before a full explanation of our methods and results. We conclude by discussing the results and outlining future work.

2 Related Work

2.1 "Most" and the Visual Identification Task

As discussed in the introduction, different representations of a quantifier's meaning may reflect different default verification strategies. This raises the question: given the many psychologically plausible verification strategies, can we determine whether any are favoured by speakers? Pietroski et al. (2009) addressed this question using the methods described above. Consequently, by identifying where speakers were most accurate, they were able to determine which strategy speakers favour and, thus, how 'most' is represented.

Their results suggested that speakers favour a cardinality comparison strategy, computed via the approximate number system (ANS) (Dehaene, 1997). The ANS is a cognitive system for representing magnitudes. Instead of relying on discrete symbols, such as precise cardinalities, the ANS's representations are imprecise and distributed. They can be described using a series of overlapping Gaussian curves across a continuous 'number line': each curve's mean is the cardinality which it corresponds to and the standard deviations increase linearly with the cardinality. Thus, the greater the magnitude of a cardinality, the less precise is its ANS representation. Because the ANS follows what's known as Weber's law (Feigenson et al., 2004), the discriminability of any two ANS representations is determined by the extent of their overlap. Consequently, the difficulty of a cardinality comparison made using the ANS is dependent upon the ratio of the cardinalities. For instance, 6:12 is equally as discriminable as 12:24, or 30:60 or 1:2. This is because the distributions of the ANS representations used to describe these ratios overlap by an equal amount — they each have a Weber ratio of 2. The dependence of accuracy on ratio follows a psychophysical model that generates what are called Weber curves (to be described precisely in our Results section).

Pietroski et al. (2009) found that these curves fit participant data very well (in three of four image types) and thus suggest that speakers may employ the ANS as a "numeralising waystation" to interface with precise cardinal values. This would allow speakers to understand 'most' as a cardinality comparison, but to implement it using the imprecise representations of the ANS. Thus, they claim the semantics for "most" is specified in a way that includes cardinality comparison. We will subject neural models to the same experiment, to see whether they exhibit the same reliance on cardinality and approximation behavior.

Register et al. (2018) argued that it is likely that the participants in Pietroski et al. (2009) were implementing a speed-accuracy trade off due to the number (360) and duration (200ms) of the trials. As such, rather than the preferred semantics for "most", they suggest ANS usage may be a result of task-based strategising: participants relied on the speed and the low cognitive effort of an ANS-based strategy in order to cope with unrealistically high demands resulting from the brevity and quantity of the trials. They tested this by running several variations of the experiments from Pietroski et al. (2009). One experiment asked participants to verify a single trial with unconstrained response time (RT). Participants' RT and accuracy were negatively correlated, as would be expected were they implementing a speed accuracy trade-off. Nonetheless, their self-reports indicated that most participants used a cardinality comparison based strategy (i.e. either counting or estimating). A second experiment also manipulated the number of trials. Participants who completed more trials were more likely to report using an estimation-based strategy. Additionally, participants' RTs for individual trials decreased as they completed trials. Both of these findings suggest that use of the ANS in Pietroski et al. (2009) was in fact due to task-based strategising. These two findings show that while cardinality comparison is the preferred strategy, it may be computed by different means, depending upon the particular context. As such, the semantics of "most" are, to a degree, context dependent.[2] Our model(s) will incorporate an element of this context-sensitivity, by manipulating a variable not yet tested on humans: task duration, i.e. how long each trial takes.

---

[2]In a similar vein, Steinert-Threlkeld et al. (2015) show that 'most' and 'more than half' are differently effected by context under working memory load.

2.2 Quantifiers and Neural Networks

Steinert-Threlkeld and Szymanik (2018) investigated the hypothesis that semantic universals for quantifiers arise because expressions that satisfy a universal are easier to learn than those that do not. By treating the verification and falsification of quantified sentences as a sequence classification task, they trained long short-term memory networks (LSTMs) to learn the meaning of various quantifiers. These quantifiers corresponded to one of three universals (quantity, monotonicity or conservativity), and came in pairs: a real one satisfying the universal and a hypothetical one that does not. By observing whether the LSTMs could learn the expressions satisfying the universals faster (and by extension, more easily), they were able to test this hypothesis. They found that the LSTMs were able to learn to verify expressions which satisfied the quantity and monotonicity universals faster than those which did not, confirming their hypothesis. Not only does this show neural networks are capable of verifying quantifiers, but it suggests that they may do so in a similar way to human speakers. Nevertheless, their motivation was of a more abstract and theoretical nature; consequently, the networks are not tested on a concrete psycholinguistic task and compared to human performance, as we do here.

Kuhnle and Copestake (2018) aimed to show how psycholinguistic tasks may provide more informative methods for evaluating how neural networks solve natural language tasks. They trained the FiLM visual question-answering model from Perez et al. (2018) (a CNN + GRU hybrid) to complete a version of the VIT. Using the Shape World framework (Kuhnle and Copestake, 2017), they generated stimuli consisting of images containing coloured shape objects, a corresponding quantifier statement and a truth value for that statement. The objects were either entirely one colour but from two different shape sets (e.g. red squares and circles) or vice versa (e.g. red and blue squares). The ratio and arrangement of the objects was manipulated. The object set ratios ranged linearly from 1:2 to 7:8, and no image contained more than 15 objects. The objects were either randomly distributed, sorted into contrasting pairs which were randomly distributed, or partitioned by contrasting feature. They trained two instances of the network. The "Q-half" network trained on stimuli with "less/more than half" statements, whereas the

"Q-full" network trained on stimuli with a broader range of quantifier statements (e.g. "some" and modified numerals such as "at least 4"). Both networks' test phases exclusively used "less/more than half" statements.

Although they found differences in performance according to object arrangement, these did not indicate that the networks favoured any one verification strategy. They suggest the networks may have learned an "adaptive strategy" to optimise performance across trial types. Both networks attained high accuracy (100-72% between ratios 1:2 and 7:8) and became less accurate as the object set ratios became more balanced. The Q-full network was also tested on an evaluation set including the object ratios 8:9, 9:10 and 10:11 (and consequently 17-21 objects). By fitting Weber curves to these data, they found the network's Weber fraction was similar to human speakers'. They interpreted these last two findings as evidence that the network learned an ANS-like system. While these are promising results, because of different motivations, their stimuli differ in certain ways from those used by Pietroski et al. (2009), which prevents their models from being cognitive models of the latter task. Moreover, they have no operationalisation of task duration, to see in what way that affects performance.

3 Hypotheses

In the present experiment, we trained two types of neural network to complete a close replica of the VIT in Pietroski et al. (2009), with one major addition: we also manipulate task duration (as operationalised by parameters of our neural networks). Based on the VIT research with human speakers discussed in the previous section, we selected three 'behavioural traces' which neural networks ought to exhibit if they verify "most" in an algorithmically similar manner to human speakers. As such, replicating these behavioural traces is essential for the models to be candidate cognitive models. Note that we do not assume these traces correspond to, or are necessary evidence of underlying algorithmic similarity between neural networks and human speakers. However, such similarities would be sufficient causes of these traces. The behavioural traces and their associated hypotheses are:

1. ANS usage: Network accuracy is negatively correlated with the stimulus dot ratio size.

2. Verification strategy preference: Network accuracy is dependent upon the arrangement of the stimulus.

3. Speed-accuracy trade-off: Network accuracy is positively correlated with an appropriate operationalisation of task duration.

4 Methods

We generated a range of dot matrix stimuli, each of which consisted two dot sets in a particular ratio and spatial arrangement. Like Pietroski et al. (2009), we used up to 22 total dots per image, in ratios from 1:2 to 9:10 in one of four arrangements. These were: column pairs sorted (parallel columns of colour sorted dots), column pairs mixed (unsorted parallel columns), scattered pairs (randomly distributed colour-contrast dot pairs) and scattered random (randomly distributed dots). Figure 1 contains an example of each. Each image was labelled with a truth value for the statement "Most of the dots are blue". The stimuli were split into a training set (18000 images), a validation set, and a test set (3600 images each). All three sets were balanced to contain equal proportions of each ratio/image type/truth-value combination. While we refer to our dot sets as blue and yellow for consistency with the existing literature, we made the input to the networks grayscale in order to reduce dimensionality.

We used two types of neural network and as such, ran two adjacent experiments. The first of these was an off-the-shelf convolutional neural network (CNN) architecture: the VGG networks from Simonyan and Zisserman (2014).

The second was a variation of the recurrent model of visual attention (RAM) from Mnih et al. (2014).[3] This model processes its input serially in a manner that aims to replicate the saccades and fixations of human visual attention. It does this by taking a series of retina-like samples (called 'glimpses') of its 'environment' in order to extract the information needed to determine the best location for future glimpses and to solve its task. This process of visual search and attention reflects a core component of human visual scene representation (Rensink, 2000; Hayhoe and Ballard, 2005; Wolfe and Horowitz, 2017).

---

[3]In particular, the glimpse network described below did not have convolutional layers and used vector addition instead of component-wise multiplication in Mnih et al. (2014).

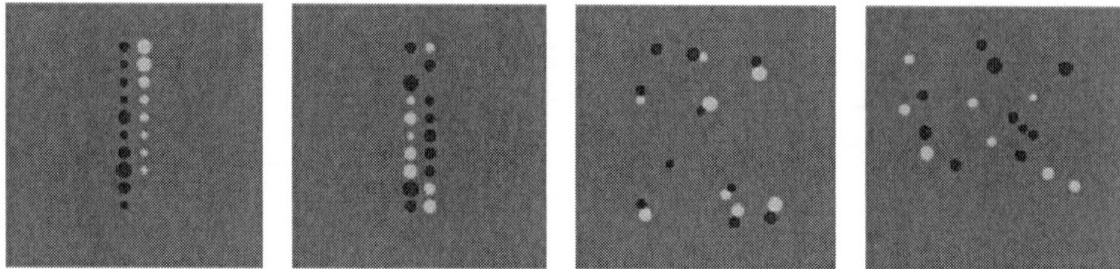

Figure 1: Example stimuli. All four have a ratio of 5:4, have a positive truth value (i.e. most of the dots are blue). From left to right, image types are: column pairs sorted, column pairs mixed, scattered pairs and scattered random.

The network processes an image by using several 'sub-networks' operating across a number of time steps (t), as depicted in Figure 2:

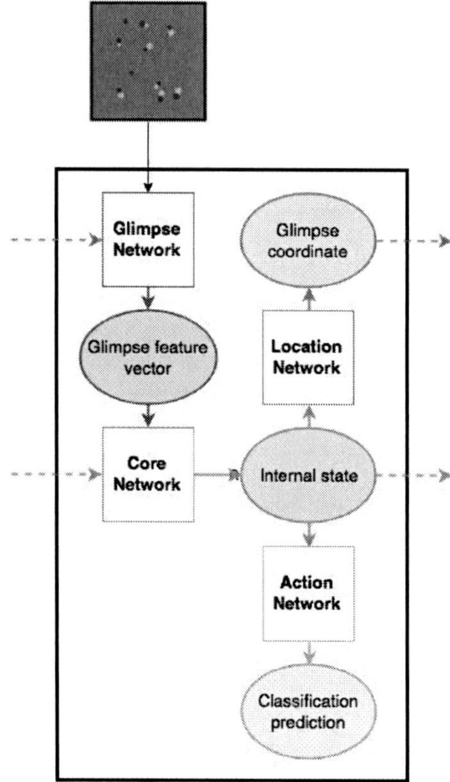

Figure 2: One time-step of the RAM model.

- The glimpse network. It takes the environment (which in the current experiment is the image stimulus) and a location co-ordinate as its inputs. At t_0, the location co-ordinate is randomly generated. At all subsequent ts, it is selected by the location network (described below) at $t - 1$. The network takes a series of samples centred around the co-ordinate and concatenates them into a glimpse. Each consecutive sample is larger than the previous, but at a lower resolution. We used 2 samples, the second of which was twice as large and at half the resolution of the first. These are then processed by 3 convolutional layers and one fully-connected ReLU layer to generate a "what" vector. In parallel, the co-ordinate is processed by a ReLU layer outputting a "where" vector. The "what" and "where" vectors are point-wise multiplied to generate the glimpse feature vector.

- The core network. An LSTM cell, which takes the glimpse feature vector at t and its own internal state at the previous time-step as its inputs.

- The location network. A fully connected layer which takes the core network's internal state at t as its input, and outputs two values ranging between -1 and 1 (via tanh) as its output. These are the means of Gaussians (we fixed the standard deviation at 0.03), one for the x coordinate and one for the y. Actual coordinates are samples from them and are fed in to the glimpse network at $t + 1$.

- The action network. A fully connected layer which takes the core network's internal state at t as its input and outputs a binary image classification. The action network produces a classification at every t, but we only record the classification decision that occurs at the final t.

Neural networks are not bound by 'wall clock time', so it is not possible to directly manipulate the amount of time they use to do a task. To operationalise trial duration, we use the networks'

144

architectures to implement processing constraints which reflect those faced by human subjects operating under urgency. The operationalisations reflect two complementary ideas about the effect that task duration will have on human speakers: as duration increases, (i) the amount of information processing and (ii) the number of saccades and fixations possible increases. For CNNs, we manipulate network depth (thus manipulating the amount of information processing possible) and for the RAM model, we manipulate the number of glimpses made by the network. Each experiment used four levels of task duration: we use the VGG7, 9, 11 and 13 architectures and RAM networks with 4, 8, 16 and 24 glimpses.

The VGG models are trained using the Adam optimizer (Kingma and Ba, 2015). For the RAM models, we adopted the hybrid supervised learning approach described in Mnih et al. (2014), where cross-entropy is back-propagated to train the action, core, and glimpse networks, and the REINFORCE rule (Williams, 1992; Sutton et al., 1999) is used for the location network. Complete hyper-parameters and training details are included in the Supplementary Materials section. The source code and data may be found at `https://github.com/shanest/neural-vision-most`.

5 Results

5.1 Descriptive

Figure 3 shows the accuracy of all networks by dot ratio, averaged across all image types. In both network types, there is a clear trend of decreasing accuracy as ratios become more balanced. There is a notable clustering of the three VGG9+ networks: they appear to have very similar accuracies across all ratios, and follow a pattern that differs dramatically from VGG7, which is significantly less accurate. Notably, VGG7 is the only CNN network not to attain 100% accuracy at any ratio. Moreover, its performance collapses much more rapidly than the other CNNs as the ratios become more balanced. Whilst the RAM networks appear to cluster together a bit, their performance at each ratio shows a broader degree of variability at each ratio than the CNNs.

Figure 4 shows the accuracy of all networks by image type, averaged across all ratios. As above, there are easily observable differences in the performance of the VGG7 and VGG9+ networks.

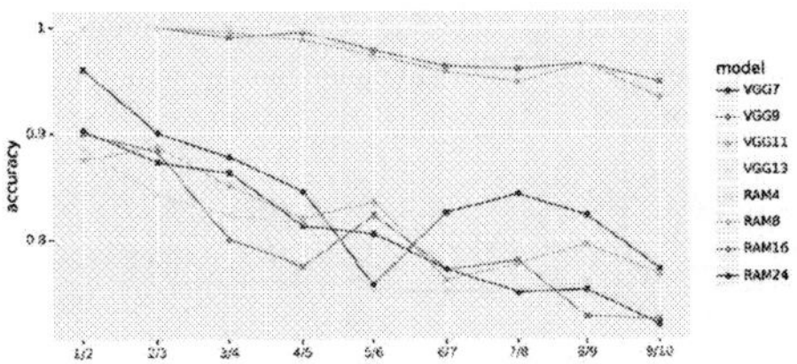

Figure 3: Accuracy by ratio, across image type.

The former performed more poorly on the scattered type images than the column types, whereas the latter attained near-or-at-ceiling accuracy on all but the scattered random trials. The RAM networks' response pattern was similar to VGG7's, albeit somewhat more pronounced. With the exception of instances where near-or-at-ceiling responses make the data less legible, for the column and scattered image sets, all networks performed more accurately on the image types that contained paired dots than their unpaired equivalent.

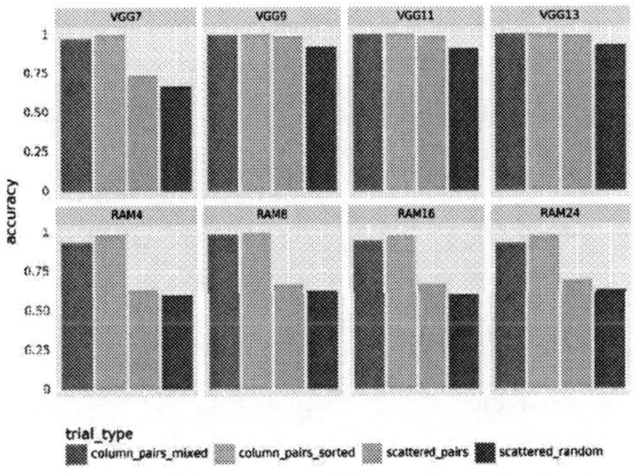

Figure 4: Accuracy by trial type, averaged across ratio.

Figure 5 shows the learning curves for both model types. The VGG7 model hits peak performance quickly, and does not improve thereafter. The VGG13 hits near-ceiling performance very quickly. VGG9 and 11 show more involved learning patterns, with significant decreases in accuracy before hitting their ceilings. These results reflect the VGG7's limited computational capacity relative to the other three.

The RAM models show an interesting pattern: the two models with fewer glimpses (4 and 8) have very similar learning trajectories, as do the two models with more glimpses (16 and 24). And while all four end up at roughly the same accuracy, the former models begin improving much earlier.

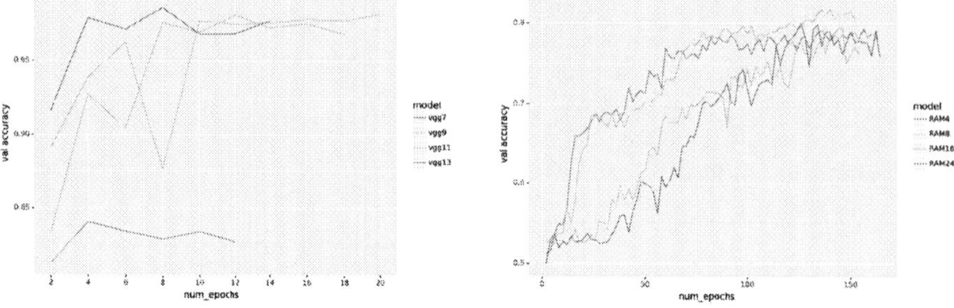

Figure 5: Learning curves for VGG (left) and RAM (right) models.

This suggests that learning how to choose a large number of glimpse location choices is a difficult reinforcement problem. A more detailed analysis of model behavior throughout learning will be left for future work.

5.2 Regression Analysis

To test the significance of these apparent trends, we fit separate multiple logistic regression models to the data from each network type.[4] Correct prediction was the outcome variable. Three predictor variables relating to the hypotheses were included: image type, a categorical variable; operationalised task duration, an ordinal variable; and dot ratio (converted to real numbers), a continuous variable. Dot ratio was ordered from least balanced (1/2) to most balanced (9/10). We also included two control predictor variables to verify whether dot ratio is the primary explanatory variable for differences in performance following manipulations of dot ratio sizes, rather than related or potentially confounding factors. These were: absolute set size difference, a continuous variable; and total dots, a continuous variable. The model also included one interaction term, between dot ratio and network type. The CNN model could not produce reliable statistical estimates for some variable levels due to response invariance (i.e. when performance was at-or-near-ceiling, there were not enough incorrect predictions to reliably estimate paramters). As such, these were excluded from the analysis. These were the data corresponding to column-type images and VGG13. Of the variables included in each analysis, the network with the greatest operationalised task duration (i.e. VGG11 and RAM24)

and the 'most organised' image type (i.e. scattered pairs in the CNN analysis and column pairs sorted in the RAM analysis) acted as the comparison class.

Variable	Estimate	Std. Error	z value	$Pr(> |z|)$
Image: Scattered pairs (Intercept)	16,20	4,15	3,91	9.42e-05 ***
Image: Scattered random	-0,79	0,09	-8,63	<2e-16 ***
Network: VGG9	-0,73	3,47	-0,21	0,83
Network: VGG7	-12,22	2,45	-4,98	6.37e-07 ***
Dot ratio	-14,90	4,93	-3,02	0.00253 **
Absolute difference	0,17	0,37	0,46	0,64
Total dots	-0,03	0,04	-0,87	0,39
Ratio * Network: VGG9	1,09	4,00	0,27	0,78
Ratio * Network: VGG7	11,81	2,83	4,18	2.97e-05 ***

Table 1: Multiple logistic regression of the CNN trials. Significance: 0 '***' 0.001 '**' 0.01 '*' 0.05 '.' 0.1.

The output of the CNN logistic regression can be seen in Table 1. The model shows that the log-odds of the VGG7-11 networks correctly predicting a stimulus' label are significantly reduced as the stimulus' dot set ratio becomes more balanced. We found no significant effect for either of our control variables (absolute difference and total number). These findings strongly support Hypothesis 1. Holding all other variables constant, VGG7-11 were significantly less likely to predict the correct label of scattered random images than scattered pairs images. Given that the lack of difference between the images types that could not be included in the analysis appears to be due to ceiling effects, we interpret these findings as supporting Hypothesis 2. Holding all other variables constant, VGG7 was significantly less likely than VGG11 to make a correct classification. No difference was found between VGG9 and 11. Again, as the lack of difference between the VGG9+ networks appears to be best explained by response invariance due to ceiling effects, we cautiously interpret these findings as supporting Hypothesis 3. Finally, we found a significant positive interaction

---

[4]See, among others, Kotek et al. (2011) (§3.3.2) for a multiple logistic regression analysis of experimental data on truth-value judgments of 'most' sentences.

between dot ratio and VGG7. Together with the negative coefficient for VGG7, the result is that the predicted log-odds for a correct prediction by VGG7 are robustly lower across ratios than for VGG9 and VGG11, as expected. The positive interaction term means that the log-odds decrease at a slower rate for more balanced ratios for VGG7 than the other two; this is due to the at-or-near-ceiling performance of the other two at many of the less-balanced ratios.

Variable	Estimate	Std. Error	z value	$Pr(> \vert z \vert)$
Image: Column pairs sorted (Intercept)	9,57	1,52	6,28	3.41e-10 ***
Image: Column pairs mixed	-1,18	0,16	-7,55	4.37e-14 ***
Image: Scattered pairs	-3,54	0,14	-25,15	< 2e-16 ***
Image: Scattered random	-3,75	0,14	-26,73	< 2e-16 ***
Glimpses: RAM16	-0,32	0,51	-0,63	0,53
Glimpses: RAM8	-0,97	0,51	-1,91	0,06
Glimpses: RAM4	-0,77	0,50	-1,54	0,12
Dot ratio	-6,91	1,84	-3,75	0.000179 ***
Absolute difference	-0,25	0,15	-1,64	0,10
Total dots	0,04	0,02	2,24	0.025427 *
Ratio * Glimpses: RAM16	0,33	0,63	0,52	0,60
Ratio * Glimpses: RAM8	1,34	0,62	2,14	0.032372 *
Ratio * Glimpses: RAM4	0,81	0,62	1,31	0,19

Table 2: Multiple logistic regression on RAM trials.

The output of the RAM logistic regression can be seen in Table 2. According to the model, the log odds of a RAM network correctly labelling stimuli is significantly reduced as set ratios become more balanced. We also found a small but significant effect of total dots, indicating that the likelihood of a correct prediction increases with total dots. This is unsurprising, as increasing total dots reduces image sparseness, increasing the odds that glimpses will contain dots. This can be especially important for the initial glimpse, which has a random location. This does not invalidate the dot ratio finding, given their comparative effect sizes. No significant effect was found for absolute difference. These findings support Hypothesis 1. The log odds of a RAM network predicting the correct labels for column pairs mixed, scattered pairs or scattered random images was significantly lower (by varying degrees) than for column sorted pairs images. This strongly supports Hypothesis 2. We found no significant difference in the likelihood of the 4-16 glimpse RAM networks correctly labelling stimuli than their comparison class, the 24 glimpse RAM network. These findings do not support Hypothesis 3. Finally, we found a small but significant positive interaction between dot ratio and RAM8, suggesting that the increase in log-odds of correct prediction per unit increase in dot ratio is stronger for RAM8 than for RAM24. Because the effect size is small, we caution against over-interpreting

this result. And, as before, this effect is somewhat offset by a negative coefficient for RAM8, lowering the intercept in this case.

5.3 ANS Model Fitting

For each model, we also fit a psychophysical model of the Approximate Number System (ANS) to the mean accuracy data, broken down by ratio and by image type (Pica et al., 2004; Nieder and Miller, 2004; Halberda and Feigenson, 2008). For this model, ratio is ordered from most balanced (10/9) to least balanced (2/1). The model represents numerosities as Gaussians, and comparisons between numerosities via the difference in Gaussians. In particular, there is one free parameter w – the Weber fraction – which represents increase in accuracy with increase in ratio. More precisely, we fit the following model:

$$\mathrm{acc} = 1 - \frac{1}{2}\mathrm{erfc}\left(\frac{n_1 - n_2}{w\sqrt{2}\sqrt{n_1^2 + n_2^2}}\right)$$

where n_1 represents the larger number and n_2 the smaller. Figure 6 shows the fit curves for the VGG7 and RAM24 networks, which exhibited the most human-like behavior. An Appendix includes these for all eight models.

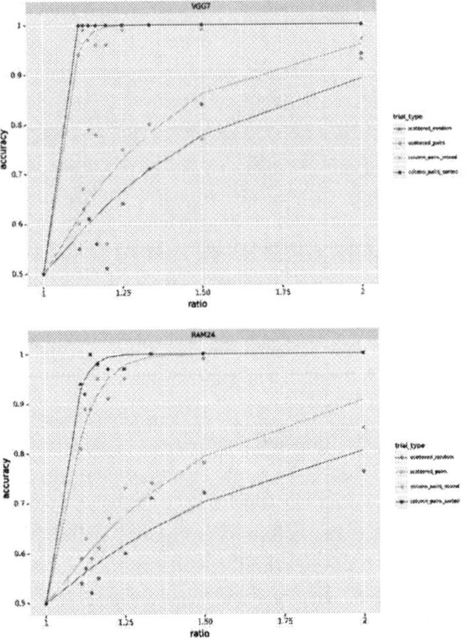

Figure 6: Accuracy by trial type and ratio for VGG7 (top) and RAM24 (bottom), with Weber curves.

For both networks, both column image types have a significantly higher degree of accuracy than both scattered types, with scattered pairs being a bit easier than scattered random. The psychophysical model provides a good fit to the data: Table 3 provides the Weber fractions and R^2 for these cases. For human participants, Pietroski et al. (2009) found w to be roughly 0.3 on all but the column sorted trials, where w was 0.04. Our models are not too far off of these Weber fractions, with one noticeable difference: our models treat column mixed trials much more similarly to column sorted trials, whereas for humans column mixed trials pattern with the two scattered trial types.

type	VGG7		RAM24	
	w	R^2	w	R^2
scattered random	0.363	0.843	0.524	0.801
scattered pairs	0.256	0.581	0.340	0.913
column mixed	0.047	0.979	0.078	0.975
column sorted	0.012	1.0	0.051	0.984

Table 3: Weber fractions and R^2 for the ANS model.

6 Discussion

We subjected convolutional networks of varying depths and recurrent models of visual attention with varying number of glimpses to the psychosemantic experiment of Pietroski et al. (2009). Our first two hypotheses are confirmed: all networks show decreased accuracy with decreasing dot ratio as well as a strong sensitivity to image type. The third hypothesis is partially confirmed: increasingly deep CNNs do show increased performance (with all VGG9+ networks being near ceiling), while increasing the number of glimpses for a RAM model has little effect on overall accuracy. The psychophysical model of approximate number fits network data well, with some Weber fractions being near those found for human participants. For the RAM models, this suggests that visual attention and search may be a causal mechanism underlying some ANS-like responses. The primary qualitative difference between model performance and human performance is that the models do roughly equally well on both column image types, whereas humans are significantly better on column sorted as opposed to column mixed trials. This suggests that the strategies learned by the models differ in some interesting ways from those employed by human participants.

These results exhibit initial promise in using neural models as cognitive models in psychosemantics. In particular, while the fit with existing human data is good (criterion (i) above), it is not quite strong enough to warrant generating robust predictions about manipulations like task duration (criterion (ii) above). Nevertheless, these initially promising results also suggest interesting avenues for future work.

(1) More detailed hyper-parameter searches may improve fit with the human data, thus allowing us to use the models to generate predictions. (2) RAM model performance could be improved by giving the network a low-resolution version of the whole image to help it make location choices (Ba et al., 2014). (3) While our depth manipulation for CNNs was designed to reflect increased information processing capacity as duration increases, one could control for capacity (number of parameters in the model) by making the deeper networks narrower or the shallow networks wider, and seeing if depth still has an effect. (4) To better understand what strategies the models are using to solve the task, techniques such as transfer learning and diagnostic classifiers (Hupkes et al., 2018; Giulianelli et al., 2018) could be applied to our models. (5) Similarly, one can investigate whether any neurons or groups thereof in the models exhibit activation curves consistent with Weber's law (Nieder and Miller, 2004). (6) Independent neural models that exhibit ANS-like behavior—or, more generally, that are trained on other image processing tasks—could be used in this task (Stoianov and Zorzi, 2012); a key challenge here will be operationalizing task duration. (7) The models could be used to model performance against more image manipulations, such as the number of colors in a scence (Lidz et al., 2011). We leave these and other avenues for improving neural models of psychosemantic tasks to future work.

Acknowledgments

Thanks to Alexandre Cremers and Jakub Szymanik for helpful discussion and to three anonymous CMCL reviewers for valuable comments. We thank SURFsara (`www.surfsara.nl`) for the support in using the Lisa Compute Cluster. SS-T has received funding from the European Research Council under the European Union's Seventh Framework Programme (FP/20072013)/ERC Grant Agreement n. STG 716230 CoSaQ.

References

Martín Abadi, Paul Barham, Jianmin Chen, Zhifeng Chen, Andy Davis, Jeffrey Dean, Matthieu Devin, Sanjay Ghemawat, Geoffrey Irving, Michael Isard, Manjunath Kudlur, Josh Levenberg, Rajat Monga, Sherry Moore, Derek G Murray, Benoit Steiner, Paul Tucker, Vijay Vasudevan, Pete Warden, Martin Wicke, Yuan Yu, and Xiaoqiang Zheng. 2016. TensorFlow: A System for Large-Scale Machine Learning. In *12th USENIX Symposium on Operating Systems Design and Implementation (OSDI '16)*, pages 265–284.

Jimmy Ba, Volodymyr Mnih, and Koray Kavukcuoglu. 2014. Multiple Object Recognition with Visual Attention. pages 1–10.

Stanislas Dehaene. 1997. *The Number Sense: How the Mind Creates Mathematics*. Oxford University Press, Oxford.

Lisa Feigenson, Stanislas Dehaene, and Elizabeth Spelke. 2004. Core systems of number. *Trends in Cognitive Sciences*, 8(7):307–314.

Mario Giulianelli, Jack Harding, Florian Mohnert, Dieuwke Hupkes, and Willem Zuidema. 2018. Under the Hood: Using Diagnostic Classifiers to Investigate and Improve how Language Models Track Agreement Information. In *Proceedings of the 2018 EMNLP Workshop BlackboxNLP*, pages 240–248.

Justin Halberda and Lisa Feigenson. 2008. Developmental change in the acuity of the "Number Sense": The Approximate Number System in 3-, 4-, 5-, and 6-year-olds and adults. *Developmental Psychology*, 44(5):1457–1465.

Mary Hayhoe and Dana Ballard. 2005. Eye movements in natural behavior. *Trends in Cognitive Sciences*, 9(4):188–194.

Dieuwke Hupkes, Sara Veldhoen, and Willem Zuidema. 2018. Visualisation and 'Diagnostic Classifiers' Reveal how Recurrent and Recursive Neural Networks Process Hierarchical Structure. *Journal of Artificial Intelligence Research*, 61:907–926.

Diederik P. Kingma and Jimmy Ba. 2015. Adam: A Method for Stochastic Optimization. In *International Conference of Learning Representations (ICLR)*.

Hadas Kotek, Yasutada Sudo, Edwin Howard, and Hackl. 2011. *Most* Meanings are Superlative. In *Experiments at the Interfaces*, volume 37 of *Syntax and Semantics*, pages 101–145. Emerald Group Publishing.

Alexander Kuhnle and Ann Copestake. 2017. ShapeWorld: A new test methodology for multimodal language understanding.

Alexander Kuhnle and Ann Copestake. 2018. The meaning of "most" for visual question answering models. pages 1–11.

Jeffrey Lidz, Paul Pietroski, Justin Halberda, and Tim Hunter. 2011. Interface transparency and the psychosemantics of most. *Natural Language Semantics*, 19(3):227–256.

Volodymyr Mnih, Nicolas Heess, Alex Graves, and Koray Kavukcuoglu. 2014. Recurrent Models of Visual Attention. pages 1–12.

Andreas Nieder and Earl K Miller. 2004. A parietofrontal network for visual numerical information in the monkey. *Proceedings of the National Academy of Sciences*, 101(19):7457–7462.

Ethan Perez, Florian Strub, Harm de Vries, Vincent Dumoulin, and Aaron Courville. 2018. FiLM: Visual Reasoning with a General Conditioning Layer. In *Thirty-Second AAAI Conference on Artificial Intelligence (AAAI-18)*, pages 3942–3951.

Pierre Pica, Cathy Lemer, Véronique Izard, and Stanislas Dehaene. 2004. Exact and approximate arithmetic in an Amazonian indigene group. *Science*, 306(5695):499–503.

Paul Pietroski, Jeffrey Lidz, Tim Hunter, and Justin Halberda. 2009. The Meaning of 'Most': Semantics, Numerosity and Psychology. *Mind and Language*, 24(5):554–585.

Jenna Register, Francis Mollica, and Steven T. Piantadosi. 2018. Semantic verification is flexible and sensitive to context.

Ronald A Rensink. 2000. The Dynamic Representation of Scences. *Visual Cognition*, 7:17–42.

Karen Simonyan and Andrew Zisserman. 2014. Very Deep Convolutional Networks for Large-Scale Image Recognition. pages 1–14.

Shane Steinert-Threlkeld, Gert-Jan Munneke, and Jakub Szymanik. 2015. Alternative Representations in Formal Semantics: A case study of quantifiers. In *Proceedings of the 20th Amsterdam Colloquium*, pages 368–378.

Shane Steinert-Threlkeld and Jakub Szymanik. 2018. Learnability and Semantic Universals. *Semantics & Pragmatics*.

Ivilin Stoianov and Marco Zorzi. 2012. Emergence of a 'visual number sense' in hierarchical generative models. *Nature Neuroscience*, 15(2):194–196.

Richard S Sutton, David McAllester, Satinder Singh, and Yishay Mansour. 1999. Policy Gradient Methods for Reinforcement Learning with Function Approximation. In *Proceedings of the 12th International Conference on Neural Information Processing Systems (NIPS '99)*, pages 1057–1063.

Ronald J Williams. 1992. Simple statistical gradient-following algorithms for connectionist reinforcement learning. *Machine Learning*, 8(3-4):229–256.

Jeremy M. Wolfe and Todd S. Horowitz. 2017. Five factors that guide attention in visual search. *Nature Human Behaviour*, 1(3):1–8.

A Supplementary Material

Images were 128x128 pixels, converted to grayscale. The TensorFlow Python library (Abadi et al., 2016) was used to implement everything. The networks were trained and tested on an NVIDIA GeForce 1080Ti GPU. The source code and data may be found at `https://github.com/shanest/neural-vision-most`.

The RAM models had the following hyper-parameters (found by a small grid search):

- Number of patches: 2

- Size of patches: 12, 24 pixels

- Glimpse network:

  - three convolutional layers with 64, 64, and 128 filters and kernel size 5, 3, and 3, respectively
  - Output vector size: 512

- Core network: LSTM with hidden state dimension 1024

We trained using the Adam optimizer with learning rate 1e-5. The RAM models were trained for up to 200 epochs, with early stopping with a patience of 10 epochs (i.e. training was stopped when loss did not improve over a ten epoch time-frame, as measured every 2 epochs).

The CNN models were trained using 0.25 dropout (on the final fully-connected layers) and the Adam optimizer, with learning rate 1e-4. We used early stopping with a patience of 10 epochs, with maximum training length of 40 epochs. For each model, we saved the best version, as measured by loss on the validation set.

B Appendix

Here we include results of fitting the psychophysical model of approximate number to all 8 of our models. Figure 7 shows the VGG models, and Figure 8 shows the RAM models.

As can be seen, VGG9-13 look very similar, with the only non-ceiling performance coming on scattered random trials, which it still learns perfectly for large enough (imbalanced enough ratios). VGG7 shows highly ratio-dependent performance for both scattered random and scattered pairs trials.

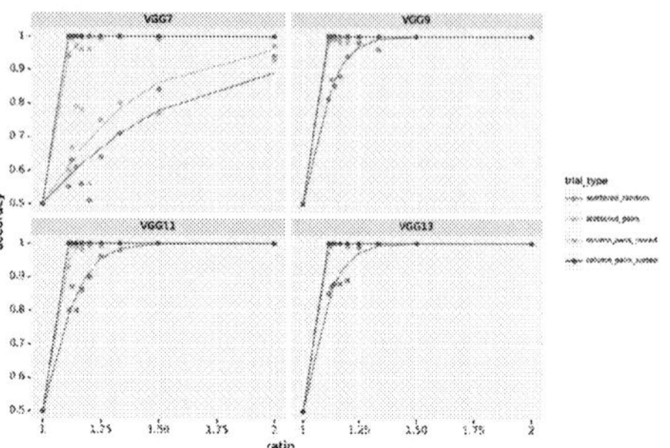

Figure 7: Fit Weber curves for all VGG models.

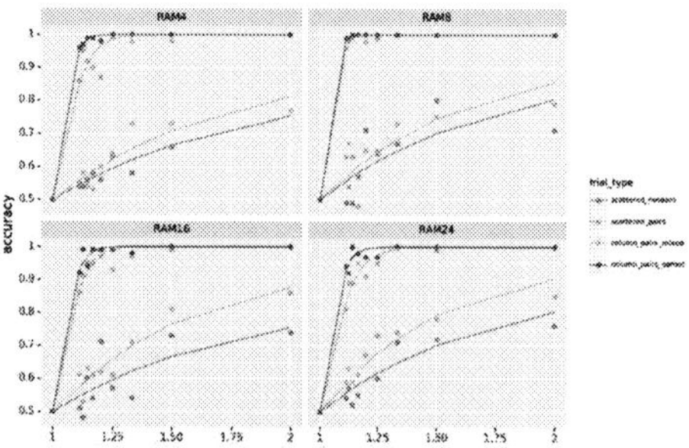

Figure 8: Fit Weber curves for all RAM models.

The RAM models show subtle patterns. The model with 8 glimpses (RAM8) was very slightly the best overall performer, but this looks due to the two column trial types. RAM24 appears to have the best performance on the scattered trial types, at the expense of the column types. For the scattered types, performance is approaching human levels of accuracy (roughly 89%, compared to the model being roughly 85%).

As mentioned in the paper, all models perform similarly on both column trial types, in contrast to human participants, who are significantly better on column sorted than column mixed trials.

Table 4 provides the results of fitting the psychophysical model to mean accuracy for each model and trial type. In particular, we report the one parameter of the model (Weber fraction, w), and the goodness of fit of each model (R^2).

	scattered random		scattered pairs		column mixed		column sorted	
model	w	R^2	w	R^2	w	R^2	w	R^2
VGG7	0.363	0.843	0.256	0.581	0.047	0.978	0.012	1.0
VGG9	0.085	0.985	0.085	0.997	0.015	0.999	0.012	1.0
VGG11	0.093	0.971	0.045	0.994	0.015	0.999	0.012	1.0
VGG13	0.081	0.973	0.038	0.999	0.012	1.0	0.012	1.0
RAM4	0.0650	0.929	0.503	0.845	0.071	0.917	0.043	0.998
RAM8	0.522	0.593	0.420	0.592	0.042	0.998	0.033	0.999
RAM16	0.646	0.574	0.384	0.912	0.049	0.986	0.049	0.986
RAM24	0.524	0.801	0.340	0.913	0.078	0.975	0.051	0.984

Table 4: Weber fractions (w) and correlations (R^2) for all models and all trial types.

The Role of Utterance Boundaries and Word Frequencies for Part-of-speech Learning in Brazilian Portuguese Through Distributional Analysis

Pablo Faria

University of Campinas

Linguistics Department

Campinas, SP, 13083-859

`pablofaria@iel.unicamp.br`

Abstract

In this study, we address the problem of part-of-speech (or syntactic category) learning during language acquisition through distributional analysis of utterances. A model based on Redington et al.'s (1998) distributional learner is used to investigate the informativeness of distributional information in Brazilian Portuguese (BP). The data provided to the learner comes from two publicly available corpora of child directed speech. We present preliminary results from two experiments. The first one investigates the effects of different assumptions about utterance boundaries when presenting the input data to the learner. The second experiment compares the learner's performance when counting contextual words' frequencies versus just acknowledging their co-occurrence with a given target word. In general, our results indicate that explicit boundaries are more informative, frequencies are important, and that distributional information is useful to the child as a source of categorial information. These results are in accordance with Redington et al.'s findings for English.

1 Introduction

Complementary to more standard methods of investigation in the field of language acquisition (such as manual corpora analysis and experimental studies), computational approaches aim to provide models that incorporate what is currently known about acquisition, language, and human cognition. In this way, they can be taken as psychologically plausible simulations that may throw light onto early aspects of language acquisition which are otherwise empirically difficult to observe. In the study described below, we developed a computational model to address the problem of learning the syntactic categories of words during language acquisition through the distributional analysis of utterances. In the present approach, this problem may be seen as a more specific instance of the general problem of finding associations between words through distributional analysis (Turney and Pantel, 2010; Lenci, 2018).

Although it is primarily meant to inform language acquisition theories, we expect that the present work may be of relevance for the general task of categorizing and grouping words through the use of distributional information. Particularly, as we apply the method to Brazilian Portuguese (BP) input data, it may help comprehending cross-linguistic differences between languages, which is a central goal of language acquisition theories and also an important one for the development of NLP techniques. Given that BP has a relatively fixed word order, we expect distributional information to have an important role in signaling the syntactic category of words.

Our model is a (local) reimplementation of the distributional learner described in Redington et al. (1998).[1] We present preliminary results from two experiments, originally, experiments 5 and 6 of the nine experiments carried out in Redington et al.'s study. We decided to reimplement their algorithm as both a way of achieving a deeper understanding of their method and also to assess its replicability, given the description found in their paper. Although being relatively old, Redington et al.'s study was chosen for being – to our knowledge – the first and most comprehensive computational study on the distributional properties of child directed speech. It investigates many aspects of the problem, such as the effects of distinct context windows, corpus sizes, number of target and context words, etc. In this sense, the present work contribution is very specific: aside from attesting the replicability of Redington et al.'s study, it also shows that distributional information is useful for

---

[1]The source code of the present model will be available at `https://gitlab.com/pablofaria/dlearner`.

Proceedings of the Workshop on Cognitive Modeling and Computational Linguistics, pages 152–159
Minneapolis, USA, June 7, 2019. ©2019 Association for Computational Linguistics

a child learning BP, a picture that will become fully clear as we publish results of the remaining experiments.

The paper is organized as follows. We first situate the present study regarding the field of language acquisition (section 2). Next, the corpus used and its preparation are described, along with a presentation of the distributional learner implemented (section 3). In section 4, we describe the two experiments and conduct a discussion on their quantitative and some qualitative results, focusing on a comparison with Redington et al. (1998). Final remarks come in section 5.

2 Language Acquisition and the Role of the Input

As a natural part of a typical human child development, learning a language - whether oral or gestual - emerges as a spontaneous, effortless, rapid, and ultimately successful process. In the field of language acquisition studies, theorists diverge on the actual explanations for this phenomenon, some arguing for mainly inductive processes based on qualities of the linguistic experience the child is exposed to and general cognitive capabilities (Tomasello, 1995; Pullum, 1996, and others), while other theorists minimize the role of the input, arguing that a specialized biological basis is necessary for language to be acquired (Yang, 2002; Berwick et al., 2011, and others). As one can see, at the core of such debate is the need for precise and exhaustive investigations of the informativeness of the input the child receives. Surprisingly, comprehensive computational and corpora studies are still restricted and scarce. For instance, although there are many studies about distributional properties of words in the literature (Clark, 2003; Turney and Pantel, 2010; Lenci, 2018, for instance), the study presented here is the first to our knowledge to investigate the distributional properties of a language other than English, *in the context of computational modelings of language acquisition.*

Acting on this gap, our study investigates the informativeness of distributional information to the task of syntactically categorizing words, also termed part-of-speech learning. As Harris (1954) points out, the "distribution" of an element can be described as "the sum of all its environments", where by "environment" Harris means an array of co-occurring elements and their positions in re-

spect to a given (target) word. There are plenty of evidence showing that not only a distributional structure exists in language data, but also that speakers are sensitive to it (Brown, 1957; Landau and Gleitman, 1985; Bernal et al., 2007, to cite some). Although distributional information is broadly known to be insufficient for correctly categorizing words, it is important to investigate how much information it can contribute to the success of this task and that is precisely what the experiments shown below help understand.

Finally, we would like to emphasize that the problem dealt with here is similar but not the same as the problem of finding (semantic) associations between words, as seen in the long tradition of distributed semantic models (DSMs) developed in the last 30 years (Turney and Pantel, 2010; Lenci, 2018). For instance, here it is fundamental that the model categorizes function words correctly, while in DSMs they are in general left aside. Certainly, syntactically categorizing words involves, in part, detecting semantic associations between them. However, in order to detect the abstract syntactic nature of words we need to move beyond purely semantic association to find out what level of similarity allows us to cluster words together that behave syntactically the same. This is not a simple task and, of course, distributional information is surely not sufficient for fully solving the problem, in particular, because syntactic categories may differ substantially in their distributional properties and in their number of elements. For this reason, we expect to find many overlappings between our study and DSMs in general, without nonetheless taking into account important distinctions between these related tasks.

3 Methodology

For simulations, it was necessary to prepare a corpus of child directed speech (CDS) in Brazilian Portuguese, partially obtained from the CHILDES Database (MacWhinney, 2000) and partially obtained from the "Projeto de Aquisição da Linguagem Oral"[2]. The preprocessing of this material included the removal of metadata, children's utterances, and all kinds of annotation and commentaries made by those who built these corpora. There was also the need for a normal-

---

[2]Available online (in Portuguese) for visualization at `https://bit.ly/2sxOKBi`. Last accessed on January 17th, 2019.

ization of the orthography of transcriptions (e.g., "nene/baby" to "nenê"), specially for the second corpus mentioned above. It was carried out in a semi-automatic way in order to cover the most recurrent cases. No lemmatization was carried out.

Besides speech data, it is also necessary a "benchmark classification" against which the performance of the learner is evaluated. For this, we use the tagged version of the Tycho Brahe Corpus of Historical Portuguese (TBC)[3], consisting of part-of-speech annotated text from various authors and centuries. For some uncovered target words in the experiments, we manually assigned their most common tag for all non-ambiguous cases, such as proper nouns and diminutive forms of nouns (e.g., "menininho" which means "little boy"). Ambiguous and other idiosyncratic forms were left unclassified. In general, we basically followed the procedures found in Redington et al. (1998).

It is worth mentioning a distinction between English and Portuguese which posed a methodological and conceptual problem not faced in Redington et al. (1998). In Portuguese, nouns can be inflected in many ways, such as diminutive, augmentative, for grammatical gender, and so on. We first thought that all inflected forms could be replaced by a default form, in all cases where there is no change in the class of the word. However, there are inflected forms that exhibits specialized meanings, such as "calcinha" (literally "small pants") which means (woman) underwear. Thus, inflected forms were kept in the corpus for the model must reflect the ability of the child to learn both the regular behavior of inflected forms and also the exceptions (when distributively distinct). Furthermore, we aim to model the lexical acquisition process from its first steps, when morphological decomposition of words is not yet available.

Finally, punctuation is treated as in the original study: all intermediary punctuation is removed and all final punctuations (where present) are replaced by single end points. After all these procedures, our CDS corpus comprises approximately

1.4 million tokens, including punctuation. In Redington et al.'s study, they used a corpus of 2.5 million tokens.

3.1 The Distributional Learner

Our method is a local implementation of Redington et al.'s (1998) learner. Therefore, only a very brief description of the method is presented here. The learner goes through three stages in accomplishing the task: (i) measuring the distributional contexts for each target word; (ii) comparing distributional contexts for pairs of words; and (iii) grouping words based on distributional context similarity. The first stage produces a *contingency table* (a co-occurrence matrix) in which each line represents a context vector for a given target word. Each column corresponds to a context word in a particular position in respect to the word. Thus, if only the preceding word is used as context and 150 contextual words are considered, the vector will be of size 150. If two contextual positions are considered, then the vector will be of size 300, and so on.

Once the table is built, the second stage generates similarity measures for all possible pairs of target words. Although cosine similarity is currently a standard for comparing word vectors (Turney and Pantel, 2010; Lenci, 2018), for replication purposes, we use the Spearman rank correlation coefficient, ρ, which Redington et al. argue as the most successful measure in their study.[4] In the last stage, target words must be grouped together. This is carried out using a standard hierarchical cluster analysis, known as average link clustering. Once the hierarchy is produced – which can be represented as a dendrogram – the method identifies the optimum cut level which maximizes the performance of the learner in classifying words relative to the "benchmark classification" provided by the tagged corpus.

In order to demonstrate the relevance of the distributional information, that is, that the method produces results above chance classification, a "baseline classification" is calculated for each cut level analyzed. It goes as follows: for each cut level, the number of clusters obtained is kept constant but words are randomly distributed across these clusters and then performance is calculated. This is done ten times and the baseline derived for

---

[3] Available at `http://www.tycho.iel.unicamp.br/~tycho/corpus/texts/pos.zip`. Last accessed on January 17th, 2019. The choice for TBC over other available corpora (such as Universal Dependencies) was for mere convenience (easy of access). The fact that it is historical data is not to be seen as a problem, given that we are targeting the most frequent words in our study, for which it is hardly the case that there was any historical change in their syntactic category. Nonetheless, ideally we would like to annotate the CDS data itself and use it as the gold standard for generated clusters.

[4] Of course, it leaves opened the question of whether cosine similarity would improve the model's performance, something we will address in the near future.

that cut level is the mean performance obtained.

3.2 Benchmark Classification

As a result of choosing the TBC as the tagged corpus of reference and in order to use the same categories assumed in the original study, a conversion between the two systems of classification was necessary. We have basically stripped off subtags from the TBC and established equivalence relations between the resultant tag system and Redington et al.'s classes. Table 1 summarizes the conversion schema.

3.3 Measuring Performance

The performance of the learner is evaluated through three measures, here applied across categories.[5] The first two are the traditional *precision* and *recall* measures. A third integrated measure is necessary in order to balance these two. In Redington et al. (1998), a measure called *informativeness* is proposed along with its justification. Although following the description given by the authors, we were still unable to obtain a satisfactory measure[6], reason why we decided to use the traditional F-measure, combined with a $\beta = 0.3$ coefficient to favor precision over recall. This (still tentative) option seemed in our simulations to compensate for the unbalanced nature of grammatical categories, in the sense that some are *open-ended*, that is, might in principle cover an unlimited number of elements, while others, such as "article" or "preposition", are "closed classes" with a fixed (and often small) number of elements. This fact tends to favor the recall measure over precision, because less clusters covering the largest categories will compensate for lower precision, something we would like to avoid.

4 Results and Discussion

In their original study, Redington et al. (1998) conduct nine experiments. From these, the authors established a "standard analysis", used as a reference in the analysis of other experimental conditions. Our standard analysis here follows the same settings: the 1000 most frequent words were used as target words for categorization, along with the

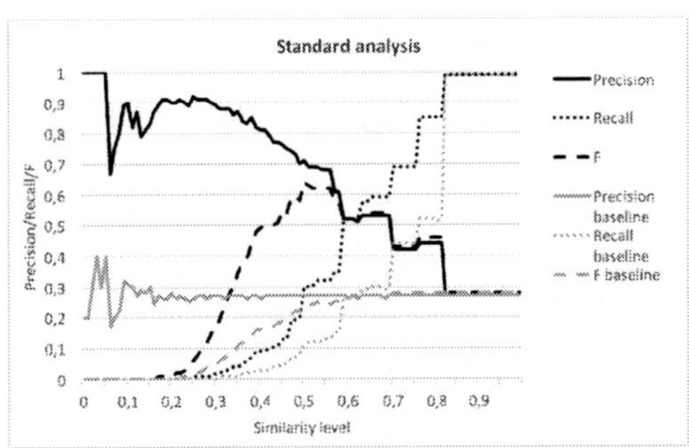

Figure 1: Performance of the learner for the standard analysis. For a similarity level of 0.5 (cut level), 25 clusters are obtained, with $F = 0.64$ (prec. = 0.71, recall = 0.30).

150 most frequent words as (relevant) contextual words. The context window included both the two immediately preceding and the two immediately succeeding words. Thus, each context vector consisted of 600 elements – four contextual positions for 150 words – each consisting of the frequency of a given context word in a specific position regarding the target. All final punctuations are removed and the data is treated as single long utterance.

Figure 1 shows that the learner's performance is significantly above the baseline. As expected, categorization is much easier for the open-ended categories, specially nouns and verbs, with some clusters coming close to be "pure" (e.g., a cluster of infinitival verbs). For other categories, however, clusters tend to be mixed and more sensitive to syntactic function than to morphosyntactic properties. Thus, one of the clusters seems to capture the distribution of elements that may appear as heads[7] of noun phrases (articles, adjectives, nouns, pronouns, etc.), while another includes elements that appear in a predicative context, such as Y in "X is Y". An interesting feature observed is that many pairs of elements that vary only in gender, such as "do/da" ("of the", masculine and feminine), were very close to each other. This is an indication that distributional information can be of much help for the child to extract the grammatical gender feature

---

[5]One specific experiment, not reported here, assess performances for each category.

[6]Our implementation of this measure for some reason produced useless (i.e., non-discriminating) values for finding the best cut level for dendrograms. We are pretty sure it is our misunderstanding of it.

[7]For instance, in Portuguese one may say "o do Pedro" ("the of Peter"), with "o" playing the role of the head of the noun phrase. Something even more complex happens in "o vermelho do Pedro" ("the red of Peter"), where "do Pedro" can be seen as the modifier of "o", of "vermelho", or of both. The common property here is the absence of the noun itself, which impacts the distributional categorization of words. Of course, the actual syntactic analysis of such phrases will depend on the theory assumed.

Category	TBC tags	Examples	n
Noun	N, NPR	ademir, adriana, ajuda/*help*	375
Adjective	ADJ, OUTRO	alto/*tall*, amarelo/*yellow*, baixo/*low*	82
Numeral	NUM	cinco/*five*, dez/*ten*, duas/*two*	14
Verb	VB, HV, ET, TR, SR	abre/*opens*, abrir/*to open*, abriu/*opened*	331
Article	D	a/*the*, aquele/*that*, os/*the*	45
Pronoun	CL, SE, DEM, PRO, PRO$, SENAO, QUE, WADV, WPRO, WD, WPRO$, WQ	aonde/*whither*, aquilo/*that*, cadê/*where*	53
Adverb	ADV, Q, NEG, FP	agora/*now*, ainda/*still*, algum/*any*	62
Preposition	P	até/*until*, com/*with*, de/*of*	11
Conjunction	CONJ, CONJS, C	como/*how*, e/*and*, enquanto/*while*	11
Interjection	INTJ	ah, ahn, ai	16

Table 1: Categories, examples, and quantities for the 1000 most frequent words of the CDS corpus.

in the acquisition of Portuguese as well as for other similar alternations such as diminutive forms, plurals, etc. This is only a summary of some core aspects of a qualitative analysis of the clusters and categorizations obtained.

4.1 Utterance Boundaries: Testing Different Assumptions

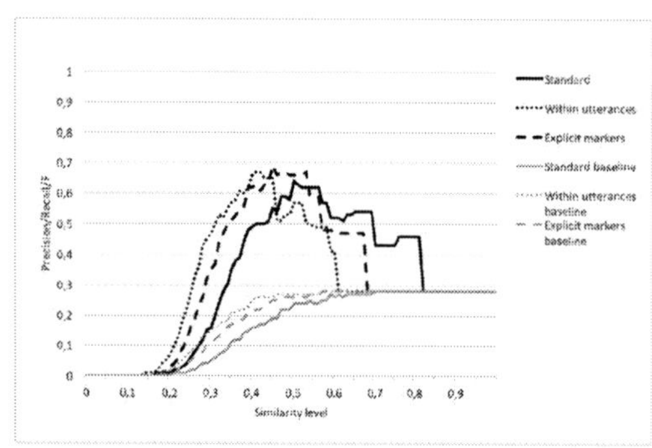

Figure 2: Comparison of performances (F-scores) when different assumptions about utterance boundaries are evaluated. Baselines for each are also shown.

In the standard analysis, all data is treated as a single long utterance, with punctuation marks removed. This is unrealistic, of course, because a child is surely sensitive to the beginning and end of utterances as well as to interruptions in speech, alternation of speakers, and so on. Thus, in order to investigate this issue, Redington et al. (1998) designed two specific conditions. First, utterances were taken one at a time, with contextual information limited to the boundaries of each utterance ("within utterance only"). This seems more realistic, although one-word utterances, be-

ing "contextless", become useless for the method. A second condition tests whether the addition of explicit boundary markers (i.e., final punctuation marks) helps the learner. In this case, punctuation marks are expressing the speaker's sensitiveness to phonological properties of speech, such as phonological phrase or utterance boundaries.

Figure 2 shows the distinct performances obtained for each condition. In general, curves are alike, although both alternative conditions have their peaks on a lower level of similarity. More specifically, in condition "within utterances only", the best $F = 0.67$ is obtained for the cut level 0.41, producing 17 clusters with precision 0.7 and recall 0.48. Recall is substantially higher (60%) than in the standard analysis, while keeping basically the same precision. Furthermore, the number of clusters decrease to 17, which is much closer to the benchmark. Considering only these general results, it seems that utterances boundaries benefit the learner. If this is indeed the case, explicit markers should help even more and that is what the condition "explicit markers" shows.

As we can see, its $F = 0.69$ is the highest obtained so far. Although recall decreases a bit, to 0.44, precision increases to 0.72, and the number of clusters is 18 (for cut level 0.45). The main difference between this and the previous condition is the use of one-word utterances, which now has an explicit boundary marker functioning as a minimum contextual information. Given these results, we can more confidently claim that utterance boundary information indeed helps the learner. This is, of course, compatible with what language acquisition theory says, specially the advocates of the important role phonology plays in the acquisition by helping the child segment the speech stream (Christophe et al., 2008, for instance).

4.2 Context Words: Attesting Occurrence Instead of Frequency

In this experiment, the goal is to observe how the learner behaves when, instead of the frequency of each context word, only the occurrence (or not) of it is recorded. Although children do extract statistics from input data (Romberg and Saffran, 2010), it may be the case that the actual learning procedure is *in between* mere occurrence and precise statistics about context words. This experiment allows us to explore this radical alternative learning strategy, see how it plays out, and hopefully learn something from it. In order to do that, after collecting statistics about context words, all context vector values greater than zero are converted to 1. And, because rank correlation is not well suited to binary vectors, following Redington et al., the "cityblock" metric is used in the "Occurrence" condition. A third condition, "Cityblock", uses frequencies *and* the "cityblock" metric, allowing for a better comparison with the standard analysis.

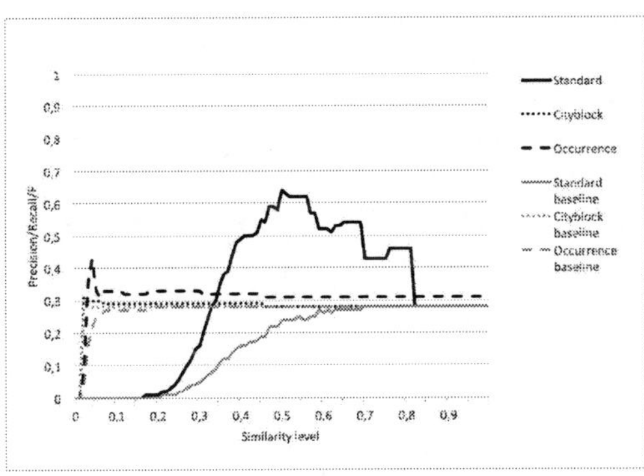

Figure 3: Comparison of performances (F-scores) for different ways of counting context words (i.e., frequency or binary context vectors). Baselines for each are also shown.

As one can see in Figure 3, the learner's performance drops significantly for both "Cityblock" and "Occurrence" conditions, when compared to the standard analysis. The "Cityblock" condition, with $F = 0.3$, precision 0.29, recall 0.91, and 9 clusters, demonstrates the inappropriateness of the "cityblock" metric when actual frequencies are taken into account, as Redington et al. (1998) point out. Its very low precision shows

that it poorly categorizes words, basically creating large clusters, which explains its high recall. Instead, when binary vectors are used with the cityblock metric, performance increases, as the "Occurrence" condition shows. It obtains $F = 0.43$, with precision 0.53, recall 0.14, and 48 clusters. While still being a low performance, it demonstrates some ability to categorize (precision 0.53), although its high number of clusters prevents it from reaching a good recall. A possible interpretation is that it performs better in recognizing differences among categories than similarities between elements of the same category. Finally, these results, in general, indicate that some tracking of frequencies of contextual elements is necessary for the learner to extract the full potential of distributional information.

4.3 Related Work

In their original study, Redington et al. (1998) evaluate the effects of different assumptions about utterance boundaries. In Mintz et al. (2002), this aspect is also investigated, but they move a step further to investigate the effects of intrasentential boundaries. This is a study we plan to conduct in the near future. When we consider Redington et al.'s results on this issue (p.457-458), we find the same tendency observed in our experiment. Both conditions, within utterance and explicit markers, help improve the learner's performance, with the latter producing the best performance overall. As Redington et al. point out, "information recorded across utterance boundaries effectively act as noise."

In our second experiment, we have found that collecting actual frequencies of contextual elements improves the learner's performance. In Redington et al.'s study (p.458-459), results show similar tendencies, but with some key differences worth emphasizing. First, in the "Cityblock" condition, in which our learner performs very poorly, their learner performs quite well, although worse than for the standard analysis. This opposite behavior is puzzling to us and we cannot find reasonable explanations for it, apart from some unnoticed technical misunderstanding in our replication of their study or, in part, due to the distinct performance measures applied in each study. For the "Occurrence" condition, however, although it performs second in our study, both here and there we observe a significant decline in performance and a very small advantage of the method over the random baseline.

In general, a precise comparison of these studies is not totally straightforward. First, as already pointed out, because each uses its specific performance measure. In the future, we expect to overcome this limitation through appropriate implementations of the measures used in Redington et al. (1998) and Mintz et al. (2002). Furthermore, with these in hand, we will be able to compare measures and try to understand whether they are complementary or substitutes. Second, and more subtle, are the way values for similarity are obtained. We cannot claim our method produces equivalent similarity values, particularly in the sense that, in our study, similarity values do not generalize across experiments, as they appear to do in Redington et al.'s study. Consequently, they are able to consider a cut level of 0.8 as an "optimum" cut level for all experiments, while this is not possible in our study. We are also working on this issue.

5   Conclusions

In this paper, distributional properties of Brazilian Portuguese are investigated through the replication of the study in Redington et al. (1998). Two aspects were analyzed here: the effects on performance of different assumptions about utterance boundaries and the effects of distinct learning strategies regarding the use of statistical information about contextual items. Our results tend to support the original study, although we have pointed out some differences that deserve more investigation. In sum, results support the claims that distributional information is informative to the task of learning word categories, that explicit utterance boundaries help the learner in this task, and that frequency of contextual elements, instead of merely attesting their occurrence, is necessary in order to extract the full potential of this source of information.

Many issues remain open for future work. Some are already under investigation, such as the remaining experiments in Redington et al. (1998), the first of them (evaluation of different context windows) reported in Faria and Ohashi (to appear). A central goal of ours is to provide a more in-depth comparison between English and Brazilian Portuguese regarding the role of distributional information, specially in terms of how morphological and word ordering differences between these two languages affect category identification. Aside from completing the set of experiments, we will also expand it by evaluating the suitability and plausibility of more recent models (Baroni and Lenci, 2010; Mikolov et al., 2013; Pennington et al., 2014) to this task. In addition, other relevant factors must also be studied, as indicated in Turney and Pantel (2010) and in Lenci (2018), such as using cosine and other vector similarity measures, as well as trying mathematical techniques to deal with lower frequencies and noise, weighting, sparsity, and optimizations.[8] Given that BP has rich morphology, exploring also how such information may help the learner, as in (Clark, 2003), is also something in our sight.

Finally, it is important to note that although the present study strongly relates with DSMs and all its literature, the distributional learning of syntactic categories is approached here as part of the language acquisition process of a child learning her native language. Consequently, matters of psychological, developmental, and empirical plausibility strongly applies to the computer model which aims to increasingly approximate what we observe in real life. Moving towards a gradual presentation of input data, for instance, is a condition for psychological plausibility we aim to meet in the future and which may be in conflict with other DSMs found in the literature, primarily conceived for massive NLP tasks with manipulation of the whole set of data. Nonetheless, assessing the suitability of the various models is the kind of question we hope to be able to answer as our research moves forward.

Acknowledgments

We would like to thank the reviewers for their thoughtful feedbacks on the present study. Their comments and suggestions not only helped improving the present paper, but also indicated interesting directions for future work.

---

[8]All reviewers stressed the fact that these are important issues to explore, not only to better understand the phenomenon *per se* but also as a way approximating the state-of-the-art in this topic. We have good reasons to expect that as we gather the results of the full collection of experiments while expanding to new ones, we will be able to provide some interesting reflections on these.

References

Marco Baroni and Alessandro Lenci. 2010. Distributional memory: A general framework for corpus-based semantics. *Computational Linguistics*, 36(4):673–721.

Savita Bernal, Jeffrey Lidz, Séverine Millotte, and Anne Christophe. 2007. Syntax constrains the acquisition of verb meaning. *Language Learning and Development*, 3:325–341.

Robert C. Berwick, Paul Pietroski, Beracah Yankama, and Noam Chomsky. 2011. Poverty of the stimulus revisited. *Cognitive Science*, 35:1207–1242.

Roger W. Brown. 1957. Linguistic determinism and the part of speech. *Journal of Abnormal & Social Psychology*, 55(1):1–5.

Anne Christophe, Séverine Millotte, Savita Bernal, and Jeffrey Lidz. 2008. Bootstrapping lexical and syntactic acquisition. *Language and Speech*, 51(1-2):61–75.

Alexander Clark. 2003. Combining distributional and morphological information for part of speech induction. In *Proceedings of the Tenth Conference on European Chapter of the Association for Computational Linguistics - Volume 1*, EACL '03, pages 59–66, Stroudsburg, PA, USA. Association for Computational Linguistics.

Pablo Faria and Giulia Osaka Ohashi. to appear. A aprendizagem distribucional no português brasileiro: um estudo computacional. *Revista LinguíStica*, 14(3).

Zellig Sabbetai Harris. 1954. Distributional structure. *Word*, 10(2-3):146–162.

Barbara Landau and Lila R. Gleitman. 1985. *Language and experience: evidence from the blind child*. Harvard University Press, Cambridge, MA.

Alessandro Lenci. 2018. Distributional models of word meaning. *Annu. Rev. Linguist.*, 4:151–171.

B MacWhinney. 2000. *The CHILDES Project: Tools for analyzing talk*, third edition edition. Lawrence Erlbaum Associates, Mahwah, NJ.

Tomas Mikolov, Ilya Sutskever, Kai Chen, Greg Corrado, and Jeffrey Dean. 2013. Distributed representations of words and phrases and their compositionality. In *Proceedings of the 26th International Conference on Neural Information Processing Systems - Volume 2*, NIPS'13, pages 3111–3119, USA. Curran Associates Inc.

Toben H. Mintz, Elissa L. Newport, and Thomas G. Bever. 2002. The distributional structure of grammatical categories in speech to young children. *Cognitive Science*, 26:393–424.

Jeffrey Pennington, Richard Socher, and Christopher D. Manning. 2014. Glove: Global vectors for word representation. In *In EMNLP*.

Geoffrey K. Pullum. 1996. Learnability, hyperlearning, and the poverty of the stimulus. In *Proceedings of the Twenty-Second Annual Meeting of the Berkeley Linguistics Society: General Session and Parasession on The Role of Learnability in Grammatical Theory*, pages 498–513. Berkeley, California: Berkeley Linguistics Society.

Martin Redington, Nick Chater, and Steven Finch. 1998. Distributional information: A powerful cue for acquiring syntactic categories. *Cognitive Science*, 22(4):425–469.

Alexa R. Romberg and Jenny R. Saffran. 2010. Statistical learning and language acquisition. *Wiley interdisciplinary reviews. Cognitive science*, 1(6):906–914.

Michael Tomasello. 1995. Language is not an instinct. *Cognitive Development*, (10):131–156.

Peter D. Turney and Patrick Pantel. 2010. From frequency to meaning: Vector space models of semantics. *Journal of Artificial Intelligence Research*, 37(1):141–188.

Charles Yang. 2002. *Knowledge and learning in natural language*. Oxford University Press.

Using Grounded Word Representations to Study Theories of Lexical Concepts

Dylan Ebert
Brown University
dylan_ebert@brown.edu

Ellie Pavlick
Brown University
ellie_pavlick@brown.edu

Abstract

The fields of cognitive science and philosophy have proposed many different theories for how humans represent "concepts". Multiple such theories are compatible with state-of-the-art NLP methods, and could in principle be operationalized using neural networks. We focus on two particularly prominent theories–Classical Theory and Prototype Theory–in the context of visually-grounded lexical representations. We compare when and how the behavior of models based on these theories differs in terms of categorization and entailment tasks. Our preliminary results suggest that Classical-based representations perform better for entailment and Prototype-based representations perform better for categorization. We discuss plans for additional experiments needed to confirm these initial observations.

1 Introduction

There are many theories and proposed definitions for what exactly constitutes a "concept". Which definition is the right one is a hotly debated topic in philosophy and psychology, which has involved a wide range of in-principle as well as empirical arguments (Laurence and Margolis, 1999). Despite the lack of consensus as to their definition, it's generally agreed that representations of concepts play a key role in natural language understanding, as the meaning of natural language expressions are necessarily defined in terms of their denotations–i.e. the aspects of the grounded (non-linguistic) world to which the expression refers. For example, reasoning about how the word *"owl"* relates to the word *"bird"* requires consideration of how *the thing or things referred to by "owl"* relates to *the thing or things referred to by "bird"*. Thus, representations of the concepts to which language refers is a key part of general language understanding.

It is not obvious, however, how one should chose to represent concepts computationally, especially given that current state-of-the-art neural models of grounded language can be seen as compatible with a number of theories for concepts, depending on how the architectures and algorithms are constructed. Thus, in this paper, we focus in particular on lexical concepts, and study two prominent theories which have both wide support–as well as substantial criticism–within the psychology and philosophy communities (Laurence and Margolis, 1999). The first, Classical Theory, represents concepts as the set of necessary-and-sufficient conditions which define the extension of the concept. For example, the representation of *owl* is the set of conditions such that, if and only if some entity meets every condition, that entity is an *owl*. Classical Theory is the most frequently cited in linguistics and NLP– it is the theory underlying traditional formal semantics–and is often formalized in terms of set theory, i.e. the extension of *"owl"* is the set of all owls. The second theory we explore is Prototype Theory, which represents concepts as a single, prototypical instance of that concept. For example, the representation of *owl* would be a particular instance of owl that captures the most characteristic, salient, typical, or otherwise important properties associated with owls. The degree to which some entity falls within the extension of *owl* is then a function of how "similar" that entity is to the prototype of owl. Thus, unlike Classical Theory, there is no clear notion of what is required in order to be an owl, and an entity may be judged to be an owl on the basis of "resemblance" despite having few definable properties in common with the prototype.

There are many points of differentiation that one might make between Classical Theory and Prototype Theory. In particular, Classical Theory is typically associated with discreteness and binary-ness

Proceedings of the Workshop on Cognitive Modeling and Computational Linguistics, pages 160–169
Minneapolis, USA, June 7, 2019. ©2019 Association for Computational Linguistics

(e.g. an entity either is an owl or it is not) while Prototype Theory is associated with graded judgements. By this distinction, it seems that Classical Theory is at odds with the state-of-the-art in NLP, which hinges on continuous representations and probabilistic judgements. However, in this paper we highlight a different distinction between Classical and Prototype Theory, which enables both theories to be operationalized in terms of continuous representations. Specifically, we frame Classical Theory as concerned primarily with representing *boundaries between classes* and Prototype Theory as concerned primarily with representing the *centers of classes*. That is, Classical Theory strives to determine the line that separates the least owl-like owl from most owl-like non-owl, while Prototype Theory strives to determine the properties that are most likely true of owls in general.

We conduct an empirical comparison of these two theories by providing computational instantiations of each in the context of visually-grounded word representations. Specifically, we use images with a given label (i.e. images of owls) to represent observed instances of each concept, and encode all images into a shared space using a Variational Autoencoder (VAE). We then build a Classical-based representation by computing the boundary which encompasses all instances of a given concept, and build a Prototype-basesd representation by computing the center of mass among all instances of a given concept. We compare these two models in terms of their performance on two tasks: 1) categorization (i.e. determining whether an instance falls within the extension of the concept) and 2) entailment (deciding whether one concept subsumes another). Our initial results suggest that the Classical-based representation consistently outperforms the Prototype-based representation on tasks related to entailment, even when we take into account the gradability of human entailment judgments. However, our results also suggest that the Prototype-based representation is better suited to perform the categorization task, although further investigation is needed to draw a complete comparison.

2 Definitions

2.1 Notation

We will use C to represent a concept and x to represent a potential "instance" of the concept. Intuitively, we can think of x as an entity when C is a concept corresponding to a noun like *"cat"*, but x might also be an event, property, or any other more abstract possible referent which might be considered to fall within the extension of C. $\mathcal{C}$ and $\mathcal{X}$ represent the space of concepts and of instances, respectively. We assume that a representation of a concept must support the tasks of categorization and entailment, as follows:

Categorization: A function $f_C : \mathcal{X} \rightarrow [0, 1]$ which returns the probability that x falls within the extension of C.

Entailment: A function $entail : \mathcal{C} \times \mathcal{C} \rightarrow [0, 1]$ which returns the probability that $C2$ can be inferred from $C1$.

2.2 Classical Theory

In Classical Theory, a concept is represented as a set of conditions which are necessary and sufficient in order for an entity to fall within the extension of the concept. Typically, in formal linguistics, this is discussed in terms of set theory: i.e. the denotation of a word is the set of instances in $[\![C]\!] \subseteq \mathcal{X}$ which forms the extension of that word. Thus, f_C is simply the characteristic function of this set. As classical theory is primarily concerned with defining clear boundaries between what can and can not be considered a member of the concept, this is best captured as a binary function (instances either are in the set or they are not):

$$f_C(x) = \begin{cases} 1 \text{ if } & x \in [\![C]\!] \\ 0 & \text{otherwise} \end{cases} \tag{1}$$

Then, C_1 is said to entail C_2 if $[\![C_1]\!] \subseteq [\![C_2]\!]$:

$$entail(C_1, C_2) = \begin{cases} 1 \text{ if } & \forall x (f_{C_1}(x) \leq f_{C_2}(x)) \\ 0 & \text{otherwise} \end{cases} \tag{2}$$

That is, whenever $f_{C_1}(x) = 1$, we must also have $f_{C_2}(x) = 1$. We also can consider a relaxed definition that supports graded (probabilistic) judgments of entailment. Specifically, we can say that the degree to which $C1$ entails $C2$ is determined by the degree of overlap between these sets:

$$entail(C_1, C_2) = \frac{\sum_{x \in \mathcal{X}} f_{C1}(x) \times f_{C2}(x)}{\sum_{x \in \mathcal{X}} f_{C1}(x)} \tag{3}$$

That is, the probability that $C1$ entails $C2$ is exactly the probability that a given instances of $C1$ is also an instance of $C2$.

2.3 Prototype Theory

In Prototype Theory, a concept is represented as a single "prototype"–i.e. an instance that falls within the extension of the concept and captures the most relevant, salient, or important properties of the concept. In contrast to Classical Theory, the features of the prototype do not represent necessary criteria–it is possible for an instance to fall within the extension of the concept despite having few features in common with the prototype. Concepts, then, are represented as a tuple containing an exemplar x_C and a distance function $d : \mathcal{X} \times \mathcal{X} \to \mathbb{R}$ which specifies how similar an arbitrary instance is to the exemplar. While there is no crisp definition of the extension of the concept, it is generally accepted that the criteria for inclusion in the extension must be proportional to the distance function (Osherson and Smith, 1981; Kamp and Partee, 1995):

$$f_C(x) \propto d(x, x_C) \tag{4}$$

That is, for any pair of instances x, y, if $d(x, x_C) < d(y, x_C)$, it cannot be the case that y is in the extension of C but x is not.

Traditional descriptions of Prototype Theory– i.e. those described in Rosch and Lloyd (1978); Kamp and Partee (1995)–do not explicitly define how to reason about entailment under Prototype Theory. Osherson and Smith (1981) proposed the use of fuzzy set theory (Zadeh et al., 1996) as a means for incorporating Prototype Theory within the familiar logical framework for reasoning about entailment. However, this approach has received significant criticism regarding the predictions it makes about compositionality (Osherson and Smith, 1981). Thus, we consider an alternative, simple definition of entailment which simply says that C_1 entails C_2 to the extent that the exemplar of C_1 falls within the extension of C_2:

$$entail(C_1, C_2) = f_{C_2}(x_{C_1}) \tag{5}$$

We begin with this definition as it is straightforward and reflects the basic spirit of Prototype Theory, without forcing it to look like set theory. We will consider alternative definitions in future work.

3 Instantiation

We focus on lexical concepts, specifically those corresponding to common nouns. We instantiate the definitions given in Section 3.1 using images to represent "instances". That is, our $\mathcal{X}$ is the space of all images and our $\mathcal{C}$ maps one-to-one onto English nouns. A similar approach, using images as a representation of "the world", has been used previously (Young et al., 2014). We adopt this approach as it enables a fairly direct way to instantiate abstract formal theories using representations (pixels) which can be handled straightforwardly by current computational models. We do not make the claim that visual attributes are the only relevant attributes which factor into representations of concepts. Rather, our focus is on testing in general how the choice of representation affects the predictions made by models, assuming that some representation of "the world" is given *a priori*. In other words, our choice to use only visual attributes is a methodologically-motivated choice, not a theoretically-motivated one.

3.1 Models

VAE. We encode all of our images into a shared space using a standard variational autoencoder (VAE) (Kingma and Welling, 2013). An advantage of using a VAE in this research is that latent features are encouraged to match a normal distribution, enforcing a structure on the latent space that allows euclidean geometric manipulations such as interpolation. This allows us to instantiate simple and intuitive euclidean evaluations when comparing theories. We train a VAE to reconstruct image encodings from a pretained CNN. In the following descriptions, $\vec{x} = VAE(CNN(x))$, i.e. the d-dimensional encoding of an image obtained by applying a pertained image classifier followed by our VAE encoder.

Classical-Based Method. Our definition of Classical Theory requires only that we can define the boundary for each concept. Given a set $\mathcal{X}_C$ of instances of a concept C–i.e. the set of images x observed with label C–we define this boundary to be the convex hull $\mathcal{H}_C$ computed over $\vec{x}$ for every $x \in \mathcal{X}_C$. That is, we compute the literal boundary surrounding a set of encoded instances (shown as solid lines in Figure 1). We can then evaluate whether an arbitrary new instance x is a member of C by computing whether $\vec{x}$ falls within this boundary (Eq. 6). We can then produce entailment judgments using Eq. 2 or 3 exactly.

$$f_C(x) = \begin{cases} 1 \text{ if} & \vec{x} \cdot \mathcal{H}_C \leq 0 \\ 0 & \text{otherwise} \end{cases} \tag{6}$$

When evaluating on the entailment tasks (Section 5.2) we consider two variants of this Classical-based representation. First, we consider a "strict" interpretation of entailment, where $C_1 \rightarrow C_2$ iff *every* instance in C_1 is also in C_2. Second, we consider a soft representation in which which $C_1 \rightarrow C_2$ if the proportion instances from C_2 that are in C_1 (i.e. Eq. 3) is at least τ. When we use this soft representation, we set τ using performance on a held-out validation set.

Prototype-Based Method. Our definition of Prototype Theory requires that we can define a prototype instance and a distance function for each concept. Again, given $\mathcal{X}_C$, the set of images x observed with label C, we approximate a probability density function ϕ_C - in this case, as a multivariate normal distribution. We then define the prototype $\vec{x_C}$ to be the mode of ϕ_C. The distance function d can then be defined as:

$$d(\vec{x}, \vec{x_C}) = \frac{\phi_C(\vec{x})}{\phi_C(\vec{x_C})} \qquad (7)$$

or the density at point $\vec{x}$ in ϕ_C. Because the density may evaluate to a value greater than 1, we normalize by density at the prototype $\phi_C(\vec{x_C})$. This results in values in the range $[0, 1]$, which are more interpretable and comparable across scenarios. We parameterize density function ϕ_C as a multivariate normal distribution with mean μ_C and covariance σ_C^2, resulting in prototype $\vec{x_C} = \mu_C$. We chose this distance function as it is arguably the simplest way to compute "distance to the prototype" which still allows asymmetry. That is, pure euclidean distance would be simpler, but would lose the ability to represent directionality, meaning e.g. *"owl"* would be as prototypical of *"bird"* as *"bird"* is of *"owl"*. In future work, we will consider different definitions of prototype and/or more complex distance functions, as well as alternative, i.e. non-Gaussian, representations.

When evaluating on the categorization tasks (Section 5.2), we must use this distance function to make a binary decision about whether or not an instance falls within the extension of the concept. Thus, analogous to how we softened the Classical-based representation, which stricten our Prototype-based representation by defining threshold τ, and saying that $f_C(x) = 1$ *iff* $d(\vec{x}, \vec{x_C}) \leq \tau$. Again, when used, we set τ empirically based on performance on a validation set.

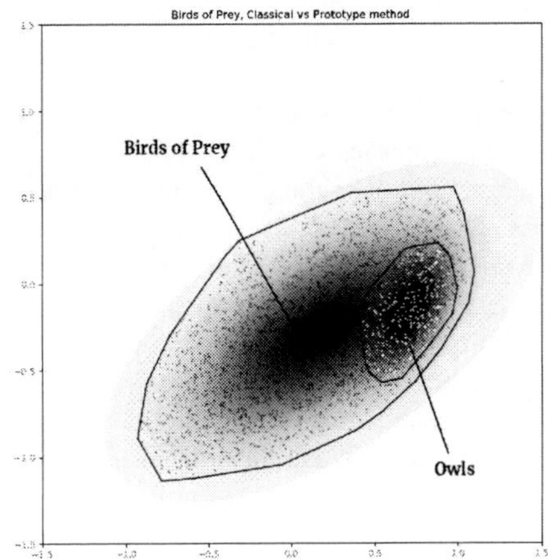

Figure 1: Encodings of *"bird_of_prey"* and *"owl"* as black and white dots respectively. The convex hull (Classical-based representation) is represented by the black lines. Colored gradients show multivariate normal distributions (Prototype-based representation).

3.2 Training

We train our VAE on IMAGENET (Deng et al., 2009), which consists of approximately 1,000 images for each of 1,000 fine-grained, mutually exclusive categories corresponding to common nouns/noun phrases (e.g. *"great_grey_owl"*, *"knee_pad"*). These class labels have been mapped onto the WORDNET (Miller et al., 1990) ontology, which provides a tree structure of hypernym-hyponym relationships. Since we want representations for both fine-grained concepts as well as higher-level concepts (in order to evaluate entailment), we compose data of high-level concepts from their lower-level hyponyms. For example, for the high-level concept *"bird_of_prey"*, we take all hyponyms of *"bird_of_prey"* according to WORDNET (e.g. *"great_grey_owl"*, *"kite"*). Of these, we identify those in IMAGENET and gather instances of these subclasses to comprise the set for the superclass *"bird_of_prey"*.

We hold out 100 instances of each low-level class to keep for testing. We split our data evenly between hypernym/hyponym labels and between train/test sets to ensure that, e.g., if a particular image of an owl is used as a *"bird_of_prey"* during training, then that same instance is not seen as an *"owl"* nor as a *"bird_of_prey"* during test. The same image might be seen as both an *"owl"* and a *"bird_of_prey"* during training.

We feed each image through a pretrained image classifier (Inception v3) (Szegedy et al., 2016), and extract the 2048-dimensional output of the final hidden layer, to be treated as the representation of that image. We use these data to train several different configurations for the VAE. Our VAE consists of a feed-forward encoder and decoder network, each with two dense hidden layers with ReLU activation. We define the hyperparameter d, the dimensionality of the latent space. We experiment with $d \in 2, 3, 4, 8, 16, 32, 64, 128, 256$. Hidden layers are scaled proportionally to the size of the latent space, while input/reconstruction layer sizes are fixed at 2048. We train each of these with an Adam optimizer with a learning rate of 0.001. We save the weights with the best validation loss, stopping training after 5 epochs without improvement. Training takes only a few minutes on a desktop with an Nvidia GTX 1070 GPU.

3.3 Dimensionality Reduction

Due to the exponential complexity of algorithms used to compute convex hulls (specifically Quick-Hull (Barber et al., 1996)) we are unable to compute Classical-based representations for values of $d > 4$. For now, we address this by training the VAE with higher dimensional encodings, then projecting into a lower dimension before applying the Classical-based method. We report results for projected and unprojected variants of both Classical-based and Prototype-based methods in Section 5. Although initial experiments do not suggest a benefit to using higher dimensions (i.e. $d = 4$ dimensions did not outperform $d = 2$ in our early experiments), a priority of our future work is to employ more sophisticated algorithms from computational geometry which will allow us to compute convex hulls in higher-dimensional spaces.

4 Evaluation

4.1 Entailment

For entailment, we consider both the traditional version of the task, in which entailment judgments are binary, as well as a graded variant of the task, in which concepts are said to entail one another to varying degrees (e.g. a *"robin"* is said to be a better instance of *"bird"* than a *"penguin"* is, and thus *"robin"* entails *"bird"* more than *"penguin"* entails *"bird"*). The observation that humans produce graded entailment judgments is what spurred Prototype Theory initially (Rosch

and Lloyd, 1978), and thus is a relevant evaluation task. Examples of binary and graded entailment judgements are given in Table 1.

Standard		Graded	
WBLESS		HYPERLEX	
stove→object	✓	kangaroo→animal	6.0
scarf→garment	✓	mammal→animal	6.0
pistol→ weapon	✓	grape→food	5.9
grain→corn	X	animal→mammal	0.8
telephone→stove	X	horn→car	0.9
jacket→raincoat	X	plate→spoon	0.2

Table 1: Positive and negative examples from each of our lexical entailment (LE) evaluation sets.

WBLESS. For the standard (binary) lexical entailment task, we use the WBLESS lexical entailment dataset (Weeds et al., 2014), which consists of 1,168 word pairs, containing an equal number of positive and negative lexical entailment examples. Positive examples are hyponym-hypernym pairs, where negative examples include reversed entailment pairs, co-hyponyms, holonym-meronym pairs, and random word pairs.

HYPERLEX. For the graded entailment task, we use the HYPERLEX (Vulić et al., 2017) dataset, which contains human judgements of the degree of lexical entailment in the range $[0, 6]$. We use the noun component of HYPERLEX, which contains 2,163 noun pairs with a mean score of 3.3.

IMAGENET Mapping. For each word/concept C in WBLESS, we want to obtain a set of images $\mathcal{X}_C$ that are considered instances of that concept. To do this, we compute the hyponym closure of C in WORDNET (containing all hyponym descendants, or all words that entail C), and gather any that exist as IMAGENET class labels. For example, for the WBLESS concept *"bird_of_prey"*, we identify IMAGENET class labels {*"kite"*, *"bald_eagle"*, *"vulture"*, *"great_grey_owl"*}. All image instances in these classes are then considered to comprise $\mathcal{X}_{bird\_of\_prey}$. Often, different concepts map to the same synset. For example, *"toad"*→*"frog"* becomes *"frog"*→*"frog"*. Different pairs also map to identical pairs in IMAGENET. For example, *"lizard"*→*"animal"* and *"lizard"*→*"creature"* each map to *"lizard"*→*"animal"*, despite having different human judgement values. Finally, some pairs might map onto multiple synsets. In the former two cases, we leave these flaw as-is. In the third case, we assign words to their first sense. Experiments with multiple ways of processing these conflicts showed no noticeable impact on results.

After filtering out pairs in which one or both words have no corresponding images in IMAGENET, both of our datasets are left with a slight entailment bias. Specifically, for WBLESS, we are left with 463 examples (325 entailing, 138 non-entailing). For HYPERLEX, we are left with 362 pairs, with a mean score of 4.0.

4.2 Categorization

We frame categorization as a binary classification task for each of the 1000 base-level IMAGENET categories. For each category, we take the 100 positive examples, and 100 random negative examples (from test data). We then evaluate whether each instance belongs to that category.

5 Results

Quantitative results are shown in Table 2. Figure 2 shows illustrative examples of instances occurring near the prototype vs. on the boundary, to provide an intuition of the differences between the two representations.

5.1 Model Variants

We consider several variants of each representation. For the Classical-based representation, we consider both strict and soft variants (Section 3.1). For the Prototype-based method, we train at various dimension sizes and find that $d = 64$ consistently performs best on a held-out validation set. For the Classical-based methods, we find that $d = 2$ consistently performs best on validation. To make as fair a comparison as possible, we also evaluate both methods on representations achieved by training the VAE with $d = 64$ and then projecting down to 2 dimensions. We note that this leads to rough comparisons, and in future work, we intend to find computational approaches which will allow us to compute the Classical-based representations directly in high dimensions.

5.2 Lexical Entailment.

On lexical entailment, the best variant of the Classical-based approach achieves a very high accuracy of 0.90. The method based on a strict interpretation of Classical Theory ($\tau = 1$) achieves a

Figure 2: Examples instances of *great_grey_owl*. Instances (a) on the Classical-based convex hull boundary are on the left; instances (b) of the most "prototypical" owls are on the right.

very high precision of 0.99 on WBLESS. While our results are not directly comparable to prior work (since we are using only a subset of WBLESS), we note that this accuracy is quite high for the task. For reference, prior work which used image generality for lexical entailment achieves a maximum accuracy of 0.75 on WBLESS (Kiela et al., 2015a); an approach using hierarchical embeddings achieves an accuracy of 0.87 (Nguyen et al., 2017); and recent work using a retrofitting approach reports an accuracy of 0.91 (Vulić and Mrkšić, 2017). In contrast, the Prototype-based approach greatly over-predicts lexical entailment, yielding high recall and low precision. The two-dimensional and downward-projected configurations perform no better than random, and the 64-dimensional case is only marginally better.

We were surprised to find that the Classical-based method also performed better than Prototype-based on graded lexical entailment (HYPERLEX), achieving a Spearman ρ score of 0.55 in both the strict and soft two-dimensional cases. By comparison, Vulić and Mrkšić 2017 achieve a maximum Spearman ρ of 0.71 on HYPERLEX nouns, while work using Poincaré embeddings for learning hierarchical representations achieves a ρ of 0.51 (Nickel and Kiela, 2017). The Prototype-based approach again performs only somewhat better than random on

Model	Dim.	Proj.	Standard LE (WBLESS)				Graded LE (HyperLex)	Categorization (ImageNet)			
			Acc.	Prec.	Rec.	F1	Spearman ρ	Acc.	Prec.	Rec.	F1
Random			0.70	0.70	1.00	0.82	0	0.50	0.50	1.00	0.67
Classical-based (strict)	2	–	0.81	**0.99**	0.72	0.83	0.55	-	-	-	-
Classical-based (soft)	2	–	**0.90**	0.95	0.89	**0.92**	**0.55**	0.55	0.52	1.00	0.69
Classical-based (soft)	64	2	0.87	0.90	0.90	0.90	0.51	0.50	0.50	1.00	0.67
Prototype-based	2	–	0.67	0.67	0.97	0.80	0.08	0.59	0.56	0.9	0.67
Prototype-based	64	2	0.67	0.67	**0.98**	0.80	0.04	0.50	0.50	1.00	0.67
Prototype-based	64	–	0.76	0.76	0.95	0.84	0.20	**0.72**	**0.66**	**0.92**	**0.77**

Table 2: Results comparing Classical-based and Prototype-based approaches on lexical entailment (WBLESS and HYPERLEX) and categorization (IMAGENET).

HYPERLEX, with the 64-dimensional configuration performing best. We were surprised to find that the Prototype-based method performed worse on graded entailment, since Prototype Theory should be well-suited to capturing graded judgements. Further experiments are required to diagnose the extent to which the poor performance of the Prototype-based methods on lexical entailment are due to theory vs. in particulars of our instantiation.

Categorization. The only approach that performs significantly better than random on categorization is 64-dimensional Prototype-based. All 2-dimensional cases (real and projected) perform at chance, over-predicting positive categorizations. This is unsurprising, as it can be expected that more dimensions are needed to capture sufficient information for differentiating classes. We note that, since our image instances are represented as pretrained IMAGENET classifier embeddings, high categorization accuracy can be achieved with a simple perceptron. However, we are not interested in the task of categorization *per se*. Rather, our goal is to assess the extent to which a single representation of a concept can be used to perform both categorization and entailment, without training task-specific modules.

6 Discussion

Several aspects of these initial results prevent us from drawing strong conclusions. In particular: the fact that we cannot compare the representations directly in high dimensions, the fact that we focus on a small number of concrete nouns only, and the fact that we choose one particular definition of prototype and distance function despite the existence of many equally-plausible alternatives.

Nonetheless, despite being preliminary, our results suggest trends which are intuitive as well as some which are counter-intuitive. In particular, we were unsurprised to find that Classical-based representations achieve high precision and all-around high accuracy for tasks related to entailment. As this theory was largely developed with the goal of explaining logical inferences, it is intuitive that such representations would be more sensitive to distinctions which explain judgements about entailment. Similarly, we were unsurprised to see that the Prototype-based representations achieve better performance at categorization, as such theories were originally motivated in terms of categorization (rather than inference) phenomena.

The strong performance of the Classical-based method on the graded entailment evaluation was highly unexpected. Further investigation is required in order to understand whether these results are attributable to something superficial (e.g. artifacts of the dataset), something methodological (e.g. our choice of distance function), or something deeper about the relationship between these two theories. However, this counter-intuitive result does emphasize how aspects of Classical Theory (i.e. the explicit representation of a "boundary") can play a role in the representation of concepts without sacrificing the ability to make graded or probabilistic predictions.

7 Related Work

Our work is very closely related to the work of Young et al. (2014), which sought to instantiate the formal semantics notion of set-theoretic entailment using images to represent the "worlds" to which natural language refers. Their work focused on representations motivated by Classical Theory, and dealt with literal sets of discrete images, meaning it could not generalize to referents outside the training data. Our Classical-based method can be viewed as an updated version of their approach, which uses a VAE in order to represent the visual world in a more flexible way. Our Prototype-based method is novel with respect to the work done by Young et al. (2014).

Also very closely related is Kiela et al. (2015b), which represented a lexical concept as a set of image encodings, and sought to make lexical entailment decisions by comparing how dispersed versus compact images within a category were. We note many aspects of Kiela et al. (2015b)'s approach which overlap with our own–namely, the use of sets of images to derive representations of concepts and the use of set overlap to determine entailment. However, our focus is on a particular question which is tangential to Kiela et al. (2015b). That is, we are interested in the differences between boundary-focused (Classical) representations compared to center-focused (Prototype) representations, acknowledging either representation is equally capable of capturing properties like dispersion and "generality" of a concept, the focus of Kiela et al. (2015b)'s work.

In general, the present study relates to the ample prior work on visually-grounded meaning representations. Beinborn et al. (2018) gives an in-depth survey of work in this area, from both a computational and a cognitive perspective. Of particular relevance to our work is prior work on multimodal lexical semantics, e.g. work which extends skipgram-like training procedures to include both visual and text information Lazaridou et al. (2015); Silberer and Lapata (2012); Silberer et al. (2017); Collell et al. (2017); Kiela et al. (2016); Kiros et al. (2018). Such representations not only perform better in practice, but have been shown to be more cognitively-plausible in terms of their ability to predict human brain activity (Bulat et al., 2017). Beyond lexical representations, multimodal representations have been incorporated representations of more complex concepts such as frames (Shutova et al., 2017) and full sentences (Han et al., 2017). Again, our work differs in that we are not focused on harnessing visual data *per se*; rather, our focus is on how, given a representation of the world to which we can "ground" meaning, different theories can be operationalized, and how the assumptions of these theories affect performance on basic tasks. That is, we view our work as complementary to, rather than competing with, existing ongoing work on multimodal and grounded representations.

Finally, there is an enormous body of work aimed at modelling lexical entailment using text-only training data, recently (Shwartz et al., 2016; Chang et al., 2017; Vulić and Mrkšić, 2017; Pavlick and Pasca, 2017; Pavlick et al., 2015). Such work often treats lexical entailment as a supervised learning problem, or at least as a task to which we should tune directly. We view such approaches as fundamentally different from what we present here. That is, our work focuses on how to form concepts which relate language to the world, with the assumption that inferences about entailment should come from reasoning directly about the extensions of these concepts, rather than indirectly by relating the surface forms which refer to those denotations.

8 Conclusion

Using a VAE to encode image embeddings into a shared low-dimensional space, we compare a Classical-based with a Prototype-based model of concepts using common evaluations on lexical entailment and categorization. The Classical-based approach performed exceptionally well on lexical entailment detection, and relatively well on graded entailment judgements. While the higher-dimensional Prototype-based approach performed well on categorization, in general our Prototype-based approach performs subpar. The extent to which this is theory vs. approach can't be determined by this research - the vagueness of the distance function d proposed by Prototype Theory gives way to a vast world of unexplored cognitively plausible instantiations that we look forward to exploring.

Acknowledgements We would like to thank Roman Feiman, Eugene Charniak, and members of the Brown NLU group and LUNAR lab for their valuable feedback.

References

C Bradford Barber, David P Dobkin, David P Dobkin, and Hannu Huhdanpaa. 1996. The quickhull algorithm for convex hulls. *ACM Transactions on Mathematical Software (TOMS)*, 22(4):469–483.

Lisa Beinborn, Teresa Botschen, and Iryna Gurevych. 2018. Multimodal grounding for language processing. In *Proceedings of the 27th International Conference on Computational Linguistics*, pages 2325–2339, Santa Fe, New Mexico, USA. Association for Computational Linguistics.

Luana Bulat, Stephen Clark, and Ekaterina Shutova. 2017. Speaking, seeing, understanding: Correlating semantic models with conceptual representation in the brain. In *Proceedings of the 2017 Conference on Empirical Methods in Natural Language Processing*, pages 1081–1091, Copenhagen, Denmark. Association for Computational Linguistics.

Haw-Shiuan Chang, Ziyun Wang, Luke Vilnis, and Andrew McCallum. 2017. Distributional inclusion vector embedding for unsupervised hypernymy detection.

Guillem Collell, Ted Zhang, and Marie-Francine Moens. 2017. Imagined visual representations as multimodal embeddings. In *AAAI*, pages 4378–4384.

Jia Deng, Wei Dong, Richard Socher, Li-Jia Li, Kai Li, and Li Fei-Fei. 2009. Imagenet: A large-scale hierarchical image database. In *Computer Vision and Pattern Recognition, 2009. CVPR 2009. IEEE Conference on*, pages 248–255. Ieee.

Dan Han, Pascual Martínez-Gómez, and Koji Mineshima. 2017. Visual denotations for recognizing textual entailment. In *Proceedings of the 2017 Conference on Empirical Methods in Natural Language Processing*, pages 2843–2849.

Hans Kamp and Barbara Partee. 1995. Prototype theory and compositionality. *Cognition*, 57(2):129–191.

Douwe Kiela, Laura Rimell, Ivan Vulić, and Stephen Clark. 2015a. Exploiting image generality for lexical entailment detection. In *Proceedings of the 53rd Annual Meeting of the Association for Computational Linguistics and the 7th International Joint Conference on Natural Language Processing (Volume 2: Short Papers)*, volume 2, pages 119–124.

Douwe Kiela, Laura Rimell, Ivan Vulić, and Stephen Clark. 2015b. Exploiting image generality for lexical entailment detection. In *Proceedings of the 53rd Annual Meeting of the Association for Computational Linguistics and the 7th International Joint Conference on Natural Language Processing (Volume 2: Short Papers)*, pages 119–124, Beijing, China. Association for Computational Linguistics.

Douwe Kiela, Anita Lilla Ver, and Stephen Clark. 2016. Comparing data sources and architectures for deep visual representation learning in semantics. In *Proceedings of the 2016 Conference on Empirical Methods in Natural Language Processing*, pages 447–456, Austin, Texas. Association for Computational Linguistics.

Diederik P Kingma and Max Welling. 2013. Auto-encoding variational bayes. *arXiv preprint arXiv:1312.6114*.

Jamie Kiros, William Chan, and Geoffrey Hinton. 2018. Illustrative language understanding: Large-scale visual grounding with image search. In *Proceedings of the 56th Annual Meeting of the Association for Computational Linguistics (Volume 1: Long Papers)*, pages 922–933, Melbourne, Australia. Association for Computational Linguistics.

Stephen Laurence and Eric Margolis. 1999. Concepts and cognitive science. *Concepts: core readings*, pages 3–81.

Angeliki Lazaridou, Nghia The Pham, and Marco Baroni. 2015. Combining language and vision with a multimodal skip-gram model. pages 153–163.

George A Miller, Richard Beckwith, Christiane Fellbaum, Derek Gross, and Katherine J Miller. 1990. Introduction to wordnet: An on-line lexical database. *International journal of lexicography*, 3(4):235–244.

Kim Anh Nguyen, Maximilian Köper, Sabine Schulte im Walde, and Ngoc Thang Vu. 2017. Hierarchical embeddings for hypernymy detection and directionality. *arXiv preprint arXiv:1707.07273*.

Maximillian Nickel and Douwe Kiela. 2017. Poincaré embeddings for learning hierarchical representations. In *Advances in neural information processing systems*, pages 6338–6347.

Daniel N Osherson and Edward E Smith. 1981. On the adequacy of prototype theory as a theory of concepts. *Cognition*, 9(1):35–58.

Ellie Pavlick, Johan Bos, Malvina Nissim, Charley Beller, Benjamin Van Durme, and Chris Callison-Burch. 2015. Adding semantics to data-driven paraphrasing. In *Proceedings of the 53rd Annual Meeting of the Association for Computational Linguistics and the 7th International Joint Conference on Natural Language Processing (Volume 1: Long Papers)*, pages 1512–1522, Beijing, China. Association for Computational Linguistics.

Ellie Pavlick and Marius Pasca. 2017. Identifying 1950s american jazz musicians: Fine-grained isa extraction via modifier composition. In *Proceedings of the 55th Annual Meeting of the Association for Computational Linguistics (Volume 1: Long Papers)*, pages 2099–2109, Vancouver, Canada. Association for Computational Linguistics.

Eleanor Rosch and Barbara Bloom Lloyd. 1978. Cognition and categorization.

Ekaterina Shutova, Andreas Wundsam, and Helen Yannakoudakis. 2017. Semantic frames and visual scenes: Learning semantic role inventories from image and video descriptions. In *Proceedings of the 6th Joint Conference on Lexical and Computational Semantics (*SEM 2017)*, pages 149–154, Vancouver, Canada. Association for Computational Linguistics.

Vered Shwartz, Enrico Santus, and Dominik Schlechtweg. 2016. Hypernyms under siege: Linguistically-motivated artillery for hypernymy detection.

Carina Silberer, Vittorio Ferrari, and Mirella Lapata. 2017. Visually grounded meaning representations. *IEEE transactions on pattern analysis and machine intelligence*, 39(11):2284–2297.

Carina Silberer and Mirella Lapata. 2012. Grounded models of semantic representation. In *Proceedings of the 2012 Joint Conference on Empirical Methods in Natural Language Processing and Computational Natural Language Learning*, pages 1423–1433, Jeju Island, Korea. Association for Computational Linguistics.

Christian Szegedy, Vincent Vanhoucke, Sergey Ioffe, Jon Shlens, and Zbigniew Wojna. 2016. Rethinking the inception architecture for computer vision. In *Proceedings of the IEEE conference on computer vision and pattern recognition*, pages 2818–2826.

Ivan Vulić, Daniela Gerz, Douwe Kiela, Felix Hill, and Anna Korhonen. 2017. Hyperlex: A large-scale evaluation of graded lexical entailment. *Computational Linguistics*, 43(4):781–835.

Ivan Vulić and Nikola Mrkšić. 2017. Specialising word vectors for lexical entailment.

Julie Weeds, Daoud Clarke, Jeremy Reffin, David Weir, and Bill Keller. 2014. Learning to distinguish hypernyms and co-hyponyms. In *Proceedings of COLING 2014, the 25th International Conference on Computational Linguistics: Technical Papers*, pages 2249–2259. Dublin City University and Association for Computational Linguistics.

Peter Young, Alice Lai, Micah Hodosh, and Julia Hockenmaier. 2014. From image descriptions to visual denotations: New similarity metrics for semantic inference over event descriptions. volume 2, pages 67–78.

Lotfi Asker Zadeh, George J Klir, and Bo Yuan. 1996. *Fuzzy sets, fuzzy logic, and fuzzy systems: selected papers*, volume 6. World Scientific.

Author Index

Agarwal, Sumeet, 30

Bernardi, Raffaella, 105
Broersma, Mirjam, 20
Bushong, Wednesday, 62

Cho, Pyeong Whan, 53

Danet, Lola, 71
De Boissezon, Xavier, 71
De Santo, Aniello, 93
Demberg, Vera, 134
Dunn, Jonathan, 117

Ebert, Dylan, 160

Fabre, Cécile, 71
Farinas, Jérôme, 71
Feliciano de Faria, Pablo Picasso, 152
Fourtassi, Abdellah, 129
Frank, Michael, 129
Frank, Stefan L., 20, 77

Gaume, Bruno, 71

Hathout, Nabil, 71
Hunter, Tim, 1

Jaeger, T. Florian, 62
Jucla, Mélanie, 71

Lewis, Richard, 53
Lindemann, Matthias, 134
Lopopolo, Alessandro, 77

Mai Ho-Dac, Lydia, 71
Marantz, Alec, 43
Melnick, Robin, 11

Oseki, Yohei, 43
O'Sullivan, Lewis, 140

Pavlick, Ellie, 160
Péran, Patrice, 71
Pezzelle, Sandro, 105
Pierrejean, Bénédicte, 71   .
Pinquier, Julien, 71

Rajkumar, Rajakrishnan, 30
Ranjan, Sidharth, 30

Sayeed, Asad, 134
Scheinfeld, Isaac, 129
Stabler, Edward, 1
Stanojević, Miloš, 1
Steinert-Threlkeld, Shane, 140

Tanguy, Ludovic, 71
Testoni, Alberto, 105
Tsoukala, Chara, 20

Valdes Kroff, Jorge, 20
van den Bosch, Antal, 20, 77

Wasow, Thomas, 11
White, Aaron Steven, 86
Willems, Roel, 77

Yan, Shaorong, 86
Yang, Charles, 43